Village France

AA

AA PUBLISHING

Village France

Contents

Copy editor: Janet Tabinski

Contributors: David Applefield (Loire);
Liz Ayre/Tina Isaac (Alsace & Lorraine,
Rhône Valley); Patricia Caffrey (Languedoc);
Lisa Davidson (Paris & Île-de-France,
Burgundy); Teresa Fisher (Normandy,
Franche-Comté, Périgord & Quercy,
Pyrenees, Provence & Côte d'Azur); Rob
Moore (Corsica); Ingrid Morgan (Atlantic
Coast, Berry & Limousin, Auvergne);
Caroline Sunderland (North, Champagne,
Alps); Marina Urquidi (Brittany)

Produced by AA Publishing

Published by AA Publishing (a trading
name of Automobile Association
Developments Limited, whose registered
office is Norfolk House, Priestley Road,
Basingstoke, Hampshire RG24 9NY;
registered number 1878835).

ISBN 0 7495 1278 4

A CIP catalogue record for this book is
available from the British Library.

The contents of this book are believed correct at the time of printing. Nevertheless,
the publishers cannot be held responsible
for any errors or omissions or for changes
in the details given in this book or for the
consequences of any reliance on the information provided by the same. Assessments
of attractions and locations are based upon
the author's own experience and,
therefore, descriptions given in this guide
necessarily contain an element of
subjective opinion which may not reflect
the publisher's opinion or dictate a reader's
experiences on another occasion. We have
tried to ensure accuracy in this book, but
things do change and we would be grateful
if readers would advise us of any
inaccuracies they may encounter.

Colour Separation by Daylight Colour Art,
Singapore

Printed and bound in Spain by
Graficromo, Cordoba

Regions & Départements

In this book France has been divided into 19 regions as numbered and colour-coded on the map opposite. Individual maps of these regions appear at the beginning of each section.

The map also shows the départements into which France is divided. Each département has a standard number, as shown on the map and in the key below, which for postal purposes replaces its name. These numbers also form part of the registration number of French cars, thus indicating the département in which the car was registered. They are listed here alphabetically under the regional headings of the book.

Brittany (Bretagne)
Côtes d'Armor 22
Finistère 29
Ille-et-Vilaine 35
Morbihan 56

Normandy (Normandie)
Calvados 14
Eure 27
Manche 50
Orne 61
Seine-Maritime 76

The North (Nord)
Aisne 02
Ardennes 08
Nord 59
Oise 60
Pas-de-Calais 62
Somme 80

Champagne (Champagne)
Aube 10
Marne 51
Marne (Haute-) 52

Alsace & Lorraine
(Alsace et Lorraine)
Meurthe-et-Moselle 54
Meuse 55
Moselle 57
Rhin (Bas-) 67
Rhin (Haut-) 68
Vosges 88

The Loire (Loire)
Eure-et-Loir 28
Indre-et-Loire 37
Loir-et-Cher 41
Loire-Atlantique 44
Loiret 45
Maine-et-Loire 49
Mayenne 53
Sarthe 72

Paris & the Île-de-France
(Paris et Île-de-France)
Essonne 91
Hauts-de-Seine 92
Paris 75
Seine-et-Marne 77
Yvelines 78
Seine-St-Denis 93
Val-de-Marne 94
Val-d'Oise 95

Burgundy (Bourgogne)
Côte-d'Or 21
Nièvre 58
Saône-et-Loire 71
Yonne 89

Franche-Comté
(Franche-Comté)
Belfort (Territoire-de-) 90
Doubs 25
Jura 39
Saône (Haute-) 70

The Atlantic Coast
(Côte Atlantique)
Charente 16
Charente-Maritime 17
Gironde 33
Landes 40
Sèvres (Deux-) 79
Vendée 85

Berry & Limousin
(Berry et Limousin)
Cher 18
Corrèze 19
Creuse 23
Indre 36
Vienne 86
Vienne (Haute-) 87

The Auvergne (Auvergne)
Allier 03
Cantal 15
Loire (Haute-) 43
Puy-de-Dôme 63

The Rhône Valley
(Vallée du Rhône)
Ain 01 (part)
Ardèche 07 (part)
Drôme 26 (part)
Isère 38 (part)
Loire 42
Rhône 69

The Alps (Alpes)
Ain 01 (part)
Alpes (Hautes-) 05
Drôme 26 (part)
Isère 38 (part)
Savoie 73
Savoie (Haute-) 74

Périgord & Quercy
(Périgord et Quercy)
Aveyron 12 (part)
Dordogne 24
Lot 46
Lot-et-Garonne 47
Tarn-et-Garonne 82

Languedoc (Languedoc)
Ardèche 07 (part)
Aveyron 12 (part)
Gard 30 (part)
Hérault 34
Lozère 48
Tarn 81

The Pyrenees (Pyrénées)
Ariège 09
Aude 11
Garonne (Haute-) 31
Gers 32
Pyrénées-Atlantiques 64
Pyrénées (Hautes-) 65
Pyrénées-Orientales 66

Provence & the Côte d'Azur
(Provence et Côte d'Azur)
Alpes-de-Haute-Provence 04
Alpes Maritimes 06
Bouches-du-Rhône 13
Drôme 26 (part)
Gard 30 (part)
Var 83
Vaucluse 84

Corsica (Corse)
Corse-du-Sud 2A
Corse (Haute-) 2B

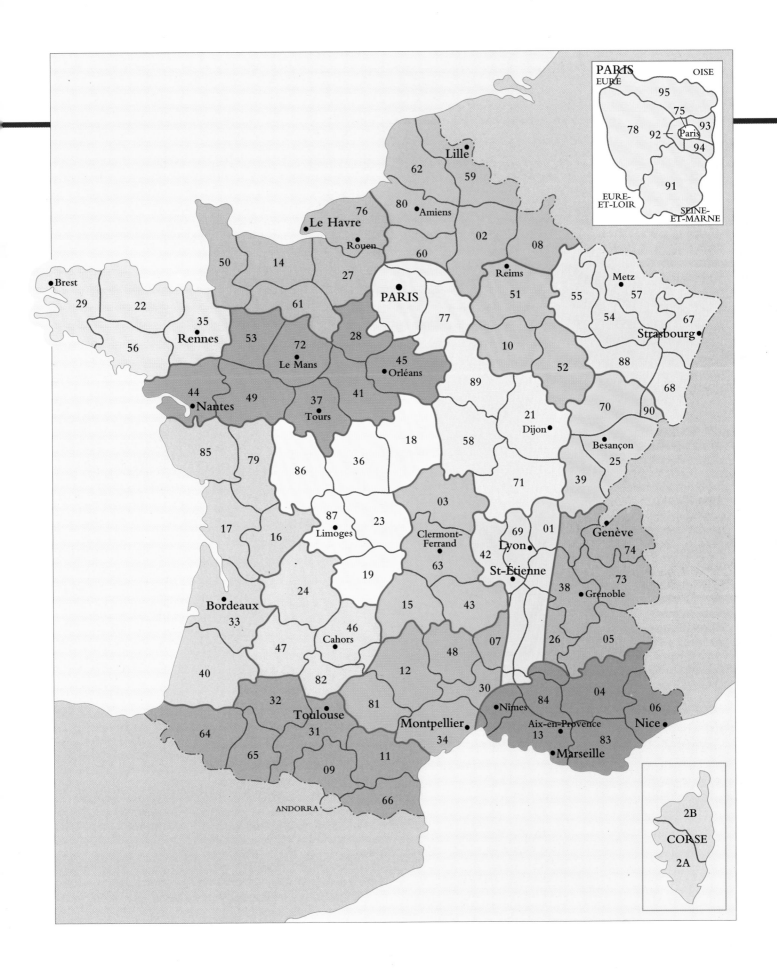

PARIS

OISE

EURE

95

75

78   92 — Paris   93

94

EURE-
ET-LOIR

91

SEINE-
ET-MARNE

•Lille

62   59

80 •Amiens

76
•Le Havre   02   08

•Rouen

50   14   60

•Brest   27   •Reims   •Metz

29   61   PARIS   51   55   57

22   54   67

35   77   •Strasbourg

Rennes•   53   28   10   88

72   45   52   68

Le Mans   •Orléans

44   49   89   70   90

•Nantes   37   41   21   •Besançon

Tours   •Dijon   25

85   79   18   58   71   39

86   36

87   03   69   01   •Genève

•Limoges   23   42   •Lyon   74

17   16   Clermont-   •St-Étienne   73

19   Ferrand   43   38   •Grenoble

24   63   05

Bordeaux•   15   07   26

33   46   48   30   04

•Cahors   12   84   06

47   82   •Nîmes   •Nice

40   81   Montpellier•   13   83

32   Toulouse   34   Aix-en-Provence   •Marseille

64   31   11

65   09

ANDORRA   66

2B

CORSE

2A

VILLAGE FRANCE has been divided into 19 sections according to the regions listed and shown on pages 6–7. Each section opens with a brief general introduction and a detailed map of the region, showing the villages included in the chapter and clearly indicating the locations of the mapped village walks. Selected walks have specially commissioned maps to accompany the easy-to-follow directions, and the key symbols for these maps are shown below. The information panels included with the walk directions include useful details on the distance covered, the terrain and accessibility, places offering refreshments and openings times (where available) of places of interest. There is also a selection of village walks without accompanying maps, and the directions for these are a little less detailed and do not include as much information, but

this offers great scope for individual exploration.

Eight selected regions have double-page features highlighting particular aspects of the area. Topics include arts and crafts, food and drink and artistic links. The sections of the book are then completed in most cases by a page of gazetteer entries describing a number of selected other villages of interest in the region.

Montrésor   *(Indre-et-Loire)*

WHEN THE CHURCH BELLS RING IN MONTRÉSOR, THE CLOCK SEEMS TO TURN BACK. SET BETWEEN A SUBLIME CASTLE AND THE SHADY RIVER INDROIS, THIS 16TH-CENTURY GEM REVEALS ITS INTRICACIES TO THOSE WHO PERSEVERE.

Montrésor's modern and well-stocked tourist office sits near the base of the drive leading to the gates of the 11th-century fortress. As a first stop it is invaluable and not only for its brochures, maps and helpful suggestions. Special offers from makers of goats cheese, vineyards offering their Touraine labels and artisans opening their *atelier* to interested visitors all leave invitations here.

Having obtained a preview of what the area has to offer, visitors can then set out to see the château built by Foulques Nerra, the Gothic church and the beautiful medieval houses that overhang the River Indrois.

MEMORIES OF THE CRIMEA

In the charming and lush grounds of the château, a bone-dry fish pond has filled up with crushed leaves. Large black birds and bats flap out of the tall evergreens, cats dart from under wrought-iron lawn furniture and stone angels seem always to be watching. Mystery is in the air, and one begins to imagine the days when Captain Roger the Little Devil built this fortress to defend the Count d'Anjou. The château as seen today was renovated in 1849 by a Polish count who accompanied Prince Napoleon to Constantinople in the Crimean War, which explains the adornment of the interior with hunting trophies, military souvenirs and a carved wooden relief depicting the Polish King Jean III Sobieski battling the Ottomans in the 17th century.

Down in the village great pleasure comes from a stroll along the river where a few retired villagers can always be seen with long fishing rods dangling in the cool green ponds, angling for perch and red-eyed rudd under the fig trees, and children dive into the water from their bankside back gardens or splash along the edge among the lily pads. Crossing an old wood-and-metal footbridge, you step back across the centuries (if you do not yet paint with watercolours, this may be the inspiration you need). The village can be seen above. Entering a field in which a horse and a gypsy basketweaver live, near a large manor house, tourists may feel like trespassers, but this is happily not the case. The

Hidden within Montrésor's simplicity is its irresistible power to charm. Whether walking its crooked streets, above, or catching sight of a patient fisherman, right, visitors enter another world.

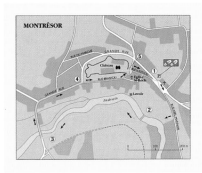

Another bridge crosses back into the village past a supermarket, and the road wraps round past the *Mairie* and a little cinema. The road makes a dramatic bend to the left, at which a 16th-century turret, now housing the local *gendarmerie*, overhangs the street.

OUT AND ABOUT

For something requiring more energy than a stroll, the tourist office has mapped out walking and cycling tours. The cycle tour consists of a 29-km route heading east of the village on the D10 turning north to Beaumont village on the D89, veering south-west at Chassenay on the D39, circling round the Plan d'Eau at Chemillé-sur-Indrois and returning to Montrésor on the D10. The walking tour covers 17km and cuts north from the village through the Bois de Beaumont, the Village du Bois, Chanteloup, La Perruche round the Plan d'Eau and back to Montrésor along the Indrois.

If the weather is particularly warm, visitors may enjoy swimming in a small lake 2km away – a refreshing relief during a summer road trip. Drive anticlockwise through the lower part of the village to reach a turn-off to the right just before a shop. Signs marked Plan d'Eau and Chemillé-sur-Indrois show

❶ Park in front of the tourist office or near the church (église) in Grande Rue. Opposite the church take the path marked rue Abel-Marinier down towards the river, with its lovely view of the fortress across the village. Continue for 100m, then turn down an unpaved lane to the river bank.

❷ Continue along the river to your right until you reach a dubious-looking footbridge. Cross it (the locals will vouch for its safety). At the end, turn right. Pass through the open spot in the fence and head across the pasture. From here there is an excellent perspective of Montrésor and its château. The old village lavoir (public washing area) comes into view on the other bank.

Proceed along the river, past the cascade, until the river narrows. Reaching a stone bridge, look for the easiest spot to climb on to the rue des Ponts. Cross the bridge and follow the road which passes a supermarket and leads into the village, with the Hôtel de France on your left. The château is straight ahead.

❹ At the 16th-century turret, continue straight along a street marked 'Sans Issue' (dead end), this is rue Branicki, named after the Polish count. Note the fine statue at number 13 and the medieval alley and ramparts between 13 and 15. Opposite number 29, turn left up the cobblestone path (ruelle des Roches) and follow it to the right. Go up the hill (you are between the château and the Église St-Roch).

At rue Nicholas-Potocki turn left for the château, moving through the iron gates into the enchanting park. Return along rue Nicholas-Potocki and back to the church.

▷ Length of walk: 1.5km
▷ Approximate time: 1 to 2 hours
▷ Terrain: Unsuitable for wheelchairs and pushchairs
▷ Open: Château guided tours Apr–Nov
▷ Refreshments: Restaurants, pâtisserie

Map Symbols

Main road	————	Château	🏰
Minor road	═══════	Church	✝
Track	═ ═ ═ ═	Place of interest	◼
Footpath	- - - - -	Post Office	PTT
Steps	▥▥▥▥	Tourist information	𝑖
Railway	—⊣—	Parking	Ⓟ
Bridge	⤳	Start point of walk	👣
Spot height	▲	Walk route	▬▬
Viewpoint	☼	Optional walk route	▸▸▸)▸
Cliff	〰	Direction of walk	➡
Castle wall	▬▬	Stage of walk	①

9

VILLAGE FRANCE

FRANCE IS A PERENNIAL FAVOURITE FOR HOLIDAY-MAKERS FROM ALL OVER THE WORLD, BUT IS SEEMS TO HOLD A PARTICULAR FASCINATION FOR THE BRITISH TRAVELLER, WHO MAY APPEAR TO HAVE A 'LOVE-HATE' RELATIONSHIP WITH THE COUNTRY, BUT WHO IS STILL DRAWN TO IT TIME AND TIME AGAIN.

THIS BOOK AIMS TO PRESENT THE ARMCHAIR TRAVELLER AND THE SEASONED VISITOR WITH SOME OF THE MOST DELIGHTFUL AND INTERESTING VILLAGES IN THIS DIVERSE COUNTRY, FROM POPULAR FAVOURITES TO THE RELATIVELY LITTLE-KNOWN, FROM SLEEPY SEASIDE PORTS TO BUSTLING MARKET TOWNS.

THEY MAY BE LARGE OR SMALL, BUT ALL HAVE THAT VILLAGE ATMOSPHERE SO DIFFICULT TO CAPTURE OTHER THAN BY PERSONAL EXPLORATION.

Brittany

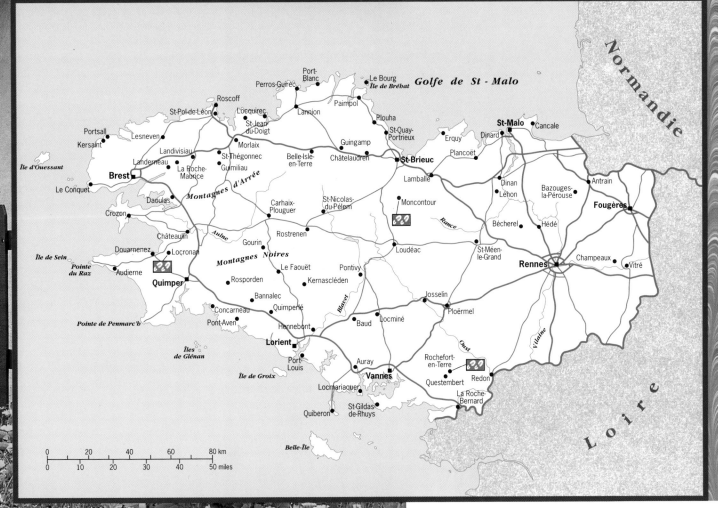

Normandie

Golfe de St - Malo

Port-Blanc
Le Bourg
Île de Bréhat
Perros-Guirec
Roscoff
St-Pol-de-Léon
Locquirec
Lannion
Paimpol
Plouha
St-Quay-Portrieux
St-Malo
Cancale
Portsall
Lesneven
St-Jean-du-Doigt
Erquy
Dinard
Kersaint
Landivisiau
Morlaix
Guingamp
Châtelaudren
St-Brieuc
Plancoët
Île d'Ouessant
Landerneau
St-Thégonnec
Belle-Isle-en-Terre
Lamballe
Antrain
Brest
La Roche-Maurice
Guimiliau
Montagnes d'Arrée
Dinan
Léhon
Bazouges-la-Pérouse
Fougères
Le Conquet
Daoulas
Carhaix-Plouguer
St-Nicolas-du-Pélem
Moncontour
Bécherel
Hédé
Crozon
Rostrenen
Rance
St-Méen-le-Grand
Châteaulin
Aulne
Gourin
Loudéac
Rennes
Champeaux
Île de Sein
Douarnenez
Locronan
Montagnes Noires
Le Faouët
Pontivy
Vitré
Pointe du Raz
Audierne
Quimper
Rosporden
Kernascléden
Josselin
Bannalec
Blavet
Ploërmel
Vilaine
Pointe de Penmarc'h
Concarneau
Quimperlé
Baud
Locminé
Pont-Aven
Hennebont
Oust
Lorient
Rochefort-en-Terre
Îles de Glénan
Port-Louis
Auray
Redon
Loire
Île de Groix
Vannes
Questembert
La Roche-Bernard
Locmariaquer
Quiberon
St-Gildas-de-Rhuys

Belle-Île

| 0 | 20 | 40 | 60 | 80 km |
| 0 | 10 | 20 | 30 | 40 | 50 miles |

*C*enturies of conflict and resistance have given Brittany its distinctive flavour. A mellow land married to the sea, it is a blend of Celtic mystery and an independent spirit that has traded and warred with France, England and beyond.

Locronan

(Finistère)

FIRST A HOLY PLACE, THEN A BUSTLING SAILCLOTH-PRODUCING CAPITAL, LOCRONAN TODAY IS A 15TH-CENTURY TOWN PRESERVED TO PERFECTION FROM THE RAVAGES AND DESECRATION OF TIME AND STEEPED IN A DEEP RELIGIOUS SPIRIT.

The name Locronan marks the transformation of an ancient Druidic ceremonial site to Christianity by the hand of St Ronan (*loc* meaning 'holy place'). According to some accounts, Ronan was a 5th-century Irish bishop seeking a retreat in Brittany. He set up his first hermitage near Brest in what was later named St-Renan in his honour. However, his reputation as a healer left him no peace, so he fled to settle on the slope of a hill in the Forest of Névet, a place which was sacred to the local pagans.

The tomb of St Ronan. In July and August there is an excellent free tour of the church, whose stone has acquired a particular character from ambient humidity

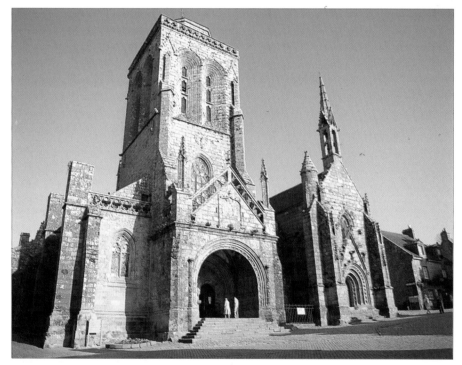

THE SAINT AND THE SORCERESS

It was here in the forest that Ronan encountered a formidable challenge: Keben, a local sorceress, probably a Druidess, claimed that Ronan's miracles were in fact witchcraft, and that he could pacify wolves because he was himself a werewolf. She tricked him into getting arrested, and after his release (having proved his innocence by performing a miracle), her continued harassment finally drove him to find tranquillity elsewhere. Upon Ronan's death shortly thereafter, the oxen pulling his mortal remains refused to go where directed and spontaneously brought him back to be buried in Névet Forest. The sorceress was washing clothes at the foot of Ronan's hill when she saw the oxen drawing her enemy back. Enraged, Keben struck one of the animal's horns. The earth swallowed Keben in a gust of fire, and Ronan was buried where the ox horn had fallen. The miracles that proliferated at Ronan's tomb gave birth to a monastic community, and later to the famous troménies.

Locronan's Troménie (from 'tro minihy', a walk round the monastery) is a yearly procession. The Petite Troménie, on the second Sunday in July, follows a 5-km (3-mile) path, thought to have been Ronan's daily penitential walk, with stops at three hallowed sites. The Grande Troménie, celebrated every six years (the next is in 2001), is a week-long pro-

The church of St Ronan is an imposing sight, above; *below, fine stone buildings in the centre of Locronan*

cession that traces the sanctification hike Ronan undertook every six days. Four thousand pilgrims gathered in 1995 behind Ronan's remains and his bell in a 13-km (8-mile) trek with 12 stops for prayer. Bretons say that entry into Paradise depends on your having accomplished in your lifetime one Grande Troménie or three Petites Troménies.

THE WEALTH OF LOCKRAM

The elegant 15th- to 18th-century residences lining the streets of Locronan attest to its past glory. 'Lockram', as the British called the rough linen sailcloth produced here from the 15th century, was exported to England, Holland and Spain for over 300 years, covering the town with wealth and prestige. But industrialisation sounded the death knell of this trade in the 19th century. Thus began the decline of the village until the early 1900s, when its fortunes were reversed by the unlikely alliance of a local farmer and a town councillor. Their efforts sparked off a long process of restoration, aided over the years by government subsidies and official recognition as a historic site. Tourism has become the lifeblood of the village and has kept alive its many interesting arts and crafts. Today Locronan offers the enchantment of a town where time seems to have stood still. Visiting

A welcoming sign of Brittany's speciality beckons the hungry visitor. Regional pastries are worth sampling

on a summer's evening, you might come across St Ronan's legend being enacted in the street, or have the chance of listening to an organ recital in the magical atmosphere of the ancient church.

The Walk

1

Begin your visit in the *musée*, with its fine exhibition of 1930s paintings of the Locronan area and a film showing the 1929 Grande Troménie.

2

Walk round to the Église St-Ronan. Inside, a striking pulpit (1707) tells St Ronan's legend in 10 medallions. The Pénity Chapel contains St Ronan's tomb (1430 sculpture) and a remarkable 16th-century sculpture of the Deposition of Jesus from the Cross. Facing away from the church on the square, admire the second house from the right, the Bureau des Toiles (Linencloth Office), built in 1669.

3

Take a downhill stroll along rue Moal. About 200m down on the left, a calvary stands before the Chapelle de Bonne-Nouvelle (15th and 17th century), the 1668 Fontaine St Eutrope and a washing place still in use.

4

Returning up rue Moal, the second dirt road on your left leads you to a view of the church and the town of Plonévez-Porzay. Continue uphill and turn right into rue des Charettes towards the church, taking in the 17th-century houses on both sides.

5

Cross the Grande Place and turn down rue Lann to the Maison Yves Tanguy on the left where the Surrealist painter was raised. Go left at the end of rue Lann, then left again, and swing round the outskirts of the town to the calvary that marks the site of a former ancient chapel, the Emplacement chapelle et cimetière St Maurice.

6

Turn left again to the main square, for the pleasure of the shops, traditional musicians and refreshment possibilities.

i

▷ Length of walk: 1km
▷ Approximate time: 2½ hours
▷ Terrain: Mostly easy, with some down- and uphill walks (not too steep), and partly unsurfaced
▷ Parking: Six car parks, small fee covers all summer
▷ Open: Museum: daily 10–6:30 15 Jun to 15 Sep; small fee. Chapelle de Bonne-Nouvelle: 10–7 from Easter to end Sep. An excellent free tour of the church is offered by the SPREV (tel: 98.91.70.14) in July and August
▷ Refreshments: Tea, ice cream and some exceptional regional pastries at the bend in the rue Lann. Restaurants and cafés on the main square.

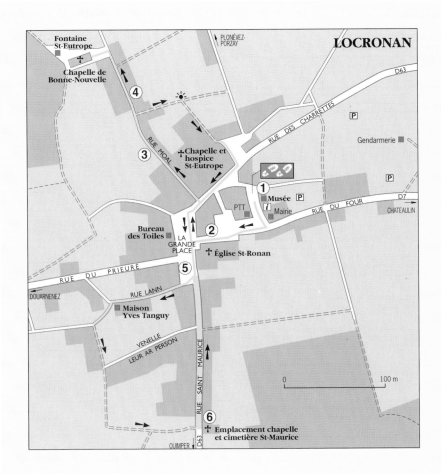

Moncontour

(Côtes d'Armor)

MONCONTOUR MAY BE SMALL, BUT THERE IS SOMETHING INDISPUTABLY GRAND ABOUT THIS CITADEL STANDING GUARD OVER TWO VALLEYS, READY TO DEFEND THE CITY OF LAMBALLE AGAINST AN ATTACK FROM THE SOUTH.

Today's peaceful, graceful town of Moncontour – where wrought-iron picture signs identify businesses and public buildings – looks back on a history of violent turmoil. Indeed, after its fortification in the 11th century, the *cité* was to be the object of continuous sieges and attacks. A prized strategic possession, it was, among other afflictions, coveted by a duke's son rebelling against his father, fought

over by rival families, and lost by the Breton camp to the French. It was bitterly disputed during the war against the Huguenots, after which, in 1626, the infamous Cardinal Richelieu had most of its fortifications and its castle dismantled.

FROM CONFLICT TO COMMERCE

Turning their energy then to the production of leather and linen, the Moncontourais developed a flourishing trade which extended from Amsterdam to Cadiz. Almost all the magnificent town houses lining the medieval streets of the old district date back to this prosperous 17th- and 18th-century period. The arrival of the Sisters of St Thomas de Villeneuve in 1663 and their establishment of a nearby hospice (now a retirement home run by the same order) completed Moncontour's

Capping a commanding hilltop position, Moncontour proudly recalls its medieval days with elegant shop signs of artful images and finely turned wrought iron

opening up and accession to tranquillity.

One last skirmish was to trouble the town when, held by the Republicans, it was attacked by Royalist rebels during the counter-revolutionary Chouan insurrection.

Peace treaties were finally signed in the house now occupied by the tourist information centre.

A LIVING FAITH

If you look up as you meander through the streets and alleys of Moncontour, you are bound to notice an abundance of statues of

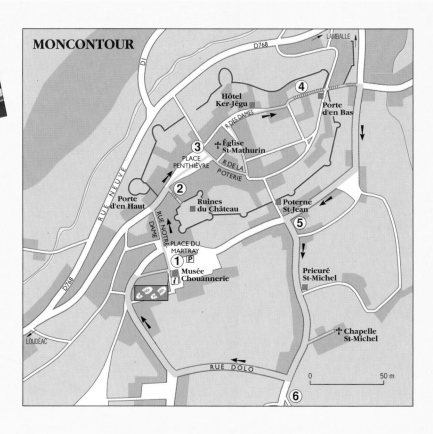

The Walk

Visit the Musée Chouannerie in the tourist office, with its superb model of the village in 1809. The diminutive place du Martray, where the pillory once stood, leads to rue Notre-Dame, with the 1773 statue of the Virgin in a niche mentioned in the text. The Porte d'en Haut (High Gate) is on your left.

Open a gate on your right and go up the steps and through a 'hidden' door to a small fruit, flower and vegetable patch. These Ruines du Château are all that remain of the former castle.

At place Penthièvre, the 18th-century house at No 2 is where General Hoche set up quarters during the Revolution. The stained-glass windows in the Église St-Mathurin, erected in the 16th century and rebuilt in the 18th, are among the most beautiful in Brittany. Turn right down rue de la Poterie, noting the sculpted face at the top right-hand side of the Post Office (1616). Turn left and then right down rue des Dames. The Hôtel Ker-Jégu houses the town hall and an exhibition room.

Go down the steps through the Porte d'en Bas (Low Gate). Stop in the small park for a breather and enjoy the view. At the bottom of the steps, go right and walk along the remains of the ramparts till you reach the 14th-century gate, Poterne St-Jean.

Go left, up the hill past the ruins of the 11th-century Prieuré St-Michel, then on to the Chapelle St-Michel.

⑥

Keep climbing till you get to a small stone wall on your left, over which you can admire the landscape. Turn back and take the rue Dolo, quite soon on your left. Halfway along, just before it bends, turn round to look down on the chapel. Turn right at the end of the street, then descend to the city and return to the starting point through the tiny rue de la Chouannerie.

the Virgin gazing down from cosy little niches. At the one in rue Notre-Dame (point 1 of the walk), a prayer is gently urged: 'If Mary's love be engraved in thy heart, thou who goest by, do not forget to pray to her'.

Living proof of the town's piety can be witnessed on Whitsun (Pentecôte) weekend, in June, when the townsfolk celebrate the St Mathurin *pardon*. St Mathurin was not, oddly enough, a Breton saint. Born in Burgundy in the 3rd century, he was renowned for healing mental diseases. Though he died in Rome, a relic (the frontal bone) was brought in the 9th century to Moncontour where, as the object of fervent devotion, he was attributed with unlimited healing powers (many believe him to have replaced an ancient pagan divinity).

The rue des Dames, one of Moncontour's many delightful streets where houses have stood unaltered for centuries, rewards an appreciative leisurely stroll

St Mathurin's *pardon* opens on the Saturday night with a torch-lit procession ending in a huge bonfire reminiscent of a solar cult, Sunday continues with a well-attended procession behind the saint's marble bust and relic, while Monday rounds off the feast with lively dancing.

The town stages an annual medieval festival on the third Sunday in August, hosts a Celtic music festival in July and holds a busy market every Monday morning. Immersed in Moncontour's medieval character at every turn, you cannot but fall under its spell.

The sea – for the moment a calm turquoise – provides a living for these Cancale fishermen, above, returning from work. The embroidered banner, left, is carried in processions in Josselin, where Olivier de Clisson and Marguerite de Rohan are buried

Cancale
(ILLE-ET-VILAINE)

Legend has it that the pair of giant rocks rising out of the water across from Cancale's Pointe de la Chaîne are merely some loose gravel that Gargantua shook out of his shoe as he journeyed past. Driving along the favoured approach to the town from the east along the scenic coastal route D155, you can see Cancale boldly jutting out into the water, like the prow of a ship sailing into the bay – an appropriately nautical image for a place that has always made its living from the sea.

The parish of Cancale is said to have been founded in the 6th century by St Méen, a Breton monk. By the 15th century it had developed into a port, and it was not long before the infamous *corsaires*, or pirates, made

it their den – for which reason it was pillaged and bombarded by the English. The more legitimate sea trades also developed, of course, and by the 19th century such a high a proportion of its men were sailors that the women of Cancale became known throughout the land for assuming the male role at home and taking on a mannish character.

Cancale has become a well-equipped seaside resort, but its livelihood remains centred on oyster farming. Its port, La Houle, sits with its back against the cliffs at the foot of the town, built 50m up above the sea. La Houle is no longer teeming with *bisquines*, the quick, sturdy fishermen's boats of the 19th century. Nowadays people watch an army of tractors putt-putting round the oyster beds at low tide. At the Ferme Marine L'Aurore (oyster museum) you can arrange for a guided tour of the oyster beds. On a clear day you will see Le Mont-St-Michel poised on the horizon about 35km away.

A leisurely walk round Cancale should take in the Musée des Arts et Traditions Populaires (Popular Crafts and Traditions).

A *cannon stands as a reminder that not all visitors to La Roche Bernard were welcome in the past. Today a suspension bridge allows easy access to the town*

The Walk

This leisurely walk in Cancale is about 3.5km and should take approximately 2½ hours, including stops. Begin at the Musée des Arts et Traditions Populaires. Then turn left as you go out, cross the tiny square and the rue Vallés Porcon, then down the rue Duquesne to the centre of town, and the new Église St-Méen (an 1875 neo-Gothic building) and the Musée des Bois Sculptés.

Take rue du Hock, a diagonal street off the square at back of the church, to a small terrace overlooking oyster beds and the bay.

From here, go down to the Sentier des Douaniers. Go right on it and follow to the end ('Kilomètre 0') for a view of the port.

Climb down to the docks and walk out on the Jetée de la Fenêtre for a good view of Cancale and its port. Go left on the docks past the port where you will find coffee shops and restaurants in which to enjoy some well-deserved refreshment.

Formerly the Église St-Méen (1714), it is now filled with Cancale's fishing paraphernalia, costumes, furniture, everyday objects and photographs down the decades. The new St-Méen Church is an 1875 neo-Gothic building, and the 189 steps up the church steeple will lead you to a breathtaking view of Mont-St-Michel Bay. The Musée des Bois Sculptés on the northern side of the church displays more than 300 amazing examples of the venerable Breton craft of woodcarving. If you go along the Sentier des Douaniers, the old coastal footpath on which the border police made their rounds, you will appreciate a pair of binoculars, and a hat on a sunny day.

Josselin
(Morbihan)

The elegant castle of Josselin, towering beside the banks of the River Oust, is still the residence of the ancient and powerful Rohan family, who have owned it since the 15th century. They withdraw to their upstairs apartments in the daytime to let groups of visitors admire the splendours of their ground-floor rooms. The excellent guided tour is also a fascinating account of Breton history.

A short distance away, facing a pleasant sloping square, the spacious and graceful Notre-Dame-du-Roncier basilica watches over the 15th- to 17th-century houses preserved along Josselin's narrow streets.

La Roche Bernard
(Morbihan)

In the 10th century Bernard the Viking, knowing a superb defensive location when he saw one, built a fortress here. Situated on a massive promontory overlooking the Vilaine estuary, just a few kilometres inland from the Atlantic, La Roche Bernard became the scene of some of the great historic conflicts of the region, and was the stronghold of Breton Protestantism for over a century. The old fortified city, a testimony to its rich and turbulent past, still impresses with its dramatic setting, best seen from the graceful, lofty bridge that approaches it from the northwest. The Musée de la Vilaine Maritime recounts the river's remarkable activities since the turn of the century.

Rochefort-en-Terre

(Morbihan)

IN THIS TINY VILLAGE OF 650 INHABITANTS, RESTORED 16TH- AND 17TH-CENTURY TOWN HOUSES CLING TO HILLY STREETS AND CASCADES OF FLOWERS POUR OUT OF WINDOW BOXES, PROMISING A MEMORABLE VISIT.

As early as Roman times Rochefort had been singled out for its good strategic position: on a rocky spur, it afforded easy access from only one side. Appreciating its potential, the Romans erected temples and villas here, and set up a camp to the west to defend them. Thus was born the Roche Forte, literally the 'fortified rock'. The Roman defence in time gave way to a medieval one, and by the 12th century a small town had developed and a church was built.

The odd location of the church – off the town's centre – was determined by the discovery of a statue of the Virgin on that spot,

A handsome front door, hand-painted with timeless appeal, captures the imagination at every level

in a cluster of old tree trunks (a *tronchaie*). The statue is believed to have been hidden there three centuries earlier to save it from Norman looting. The church was thus dedicated to Notre Dame de la Tronchaye.

A pretty roofscape of sloping slate, dormer windows, turrets and chimneys tops the quaint grey stone and half-timbered buildings of Rochefort, above. Everywhere, flowers spill out of window boxes and tubs, as in the main street, below

A TOWN FLOURISHES, A CASTLE FALLS

In the 1300s, the Rochefort lords became influential in the duchy and the town gained prestige. The high borough, where the elite dwelt at the foot of the castle, had a wall built round it in the 15th century, leaving the craftsmen outside in the low borough. The castle and the town were to have totally different fates. The Rochefort lords' political involvement caused the castle to be dismantled twice, and it was finally demolished in the post-Revolutionary turmoil of 1793. Meanwhile, the town continued to develop on the basis of solid industries in textile, wood and slate.

A HAVEN FOR PAINTERS

At the turn of the century, many landscape painters and miniaturists began coming to Rochefort-en-Terre. Among them was an American artist, Alfred Klots; enchanted with the village, he decided to buy the castle ruins, and began building a new castle by purchasing stones, doors, turrets and dormer windows from other nearby castles. The new château, a strikingly original blend of styles and design, was completed by 1927.

Klots also launched, in 1911, a yearly 'deck your house with flowers' contest. As a result Rochefort became, and has remained, one of the most beautifully flower-adorned towns in the country. A vast investment

scheme was undertaken in 1970, at the end of which the town could boast 60 *gîtes* in the area and a regional museum at the castle; its ancient houses were restored, its streets paved, and all outward signs of modernity, such as television antennas, removed.

One day a year, in spring or summer, Rochefort is the venue of a Brittany-wide painting competition, and the streets are filled with painters of all sorts and styles displaying their entries. With its regular summer art exhibitions, outstanding restaurants, Creative Art School (painting courses all year round), Our Lady of Tronchaye pardon (first Sunday after 15 August), and the old town magnificently lit up from mid-June to mid-September for enchanting night strolls, Rochefort-en-Terre is indeed unforgettable.

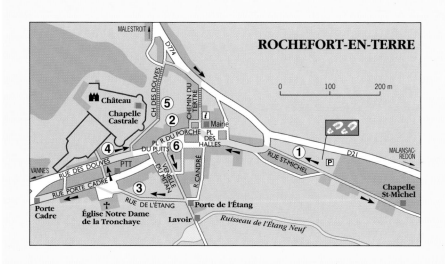

The Walk

 1 From the St-Michel car park, take rue St-Michel to the place des Halles. The tourist office and an art gallery are located in the Mairie (Town Hall).

 2 On the right-hand side of rue du Porche, note the magnificent schist-and-granite houses. Go left down the Venelle de Mitan alley in front of the turret-clad house into a 16th-century atmosphere, then continue downhill to the former *lavoir*.

 3 Turn right at rue de l'Étang to the Église Notre Dame de la Tronchaye, which was modified in the 15th century. Note the snake-shaped, horned figure on the corner of the bell tower. Inside, on top of a separation wall behind the pulpit, sits a macabre wooden sculpture of skulls, bones and ears of maize. From the church turn left along rue Porte Cadre to Porte Cadre. Returning back along rue Porte Cadre, take the second left to a 1658 gate leading to the very few remains of the fortified château and Chapelle Castrale. The entrance fee covers the museum and a guided tour of the castle, otherwise inaccessible.

 4 Leaving the castle, follow rue des Douves; when you see the castle tower over a wall on your left, go left and walk along the rampart, chemin des Douves. From the top of the long stairway down to the old borough, admire the view of the heather-covered schist mountains.

 5 Walk down the steps, turn right, then right again into chemin du Tertre (another set of steps). At the back of the covered market, turn right into a back alley, past an old well to the schist side turret of the Café Breton, which has a stunning interior.

 6 After a quick glimpse of the place du Puits, return to the car park along rue St-Michel, at the very back of which is the 11th-century Chapelle St-Michel.

i

▷ Length of walk: 2.25km
▷ Approximate time: 3 hours (including castle visit)
▷ Terrain: Suitable for pushchairs and wheelchairs, except for stairs at points 4 and 5
▷ Parking: Three car parks (small fee)
▷ Open: Castle and Museum: Jul and Aug daily 10:30–6:30; Jun and Sep daily 10:30–noon and 2–6:30; weekends only Apr, May and Oct
▷ Refreshments: Four good restaurants, four *crêperies*, plus snack bars

It is impossible to visit Brittany without soon becoming aware of the people's ever-present religious feelings. As Breton writer Anatole Le Braz said in the 19th century: 'Travelling in Brittany is to set foot on the classical soil of ossuaries and charnel-houses. There is no village too small and humble to have one of its own, or at least to be able to boast of its remains' – and a century later the statement still holds true. In fact, whatever their creed or culture – pagan or Christian, Stone Age or Information Age – Bretons have manifested their beliefs with conviction. The landscape itself tells the story, enriched not only by churches, but also by calvaries, crosses, chapels and isolated oratories, and the hauntingly inscrutable megaliths.

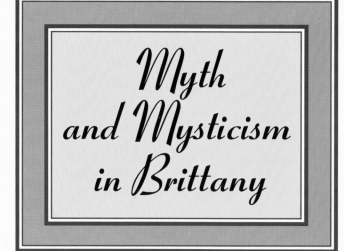

Myth and Mysticism in Brittany

Brittany's religious architecture may be centuries old, but the faith that brought it into being is still a living part of Brittany's heritage. Upcoming pilgrimages and *pardons* (religious festivals dedicated to patron saints) are advertised all over town as well as in the church porches. Locals are magnetised by such events, and major celebrations draw pilgrims from all over Brittany. Witnessing one of these gatherings, you will come away impressed by the participants' sincerity, as young and old of every station in life walk in procession (some in regional costume), ask the saint's intercession or pray for forgiveness, protection or relief from illness.

For the Breton, this interweaving of the spiritual with day-to-day living is part of the region's adherence to tradition. Until modern times, life here was hard, with much effort and suffering involved in eking out an existence from land or sea. The sea, indeed, was as much feared as loved, providing food but also bringing death. Grounded in this harsh and inescapable reality, the Breton people have long had a familiar relationship with death which some might think morbid. On the Île-de-Sein, where old ways are fiercely guarded, the age-old greeting is: 'Joy to your departed'/'Joy to yours too'. Inscriptions in ossuaries offer such sombre reflections as: 'Death, judgement, cold hell, when man thinks of it he must tremble. Mad is the man who does not pray, knowing that he must die' – or the arrestingly simple:

Giant relics of Druidic beliefs, below, defy the passage of time, while intricate lace coiffes, above, make a celebratory appearance on Christian holy days

'Me today, you tomorrow'.

Even in pre-Christian times the Bretons were a people given to mysticism. Thousands of years ago, in the Stone Age, their fervent Druidic beliefs led them to erect granite monuments that have testified to every generation since, their purpose perplexing, their construction confounding – passage graves, dolmens (table-like tombs) and the astonishing alignments of menhirs that stand, row upon row, mile upon mile, silently claiming the land. Today the alignments are interrupted by roads and fields, and individual stones can be seen forming part of a house or wall. Enough remain undisturbed, however, to intrigue us and ultimately to defeat our attempts to explain them.

Unconquered Hearts

What the Romans found on conquering the region in 56 BC was a well-organised Celtic society centred on its Druidic high priests, the all-powerful, uncontested leaders. The knowledge they claimed – preserved in the oral tradition of verse and passed on to priests-in-training and children of noble birth – covered soothsaying, healing, the casting of spells and the power to change form. Inland Brittany, known as Argoat, was covered with magical forests of beech and oak in whose deep and misty shade dwelt all manner of mythical beings. Their presence explained much of life to the Druidic faithful who lived intimately with nature – woodcutters, clog-makers, charcoal burners and other simple folk. Their beliefs are seen today in the place names and legends linked to fairies, sorcerers and giants.

Although the Romans sculpted images of their own gods on the Celtic monuments, they did little else to change the society they had found. Their departure after four centuries revealed the persistence of Brittany's indigenous form of nature worship. Christian Celts from Britain and Ireland, fleeing Saxon invasions in the 5th and 6th centuries, found a people firmly convinced of the supernatural, though pagan in form. With no idols to destroy, no sacred texts to burn, no temples to tear down, the task of Christianising depended on ingenuity. The newcomers built chapels beside myth-bound springs and, like the Romans before them, carved their own symbols into the ancient granite monuments or crowned them with crosses.

They also incorporated some Druidic concepts into the presentation of the new faith. Thus those Christians preaching the afterlife were served by the earlier entity known as Ankou (meaning death, oblivion, sorrow), who announced a person's death, then carried his soul to mysterious islands beyond a river or sea. The

Processions in regional costume mark religious festivals, like this one in Pont l'Abbé, above. Ste-Marie-de-Ménez-Hom's calvary, right, tells of faith

Christians explained that the souls of the converted then left these islands to be welcomed into Paradise.

Slow Victory for Christ

The relative isolation of the region from the rest of Christendom resulted in a number of other unconventional practices. Celtic missionaries were often 'of no fixed abode', taking along a consecrated altar stone on their wanderings; they preferred the Breton language to Latin; they observed religious feasts on different dates and – more worryingly – some lapsed into the practice of soothsaying and pagan rituals. In spite of these irregularities, Christianity had established itself by the end of the 7th century.

For a few decades, under the influence of Charlemagne and his son Louis I, an attempt at 'order' was made as Bretons were told to abandon the customs they had received 'from the Scots'. However, in 845 Brittany gained independence from the empire and, existing as a separate kingdom for about a century, developed its unique form of Christianity with many a reference to Celtic mythology.

Of this early Christian period, very few traces remain. 'Normans' (literally 'men of the North', ie Scandinavians) descended upon Brittany and, for over a hundred years, pillaged and demolished everything in sight. Monks and bishops fled, taking with them treasures and relics. In an unsettled age, legend once again stepped in, this time to promote the memory of happier, prouder days. The original Celtic missionaries, it was said, had sailed to Brittany on barges of stone, destroyed dragons, performed miracles and engaged in cosmic duels with local Druids. In life they may have been monks or hermits, but in legend they became bishops and, in the next life, saints – practically none of whom are known outside Brittany, though their numbers be in the thousands.

By the 11th century, when calm was slowly descending on the region, a more Latinised form of Christianity was taking hold. Old churches were rebuilt, and new abbeys and cathedrals were raised to God's glory. Most of those still standing today date from the 14th and 15th centuries, designed in the Flamboyant Gothic style, sometimes set on Romanesque foundations. It is no surprise to find that the further west these structures are, the less they resemble those found elsewhere in France. Brittany's religious architecture achieves uniqueness in the form of the parish close, a grouping of church, calvary, cemetery, ossuary and triumphal gate enclosed by a low wall (see Guimiliau, page 22). This typically Breton form of artistic and religious expression developed between 1550 and 1650, a time of increasing prosperity in the country districts, as much a proof of worldly rivalry between wealthy villages as of Christian devotion. Yet the lessons of faith carved in stone for all generations remain potent reminders of the mystical heritage of this land, where the presence of Death is linked with each moment of life.

At Guimiliau, the calvary contains over 200 characters playing out their role in 17 scenes from Christ's Passion; inside, ornate carving is highlighted in gilt

Guimiliau
(Finistère)

The sombre side of Breton mysticism is expressed with amazing force in the architectural entity known as the *enclos paroissial* (parish close), and an exquisite example is to be found in Guimiliau.

Ranging from fairly simple to sumptuous, an *enclos* was a closed-off area in the middle of town, made up of a low wall round the parish cemetery and three constructions: the church, a calvary and an ossuary (where disinterred bones were placed, making more room in the tiny cemeteries). The interrela-tionship of these structures and their functions, representing in a single holy place the link between everyday religious life and the afterlife, is believed to have followed on from the Bretons' pre-Christian relationship with the divinity Ankou, or Death. A *porte triomphale*, or triumphal gate, which gave access to this garden of rest and symbolised the triumphal entry of the Christian into the eternal kingdom, was opened on Sundays. For entrance at other times, the gate, built as a classical arch, usually had a permanent opening on one side of it, partially blocked off to prevent animals from wandering in.

The most striking closes were built in the west of Brittany in the 16th and 17th centuries. Their style is Flamboyant Gothic typical of the Breton Renaissance. Granite was used for the main construction, and the myriad statues and figurines were usually sculp-

The Walk

Enter through the comparatively modest triumphal gate and, after admiring the *enclos* ensemble, go to the calvary (1588), an extravagant portrayal of crowds of characters populating 17 scenes of the Passion.

Take a walk round the outside of the 16th-century church. The tri-cylindrical vestry was added in 1683. Note the ossuary when you return, to the left of the south porch. Large statues of the twelve Apostles standing inside the porch show traces of their original colours.

A sense of spaciousness prevails inside the church; take your time and look at every bit of it. In July and August, student volunteers provide a fascinating free tour.

ted out of kersantite, an easy-to-work, almost indestructible lava rock from the Brest area.

The church generally stands in the centre of the cemetery, and can be circled round without leaving the close. Its main entrance is usually a tall porch on the south side of the church, even though the chancel is on the east. The ossuary sometimes developed into a separate temple-like building. The calvary, placed between the arch and the main church entrance, is a profoundly moving Breton monument representing Christ on the Cross. At the foot of the Cross the Passion is depicted in numerous, vivid bas-relief tableaux, an effective 'teaching aid' at a time of widespread illiteracy.

The Guimiliau parish has published a helpful Visitor's Guide, available in English at the funeral chapel. A thorough tour of the close should take about 1½ hours.

St-Thégonnec
(Finistère)

Established just a few miles from each other, St-Thégonnec and Guimiliau became fierce rivals in their effort to possess the holiest, most magnificent parish close. For every element built by the one, the other tried to outdo it with something more lavish and spectacular, and show that it was a richer parish. As a result, both Guimiliau and St-Thégonnec, but especially the latter, border on the excessive. Nonetheless, they are the most complete representations of this religious architectural form, the epitome of the *enclos*. St-Thégonnec called on the most sought-after craftsmen to contribute to what became the most ornate of all Brittany's religious monuments (the organ, for example, was specially commissioned to an Englishman). The 17th- and 18th-century church interior is high baroque, with marble and gold altars in an overall background of finely sculpted oak.

In St-Thégonnec, as in Guimiliau, many of the statues, figures and the finer pieces were dismantled and hidden during the 18th-century Revolutionary period, to prevent their destruction. When everything was reassembled, much of it was put back in the wrong place; this is particularly true of the calvary figures, in which the events of the Passion are out of order. St-Thégonnec claims that, in the upheaval, Guimiliau misappropriated the baptistery that was originally theirs, leaving them the plainer of the two. It is true that the sumptuous 1675 oak baptistery in Guimiliau touches the church ceiling, while St-Thégonnec's does not even begin to fill the grandiose space allowed for it.

The ossuary in St-Thégonnec, built in 1676 by a renowned architect, was intended, not to collect disinterred bones, but to honour death, so to speak. In the crypt the Entombment of Christ is portrayed in a tableau of life-size painted oak statues with exceptionally moving, expressive faces. In its frame are the following words:

> You see this dead Man, sinner, this God who gave you life
> His death is your work, and becomes your support:
> Through this attribute of goodness, you must at least know
> That if He died for you, you must live for Him.

St-Jean-du-Doigt
(Finistère)

Somewhat off the beaten track, not far from the sea, this village is indisputably worth a special trip. In sharp contrast with Guimiliau and St-Thégonnec, the parish close of St-Jean-du-Doigt presents a sort of naked, breathtaking beauty. Each component stands within the spacious perspective of a gently sloping burial ground, where sometimes a freshly dug grave is strewn with flowers, its spiritual dimension defined by a suggestion of delicate and mysterious curves. The triumphal gate, the oldest (1584) and reputedly the finest in Lower Brittany, opens on to a superb Renaissance fountain, rather than the usual calvary, representing the Baptism of the Lord watched over by His Heavenly Father.

The church construction is very high and narrow, contributing to the awesomeness of its austere interior, most of which was destroyed by a fire in 1955 (a small exhibition presents a few contemporary newspaper articles describing the disaster). The treasure of the church contains a relic miraculously discovered at Plougasnou in 1437: a bone from the right index finger of St John the Baptist which, plunged into the water of the fountain, acquires the power to cure eye dis-

eases (this accounts for the theme of the fountain as well as for the name of the parish). The beloved Duchess Anne, ruler of Brittany in the 15th century, came here to have her eyes treated, and her grateful generosity enabled the church to be built.

Fortunately, the famous relic survived the 1955 fire unscathed, and the parish *pardon* on 23 and 24 June, celebrating the birth of the saint, continues to attract hordes of blind and sick pilgrims hoping to be healed.

The fountain at St-Jean-du-Doigt, right, flows over the scene of the Baptism of the Lord. At St-Thégonnec, below, figures on the calvary wear medieval dress, according to the custom of sculptors of the period

Other Villages

BAZOUGES-LA-PÉROUSE

The church at Bazouges-la-Pérouse was born of the marriage of two medieval buildings, the 7th-century 'High Church' and the 9th-century 'Low Church', which had stood side by side until the 19th century. The intriguing three-nave church has elements from various different centuries. Pre-Romanesque pieces include the eastern walls and two massive holy-water basins.

Bazouges has a great many art galleries, and, every summer in July and August, the place becomes an 'artists' village', where even the knitwear in the shops ranks as artwork.

Set on a hilltop, the village makes a fine starting point for a cycling tour along what is known as the 'Marquis de la Rouërie' route. Blue triangle markers guide you through Villecartier Forest, past ancient yet well-preserved farms, mills, wayside crosses and Druidic sites to the village of Antrain and the 18th-century La Rouërie Castle.

BÉCHEREL

Like a jewellery box of precious stones, this tiny, formerly fortified city perches atop a hill. A Celtic cross and a nearby Gallo-Roman funeral stele are marks of Bécherel's early history, while the largely destroyed 12th-century fortifications point to the continuous strife it suffered in the Middle Ages. Its commercial activities, however, became ever more successful, bringing a prosperity reflected in unique 16th- to 19th-century houses still standing today. The Romanesque church soars upward out of a small circular maze of streets dotted with little squares and a minute garden. Bécherel's year-round weekly book fair and other literary events organised round a constellation of rare book shops point to its present vitality.

CHAMPEAUX

On arriving at the small cluster of houses that make up Champeaux, one's first thought is that the village could never have filled up – much less afforded – such a large church. The original 10th-century parish church was, in fact, demolished in the early 15th century by the d'Espinay family, which had supplanted the Champeaux family through a fusion of their two domains. To replace it, the wealthy and well-connected d'Espinay family enlarged their own family chapel, which the Pope raised to the rank of collegiate parish church

in 1437. The five canons who made up the chapter were housed next to the church in a cloister built round a well.

Today, ordinary people live in the former cloister – part of which is now the town hall – and geraniums spill out of the well. The collegiate church, classed as a historic building at the beginning of the century, still dominates the quiet landscape. Inside, its past glory is revealed by the furniture and stained-glass windows. The ethereal chanting of canons and clerics' voices still seems to linger round the remarkable sculpted wood stalls of the chancel, which date back to about 1540. They were donated by Guy III d'Espinay and his wife, who in 1553 were buried in the recess at the left of the choir. The recumbent marble statues on their tombs represent the lord and his wife as they must have looked at their death – and nude, a reminder that they took none of their wealth into the next life.

LE CONQUET

Galerie du Bout du Monde, or 'End-of-the-World Gallery', is the name of the establishment in the rue Troadec – the next stop being the New World across the sea. In 1558 the nearby Maison des Seigneurs, the 15th-century Maison des Anglais just up the street and six other houses were the only properties spared by the English because they belonged to English subjects. Today Le Conquet is a peaceful fishing harbour bringing in mainly shellfish, and a picturesque retreat away from the crowds typical of other Breton holiday venues.

Fishing boats at rest in Le Conquet, where tourists ride mail boats to islands

LE FAOUËT

Le Faouët, with a massive 15th-century market forming its centrepiece, attracted a great many painters in the first half of this century. The former 17th-century convent, entirely restored, has their paintings permanently on show, and every summer presents an exhibition of such quality that people come from far and wide to visit it. An absolute must, however, is the St Fiacre Chapel 3km south of the village. Its magnificent, multicoloured rood screen, minutely sculpted in lace-like detail, is the most beautiful in France, an experience in itself.

ÎLE-DE-BRÉHAT

Just a 15-minute boat ride from the mainland, the Île-de-Bréhat – really two islands bridged together – makes an exceptionally pleasant day trip. This car-free island has a lovely beach, as well as a series of long, invigorating walks and cycle routes through a variety of lush landscapes to a surprising number of interesting historic sites. Hike to the Chapel of St-Michel, up a 26-m hill, for a view over the whole of both islands and an idea of the delights they offer.

ÎLE-DE-SEIN

First a Stone Age site for megaliths, then a Druidic retreat, the island of 'Sena' was described by a Roman geographer as early as AD 43. Such a venerable history seems at odds with the nature of the island itself, small, flat, apparently fragile (it has survived being entirely swamped by the sea on at least two occasions, in 1868 and 1896). Not particularly a tourist centre, it draws visitors who admire its proud

people, their unchanging traditional lifestyle and the stark beauty of their environment. The inhabitants, renowned through the ages for their bravery in rescuing shipwrecked crews, earned another distinction in 1940, when all the males crossed the Channel to join de Gaulle's Free French army.

LOCMARIAQUER

Just inside the Gulf of Morbihan, this unpretentious resort is attractive for three main reasons. First, as a holiday place it offers wonderful sandy beaches, boat tours and great sailing facilities, and surrounding countryside that was made for cycling and walking tours. Second, as an oyster-farming location it is also a good destination for gastronomes. Third, as a prehistoric site it features major Stone Age remains erected some 2,000 to 5,000 years ago. Among a complex grouping of dolmens, tumuli and 'tables' lies a 20m, 350-tonne menhir, long since fallen and broken into four gigantic pieces.

QUESTEMBERT

Every Monday morning a very special market comes alive in Questembert's 16th-century covered marketplace – a picture-book setting of medieval houses. Le Marché de la Nature, as it is called, specialises in organic produce and home-made baked goods. Not surprisingly, Questembert is also renowned for its gastronomy, with a number of multi-star restaurants as well as an exclusive hotel. The surrounding area is the site of a great Breton victory over the Normans in 890, in which Alan the Great totally destroyed a large contingent of Norman pirates.

ST-GILDAS-DE-RHUYS

This pleasant family holiday resort, with its beaches and cliffs, possesses a unique architectural treasure: the Church of St-Gildas, largely Romanesque, a reminder of the town's eminent religious history. The monastery founded here in 530 by Gildas, a Celtic monk, was destroyed in the 10th century by Vikings, then built up again round a church in the 11th. By the 12th century, however, the monks had developed unorthodox behaviour which required reining in. The famous theologian Abélard (Héloïse's former lover) was the new abbot sent to reform them; he only narrowly escaped being poisoned and fled via an underground passageway.

Normandy

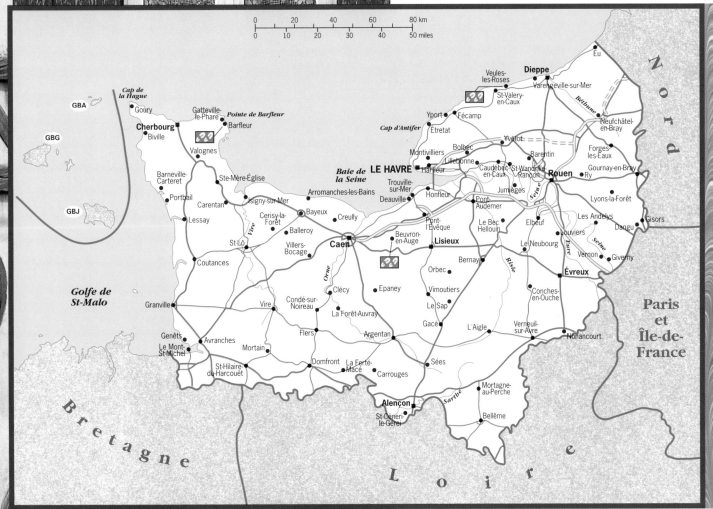

W hether you are looking for long sandy beaches or craggy cliff walks, hidden hamlets, the flavour of the Calvados orchards or the salt-air tang of traditional fishing villages, the friendly region of Normandy has something for everyone.

Barfleur

(Manche)

THIS FISHING VILLAGE ON THE COTENTIN PENINSULA WAS FORMERLY THE FAVOURITE PORT OF THE DUKES AND KINGS OF ENGLAND. WITH ITS PRETTY STREETS, BEACHES AND HARBOUR, BARFLEUR REMAINS A POPULAR TOURIST AND YACHTING CENTRE.

Seven centuries ago Barfleur, 27km east of Cherbourg, was the biggest port in Normandy and an important naval base. Its population has since dwindled, as has its prosperity, and Barfleur is now a simple working village. The busy harbour is always full of pleasure craft and fishing boats, armed with huge wheel pulleys and heaped with great lengths of netting ready for the next catch. You can sample their haul in one of the many quayside cafés and restaurants, or buy

Blue on blue: grounded vessels look out over boats bobbing in Barfleur's harbour, above. Through the old stone archway, left, is Cour Ste-Catherine House

direct from the fishermen's stands on the docks. There is also a morning market by the quay every Saturday and Wednesday.

With their quaintly shuttered cottages, crimson with geraniums, the quiet back streets hide numerous artists' and potters' *ateliers* (studios). The 17th-century granite buildings in the main street, with their blue-grey slate roofs – subject of many early Impressionist paintings – house a jumble of galleries and fishmongers, fine antiquities juxtaposed with humble fishing tackle.

Barfleur has its fair share of history, with the ruined remains of a feudal manor house near the sea wall and, surprisingly, even a fine cylindrical *colombier* (dovecot), usually the first target for destruction during the French Revolution, as the lord's pigeons used to feed off the grain from the peasants' land. The La Bretonne nunnery, founded in the 18th century by a local saint, Marie-Madeleine Postel, is still active today, and the fine 17th-century Church of St Nicolas, patron saint of mariners, looks out boldly along the coast towards the giant Gatteville lighthouse (see page 38) on the Pointe de Barfleur. The village, however, is perhaps best remembered for its naval history and the terrible shipwrecks off the coast.

NOTORIOUS COASTLINE

The port of Barfleur reached the height of its importance in Norman times, when it was frequented by the fine ships of several Anglo-Norman kings. It was here that William the Conqueror's famous ship *Le Mora* was built;

skippered by a local Barfleur sailor, it carried him to England in 1066. In 1966, to commemorate the 900th anniversary of this voyage, a bronze plaque was unveiled on a large rock at the harbour entrance. It was also from Barfleur, in 1194, that King Richard the Lionheart sailed back to England following his release from captivity in Austria.

This stretch of coast is often very treacherous and is well known for its swift currents. In fact, if not for the long stone breakwater to the north of the village, Barfleur would soon become swamped by the sea. Many ships have foundered here, especially near the Gatteville lighthouse.

The most famous wreck occurred nearly 900 years ago, when the *Blanche Nef* (White Ship) crashed into the rocks here in 1120, carrying the only son of England's King Henry I, plus 300 nobles. The prince had managed to escape in a small boat, but he returned to the doomed ship to rescue his sister. On reaching the *Blanche Nef*, his tiny boat sank under the weight of the nobles and crew who clambered on board. Perhaps unsurprisingly, Barfleur boasts France's first lifeboat station and one of its tallest lighthouses.

FRUITS OF THE SEA

Barfleur is famous throughout the region for its delicious *fruits de mer* (shellfish). Normandy's jagged coastline has recently become the main mussel- and oyster-producing area in France. Introduced in the 1960s, mussel production soon became a profitable activity and is Barfleur's main source of income. Whereas most mussels from Normandy are cultivated and collected by tractor at low tide, at Barfleur the fishermen bring in 'wild' mussels, fished by dragnet during high tide. Today over a quarter of all mussels and oysters eaten in France come from the region.

Barfleur is also well known for its extensive oyster hatcheries, producing seeds which are then reared further down the coast at St-Vaast-la-Hougue. These oysters, with their unique nutty taste, have earned accolades from gourmets round the world.

Set into a massive rock by the harbour, a bronze plaque, above, commemorates William the Conqueror's departure for England. Lichen-dotted roofs straddle typical granite buildings, below right

The Walk

❶

Start at the harbour end of the main road, rue St-Thomas-Becket, and walk along the quai Henri Chardon, past the Église St-Nicolas to the Station de Sauvetage (Lifeboat Museum) at the end.

❷

Take the narrow alleyway just before the museum to the place de l'Église. Follow the road back round to the church. Turn right into rue St-Nicolas, past the house of the late artist Paul Signac, potters' studios and antiques shops back to the quay.

❸

Turn right up the main road, take the second turning on the left, cross place Général de Gaulle into rue Pierre Salley past an unusual chimney-lighthouse, Feu Amont, walk across the bridge and past the Communauté de la Bretonne nunnery on the right. Take the next left along rue du 24 Juin on to the jetty for views of the village.

❹

Return along a path to the right by the water's edge, past a small lighthouse, Feu Aval, then retrace your steps to the bridge. Continue to hug the harbour, following a narrow gravel passage to the right.

❺

Rejoin the road opposite a gateway marked Porte Ste-Catherine. Enter through here, cross the 14th-century Cour Ste-Catherine courtyard and return to the main road.

ⓘ

▷ Length of walk: 3.25km
▷ Approximate time: 1 hour
▷ Terrain: All surfaced except two short footpath sections at point 4. Suitable for pushchairs and wheelchairs
▷ Parking: Free parking along the quay
▷ Open: Church: during services only. Lifeboat Museum: 10–noon and 2–6 Apr to Sep
▷ Refreshments: Quayside cafés, terraces and seafood stalls

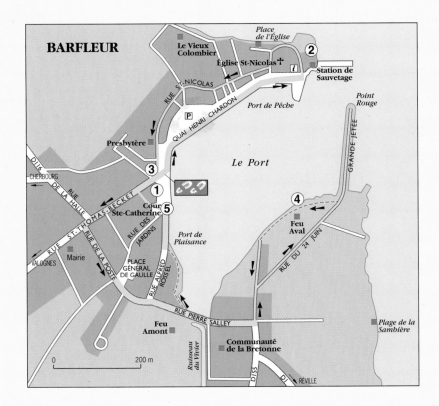

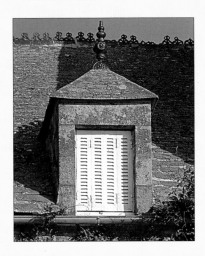

Beuvron-en-Auge

(Calvados)

DEEP IN THE PAYS D'AUGE – A LAND OF LUSH, HILLY MEADOWS AND ORCHARDS, CHEQUERBOARD MANORS, CHÂTEAUX AND CHARMING VILLAGES – LIES BEUVRON, FAMOUS FOR ITS CHEESE, CIDER AND HORSES, AND AN EXCELLENT TOURING CENTRE.

Beside Beuvron's main square stands one of the village's most impressive assets, a 16th-century *manoir*, or manor house, whose unusual wooden supports are carved with rustic figures and grimacing masks. Regardless of the season, its highly decorative half-timbering, typical of Pays d'Auge houses, is always adorned by a riot of colourful flowers. Indeed, the annual geranium fair held outside here is a spectacular sight. Elsewhere, other unusual façades combine wood panelling with brick, a fashion in the region during the 17th century.

In the main square itself, shaded by stately chestnut trees, the wooden covered market has been converted into a genteel collection of small antiques shops. Worth a browse, too, are the farm stores and *ateliers* (artists' studios) found in numerous alleyways throughout the village, along with several first-class restaurants.

Beuvron's other claim to fame is as a centre of horse-breeding. There are over a thousand privately owned *haras* (stud farms) in Calvados alone, and France's National Stud is only a short distance away at Haras du Pin. Beuvron's Manoir du Haras de Sens, with its splendid 16th-century outbuildings, is particularly well known for its trotting horses. It is possible to tour the *haras* and its fine

Provisions and beverages of all sorts are promised by this sign above shop premises in Beuvron's high street, which offers the full range of fresh local products

Calvados cellars, with their old-fashioned cider presses and heavy wooden crushers.

Behind the stud farm is the 11th-century Chapelle de Clermont, with views of the Normandy hills across the rich pastures of the Touques Valley and the Caen Plain.

SAY CHEESE

It is these rich pastures that have earned Calvados its reputation as one of France's finest gastronomic regions, with its lavish use of butter, cream and cheeses. The three main cheeses of the region are Pont-l'Évêque, Livarot and Camembert, all of which, until recently, were made exclusively on farms and sold at the local markets. The village of Camembert – a name recognised worldwide – lies to the south of Beuvron. It was here that Marie Harell, a local farmer's wife, was given the then-secret recipe by a priest from Brie whom she sheltered during the Revolution. However, Beuvron boasts its own secret recipe: the Legrand farm in the village produces its very own Petit Beuvronnais cheeses, which are quite delicious. Look out also for the local Pavé d'Auge – a large cheese, as *pavé* (paving stone) implies.

APPLES AND PEARS

It is not only dairy products for which the region is famous. The orchards here yield the best cider in France, made from apples and pears. The Normans started the custom of drinking cider and Calvados (apple brandy) as far back as the 8th century. Demand is

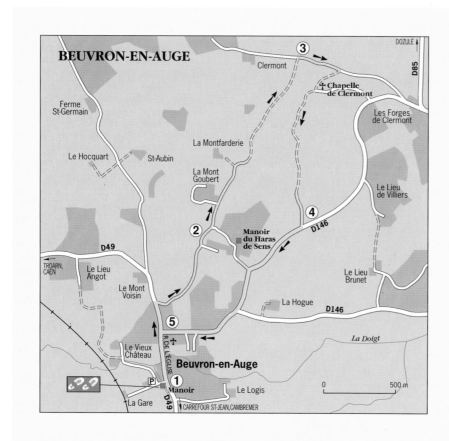

Map: BEUVRON-EN-AUGE — Clermont, Chapelle de Clermont, Les Forges de Clermont, Ferme St-Germain, La Montfarderie, Le Hocquart, St-Aubin, La Mont Goubert, Le Lieu de Villiers, Manoir du Haras de Sens, D146, D49, TROARN CAEN, Le Lieu Angot, Le Mont Voisin, Le Lieu Brunet, La Hogue, D146, La Doigt, Le Vieux Château, R. DE L'ÉGLISE, Beuvron-en-Auge, La Gare, D49, Manoir, Le Logis, CARREFOUR ST-JEAN, CAMBREMER, DOZULÉ, D85 — 0 500 m

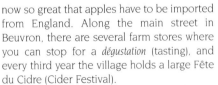

now so great that apples have to be imported from England. Along the main street in Beuvron, there are several farm stores where you can stop for a *dégustation* (tasting), and every third year the village holds a large Fête du Cidre (Cider Festival).

Many farms have a sign outside advertising Cru de Cambremer, the *appellation controllée* mark of the best ciders here. Cambremer is an attractive village 13km south-east of Beuvron. Each May, local producers bring their cider, Calvados and *pommeau* (a sherry-strength aperitif made of apple juice and Calvados) to an old barn for tasting. Proper cider, called *bon bère*, must contain at least 5

The commercial centre of Beuvron caters for the weary feet of shoppers and tourists alike, who can enjoy a break at an outdoor café. The miserable face carved on a beam, top right, unfailingly cheers up the rest of us

per cent alcohol. Calvados, colloquially called *calva*, is matured in oak casks for up to 10 years, and drunk at the end of a meal. The drink is also delicious as a sorbet or as a *trou normand*, during pauses in the meal – the traditional theory being that it makes way for more rich Norman food!

From Beuvron you can follow the Cider Trail, a 40-km route through the picturesque villages of the Auge Valley.

The Walk

① Starting from the Manoir (manor house), cross the main square and proceed along rue de l'Église. Head out of the village and, after the church, take the second road to the right.

② After you have climbed for some distance, the road becomes a dirt track and eventually turns into a grassy path, passing farm estates and orchards to a narrow surfaced lane at the top.

③ Turn right (past two picnic tables), then right again down a rough track to the Chapelle de Clermont. Follow the grass track beside the church downhill for magnificent views of the Pays d'Auge.

④ Turn right when you reach the road and right again to the Manoir du Haras de Sens to visit the stud or tour its Calvados caves. Back at the road, bear right out of the stud, right again at the next fork and head downhill towards the village.

⑤ Turn left at the T-junction and return along rue de l'Église to the main square.

---

i

▷ Length of walk: 5.5km
▷ Approximate time: 1½ hours
▷ Terrain: Mostly surfaced but steep at times. Point 2 is particularly rough underfoot (sturdy shoes recommended. Suitable for pushchairs and wheelchairs except points 2 and 3
▷ Parking: Free village car park
▷ Refreshments: Cafés and bars

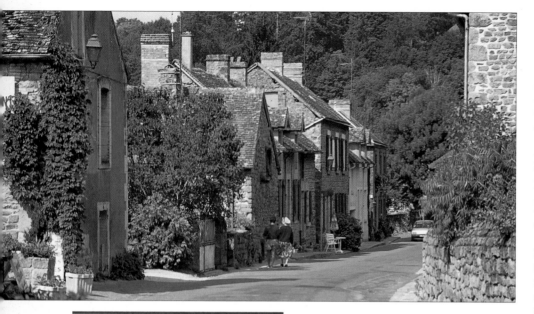

St-Cénéri-le-Gérei
(ORNE)

Listed as 'one of the prettiest villages in France', this tiny village on the edge of the Alpes-Mancelles sits on a granite spur dominating a majestic loop of the River Sarthe. Huddled at the riverside, St-Cénéri's ochre-coloured stone cottages with their steep tiled roofs have attracted many artists over the years, including the famous 19th-century painters Corot and Courbet, who stayed at

The Walk

1

This short walk of about 2km around St-Céneri-le-Gérei takes only about ¾ hour and is suitable for pushchairs and wheelchairs, except for some narrow steps at point 3. There is free parking in the village car park and cafés and bars for refreshment. Starting at the Café des Peintres, go up a pedestrian-only lane, past the church, through a gate into a meadow. Follow the path to the Chapel of St-Cénéri.

2

Return to the café, then immediately turn right down a steep slope to the bridge, watermill and artists' *ateliers*.

3

Back at the café, turn sharp right up a rough lane. At the top, turn left by the war memorial, go past the château remains (a single rock!) and down some narrow steps before the crêperie on the right.

4

Turn left at the bottom and return to the starting point at the Café des Peintres, which contains a small gallery of paintings by former inhabitants of the village.

Honey-toned houses, softened with lush greenery, follow the curving streets of St-Cénéri with artless charm

the Auberge Moisy. Since then, the village has become a haven for artists and crafts-people. Some of their studios are open to the public, especially those on the banks of the Sarthe near the old stone bridge.

Near by, in the middle of a grassy meadow on the curve of the river, stands the tiny Chapel of St-Cénéri, constructed on the site of an earlier 7th-century chapel built by the Italian ascetic and hermit, St Cénéri. The present chapel dates from the 14th century, but still contains his statue and his old stone bed. As the hermit's following grew, so did the settlement, which was named after him. A monastery built by Cénéri's followers was, sadly, destroyed by the Normans. However, the Normans built a remarkably beautiful Romanesque church in its place, perched at the summit of the village. The saddleback roof, unique in France, together with the striking 12th-century wall paintings in the choir, makes this church one of the great ecclesiastical treasures of Normandy.

The picturesque 14km drive from Alençon to St-Cénéri, through chestnut woods and the typical Norman *bocage* countryside of small hedged fields, leads you deep into the heart of the Parc Naturel Régional de Normandie-Maine. With its forests, lakes, rivers, gorges and rocky outcrops, the park offers a wide range of sporting possibilities.

Le Bec-Hellouin
(EURE)

The approach to Le Bec-Hellouin along the D39 takes you alongside a small stream, past perfect ochre-, cream- and salmon-coloured farmhouses with immaculate gardens, straight to the heart of the village. The shady main square is surrounded by charming

antiques shops and ceramic workshops and is also a surprising venue for a quaint museum devoted to mechanical musical instruments.

The village's main attraction is undoubtedly the great abbey, founded by a hermit called Herluin in 1034, and formerly one of the most important centres of learning in the Christian world. After the Conquest of England in 1066, two of his academic disciples, Lanfranc and Anselm, carried the cultural and spiritual tradition of Bec to England, and both went on to become Archbishops of Canterbury, forging an important historic link with England which is still very strong today.

Since then, however, the abbey has seen hard times, including the Hundred Years' War, the Wars of Religion and, finally, the departure of the monks in 1792. It even served as a cavalry barracks and was occupied by the army until World War II. Not until 1948 was monastic life restored.

Today white-robed Benedictine monks lead a simple life in their awe-inspiring cloisters. The whole of the Risle Valley has a tranquil, monastic feel to it, with bells echoing

Crossed lines: diagonals and verticals set between strong horizontals define Le Bec-Hellouin's fine old buildings, brightened with cascading geraniums

over the hills and the imposing tower of St Nicolas, a famous landmark, visible for miles. This 15th-century tower, with its splendid views over the valley, is all that remains of the original abbey church, once one of the largest in Europe. Today's buildings date from the 17th and 18th centuries. Recent Archbishops of Canterbury maintain the centuries-old tradition of coming here on retreat, and the abbey remains an important intellectual and spiritual centre in Normandy.

Le Mont-St-Michel
(MANCHE)

Despite the hordes of visitors, Le Mont-St-Michel is no doubt one of the great spectacles of Europe. A circular rocky island crowned by a magnificent Romanesque and Gothic fortress-abbey, it rises dramatically out of a wide sandy bay with the highest tides in Europe. During the Middle Ages, when it was not connected to the mainland, it was known as 'Le Mont-St-Michel-at-the-Mercy-of-the-Sea'. Even these days the car park is sometimes submerged.

The steep cobbled climb up the Grande Rue to the abbey is lined with half-timbered buildings tempting tourists to enter the cosy cafés, expensive restaurants and countless souvenir shops. The ramparts offer a less crowded route and magnificent sea views. The abbey itself, founded by Bishop Aubert in 708 following a vision of St Michael the Archangel, presents an extraordinary summary of architectural styles from the Middle Ages to the 16th century and is a renowned pil-

*Le Mont-St-Michel
from the causeway*

grimage site. The bishop's skull, on view at the abbey, is said to bear the mark of St Michael's finger.

Such local legends abound here. The extreme and fast-moving tides, which can result in variations of up to 15m, are said to be due to Gargantua: as the giant passed through the region centuries ago, he felt an irresistible urge to relieve himself of the excessive quantities of cider drunk earlier that day, just as he was about to stride across the gap between Carolles and the village of Cancale! (See page 16)

The bay is home to many rare sea plants and birds (nearby Tombelaine Island is a bird reserve). At low tide between here and Genêts you can sometimes see *la pêche à pièd*, a 13th-century method of fishing on foot with giant wooden V-shaped fish traps. The main catch is grey shrimps (*crevettes*), mullet and 'cockles of Genêts'. Another local speciality, available in many restaurants, is salt-meadow (*pré-salé*) lamb.

Veules-les-Roses *(Seine-Maritime)*

FIRST POPULARISED BY PARISIAN FACTORS, THIS LITTLE RESORT WAS ONCE A BUSY FISHING, MILLING AND WEAVING CENTRE. NESTLED IN A HOLLOW VALLEY 25KM WEST OF DIEPPE, THE VILLAGE BOASTS THE SMALLEST RIVER IN FRANCE.

Veules is one of the oldest ports of the coast, dating back to the Middle Ages. Over the centuries, the village has survived wars, epidemics, fires and even tidal waves. As a result many different periods of architecture coexist here, illustrating pages out of its past, with 'neo-Norman' resort-style buildings interspersed with grand bourgeois manor houses, thatched weavers' cottages and the terraced houses of fishermen, who sell their daily catch at the seafront car park.

Veules became a fashionable seaside resort at the end of the 19th century when Anaïs Aubert, a leading light at the Comédie-Française, encouraged her friends to come here, including artist Camille Marchand and writers Paul Meurice and Victor Hugo. The narrow riverside alleyway tongue-in-cheekily called the Champs Elysées is one of the reminders of those old Parisian links.

LITTLE RIVER, BIG ROLE

The River Veules, just over a kilometre in length, has divided the village into two parishes since the 11th century; indeed, the name of Veules was derived from the ancient Saxon *wael*, meaning a bridge of water. On the right bank stand the ruins of the mariners' Church of St Nicolas, built in 1095. Every August the ancient village festival, La

Hanging baskets of brilliant blossom distract the eye from the herringbone pattern of dark half-timbering

Fête des Pêcheurs, is held here, when a fish market and parade of ornately decorated fishing boats are followed by a torchlit evening Mass. On the left bank sits the Church of St Martin, a beautiful example of late 12th-century architecture, with unusual sculpted pillars depicting mermaids, shells and fishing boats. The church has more than its fair share of statues, having salvaged many from the ruins of St Nicolas. It once had a cemetery, too, for those drowned at sea. The nearby marketplace, renamed place des Écossais (Scotsmen's Square) on Liberation Day in 1944, has always been a hub of activity, and a market has taken place here weekly since the reign of Louis XIV.

The River Veules has been put to practical use for over eight centuries, with 11 watermills contributing considerably to the wealth of the village. The earliest recorded mill (1235) was the Moulin de la Mer, situated at the mouth of the river, which functioned with the ebb and flow of the tide. Only four mills remain today.

In the upper part of the village there is a series of wells that follow the line of the river. Perhaps the most unusual, attached to a typical Norman *colombier* (dovecot), is at Les Puits de Veules. The river also attracted other profitable businesses, including *auberges* (inns), and to this day the Veulais are renowned for their hospitality.

OF WATERCRESS AND CLOGS

The most attractive part of the village is at the source of the river, with its verdant watercress beds and Moulin d'Eau Vive. Veules' cress is valued for its exceptional piquancy and is still gathered in the traditional method in the winter. Before the invention of wellington boots, harvesters wore wooden clogs, extended to the knee by metal guards (the water seeped in nevertheless). These watercress beds became the 'vegetable garden' of Dieppe, providing a unique salad for the season. In former times, it was grown to help prevent scurvy.

Near by, the picturesque ford was formerly the only entrance to the village by road, and at the *abreuvoir* (drinking trough) the water was used for washing clothes and sheep's fleeces as well as for drinking.

The abreuvoir, beside quiet waters, left, has seen busier days. Opposite, beds of watercress, like a patchwork quilt, cover the ground with salad greens

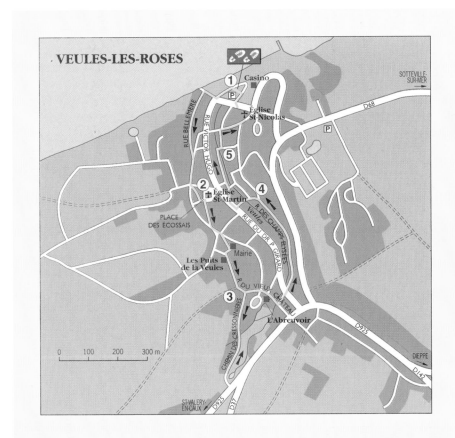

VEULES-LES-ROSES

1

Start your journey at the seafront car park and take the narrow path signposted chemin de Randonnée (not named on the map) leading up the cliff edge. Continue along rue Bellemere, turn left at rue du Marché (not named) and down into place des Écossais.

2

Go past the Église St-Martin and along rue du Manoir, and continue across the junction to the Mairie (Town Hall). Turn right, then fork to the left, passing Les Puits de la Veules. Bear left again along rue du Vieux Château, following the old stone walls (these are all that remain of the castle).

3

Take the next right turn, along chemin des Cressonnières, and cross the river to the watercress beds. Retrace your steps back to the sign and turn right, returning to rue du Vieux Château. Go through the ford at L'Abreuvoir, cross the tiny sandstone footbridge and immediately turn left. Cross the main road into rue Champs Elysées and then follow the river.

4

After two watermills take a left fork, zigzag back across the river and return to the main road. Turn right into rue du Bouloir, then take the second lane on the right, to follow the river.

5

Turn right at the road, cross the river again and turn left into rue Melingue. Bear right at the next junction, rue Paul Meurice, then left into rue A-Vasquerie to the ruined Église St-Nicolas. A flight of steps from the former cemetery leads back down to the seafront car park.

i

▷ Length of walk: 2.5km
▷ Approximate time: 1 hour
▷ Terrain: All surfaced except the initial climb up the cliff and a short stretch along the river. Suitable for pushchairs and wheelchairs
▷ Parking: Free car park at the seafront
▷ Refreshments: Cafés and bars

NORMANDY HAS PRODUCED MORE GREAT WRITERS AND INFLUENCED MORE GREAT LITERATURE THAN ANY OTHER REGION OF FRANCE. IT HAS GIVEN BIRTH AND INSPIRATION TO MANY FAMOUS WRITERS SUCH AS GUY DE MAUPASSANT AND GUSTAVE FLAUBERT, AND ATTRACTED MANY NON-NORMANS TO THE AREA, INCLUDING VICTOR HUGO, MARCEL PROUST AND JEAN-PAUL SARTRE. IN THE SAME WAY THE WORLD OF ART HAS BEEN IMMEASURABLY ENRICHED BY THE PAINTERS BORN OR DRAWN HERE. IT WAS A NATIVE OF HONFLEUR, EUGÈNE BOUDIN, WHO BEGAN THE FASHION FOR PAINTING SEA- AND SKYSCAPES AND WHOSE MEETINGS WITH OTHER PAINTERS TO DRINK CIDER IN A FARMHOUSE INN LED TO THE BIRTH OF IMPRESSIONISM. THE BELOVED WORKS OF MONET, CÉZANNE, PISSARRO AND MANY OTHERS OWE THEIR EXISTENCE TO THE MOVEMENT THAT BEGAN BESIDE A LITTLE NORMAN HARBOUR.

A Heritage in Print and Paint

The heart of Norman writing is centred on the three ports of Le Havre, Rouen and Dieppe. Rouen, on the River Seine, was home to the dramatist Pierre Corneille (1606–84), who was educated at a Jesuit college (now the Lycée Corneille) which numbers Flaubert, Maupassant and Delacroix among its past pupils. Corneille's home is now a literary museum, as is the Maison des Champs, his beautiful country retreat at Le Petit-Couronne, near Rouen. A controversial and progressive writer, he is regarded as the founder of French classical drama.

The great novelist Gustave Flaubert (1821–80) was born in Rouen. The family home is today a museum of Flaubert memorabilia, including the famous stuffed green parrot which featured in *Un Coeur Simple* and sat on his desk as he wrote it. Flaubert lived most of his later life at Croisset, near Rouen. The garden pavilion there is now a museum (which claims its green parrot as the authentic one). It was here that the great perfectionist wrote his notorious and compelling novel *Madame Bovary*. The cathedral at Rouen, which provided a romantic setting for the lovers, can still be seen today, but little now remains of the city's colourful bohemian quarter where the heroine Emma Bovary 'walked amid a smell of absinthe, cigars and oysters'. A large part of the book is centred on the pretty village of Ry, east of Rouen, which is now the centre of a thriving Madame Bovary tourist industry (see page 38).

Past Images, Present Encounters

Guy de Maupassant (1850–93), a close friend of Flaubert, featured the Normandy coast in much of his work, perhaps most vividly described in *Pierre et Jean*: 'The fallen rocks looked like the ruins of a great vanished city which formerly overlooked the ocean.' Sadly, the Le Havre described in the same novel – its 'numberless masts along several kilometres of quays ... like a great dead forest' – is a thing of the past, as the port area was destroyed during World War II. Even the striking 1930s portraits of Queneau, Salacrou and Jean-Paul Sartre have been eroded by the passing decades. However, one can still encounter the Le Havre of pre-war days presented in Sartre's first novel *La Nausée* (1938), which vividly portrays the sharp social contrasts of the city and reveals his fascination with the seedy dockside quarter of St François, where he lived while teaching philosophy for five years.

Victor Hugo, France's greatest 19th-century poet, also had strong links with Normandy. It was the tragic drowning of his beloved daughter in the Seine at Villequier which inspired him to write one of his best-known poems, À Villequier. His statue by the river is carved with a fragment of the poem:

Il faut que l'herbe pousse
et que les enfants meurent;
Je le sais, ô mon Dieu!
(Grass must grow, and children must die;
I know that, O Lord!)

The family house is now a museum devoted to Hugo.

The novelist Marcel Proust (1871–1922) was also a regular visitor to Normandy, frequently staying at the Grand Hotel in Cabourg and writing about it in his novels. Indeed, the town of Balbec in his supreme literary achievement, À *la Recherche du Temps Perdu*, is based on Cabourg. The hotel now glories in its Proustian connections: you can book into the Proust bedroom, enjoy a sea-green 'Proust cocktail' and dine in the Balbec Restaurant, described by Proust as 'the aquarium' because 'each night locals would press their faces to its windows in wonder at the luxurious life within ... as extraordinary to the poor as the life of strange fishes or molluscs'.

The Cabourg hotel which Proust frequented for over 30 years. Above, Gustave Flaubert and, above right, the poet Victor Hugo

Impressions of Life and Light

The images created by Proust in his novels find another, equally brilliant form in the evocative seascapes painted by the French Impressionists in Normandy at the turn of the 20th century. For centuries the region has produced many fine works of art, but it was during the 19th century that art truly flourished here, with the birth of Millet, Boudin, Courbet, Dufy and Léger, the arrival of Monet, Corot, Sisley, Renoir, Cézanne, Pissarro and Braque, and a wave of overseas artists including English landscapists Turner and Bonington – all attracted by the breathtaking coastline, wide vistas and bustling seaside resorts.

Eugène Boudin, from Honfleur, was one of the first French artists to paint in the open air. Famous for beach scenes featuring parasols and billowing dresses, his pictures can be seen in Honfleur's Musée Eugène Boudin along with works by his contemporaries Pissarro, Dufy, Renoir and Cézanne. He persuaded Claude Monet, the young cartoonist from Le Havre, to work outdoors and to study the ways in which changing light affects the subject. Monet's later series of haystacks and Rouen Cathedral in 20 different moods were clearly influenced by Boudin.

In 1864 Monet moved to Honfleur, where he mixed with many artists including Corot, Renoir, Sisley, Pissarro and Cézanne. Together they formed a group called the Société Anonyme des Artistes-Peintres, whose works were to become the basis for Honfleur's art museum. In those early years, though, the artists had no recognition and life was hard. They often begged, borrowed or went hungry. Once, Monet was even thrown out of a hotel, and Renoir stole bread for him!

A decade after his arrival, in 1874, Monet painted the sunrise at Le Havre and called it *Impression: Soleil Levant*. Several art critics dismissed it at the time, yet the painting marked a milestone in art, giving its name to the new movement – Impressionism. Renoir, with his sparkling 'snapshot' portrayals of real life, broke from the group in 1880, his rheumatism forcing him to leave Normandy and settle in Provence, where he finally had to paint with a brush tied to his fingers.

Monet retired to a small pink house at Giverny in the Seine Valley in 1883 (see page 36). Here he created his magnificent gardens and water-lily pond, which inspired his Nymphéas paintings. Many American artists visited him here, including James Whistler, John Singer Sargent and Theodore Robinson.

American, French and English artists also flocked to Dieppe. Walter Sickert, the London Impressionist, studied here under Degas, and Raoul Dufy and Georges Braque moved here at the turn of the century. Braque retired to Varengeville-sur-Mer (see page 36), where many visit his grave and stained-glass windows. Dufy's sailing scenes can be seen at Le Havre's André Malraux Museum alongside works by Boudin, Corot, Pissarro and Gauguin.

These coastal resorts played host to so many great artists that, as Impressionism was born, Normandy became a huge outdoor *atelier*. Today each resort is represented by many great works of art, as the local museums and galleries testify. And the countryside and towns of the region continue to inspire each new hopeful generation of artists and writers.

A crowd of boats at Honfleur, where Monet, inset, spent critical creative years

The blues of sea, sky and precious gems were used by Georges Braque in his Tree of Jesse stained-glass window, set in Varengeville's much-painted church of St Valéry. His body lies buried in the cemetery here

Varengeville-sur-Mer
(SEINE-MARITIME)

A typical Norman village of old timbered farmhouses, thatched cottages and manor houses, Varengeville is set in woodland west of Dieppe, just inland from the white cliffs of the Alabaster Coast.

Varengeville's Parc des Moutiers is the setting for the village's most unusual building, yet Britons may find it a touch familiar, for it is an English house designed by Sir Edwin Lutyens in 1898. Its garden, the first private garden opened to the public in France, was designed by the influential English horticulturalist and landscape gardener Gertrude Jekyll. It contains an extensive range of rare trees and shrubs in a series of valleys running down to the sea. The park is open daily from 10–6, closing for lunch from noon to 2pm.

Also well worth a visit is the grand Renaissance manor house Manoir d'Ango. Built as a country retreat for Jean Ango, a 16th-century Dieppe shipbuilder, its interior has been carefully restored and the court-yard contains the finest *colombier* (dovecot) in the region. Ango, deciding to embellish the mariners' church of St Valéry, added an unusual nave whose roof resembles an upturned boat. The shells, suns and scallops carved on the columns are believed to be reminders of his voyages all over the world. The Manoir can be visited daily, although like the Parc des Moutiers it is closed from noon until 2pm for lunch.

The church – known throughout France for its admirable position perched high on the edge of the cliffs which were so often painted by Monet – also attracted other artists. Georges Braque, pioneer of the Cubist art movement at the turn of the century, made Varengeville his home; he was the first living artist to have his works hung in the Louvre in Paris. In the church you can see the *Tree of Jesse*, his famous stained-glass window depicting Christ's line of descent from Jesse's son, King David. At the other end of the village, in the small barn-like Chapelle St-Dominique, other unusual Braque windows glow with golden *galets* (pebbles) from the beach. His grave is in the cemetery of St Valéry, along with the tombs of several other well-known figures, including the composer Albert Roussel.

The Walk

This suggested walk around Varengeville-sur-Mer takes something under two hours, covering about 6km, and is not suitable for pushchairs and wheelchairs. Start by descending a steep footpath to the right of the Église St-Valery, then zigzag down some steps to a tiny pebbled cove (an ideal picnic spot). Note that the cliff descent can be dangerous in wet conditions.

Climb back up the steps, then turn left and follow a path into woods until it merges with another. Bear left here and eventually curve round to the right, up to a road.

Turn right, first left and second right into a main road. Turn right past the Chapelle St-Dominique, then left to the Manoir d'Ango.

Cross the manor grounds, turn right at the road, follow the curve to the right, then turn left into the main road.

Return to the church along the main road, following signs to the Parc des Moutiers, with its 'English' house and garden.

Giverny
(EURE)

This delightful little village, spread out along a hillside near Vernon, is the most visited site in Normandy. Crowds of art- and garden-lovers flock to see the home of Claude Monet and the world's most famous lily pond, immortalised in some of the best-known works of Impressionism.

Monet settled here in a little pink house with grass-green shutters in 1883, near the Paris suburb of Argenteuil, where he had worked with Renoir, Sisley and Manet for a number of years. He himself designed the generously proportioned garden, which slopes down over 0.8ha towards the bottom of the village to the Chemin du Roy, along which ran a small local railway connecting Vernon and Gasny. Spotting the village out of the window of the train one day, Monet was inspired to move there.

At the bottom of the main garden, he created his famous water garden, with its lilies and Japanese bridge, which he went on painting until his death, aged 86, in 1926. The house is best visited in May or June when the rhododendrons and the wisteria on the bridge are in bloom. Despite the crowds of tourists, it is easy to imagine the great master at work on one of his huge canvases. As he used to say: 'I am good for nothing except painting and gardening.'

The garden, with 12 resident gardeners, still follows Monet's design and is a dazzling palette of changing colours from spring to autumn. Each month is characterised by a dominant colour, as is each room in Monet's immaculately restored house: the kitchen is cool blue, decorated wall to wall with his collection of Japanese prints, and the dining room is vibrant yellow.

As Monet's fame spread, many American painters moved to Giverny. The modern Musée Americain in the village demonstrates the influence that French Impressionism had on American painting until the outbreak of World War I, when most of the artists returned home, marking the end of an era.

Jumièges
(SEINE-MARITIME)

This small village, surrounded by meadows and orchards, lies along the Route Historique des Abbayes in one of the magnificent loops of the River Seine. The broad river valley between Rouen and Le Havre, with its wooded vales and chalk cliffs, provides a dramatic backdrop for several abbeys, none so important as the 7th-century Benedictine abbey of Notre Dame at Jumièges.

Today the abbey is a haunting ruin, with its nave open to the sky and huge ivory-coloured towers rising impressively above the trees. At one time it was among the most important and influential monastic institutions in France, and you can sense its former glory as you walk round the ruins, tracing out the vast dimensions of the original buildings. Founded in 654 by St Philibert, the original was destroyed two centuries later during the Norman invasions. The new abbey was consecrated in the presence of William the Conqueror in 1067. During the Revolution, however, the monks were dispersed again and the abbey sold for use as a stone quarry.

Charles VII, Joan of Arc's king, often stayed in the village with his favourite mistress, Agnès Sorel, who died here in 1450. A small museum in the former abbot's lodge contains the black marble slab that covered her heart, along with tombs, gargoyles, statues and other fragments salvaged from the original abbey.

Hidden amidst lovely cottages and manor houses, the Auberge du Bac offers refreshments on the banks of the Seine. From here you can cross the river on a small car ferry or *bac* into the Forest of Brotonne.

Visit Monet's home in Giverny for a first-hand impression of the artist's inspiring garden, below. Right, the remains of the fine abbey at Jumièges

Other Villages

BALLEROY

This grand village nestles in a valley at the eastern edge of the Forêt de Cerisy, surrounded by rolling hills and lush green meadows, and makes a good centre for visiting Caen, Bayeux, St-Lô and the potteries of Noron-la-Poterie. The tree-lined main avenue leads straight to the stately Château de Balleroy, the first masterpiece of Louis XIII's celebrated architect François Mansart. In the 1970s the castle was bought by an American publishing magnate who created a museum to his principal passion – ballooning – in its outbuildings. The eccentric Musée des Ballons portrays ballooning from France's invention of the *montgolfière* (hot-air balloon) to the barrage balloons of World War II. Balleroy fittingly hosts an international balloon festival in June.

BIVILLE

Biville is situated in rugged heathland near the barren Nez de Jobourg, some of the highest cliffs in France. Perched above the windswept seascape of the Anse de Vauville, this enduring granite hamlet centres on its splendid 12th-century church, which contains the vault of local missionary and priest St Thomas Hélye the Blessed, who died here in 1257. The village has been a famous local centre of pilgrimage for over five centuries, with an annual midnight pilgrimage every 18–19 October.

CARROUGES

This attractive working village, set on a low hill 21km south of Argentan, lies at the heart of one of France's largest nature reserves, the Parc Régional de Normandie-Maine. Its ornate fairy-tale château, dating from the 13th to the 17th century, is surrounded by a moat and elegant formal gardens. The castle is one of Normandy's most outstanding and unusual, being made of attractive rose-red brick with four circular towers capped with pepperpot roofs. Visitors can enter the castle by the drawbridge for a tour of its sumptuous furnishings, tapestries and paintings. Sights not to be missed include the Gatehouse, the Portrait Gallery and King Louis XI's Bedroom, where the monarch stayed during 1473. There is also a craft centre in the castle grounds.

CREULLY

It is hard to believe that this tranquil village –12km inland from Arromanches in the Baie de la Seine; where D-Day's artificial Mulberry harbour was put together – played host to many wartime dignitaries. Winston Churchill and King George VI were among the luminaries entertained by Field-Marshal Montgomery in a straw-camouflaged caravan parked in the grounds of Château de Creullet in 1944. In June of the same year, a makeshift BBC studio was set up in one of the towers of Creully's *Mairie* (Town Hall), from where news updates of the Battle of Normandy were broadcast.

The village today, with its two castles, Norman church and water mill, lies on the Route des Moulins, a round trip of 35km that focuses on the beautiful Seulles Valley.

GATTEVILLE-LE-PHARE

Guarding the treacherous, sea-lashed north coast of the Cotentin Peninsula at Gatteville-le-Phare is the tallest lighthouse in France, connected by a long causeway to the rocky headland of the Pointe de Barfleur. The towering lighthouse is something of a calendar beacon: there are 12 storeys, 52 windows and a daunting 365 steps – a climb compensated by the magnificent views.

A calm and solid counterpoint to the pounding seas, granite-built Gatteville has a spacious square, a tiny 11th-century Chapelle des Marins (Sailors' Chapel) and a cosy bar. The main church, dating from the 15th century, features an unusual Romanesque bell tower which rises high over the small village huddled around it.

GENÊTS

This attractive seaside resort with its narrow streets and medieval houses, 9km west of Avranches, was formerly a bustling port and saltworks. Its small 12th-century church was the final stop on the pilgrim route to Le Mont-St-Michel. The pilgrims would then cross the sands barefoot to the abbey. The walk can still be done today, setting out from Bec d'Andaine across the sand dunes and salt marshes of this broad bay, but the journey must not be attempted without a guide, as quicksand and rapid tides are a hazard.

LESSAY

Lessay lies in the inlet of the estuary of the River Ay. The surrounding bleak marshlands inspired many 19th-century romantic writers, including Barbey d'Aurevilly, with his tales of local folk legends and witchcraft.

The main attraction of the village is undoubtedly the abbey church of Ste-Trinité, founded in 1056 during the reign of William the Conqueror and completed by the 12th century. Built in mellow golden stone, it was the first Norman Romanesque building to be entirely vaulted with interesting diagonal ribs.

Sadly, the abbey survived the vicissitudes of the centuries only to be destroyed in 1944 in a matter of minutes. Undaunted, the locals decided to reconstruct it. The magnificent restoration – using traditional medieval tools and the original shattered fragments – took 12 years to complete. The result is one of the loveliest Romanesque churches in France.

A more fleeting attraction at Lessay is the Holy Cross Fair, four days of domestic livestock trading and festivities every September. It is also a great place to taste the fine smoked Cotentin hams.

LYONS-LA-FORÊT

This peaceful, picture-postcard village is tucked away in a deep valley in the famous Forêt de Lyons. The beech forest was once the hunting ground of the Dukes of Normandy, and it served as a regular dropping point for supplies to the Resistance in World War II.

Lyons itself comprises an appealing collection of ancient half-timbered houses, a restored 18th-century Bailiff's Court and a covered wooden marketplace.

Once the retreat of composer Maurice Ravel (who wrote *Le Tombeau de Couperin* here in 1917 at Le Fresne in rue de la République), the village makes an ideal touring centre for exploring the surrounding woodlands.

RY

Gustave Flaubert based his infamous novel *Madame Bovary* on the village of Ry (called Yonville l'Abbaye in the book), where the heroine lived with her dull, but devoted husband. The characters are based on the tragic Delphine and Eugène Delamare, who lived in the pharmacy. She died there aged 27, he later hanged himself.

The village of Ry thrives on its literary connections, and the pharmacy, which has been converted into a Musée d'Automates, features over 500 mechanical figures performing scenes from the book.

More cover than market: like squat stilts, sturdy ancient timbers support the roof of the marketplace in the centre of Lyons-la-Forêt, a village set in a forest of beech trees

The North

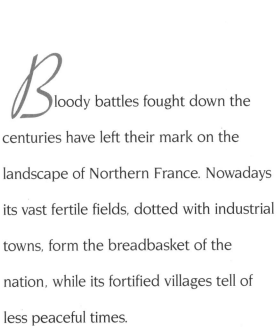

Bloody battles fought down the centuries have left their mark on the landscape of Northern France. Nowadays its vast fertile fields, dotted with industrial towns, form the breadbasket of the nation, while its fortified villages tell of less peaceful times.

Gerberoy

(Oise)

TODAY GERBEROY IS A TRANQUIL HAVEN FOR ARTISTS, BUT BACK IN THE MIDDLE AGES IT WAS AN IMPORTANT FRONTIER TOWN ON THE BORDER OF THE ILE DE FRANCE AND THE DUCHY OF NORMANDY.

The fortified village of Gerberoy occupies a natural mound some 21km north-west of the cathedral town of Beauvais. In 948, Louis d'Outremer King of France and Richard II of England signed a treaty here which recognised Richard II as the ruler of Brittany and Duke of Normandy. But after these peaceful beginnings the village saw a series of invading armies, and by the end of the Hundred Years War in 1453 it lay in ruins. Centuries later, signs of Anglo-French animosity can be detected in some of the place names: the path around the northern ramparts is named after William the Conqueror, who came to Gerberoy in 1079, and the pretty Vallée d'Arondel, which lies to the west of the village, was named after the Earl of Arundel, who was killed in battle in 1435.

A shaded lane in Gerberoy rises gently, lined with carefully tended houses of quite different characters

Although Charles VII partially rebuilt Gerberoy in the 15th century, the final blow came at the end of the 16th century, when the combination of a plague epidemic and a huge fire destroyed much of the village. Among the surviving buildings is the house where Henry IV is reputed to have stayed when he was injured in the Battle of Aumale in 1592; it is set back behind railings at the crossroads with the rue du Château.

Much of the collegiate church of St-Pierre dates from this period too. Some of the church's original 11th-century walls were rebuilt after an earlier fire in 1419, but most of it dates from the mid-15th century. Inside, the nave has a vaulted wooden ceiling and box pews, while the ornate wooden choir stalls date from the 15th century. There are two 17th-century altarpieces in the side chapels and three late 17th-century Aubusson tapestries. Louis XIII and Cardinal Richelieu visited the village In the early 17th century, but the next two centuries saw its return to obscurity.

A venerable wisteria gracefully frames a doorway, left. With its wooden structures picked out in sky blue, the corner building, below, is sure to be noticed

REVIVED BY ART

It was the landscape painter Henri Le Sidaner who 'rediscovered' Gerberoy at the turn of the century. In many respects, it is thanks to his vision that Gerberoy was classed as one of the 100 'most beautiful villages in France' in 1982. The cobbled streets, the pretty gardens and the timeless feel have attracted other artists and today, as you wander down the narrow roads, you will still find painters sketching the old well by the Hôtel de Ville (Town Hall) or the chestnut trees in the place Delchet or the rustic ruelle St-Amant.

Le Sidaner was born in Mauritius in 1862 and studied painting at the École des Beaux-Arts in Paris. His style was close to that of his

The Walk

1 Start by the Hôtel de Ville, which houses the museum. Walk through the Porte Notre-Dame, passing the free car park on your left, and turn left through a small metal gate down the chemin Vuillotte.

2 Follow the path down the hill and turn left when you join a wider path. When you reach the wood, Forêt Domaniale de Caumont, take the left-hand fork up the steps, then turn left again and follow the path for about 1km.

3 About 100m after a bench, you come to a crossroads. Turn left and follow the track until it makes a sharp bend to the right. Turn left again.

4 After crossing the stream, the path climbs quite steeply towards the village; just before it levels out, turn right. Continue straight along until you reach the surfaced road by the pond.

5 Walk through the village gates and up the rue du Logis du Roy. Note the unusual brick gateway on your left, with its stone head centrepiece. Turn right up the steep, cobbled rue du Château.

6 Go through the large stone gate (once a tower that formed part of Gerberoy's interior fortifications), passing the Église St-Pierre on your left. Continue along the road until you reach a sharp right-hand bend. Climb the steps straight in front of you and admire Sidaner's garden (*jardin*). Cross the grass until you reach the tumbled-down turret at the edge of the château wall. Turn left down the shady track by the ramparts and, when you come out into the open, turn left down the avenue of lime trees which leads back to the Porte Notre-Dame.

ⓘ

▷ Length of walk: 3.5km
▷ Approximate time: 1½ hours
▷ Terrain: Dirt paths and tracks in wood and around ramparts; surfaced road and cobbles in village; wood section not suitable for pushchairs or wheelchairs but can be missed out; steps up to bench opposite gardens cannot be avoided
▷ Parking: Free car park outside Porte Notre-Dame
▷ Open: Museum: Saturday and Sunday 2:30–6:30. Guided visits to museum, chapter house and sacristy of St-Pierre can be arranged in advance
▷ Refreshments: Le Vieux Logis sells drinks and has a medium-priced menu

Late Impressionist friends Monet, Sisley and Pissarro, and like them he was interested in the different effects of light on a subject. In 1900 he bought a house in the virtually abandoned village of Gerberoy, where he spent every summer until his death in 1939. During his time in Gerberoy, Le Sidaner created the beautiful terraced, Italianate garden in the ruins of the old château and produced nearly 200 paintings and countless drawings of the village. The museum on the first floor of the Hôtel de Ville contains a selection of his small watercolours.

It was Le Sidaner's idea to plant the hundreds of roses that grow throughout the village and climb the wood-and-daub and brick-and-flint houses dating from the 16th, 17th and 18th centuries.

One of the best times to visit Gerberoy is in the early summer months, when the roses are in bloom. The annual rose festival takes place on the third Sunday in June.

Seen from a red-brick arcade in a moment of quiet, the streets can seem like a film set waiting for actors

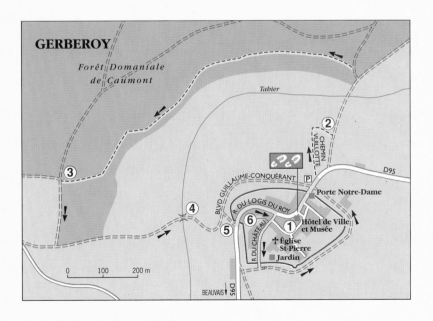

Cassel

(Nord)

BUILT ON THE SLOPES OF MONT CASSEL SOME 30KM FROM DUNKERQUE, CASSEL LIKES TO THINK OF ITSELF AS A SMALL TOWN, BUT THE PLACE IS MORE ACCURATELY DESCRIBED AS A LARGE VILLAGE.

According to a local saying, you can see five kingdoms from Mont Cassel – 'France, Belgium, Holland, England and, above the clouds, the kingdom of God' – and there is no doubt that this geographical importance has played a major role in Cassel's history. The Romans appreciated Cassel's strategic position, set 176m above the Flanders plain, and fortified the village nearly 2,000 years ago. It lay at the crossroads of seven Roman routes, six of which are still visible today from the viewing platforms in the public gardens.

Bold bouquets of red emphasise the windows of a restaurant in the Grande Place, above. Winding back streets, right, descend from Mont Cassel, while the church tower can be seen rising in the background

BATTLE FATIGUE

Cassel has been the site of three battles, in 1071, 1328 and 1677, and it also housed Maréchal Foch's headquarters during World War I. It also saw action during the English retreat to Dunkerque in World War II; much of the village was destroyed and nearly 80 per cent of the population were killed during the bombardments.

Despite this violent past and its present busy commercial life, the winding streets and cobbled paths give Cassel an air of tranquillity. The brick collegiate church of Notre-Dame dates back to the 13th century, but it has been rebuilt a number of times. In the 18th century it was redesigned, and its three parallel naves are typical of the Flemish hallekerk-style churches.

The museum of art, history and folklore is based in one of the 17th- and 18th-century houses lining the place du Général de Gaulle. The museum, which was originally the magistrates' office, was built in Renaissance style, but parts of it date back to medieval times. Maréchal Foch had an office there from October 1914 to June 1915, and it was from this room that he directed the Battle of Yser; it now contains various memorabilia from his time at Cassel. Foch used the Hôtel de Schoebeque at 32 rue du Maréchal Foch as a base during the war, and King George V and the Prince of Wales also stayed there in 1916 and 1917.

A wooden windmill, left, stands in the public gardens. Above, a slatted gate in a doorway bars access to some

The Walk

Start by the Musée in place du Général de Gaulle and walk towards the Mairie (Town Hall). Immediately after the 17th-century house at No. 12 there is a good view to the left through the Porte d'Aire. Turn right up rue du Château and go through the Porte du Château to the Jardin Public (public gardens).

On the right is the Monument des Trois Batailles and good views of the Mont des Récollets and the Mont des Cats. To the left is the southern viewing platform, where on a clear day you can see for over 60km. Follow the path behind the *moulin* (windmill) to the northern viewing platform by the statue of Maréchal Foch. Just after the statue, turn left down the cobbled path to place du Général Vandamme.

Follow the place round to the left. Turn right into rue Bollaert le Gavrian (not marked) and then almost immediately turn left down the narrow passage of rue des Remparts.

Rue des Remparts meanders between the gardens and houses on the southern edge of the village. Cross rue de l'Infirmerie and a little further on cross rue d'Aire into chemin de Tilleul.

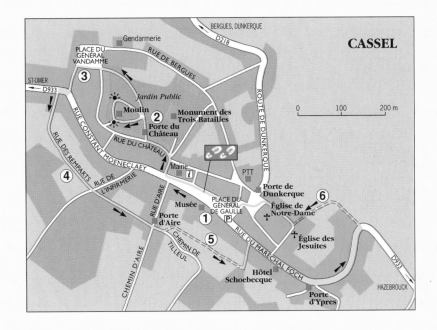

Bear left immediately and continue until a rustic-looking bridge crosses the path. Turn left up the cobbled path and then turn right into rue du Maréchal Foch. Follow the road until you reach a sharp right-hand bend by a stonemason's and then turn left.

As the track narrows you can see the 17th-century Église des Jesuites above you on the left. Climb the cobbled steps to the square in front of the chapel and then turn right, passing the Église Notre-Dame on your left. Walk down the slope and back into the place du Général de Gaulle.

---

i

▷ Length of walk: 2.5km
▷ Approximate time: 1¼ hours
▷ Terrain: All surfaced apart from some cobbled sections, two paths and steps up to Jesuit chapel; occasional 1m width restriction and narrow pavements
▷ Parking: Place du Général de Gaulle
▷ Open: Museum and windmill: Apr–Nov, daily except Tuesday, 10–12:30 and 2–6:30
▷ Refreshments: Cafés in main square; T'Kasteelhof restaurant just beneath southern viewing platform has a terrace and a wide selection of Belgian beers

FEASTS AND FOLKLORE

There are a variety of fairs and festivals held at Cassel and it is worth timing a visit to coincide with one of them. The most important takes place on Easter Monday with a carnival whose centrepiece is the Reuze giants, warrior-like figures who represent the town and the story of its origins. Legend has it that Cassel's two giants (Reuze Papa and Reuze Maman) were filling in a gully when one of the lumps of earth that they were carrying fell and became Mont Cassel. The present giant models, made from wire mesh and papier-mâché, were built in the 19th century and are paraded through the streets accompanied by much singing and dancing. The evening features traditional dances, and flares are lit as the giants leave the village for another year.

Cassel used to have a great number of windmills for wheat, cereal and oil, but now there is only one left, Casteel Meulen. The original 16th-century mill burnt down in 1911 but it was replaced in 1947 and is now open to the public. A mill fair takes place on Bastille Day, 14 July. There is a flea market in May and an antiques fair, which also sells Flemish food and drink, in September. Cassel's weekly market is every Thursday.

Other Villages

ARGOULES

Argoules is a charming village whose rustic houses are spread along the Authie Valley. A Renaissance-style château and a small 16th-century church form the heart of the village. On the other side of the square is an ancient lime tree called Sully's Tree which, according to tradition, was planted during the reign of Henry IV; there, too, is the Auberge du Gros Tilleul, with rooms, a medium-priced menu and mountain bikes for hire.

Two kilometres to the west of the village is the huge abbey of Valloires, founded in 1143 but rebuilt in the 18th century. Its beautiful gardens are open from April to November.

BOURGUIGNON

This listed village is hidden away in a narrow valley some 10km southwest of Laon. With its well-tended, large stone houses and barns, the village has a prosperous air about it. Drinking troughs and water spouts abound, and a pretty washhouse with an old stone water tank stands just beyond the Mairie.

Signposted walks take visitors round the village, and one leads up to Les Creuttes, which has a fine view across the countryside to Laon. Bourguignon's most famous inhabitants were the three Le Nain brothers. These 17th-century painters came from a family of wine-growers and owned a house on the right-hand side of the shady place des Fréres Le Nain. In mid-May each year the village holds an outdoor arts festival.

ESNES

In the middle of the cereal plains about 11km south of Cambrai, Esnes spreads along both sides of a small tributary of the River Escaut, rather grandly called the 'Torrent of Esnes'. There has been a settlement here since antiquity, and next to the church, which dates from the 12th century, are the remains of two much earlier Merovingian tombs from the first Frankish dynasty.

On the opposite side of the river is the château of Esnes. Despite many alterations it has kept its feudal style, with its huge 15th-century entrance towers and 14th-century lookout turret in the north-east corner. From April to September the château is open on the fourth Sunday of the month (afternoons only). The annual Esnes carnival is held on the fourth Sunday in June.

ESQUELBECQ

Lying beside the River Yser 20km south of Dunkerque, Esquelbecq is a typically Flemish village with its paved central square, low houses and 17th-century church, whose design with three parallel naves follows the Flemish hallekerk style. The romantic pink and yellow brick château, set back from the main square, has stepped gables, turrets and a 45m-tall watch tower, and is surrounded by a moat fed by the Yser. Unfortunately, it is closed to the public, but the façade and formal parterre garden can be admired from the square. On special occasions archery competitions are held in place Bergerot, a tradition that dates back to the Middle Ages. The annual festival takes place on the fourth Sunday in July, and there is a flea market on the second Sunday in September.

LONGPONT

Bordering the Forest of Retz 90km from Paris, Longpont grew up round a Cistercian abbey founded by St Bernard in the 12th century. A 14th-century turreted gate is all that remains of the town walls. Much of the church and abbey buildings was destroyed by fire in 1724, and the Revolution did further damage. The church was progressively dismantled until the abbey was bought privately in 1831. The cloister contains a 13th-century warming house, believed to be the only one in Europe, and includes a small manor-like building whose drawing room comprises former monks' cells (open June to mid-August). The carnival is on the second Sunday in June, and a flea market is held on Ascension Thursday.

MAROILLES

Set on a river bank 40km east of Cambrai, this village is famed for its strong Maroilles and Dauphin cheeses, reputedly the North's finest. The former, invented by a 10th-century monk, has a soft centre and a beer-washed crust; with other regional specialities, it can be sampled at Les Caves de l'Abbaye in the high street. Festivals are held in May and September, an antiques fair in June, and market day is Tuesday.

Maroilles' history is entwined with that of its Benedictine abbey, founded in 652. The 18th century saw its wealth looted by a neighbouring village. Today only a few abbey buildings still exist: a restored gatekeeper's house, which can be visited, 17th-century living quarters and a dilapidated tithe barn.

PARFONDEVAL

This hamlet of under 200 inhabitants is in the ancient border land of the Thiérache. Once covered with forest and marsh, it was settled by Irish monks in the 6th and 7th centuries. Parfondeval is a typical village here, clinging to the side of a river valley. In the Thiérache, churches as well as castles were fortified to protect the population. Parfondeval's church, entered through a gateway in a nearby house, has a turreted square tower and could be barricaded in the event of attack. Today, little disturbs the bucolic peace, which you can savour as you walk round the houses, farm buildings – mostly brick, some cob and thatch – and gardens, watched by a few cows and ducks.

ST-RIQUIER

St-Riquier developed from a 7th-century Benedictine abbey and is one of the oldest freetowns in France. The church dates from the 15th century, with 17th-century restoration work. Much of the 17th-century interior is still in place (guided visits available). The abbey buildings now serve as a hostel and cultural centre; an exhibition of rural Picardy life displays tools, furniture and reconstructed artisans' workshops, plus two traditional barns. There is also a folk museum with a collection including wine-making equipment. At the bottom of the hill is a bizarre house built by one of Napoleon's soldiers, with a roof shaped like the Emperor's hat. Every July there is a major classical music festival.

SUZANNE

Rolling countryside surrounds this sleepy little village. A shady avenue of lime trees leads down the hill through the village towards the 17th-century brick-and-stone château. which sits on a terrace overlooking the ponds of the Somme. Although the castle was not damaged in the Revolution, it was altered in the 19th century and again after World War I. It is open to the public every afternoon except Mondays from 15 July to 31 August. Apart from the château there is a restored church, a few houses, the 18th-century Auberge de Suzanne – and a peace punctuated only by birdsong. A few kilometres upriver is the Belvédère de Vaux, which has a pretty view over the watery Somme Valley.

LE WAST

Set 15km inland from Boulogne, Le Wast boasts a 100-year-old chestnut tree growing on its green, surrounded by houses with brightly painted woodwork. At one end of the green is the 18th-century Manoir du Huisbois, which houses the offices of the Parc Naturel Régional. The helpful staff offer advice and leaflets on places to visit and various activities in the area. If you turn left in front of the 12th-century church with its Romanesque portal, and then right after the Mairie, you come to a shady walk by the Wimereux River.

During the Middle Ages, some churches in the border area of the Thiérache, like St-Médard in Parfondeval, were fortified against the possibility of attack

Champagne

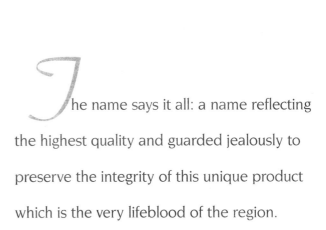

The name says it all: a name reflecting the highest quality and guarded jealously to preserve the integrity of this unique product which is the very lifeblood of the region.

Yesterday and today: champagne grapes are hand-picked, and so carefully handled and delicately pressed that the black skins impart none of their pigment

Vignory
(HAUTE-MARNE)

Snuggling at the bottom of a wooded slope, the village of Vignory has a workaday charm in its plain stone houses and simple shopfronts that sets off its splendid church. The first mention of Vignory, situated around 20km north of Chaumont, was when the Norman knight Raoul Barbeta became the owner of the land in the 10th century. There he built a fortified castle, whose ruins still stand guard over the village.

At the beginning of the 11th century Barbeta's son Guy de Vignory founded a religious order and began work on the beautiful Romanesque Church of St-Étienne, which his brother Roger completed in 1057. The brothers had very different views on religious architecture, which helps to explain the striking difference between the church's nave and choir. The nave is in the Carolingian style frequently found in the Meuse, Rhine, Oise and Aisne regions, while the choir was inspired by Benedictine monastic architecture which became popular in the 11th century in Normandy, the Loire and the Seine areas. Five chapels were added in the late Middle Ages, and the church also contains a fine collection of statuary from the 14th, 15th and 16th centuries.

The village walk covers 1.5km and takes 45 minutes. Although the path to the château is fairly steep, there is also a road. Visitors are welcome to use the picnic facilities near the château ruins.

The Walk

1

Starting from the car park by Vignory's church, walk away from the main part of the village. At a sharp left bend go down a surfaced lane (note the small signpost to the château).

2

After 200m turn right up a grassy track (another signpost to the château); follow the track round a hill beneath the tower ruins. On the far side, turn left and climb the hill to more ruins.

3

Retrace your steps, but instead of turning right (the path you came up) carry straight on towards the village. Then turn left at the bottom of the hill.

4

Keeping to the road nearest the hill, carry straight on between some houses to reach the main road. Turn right, passing the Hôtel Restaurant de l'Étoile in the market square, continue to the village *lavoir* (washhouse) and walk through.

5

Turn left along a narrow road parallel to the main road. The church car park is at the end of the road.

Hautvillers
(MARNE)

Surrounded by vineyards, the village of Hautvillers surveys the valley of the Marne from high ground just north of Épernay. Its proudest boast: it is the birthplace of champagne. With supple lines of vines blanketing the countryside, Hautvillers has a mix of residential housing and champagne manufacturers. Commercial life is active here, and almost all the shops and businesses display delightful wrought-iron signs illustrating their trade. At one end of the village is a Benedictine abbey, founded in the 7th century and owned, with its vineyards, by the Moët family since 1823. The abbey buildings and the small Musée du Vin are not open to the public but can occasionally be visited by special appointment. The abbey church, however, is open every day.

In the late 17th century, and into the 18th, the abbey's cellarmaster for 47 years was a meticulous monk called Dom Pierre Pérignon (1638–1715), whose skills as a winemaker were greatly revered. According to popular tradition, he was the creator of bubbling champagne wine as well as the sophisticated champagne press, capable of producing white wine from black grapes (Pinot Meunier

and Pinot Noir) by its swift yet gentle action. He also perfected the art of blending grapes to produce a consistent flavour and a superior *cuvée*, pioneered the use of stronger English glass to withstand the pressure of sparkling wine and reintroduced the cork stopper to France.

There is an information office on one corner of the place de la République which organises guided visits of Hautvillers. Just over the village boundary, beyond the abbey,

there is a viewpoint with a magnificent panorama over the river and the vineyards and villages of the Marne Valley.

Outines
(MARNE)

This is a typical farming village of the isolated and distinctive Der region, which takes its name from the Celtic word for oak. Known as 'Little Alsace', Outines is full of delightful houses and barns, fine examples of the local architecture and beautifully restored. The low timber buildings have a framework filled in with cob or mud and straw, and painted white or grey, with shingle-covered shallow roofs and decorative *colombiers* (dovecotes). The houses are clustered round the equally characteristic church, with its pointed spire also covered with shingles.

The buildings of this village all reflect the construction traditions of this heavily wood-

Vineyards cloak Hautvillers' hills with tight green lines of leafy vines. Each slope has its own micro-climate and unique chalky soil conditions, producing subtly varied characteristics. Inset, a view of Vignory

ed area. Indeed, part of the forest and three villages were submerged by the huge Der-Chantecoq reservoir, completed in 1974 and now a major centre for watersports, sailing, fishing and birdwatching.

Other Villages

AVENAY-VAL-D'OR

Situated on the banks of the River Livre, this old village features a church originating from the 13th century, rebuilt during the 16th century and boasting a beautiful flamboyant façade. The church contains a 16th-century organ, and paintings from the former Benedictine abbey at Breuil, which was destroyed during the excesses of the Revolution.

CIREY-SUR-BLAISE

Tucked away in the Blaise Valley some 23km north-east of Bar-sur-Aube is the village of Cirey-sur-Blaise. With its elegant bridges and simple church, Cirey seems to have been ignored by the 20th century. Voltaire took refuge in the village's lovely stone château in 1734 and spent 15 years living there with Émilie du Châtelet. He built the 18th-century wing, with its stone door surrounded by symbols of the arts and sciences, and many of his best works were written at the château. Inside, the tiny attic theatre where Voltaire's friends performed his plays is still intact. The château is open every afternoon from 15 June to 15 September.

OGER

Oger is situated 12km south-east of Épernay. Like many other villages in the Côte des Blancs wine-growing region, it is built on a fairly steep, sunny slope. Apart from a 12th-century Romanesque church, the village has no fine buildings as its whole *raison d'être* is champagne: its vines cover 370 hectares, and there are countless champagne houses where you can taste and buy wine. In the centre of the village is the recently opened Musée du Mariage et de ses Traditions, whose exhibits range from early wedding dresses to the menu for a silver wedding anniversary celebrated in 1900.

ST-AMAND-SUR-FION

The village of St-Amand-sur-Fion is about 10km north of Vitry-le-François. Its timber-framed houses meander along either bank of the Fion, a tributary of the River Marne, making the village appear much larger than it really is. The uniformity of the architecture is striking, but the main charm of the village is its superb 12th-century church with its triple-storey choir. Until the 18th century St-Amand was a wine-producing village, but the vines were destroyed by phylloxera in 1770, and the locals turned to cattle-farming. Now, however, St-Amand has been included in a new champagne *appellation* area, and the village produced its first vintage in 1994.

VERZENAY

One of several villages set amongst the vineyards north of the Parc Régional de la Montagne de Reims in the Marne Valley, Verzenay is noted for its windmill, perched dramatically on the crest of a ridge. The winding road below offers excellent views across the expansive fields towards Reims.

VERZY

Another old village famous for the quality of its champagne, Verzy originally flourished under the protection of the 7th-century Benedictine abbey of St-Basle which was destroyed during the Revolution. The village is famed for its curious Faux de Verzy, slow-growing, strangely twisted beech trees, typically umbrella-shaped, near the chapel of St-Basle.

WASSY

Today Wassy, 18km south of St-Dizier, is a tranquil riverside village, but this tranquillity belies its tragic history. It was on 1 March 1562 that the soldiers of the Guise dukedom massacred a group of Protestants in this little village, provoking outrage thoughout the French Protestant community and serving as a catalyst to the Wars of Religion (1562–98).

Formerly an area renowned for its ironworks, the demise of this industry has left Wassy a pleasant little village, with echoes of its former grandeur reflected in the late 18th-century town hall, complete with astronomical clock.

Scudding clouds in an azure sky smile upon Verzenay's vineyards, maturing beneath the village's landmark windmill

Ancient door furniture, like this knocker in Vignory, is often beautifully worked. One can only wonder at its meaning

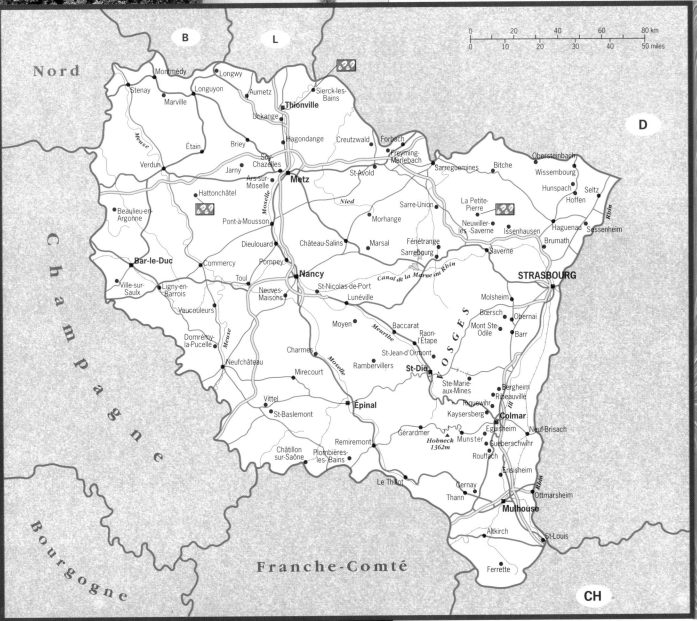

Alsace & Lorraine

The affluence of Alsace and the

no-frills approach of rustic Lorraine –

both offer treasures awaiting discovery.

Hattonchâtel

(Meuse)

NAMED AFTER A **9**TH-CENTURY BISHOP, HATTONCHÂTEL CAPS A MAJESTIC SPUR OF LAND THAT DOMINATES THE WOËVRE PLAINS. THE VINEYARDS AND ORCHARDS THAT SUPPORT THE AREA CAN BE SEEN ON A STROLL ROUND ITS PERIMETER.

This village 36km south-east of Verdun took its name from Hatton, the 9th-century Bishop of Verdun who fortified the village and built his residence here; from the construction of the château around AD 860 until the middle of the 16th century, this was the preferred residence of all Hatton's episcopal successors. Built in a quadrilateral shape, the fortified château had two wings crowned by nine towers. In 1546 Hattonchâtel became a provostship of Lorraine.

Typical shuttered houses in a peaceful byway near the village high street, above. Left, the extraordinary château, seamlessly reconstructed earlier this century

Remnants of the collegiate church are still standing, such as the half-round tower wall on the western flank of the village. The diminutive church, with its 13th-century *chevet droit* (unmissable, as it is located on the right, immediately inside the door), contains a beautiful Renaissance retable in triptych form depicting Christ's Passion, attributed to the artist Ligier Richier and dated 1523. Five religious scenes are displayed in the choir: the Scourging at the Pillar, the Carrying of the Cross, the Crucifixion (mutilated by decree in 1793 during the Revolutionary Terror), the Resurrection and the Apparition to Mary Magdalene. The church reliquary, which houses the remains of St Maur, is open every 16

STONES OF LONG STANDING

Of its original architecture, a few vestiges can still be seen, such as the skeletal remains of the two-level Maison à la Voûte (12th and 14th centuries), overlooking the place du Grand Puits, and the medieval Maison aux Arcades just down the road. The upper level of the Maison à la Voûte features two Romanesque windows in the remains of the north wall. The Maison aux Arcades, from the Middle Ages up until the 18th century, was used as a forum where the village provost proclaimed prison sentences. Built with flared sides, the house has a gallery with a double arcade on the lower level and a central round pillar. Under the gallery is original joinery of squared oak beams; on the second storey and on the north-west side of the house there are small original windows.

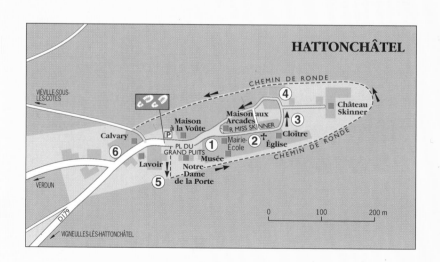

Alsace & Lorraine

The Walk

①

Starting from the car park to the left of the Maison à la Voûte, in the place du Grand Puits. Turn left and walk down rue Miss-Skinner to the Mairie-École. Pass through the archway and admire the view of the Woëvre plains from the terrace of the Mairie (which was destroyed in World War I and renovated with generous donations from Belle Skinner).

②

Exit the Mairie and turn right down rue Miss-Skinner. Stop at the church *cloître* (cloister) and view the church interior with its 16th-century Richier retable.

③

Leaving the cloister, turn right and continue along rue Miss-Skinner to Château Skinner.

④

When you leave the château, bear right to circle back, passing the Maison aux Arcades, to place du Grand Puits.

⑤

As you arrive in the place, follow signs on your left for Circuit du Château, or Chemin de Ronde, which begins along the wall of Notre-Dame de la Porte. Descend a dirt pathway and turn left to trace the perimeter of the village. Walking the Chemin de Ronde takes about 30 minutes. (A stairway leading to the front of the château provides a short-cut that follows only the most scenic portion.)

⑥

Back in place du Grand Puits, circuit completed, admire the Calvary and 1921 *lavoir*.

ⓘ

▷ Length of walk: 2km
▷ Approximate time: 45 minutes to 1 hour
▷ Terrain: Surfaced roads; dirt pathway round perimeter with stairs leading up to castle. Sturdy shoes recommended. Chemin de Ronde not suitable for wheelchairs
▷ Parking: Free car park next to Maison à la Voûte
▷ Open: Castle: 9–noon and 2–7 (closed Tuesdays); guided tour recommended
▷ Refreshments: Small bistro in front of château, with simple limited menu

November, the feast day of the parish's patron saint.

Despite its exceptional strategic positioning, conflicts down the centuries took a heavy toll on Hattonchâtel. The village was ravaged during the Thirty Years War (1618–48), and in 1634 Cardinal Richelieu ordered its citadel destroyed. The village also sustained heavy damage from bombardments during World War I, leaving the remains of this formerly fine village in an even sorrier state.

SAVED BY BELLE

In the 1920s, American heiress Belle Skinner came to the rescue of Hattonchâtel, erecting a neo-Gothic château on the site of the devastated medieval bishop's castle. Working with the help of French architect Jacquelin d'Evreux, Miss Skinner managed to preserve several elements of the original structure, including part of the western moat and much of the northern wall and the lower southern façade. The arch of the castle's main portal remains (though it has been moved) and the original dimensions of its chapel were kept.

Miss Skinner also funded the restoration of the village, hiring American architect John Sanford to rebuild the Mairie-École (Town Hall and School) in 1923; today the former classrooms are occupied by a museum devoted to the works of the painter Louise Cottin. The terrace overlooking the Woëvre and the Côtes de Meuse gives on to French gardens and a stairway leading to the Chemin de Ronde circling the village.

Much of the architecture in renovated Hattonchâtel was influenced by the work of the innovative and sometimes controversial Frank Lloyd Wright: note the modern 'medieval' details and the lines of the *lavoir* (washhouse), which has a gently sloping roof recalling those found on Japanese palaces.

Treasure within Hattonchâtel's collegiate church: a glorious retable depicting scenes from Christ's Passion. Here, the artist's skill brings the moment alive with movement, expression and undiminished pathos

Hunspach
(BAS-RHIN)

Of the constellation of tiny villages scattered throughout northern Alsace, Hunspach is doubtless one of the most picturesque and has been voted one of France's most beautiful villages several years running.

Hunspach, unlike many of its neighbours, emerged relatively unscathed from the Liberation during World War II. Located 10km south of Wissembourg, it is separated from the rest of the Alsatian countryside by the 19,000-hectare Hagenau Forest (one of the largest forests in France), where St Arbogast, Bishop of Strasbourg and the patron of Alsace, lived as a hermit.

Devastated by the Thirty Years' War, Hunspach owes its impressive unity of style and proportion to Louis XIV, who ordered the town rebuilt at the end of the 17th century in an effort to repopulate the northern Alsatian countryside – which drew several Swiss families to the area as well. Such architectural harmony has not, however, precluded individuality. The timber framework of each house often carries symbolic significance: diamond-shaped lozenges, for example, were a symbol of fertility, while the *chaises curiales* (rounded X-shaped beams) often signified the judicial power or prosperity of its occupants. With practice, one can distinguish originally Protestant homes from Catholic ones at a glance. Simply put, the former are more ornate because these families had fewer children and a lighter financial obligation to their church, leaving them with more to spend on their possessions. Note, too, that the windows in many houses are *bombée*, or convex, thereby allowing occupants to look out but preventing passers-by from peering in.

Hunspach has its share of fine old farmhouses. One of the oldest (dated 1713), at 12 rue des Moutons, is said to be one of two in town that still have the original *toit long* (extended roof). Another farmhouse, in an impasse off rue de l'Ange, is festooned with antique lanterns and assorted farm implements, and also has a communal well which is several hundred years old.

On Sundays, village elders may be seen wearing traditional costumes, and in neighbouring Seebach, locals don what are arguably the most striking of traditional Alsatian costumes – particularly on the Sunday which follows the 14th of July.

A Hunspach house bursting with character, above. A carved door, below left, speaks proudly of abundance

Women's *coiffes*, or bonnets, are small and worn high on the head; the ones worn by Protestant women are in embroidered silk brocade with sequins or black and white pearls, crowned with a red or black lace-bordered ribbon which is tied in a delicate bow. Catholic *coiffes* are made of white tulle embroidered with flower motifs. Scarves, the centrepiece of the Alsatian costume, are richly coloured, in red, mauve or green silk, and highly embellished.

Hunspach's annual Forest Festival is held the first Sunday in July. The village tourist office (where the staff are very helpful) is hidden behind an ivy-covered arch.

Neuwiller-les-Saverne
(BAS-RHIN)

Situated amid undulating vineyards and woodlands between the foot of the Vosges Mountains and the Alsatian plain, some 13km from Issenhausen (see page 60), the village of Neuwiller-les-Saverne began life in the 8th century, when a Benedictine abbey dedicated to SS Peter and Paul was erected on this site by Siegbad, Bishop of Metz. It was a popular pilgrimage destination in the 9th century, which fostered prosperity. By the 12th century, the 15 or so churches belonging to the abbey gave it a certain importance, as several of these churches fell outside the diocese of Metz.

At about the same time, Neuwiller's moat and a succession of ramparts were built, which account for the well-contained elliptical development of the town over the centuries – although the linear extension built in the 18th century along the Dossenheim-sur-Zinsel road has given the town a peculiar tennis-racquet shape.

The portal near the entrance of the Roman Catholic parish church is the most important vestige of the ancient former Benedictine abbey. Itself an interesting compilation of Romanesque chapels, the church has a transitional Romanesque transept and choir, an early Gothic nave (13th century) and

a baroque tower, making it one of the most remarkable churches in lower Alsace. The Dupont organ dates from 1772.

Do not miss the superb late 15th-century tapestries in the upper chapel of St Sebastian which recount the life of St Adelphus, who gave his worldly goods to the poor and restored sight to the blind, hearing to the deaf and voices to the mute (the tapestries can be viewed by appointment with the parish priest of St Peter's).

main street is the Dolder belfry with its elaborate rounded-X motifs dating back to the town's earliest days. At the end of the diminutive rue des Juifs stands the Voleurs (Thieves) tower which, as its name suggests, served as a prison. At the southern end of town stood another tower, the Tour des Bourgeois, destroyed in 1846 to make room for a Catholic church. To the east was the fourth tower, which was removed to make way for the current Empire-style town hall.

The Walk

This walk in Hunspach is 1.5km long and takes about 45 minutes. From place de la Mairie (Town Square), follow rue Principale towards the post office. Note the farmhouse at 12 rue des Moutons, on the right at the top of the street.

Go back along rue Principale, turning right into rue de l'Ange. Continue straight on into an impasse to see the farmhouse at number 13 and the old communal well. Leave the impasse, then turn right on the continuation of rue de l'Ange.

Approaching place de la Mairie again, take the surfaced garden pathway running beside the house at 1 rue de l'Ange and follow a gently rising path. At the top is a small church on the left; on the right, a cemetery.

From the cemetery, bear right and continue on a broken pathway for about 5 minutes, emerging at rue St-Paul. Turn left.

Keep bearing left into the continuation of rue Principale. Opposite number 50, turn up a surfaced path lined with chestnut trees towards the church.

At the front of the church, you can either turn right towards the cemetery and right again to follow a garden path down to place de la Mairie, or retrace your steps down to rue Principale and then turn left towards place de la Mairie.

▷ Length of walk: 1.5km
▷ Approximate time: 45 minutes
▷ Terrain: Surfaced roads sometimes in disrepair; gentle slopes; garden path may be difficult for wheelchairs
▷ Parking: Free car park opposite the town hall.
▷ Open: Tourist office
▷ Refreshments: Two restaurants, À la Couronne in rue Principale and Au Cerf in rue de la Gare. Tea salon opposite church in rue Principale

Despite its clock tower surveying the land, Riquewihr and its vineyards tell of timeless traditions

Riquewihr
(HAUT-RHIN)

Tucked into the foothills of the Vosges, Riquewihr lies in one of the richest wine-growing pockets of the *département*. The village has long been a major tourist draw along the Alsatian wine route, and since time immemorial has been prized as a viticultural gem. The first historical mention of the village surfaces in 1094, though Merovingian tombs excavated locally indicate that the area was inhabited well before that date. This *perle du vignoble* displays a remarkable architectural homogeneity within its original medieval fortifications, first erected in 1291. Of the quadrangular layout, three fortified walls still stand, with bastions at the north-east and south-west corners. At either end of the village stand two towers: opening on to the

Lift your gaze above the town's wealth of souvenir shops to see the most harmonious ensemble of geranium-bedecked 16th- and 17th-century houses Alsace has to offer, ranging from the very simple to the unabashedly ornate. Note house number 16, called 'Nid de Cigognes' ('Stork's Nest'), which dates from 1535 and has sculpted columns, a well from 1603 and a large wine press from 1817. Be sure to visit the surprisingly fascinating Musée d'Histoire des PTT, in a restored 16th-century château.

At La Couronne Hôtel, renovations have uncovered striking hand-painted ceilings in rooms 10 and 11. A Christmas market features concerts, local handicrafts and a range of gourmet items.

La Petite-Pierre

(Bas-Rhin)

HALFWAY BETWEEN PLAIN AND PLATEAU, THIS FORTIFIED TOWN IS ENHANCED BY FINE, FLOWER-STUDDED 18TH-CENTURY HOUSES WITH ELABORATELY SCULPTED PORTALS. THE LOCAL GASTRONOMY FEATURES GAME, TROUT AND GOOSE-BASED POT-AU-FEU.

Located 22km north-west of Saverne, the bourg of La Petite-Pierre, which looks over the Imsthal Valley, has been since the Celtic era a key centre of communication between the plains of Alsace and the plateau of Lorraine, and served as an important gateway for the Romans. Given its strategic location as a mountain pass, the Bishops of Metz ordered a castle built here during the 12th century to safeguard free movement between the two regions. It was the residence of the Counts of Lutzelstein and, after 1566, the Comte Georges Jean de Veldenz (Jerri-Hans). A wealthy industrialist nicknamed 'King of the Glassmakers', whose father-in-law was the King of Sweden, the Comte embellished and restored the castle and its grounds. During the 17th century, the castle became a military fortress, and remained so until 1870.

DIVIDED IN TOLERANCE

In 1417 a church was erected by Comte Burkhardt, part of which still stands today: the Gothic-style choir containing remarkable 15th-century frescoes – among the oldest in the east of France – of the Four Evangelists and Adam and Eve, rediscovered in 1864. The church is a 'simultaneous' one, having served for both Protestant and Catholic wor-

Best seat in the house: awaiting an occupant, a garden chair is all set for watching high-street life, below

The fortified château of La Petite-Pierre served as a military fortress for about two centuries, until 1870

ship since 1737. According to the 1685 Rule of Simultaneum, Protestant villages were obliged to grant the Catholic minority use of the church choir if a minimum of seven Catholic families lived in the parish; Protestants held their services in the nave. This practice still exists in about 50 churches throughout France. Initially, this shared use met with great resistance; today it is considered a sign of religious tolerance.

While in La Petite-Pierre, visitors should take a look at the Museum of the Alsatian Seal in the rue du Château. The use of seals, such as those engraved on helms and emblazoned escutcheons, dates back to antiquity; they served as marks of identity, authority or property for popes, emperors, kings and craftsmen.

The Museum of Crafts and Folklore on the rue des Remparts is located on the site of a 16th-century gunpowder warehouse. On display here are decorative moulds, pastry recipes, imitation ingredients used in making *springerle* (aniseed biscuits) and *lebkuche* (gingerbread), and Alsatian Christmas traditions. (Guided visits to both museums can be arranged through the museum council or town hall.)

The nearby northern Vosges Mountains offer good opportunities for nature walks. The tourist office has details of a 9-km trail, and can arrange free guided theme-based excursions.

Park at the entrance to the *vieille ville* (old town) at the top of the hill, near the tourist office. Head downhill towards the church along the sloping rue du Château.

When you reach the Église de l'Assomption, note the epitaphs of the Comte Burkhardt and his wife at the entrance to the church. Both died in 1418 and were buried underneath the choir; their tomb was moved outside in 1884.

As you exit the church, turn right and enter the gates of the 12th-century Château de la Petite-Pierre. The 18th-century observation tower has a good view over the Vosges Mountains, from the Donon range to Lichtenberg.

Turn right as you leave the castle. You will come to a viewpoint. Off to the right is a narrow dirt path leading down to a *citerne* (cistern) carved out of rock (the hike down takes about 15 minutes; a torch is useful).

Take rue des Remparts which ascends to the right. The Museum of Crafts and Folklore (Musée) is located at number 11: it specialises in Alsatian Christmas traditions.

As you continue up rue des Remparts, note the wisteria-lined *ruelle* on the left which leads to the rue du Chemin de Ronde. Number 3 is one of the oldest houses in the village. Further along on your right is a staircase leading to the cistern. Continue back to the car park at the entrance to the village.

i

▷ Length of walk: about 2.5km, including the hike to the cistern (point4)
▷ Approximate time: 45 minutes to 1 hour, including the visit to the cistern
▷ Terrain: Sturdy shoes recommended. Generally unsuitable for wheelchairs, although drawbridge gives access to castle. Dirt pathway tricky
▷ Parking: Free parking at the entrance to the village
▷ Open: Church: 8–6. Seal Museum: 10–noon and 2–6 Tuesday to Sunday during school holidays; weekends only rest of year. Folklore Museum: 10–noon and 2–6 Tuesday to Sunday from Jul to Sep; Sundays only Oct to Jun. (Check with town hall or museum council for guided visits to both museums)
▷ Refreshments: Cafés and restaurants in the *vieille ville*. Try the Auberge d'Imsthal for a memorable, medium-priced meal

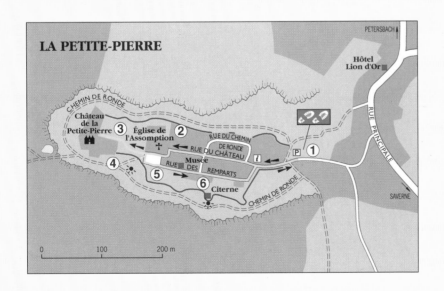

THE FRENCH REGION OF ALSACE HAS TRADITIONALLY EXISTED ENTRE DEUX CHAISES, OR 'BETWEEN TWO CHAIRS', TORN BETWEEN ITS FRENCH AND GERMAN IDENTITIES. ORIGINALLY CELTIC, THE REGION HAS ABSORBED TEUTONIC INFLUENCES FROM THE 4TH CENTURY UP THROUGH THE MIDDLE AGES AND RENAISSANCE, UNDERGOING GRADUAL GALLICISATION DURING THE 17TH CENTURY ONLY TO BE TAKEN BACK BY BISMARCK IN 1871 AND REMAINING UNDER GERMAN CONTROL UNTIL 1918. BUT THE ALSATIAN ARTIST CHARLES SPINDLER, BORN INTO AN ERA CHARACTERISED BY CONFLICT – BOTH CULTURAL AND POLITICAL – FOUND INSPIRATION IN SUCH DISPARATE TENDENCIES AND LEARNED HOW TO SYNTHESISE THIS DUALITY INTO AN AESTHETIC WHOLE, CREATING AN ALSATIAN ART NOUVEAU STYLE IN FURNITURE, ART AND DESIGN AT THE TURN OF THE CENTURY.

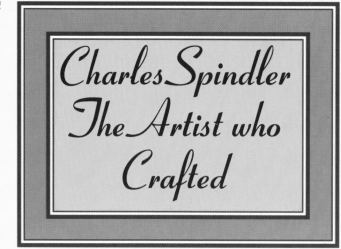

*Charles Spindler
The Artist who
Crafted*

Born in the Bas-Rhin village of Bœrsch (see page 60) in 1865, Charles Spindler attended art schools in Munich and Berlin, where he learned painting. In 1897 he founded the artistic group known as the Cercle de St-Léonard and set up his studio in the village of St-Léonard, just outside Bœrsch. At that time, reacting against the ornamental style of the École de Nancy, there had arisen a tendency towards functionalism (a harbinger of the Bauhaus movement) espoused by artists in Germany's Kunstlerkolonie, England's Arts and Crafts movement with William Morris, and Austria's Viennese School. In Charles Spindler the two opposing styles found a sympathetic and able interpreter.

'He was a link between the various opposing movements, a very important link, and they were accesssible to him given the various influences he had been exposed to during his development as an artist,' says Jean-Charles Spindler,

Below, crimson creepers blaze beside the balconied courtyard of the old Spindler workshop in the village of St-Léonard, near Bœrsch. Charles Spindler, right, devoted himself to developing the use of wood itself as an artistic medium, letting grain, colour and texture do the work of both paint and brush in the techniques of marquetry

the artist's grandson, who runs the ancestral workshop.

The art of marquetry, the ancient technique of wood inlay believed to have originated in Asia Minor in 350 BC, was revived here in large measure through the talents of Charles Spindler (indeed, marquetry is now considered typical of Alsace), who used it in decorating art nouveau furniture and also as a pictorial technique. He discovered marquetry by chance in 1893, and reinterpreted the techniques to create a new form of 'collage' that relied on various kinds of wood grain. This in turn led him to furniture design in 1898, much of which was inspired by the illustrious art nouveau artists Mucha and Grasset, and even landscape pictures using wood which, as Spindler wrote, 'is sometimes able to render to perfection the fleece of a lamb or the reflections of silk'.

The Painterly Touch

'He made a name for himself with objects of furniture which he decorated with marquetry,' says Jean-Charles. 'As he was a painter, he used wood differently from the other Art Nouveau artists.' Even in his style and influences, Spindler was *entre deux chaises*: in furniture design, he was first influenced by Gothic style, then by the ornate *style de Nancy*, then by the functional Kunstlerkolonie from Darmstadt, and especially by Olbrich Jugendstil from southern Germany and the Viennese Secession.

His work with furniture was carried out in the workshop at St-Léonard, which received such distinguished guests as Claude Debussy and Gustav Charpentier. The workshop, set within the walls of the former abbey of St-Léonard at the foot of Mont St-Odile, was handed down first to Spindler's son Paul, a painter and watercolourist who continued the marquetry tradition. It has been run by Paul's son Jean-Charles since 1975.

The large, vine-covered courtyard leading to the entrance of the workshop is filled with the fragrance of wood. More than a hundred veneering oils and several thousand varieties of veneer are used. In addition to traditional scenes of the Alsatian countryside, Jean-Charles also employs more contemporary motifs, placing a great emphasis on wood as a material. He allows himself to be guided by the natural colours and structure of the wood – the gnarls of light and red amboina from Sulawesi, violet amaranth, Brazilian redwood, and gnarls of thuja from Morocco.

Once the veneers are selected and smoothed, each element of the picture is cut out using a crossbow saw fitted with an extremely thin blade. Jean-Charles creates wall panels, pictures, folding

Details from La Chasse, above and right, by Paul Spindler. With extra-ordinary versatility the various wood grains represent earth, fabric, even flesh – a fine testimony to the skill of the maker

scenes and triptychs, which can take as long as two and a half months for the larger pieces. He has exhibited worldwide and has been awarded many prizes, as had his grandfather.

From Accolades to Obscurity

Charles Spindler's renown once spread far beyond the boundaries of Alsace. A music room he created for the 1900 World Fair won the Grand Prix (London's Victoria and Albert Museum acquired one of the walls; the Berlin Museum acquired the opposite wall, now lost), and he took another Grand Prix at the 1904 World Fair in St Louis, Missouri. At the time, the press reported that his items of marquetry were 'miles ahead of everything the French masters Galle and Majorelle, famous for their inlay work, have exhibited... They probably represent the height of that which has ever been created in this intricate and costly technique'.

Unfortunately, the fluctuating political status of Alsace was to smother the Alsatian art nouveau movement. 'The State of Alsace-Lorraine was anxious to support us, and amongst [the] buildings it was erecting, there was a natural need for our talents, but the architects it was employing were not in our field. To them, we were unknown. The government contented itself in subsidising us for exhibitions,' wrote Spindler in his memoirs. While his marriage of modern German principles with the typical French love of ornament was what made him and his movement original, it also explains why he remained an outsider, reduced ultimately to obscurity.

Sturdily made chairs are elevated to an art form when given a fanciful back in the guise of a butterfly

Spindler on View

The works of Charles Spindler and some of his *objets d'art* can be seen at various locations in Alsace. In Obernai in the Haùt-Rhin *département* there is a room he decorated at the Hôtel de la Cloche, and outside Obernai at the Château de la Léonardsau there is a salon decorated by him in 1902. In Strasbourg the Musée de l'Art Moderne exhibits some of his works, and the Spindlers also played an active role in the creation of Strasbourg's Musée Alsacien. The towns of Colmar and Mietesheim, both in the Haut-Rhin, feature works by Spindler in their musuems. In the Abbaye St-Léonard at Mont Ste-Odile there are works by father and son (Charles executed the *Chemin de Croix*). Finally, the Spindler workshop itself may be visited, but only by appointment. Contact the Marqueterie d'Art Spindler, St-Léonard – 3 cour du Chapitre, Bœrsch 67530, Ottrott, France (fax: [33] 88.95.98.31).

Sierck-les-Bains

(Moselle)

TUCKED INTO THE MEANDERS OF THE MOSELLE, SIERCK SITS ON A HILLSIDE FACING THE IMPOSING ROCKY, VINE-COVERED SWELL OF STROMBERG. UNABLE TO SPREAD OUTWARDS, IT HAS HISTORICALLY REBUILT ITSELF UPWARDS.

The village of Sierck-les-Bains, 18km north-east of Thionville, is situated near the borders of Luxembourg and Germany. Though not instantly apparent from without, its medieval streets contain many vestiges of the village's heyday. The Tour de l'Horloge (Clocktower), which is now a museum and tourist office, the Tour des Sorcières (Witches' Tower) and the Porte Neuve are the most striking remains of the fortified 13th-century town which once flourished here. This village, like many less attractive ones in the region, now stands stripped of once-lucrative local industries such as coal mining

Strong lines in warm earth tones define the upper-storey windows of this house in Sierck

and steel foundries, but in Sierck-les-Bains a rich architectural legacy lingers in the spectacular Renaissance façades crowned with ornate portals and the weather-worn family crests of the local nobility. Look along the façades for tell-tale evidence of the Moselle, which has been known to swell and lap against the villagers' front doors. (The raised ground floor of the Maison Berweiller, in fact, was intended to protect the residents and their possessions from frequent floods.)

CRUSHED BY CONFLICT

Chartered in 1295, Sierck-les-Bains was a centre of industry for *faïence* (crockery), tanneries, small crafts and the cloth trade until a succession of 17th-century wars put an end to local prosperity. The old citadel overlooking the city – of which only a massive chunk of wall remains – was a favoured residence of the Dukes of Lorraine until 1643, when the region became part of France and the residence was destroyed.

VANISHING ACT

Built right into the rocky hillside is the small 15th-century Église Paroissiale de la Nativité, the interior of which underwent a complete renovation in 1995. Inside, there is a copy of a series of wooden panels depicting the life of Christ. The originals of these reliefs were dismantled for safekeeping during World War II; they subsequently vanished. Note also the baroque high altar, as well as the primitive chapel, originally built in 1236 for the Teutonic knights.

The babbling river, shallow and picturesque, has sometimes overflowed its banks to flood the town

The Walk

①

Park across the street from the tourist office on the quai des Ducs de Lorraine.

②

Cross under under the archway of the Tour de l'Horloge, directly behind the tourist office, and walk towards the church. On your left is the Maison Berweiller (1624). Note the privately owned Tour des Sorcières beyond the Maison.

③

After visiting the church, retrace your steps and head towards a steep cobblestone *ruelle* which ascends to the Venelle St-Christophe. Note the house on the left-hand corner at the entrance of the *ruelle*: its façade has a coat of arms which bears scales, three *croix de Lorraine* and two bars, signifying the town's dependence on the duchies of Lorraine and Le Bar. At the top of the *ruelle*, turn left into the Venelle St-Christophe, which is lined with elaborate houses. You will emerge at the place de Jeanne d'Arc, at the foot of what was once the fortified castle.

④

From the place Jeanne d'Arc, turn towards the hospital and take the first left, descending a well-marked pathway towards the canal (Ruisseau de Montenach). As you cross the Pont rue du Moulin, look back towards the small, original (and privately owned) crenellated tower. Turn left into the rue du Moulin and walk towards the place du Marché, noting the Renaissance portal next to number 6.

⑤

Turn left into the Grande Rue. Known as rue des Juifs (Jews' Street) until World War II, it has many façades which merit attention, notably the inscribed Renaissance portal next to number 14 (dated 1615).

⑥

Continue along Grande Rue, passing under the archway to emerge in place Morbach, opposite the tourist office.

ⅰ

▷Length of walk: about 2km
▷Approximate time: 1 hour
▷Terrain: Steep, with surfaced roads and cobbles; dirt pathway and stairs leading up to castle; sturdy shoes recommended; not suitable for wheelchairs
▷Parking: Free car park by tourist office
▷Open: Castle: 10–7 Tuesday to Sunday, May–Sep; grounds accessible daily. Intermittent off-season fine afternoons
▷Refreshments: Several cafés; for a traditional meal, try Auberge de la Klaussthough (follow signs to Montenach) – like most of town, closed on Mondays

A view of past and present: even in ruins, Sierck's ramparts command respect, sitting heavily above the village they once guarded. The town centre below goes about its daily business, while public gardens invite a rest amid cool lawns and flowers in full glory

At the top of the hill, the grounds of an 11th-century château built on the site of a Gallo-Roman castle called Circum Castellum are sprinkled with picnic tables, and its ruined ramparts boast some glorious views.

Sierck's calendar includes the Fête de la Grenouille (Frog Festival) on 20–21 May; the Hommage à St-Jean, a major festival honouring the saint who saved Sierck from the Plague, on 22 June; and the Fête de la Choucroute et de la Bière (Sauerkraut and Beer) on 2–3 September.

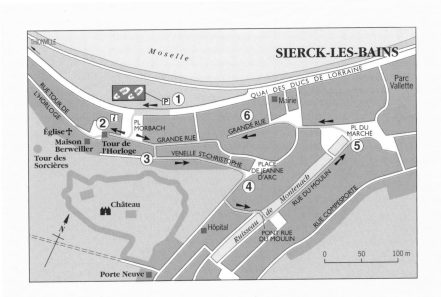

Other Villages

BEAULIEU-EN-ARGONNE

Beaulieu-en-Argonne, a *Village Fleuri*, sprang up on the site where the Scottish-born monk St Rouin founded a Benedictine abbey around the year 642. Though pillaged, burnt and destroyed over the centuries, Beaulieu has been faithfully reconstructed after each calamity. After the last abbot died in 1790, the abbey buildings were dismantled and its stones used for construction. All that remains is an outbuilding housing an enormous 13th-century *pressoir à bascule*, or lever-operated wine press, in use until 1914. At the village entrance a board charts five nature walks from 2km to 17km long.

BERGHEIM

This is a gem of a village along the Alsatian wine route. Near the 14th-century Haute Porte stands the Liberty Lime Tree, dating from 1300. Clematis and roses garland half-timbered houses, balconies and the cobblestone square with its old fountain. The 14th-century basilica contains frescoes of the Mount of Olives and St George discovered in 1959. Medieval fortifications girding the village are very well preserved. Feudal Bergheim was, unusually, a place of refuge. Several people standing trial in lay or ecclesiastic courts were granted asylum here. Until the late 1800s, a carving on the Haute Porte depicted a man thumbing his nose at authorities.

BŒRSCH

'It looks like a toy, a miniature city uniting every kind of Alsatian wine district within a confined space,' wrote French artist Hansi in reference to Bœrsch. This little village

4km west of Obernai nestles inside three fortified Gothic gateways. Traces of the 14th-century murals which ran between them are still visible. The triangular Grand Place is formed by 16th-century houses and a town hall featuring a turret, spiral stairway and mullioned windows. The rare Renaissance well opposite the town hall has elaborate columns supporting three wheels and six buckets, one of the most beautiful in Alsace. Altogether a fitting birthplace for artist-designer Charles Spindler (see page 56).

CHÂTILLON-SUR-SAÔNE

This fortress-cum-Renaissance village is approached from the pasture-lined road to Jonvelle at the confluence of the Saône and the Apance. Tall trees mark the site of a castle first recorded in 1234. Fortified to defend its exposed position between Lorraine and Bourgogne, Châtillon was attacked by Swedes and Houlans during the Thirty Years War, and was uninhabited for nearly two decades; today the Renaissance heart of the town seems frozen in time. The church with its 13th-century chevet, the Grande Place, the *grenier à sel* (salt store) and, behind it, the façade of the Hôtel de Ligniville (1554) and the Hôtels Sandrecourt and Bourbevelle all reward exploration. The Maison de l'Auditoire, with its Gothic tympana, was until 1790 a gateway to the city.

DOMRÉMY-LA-PUCELLE

This village on the edge of the tranquil Meuse Valley is named 'la Pucelle' ('the Maiden') after the

martyr whose birthplace put the site on the map. Joan of Arc was born in a simple slope-roofed home with a tympanum over the entryway bearing a statue of La Pucelle and the family coat of arms. A museum chronicles her life as well as the history of the region. St-Rémy Church contains a choir and part of a tower dating from the 13th century, and 16th-century frescoes of St Sebastian. South of Domrémy is Bois Chênu, where the uneducated but astute 13-year-old shepherd girl first heard the voices of St Michael, St Catherine and St Margaret exhorting her to deliver France from the English. A basilica here contains the statue of St Margaret in front of which young Joan allegedly prayed. The bois offers some good nature walks.

EGUISHEIM

Cro-Magnon man inhabited this area circa 3000 BC, and Romans planted the region's first vineyards here in the 6th century. Now, wrapped in a wide belt of vines at the foot of Schlossberg near Colmar, Eguisheim is one of the oldest unwalled villages in Alsace. The château fort rose from the site of a fortified residence founded around 720. For four centuries the castle was the home of the episcopal magistrat. During the Revolution, the château was sold as a national asset and its keep disappeared. In the last century the Romanesque church received a new nave, but the original clock tower and its 12th-century tympanum have been preserved. Look out for large storks' nests on the rooftops.

HOFFEN

During the Middle Ages, Hoffen belonged to the Abbey of Wissembourg 13km to the north. The houses here, with timbered gable ends and flower-decked windowsills, are aligned perpendicular to the single main street. Along one side of the street is a 19th-century timber-framed town hall, a communal well and a relatively recent church. As is customary in this region, the courtyards which separate the family hearth from the stables are open to view. On the place du Tilleul is the Liberty Tree, a majestic lime planted during the Revolution, and a rare covered well. The patois, or local dialect, varies from village to village, making each of them a living repository of regional traditions and dialect.

ISSENHAUSEN

Founded in the 13th century, minuscule Issenhausen thrived mainly on agriculture. The local population, entirely Protestant, currently stands at 78. The village's 23 farmhouses were constructed during the 18th and 19th centuries and, in contrast to northern Alsace, their courtyards are enclosed by massive metal gates. The 18th-century Ferme Michel, with covered arcades and a bell turret which called the servants at day's end, houses the only *gîte*. Above the entryway is an inscription which translates: 'Would-be pilferers keep out, our cats are masters of the art'!

KAYSERSBERG

The bailey walls, which were joined to those of this small town in 1233, still surround the grim tower guarding this medieval village, birthplace of the saintly Albert Schweitzer, winner of the Nobel Peace Prize in 1952.

MARVILLE

Sleepy Marville is of particular interest to architecture buffs. First occupied by the Romans, Martis-Villa developed a prosperous leather and cloth trade and evolved into a well-to-do Renaissance village. Iberian troops occupied it from 1555 to 1659, leaving distinctive tall, chalky-yellow houses, with sculptures often inspired by classical myths. The main square is lined with 16th- and 17th-century dwellings (note the superb loggia of Chevalier Michel's house nearby). The austere 14th-century church has a Flamboyant 16th-century balustraded organ loft. Beyond the ruins of a 1629 convent is a cemetery with impressive 15th- and 16th-century funerary sculptures.

SCY-CHAZELLES

This minuscule pair of villages 6km west of Metz are built into the ledges of Mont St-Quentin. Imposing homes, built primarily by wealthy vintners, crowd the steep, narrow streets. Though simple, many are embellished with 18th- and 19th-century decorative elements evoking the wine trade. Two fortified churches dominate these villages. The one at Chazelles is the final resting place of the father of the European Union, Robert Schuman. His house is now a museum commemorating his life and work.

Quirky shapes, pointy roofs and none-too-vertical walls give the buildings of Eguisheim the undeniable atmosphere of a fairy tale

The Loire

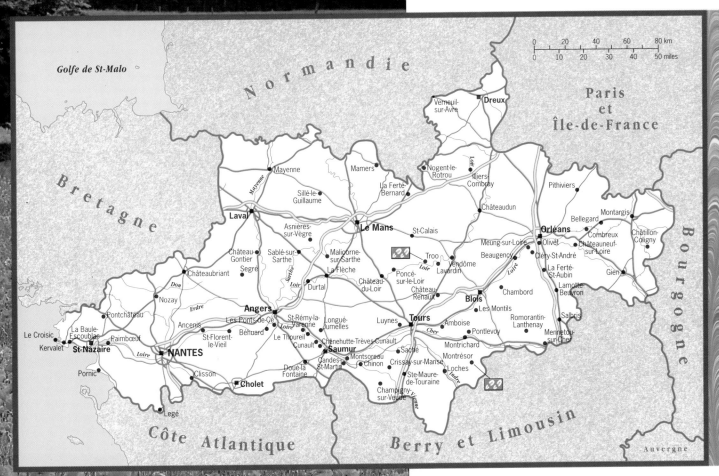

Perhaps the most pleasantly balanced and richly diverse region of France, the Loire quite simply has it all: rivered landscapes, medieval villages, unusual land formations, magical châteaux, succulent cuisine, brilliant wines and an endless labyrinth of quaint country roads.

Lavardin
(LOIR-ET-CHER)

With its medieval character intact, Lavardin's charm lies in the mysteries of its grand ruins: the once mighty Château de Lavardin, which dominates the landscape and demands to be visited. The village appears as if lifted out of the pages of a fairy tale. The only unsettling aspect of Lavardin is the impression that it has been preserved solely for its beauty, for it seems to support little indigenous life other than that serving tourism. That, however, is no reason not to visit this exquisite village.

Posted on the Gothic stone bridge at the entrance to town are the times for the tours of the Forteresse de Lavardin – worth waiting for, as the tour is fascinating. And, aside from a lazy stroll through the village or a picnic or romantic promenade along the Loir, the château-fortress is Lavardin's chief asset.

The Forteresse de Lavardin, which served as the castle of the Counts of Vendôme in the Middle Ages, looms imposingly above the village, offering an immediate insight into medieval feudalism. In its early days, King Henry II of England, son of Richard the Lionheart, set up his headquarters here.

Impressive even in ruins, the silhouetted lines of Lavardin's château rise up starkly from the slope

The fortress, which had been privately owned, was sold to the village for a single symbolic franc in 1986 and has since been subsidised by a local transport magnate. The château was then closed for eight years of restoration, and its structure proved so solid that it took two years for renovators just to build a catwalk from the outer edge to the inner plateau. It was opened to the public for the first time in 1994.

At the appropriate hours, the château guide unlocks the iron gates, leads you through a series of three outer walls into the recently renovated 11th-century ruins, then teases your imagination into overdrive with a wealth of description that brings the château's past alive. Within the walls – but separate from the areas reserved for the seigneur, his family and the nobility – a triangular field was kept as a Roman camp; here, captured slaves were locked up and forgotten in dank chambers poignantly called *oubliettes*. The bridge across to the châtelet, or small château, was fully equipped with a triple security system, and, as the guide points out such details, one realises that ancient and

contemporary concerns are essentially identical. A hollow column built into the walls, for example, served as a sort of intercom or telephone system, as sound was found to travel well in the stone-encased space.

The fortress suffered a series of attacks, and was almost totally destroyed in 1589, when the Protestant Henri IV sacked it (only later did he convert to Catholicism). It was Lavardin, after whom the village is named, who put up the longest resistance. Out of vengeance, Henry IV rendered the château virtually impotent by ordering his army to *saper les murs* – a technically fascinating but vindictive process of weakening the supporting structure of the walls.

The culmination of the guided walk is the Tour du Capitaine, the highest point of the castle, where visitors are led through a ruined chamber that was once the seigneur's private bedroom. The beds are alarmingly short, for at that time the nobility are reputed tohave slept in a sitting position; reclining was reserved for the dead, and he who lay down flat was fearful of not waking.

Every year the fortress hosts a wine exhibition in its stone entranceway, devoted to the ancient tools used for pressing grapes to make the local Coteaux du Loir wines.

Montrichard
(Loir-et-Cher)

Life in the large village of Montrichard, situated on the D176, is dominated by the River Cher. Along the quai de le République, the visitor finds the Embarquadeur, where boating activities, hired pedaloes and bathing beaches enliven the summer landscape. On the bank across from the village, over the stone bridge to Faverolles-sur-Cher, a pleasant Parc Nautique is located. Visitors can witness an unforgettable live eagle show every afternoon (3:30–5) at the Donjon des Aigles. Wild and free-flying birds of prey swoop from surrounding heights to rip titbits from the gloved hands of the falconers. The collection of diurnal and nocturnal birds from round the world is renowned.

The Église Ste-Croix, with its Romanesque architecture, is well worth a visit; Jeanne de France, daughter of Louis XI, was married here. The Caves de Champagnisation Monmousseau will appeal to anyone interested in wine-making – and tasting.

Resting on projecting prow-like supports, the old stone bridge at Montrichard crosses the broad River Cher

Candes-St-Martin
(Indre-Loire)

This village, about 1.5km south-east of Montsoreau at the confluence of the Loire and Vienne rivers, is an ideal spot for anglers. It also boasts a surprisingly large 12th-century monastic church, marking the spot where St Martin of Tours died on 11 November AD 397. Although he was initially buried here, the considerable rivalry between the local monks and those of Tours over his body resulted in the monks of Tours 'kidnapping' the saint's remains. As they rowed the body upstream, the bare trees lining the river banks are said to have bloomed miraculously, even though it was November. This led to the phrase 'St Martin's summer', meaning a freak spell of unseasonably fine weather, used by both the French and the English in days gone by.

Stone comes to life in the graceful details of carved medieval faces at the church in Candes-St-Martin

Montrésor

(Indre-et-Loire)

WHEN THE CHURCH BELLS RING IN MONTRÉSOR, THE CLOCK SEEMS TO TURN BACK. SET BETWEEN A SUBLIME CASTLE AND THE SHADY RIVER INDROIS, THIS 16TH-CENTURY GEM REVEALS ITS INTRICACIES TO THOSE WHO PERSEVERE.

Montrésor's modern and well-stocked tourist office sits near the base of the drive leading to the gates of the 11th-century fortress. As a first stop it is invaluable, and not only for its brochures, maps and helpful suggestions. Special offers from makers of goats' cheese, vineyards offering their Touraine labels, and artisans opening their *ateliers* to interested visitors all leave invitations here.

Having obtained a preview of what the area has to offer, visitors can then set out to see the château built by Foulques Nerra, the Gothic church and the beautiful medieval houses that overhang the River Indrois.

MEMORIES OF THE CRIMEA

In the charming and lush grounds of the château, a bone-dry fish pond has filled up with crushed leaves. Large black birds and bats flap out of the tall evergreens, cats dart from under wrought-iron lawn furniture, and stone angels seem always to be watching. Mystery is in the air, and one begins to imagine the days when Captain Roger, the 'Little Devil', built this fortress to defend the Count d'Anjou. The château as seen today was renovated in 1849 by a Polish count who accompanied Prince Napoleon to Constantinople in the Crimean War, which explains the adornment of the interior with hunting trophies, military souvenirs and a carved wooden relief depicting the Polish King Jean III Sobieski battling the Ottomans in the 17th century.

Down in the village, great pleasure comes from a stroll along the river, where a few retired villagers can always be seen with long fishing rods dangling in the cool green ponds, angling for perch and red-eyed rudd under the fig trees, and children dive into the water from their bankside back gardens or splash along the edge among the lily pads. Crossing an old wood-and-metal footbridge, you step back across the centuries (if you do not yet paint with watercolours, this may be the inspiration you need). The village can be seen above. Entering a field in which a horse and a gypsy basketweaver live, near a large manor house, tourists may feel like trespassers, but this is happily not the case. The banks of the Indrois belong to the castle and are freely accessible to everyone.

Hidden within Montrésor's simplicity is its irresistible power to charm. Whether walking its crooked streets, above, or catching sight of a patient fisherman, right, visitors enter another world

Another bridge crosses back into the village past a supermarket, and the road wraps round past the *Mairie* and a little cinema. The road makes a dramatic bend to the left, at which a 16th-century turret, now housing the local *gendarmerie*, overhangs the street.

OUT AND ABOUT

For something requiring more energy than a stroll, the tourist office has mapped out walking and cycling tours. The cycle tour consists of a 29-km route heading east of the village on the D10, turning north to Beaumont village on the D89, veering south-west at Chassenay on the D39, circling round the Plan d'Eau at Chemillé-sur-Indrois and returning to Montrésor on the D10. The walking tour covers 17km and cuts north from the village through the Bois de Beaumont, the Village du Bois, Chanteloup, La Perruche, round the Plan d'Eau and back to Montrésor along the Indrois.

If the weather is particularly warm, visitors may enjoy swimming in a small lake 2km away – a refreshing relief during a summer road trip. Drive anticlockwise through the lower part of the village to reach a turn-off to the right just before a shop. Signs marked 'Plan d'Eau' and 'Chemillé-sur-Indrois' show the way. The swimming is free, and massive inner tubes can be hired for a small charge.

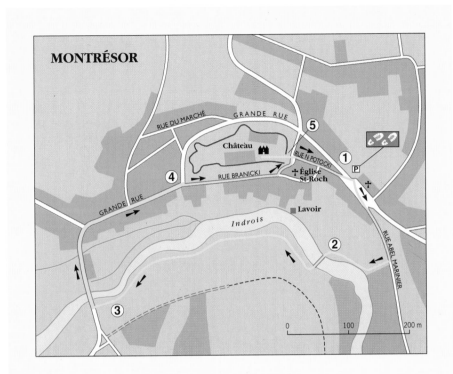

MONTRÉSOR

The Walk

❶

Park in front of the tourist office or near the church (*église*) in Grande Rue. Opposite the church take the path marked rue Abel-Marinier down towards the river, with its lovely view of the fortress across the village. Continue for 100m, then turn down an unpaved lane to the river bank.

❷

Continue along the river to your right until you reach a dubious-looking footbridge. Cross it (the locals will vouch for its safety). At the end, turn right. Pass through the open spot in the fence and head across the pasture. From here there is an excellent perspective of Montrésor and its chateau. The old village *lavoir* (public washing area) comes into view on the other bank.

❸

Proceed along the river, past the cascade, until the river narrows. Reaching a stone bridge, look for the easiest spot to climb on to the rue des Ponts. Cross the bridge and follow the road which passes a supermarket and leads into the village, with the Hôtel de France on your left. The château is straight ahead.

❹

At the 16th-century turret, continue straight along a street marked 'Sans Issue' (dead end); this is rue Branicki, named after the Polish count. Note the fine statue at number 13 and the medieval alley and ramparts between 13 and 15. Opposite number 29, turn left up the cobblestone path (ruelle des Roches) and follow it to the right. Go up the hill (you are between the château and the Église St-Roch).

❺

At rue Nicholas-Potocki turn left for the château, moving through the iron gates into the enchanting park. Return along rue Nicholas-Potocki and back to the church.

ℹ

▷ Length of walk: 1.5km
▷ Approximate time: 1 to 2 hours
▷ Terrain: Unsuitable for wheelchairs and pushchairs
▷ Open: Château: guided tours Apr–Nov
▷ Refreshments: Restaurants, *pâtisserie*

Pontlevoy
(LOIR-ET-CHER)

This sprawling white-stone village of 1,500 inhabitants is set amidst agricultural lands of grain fields, brilliant sunflowers and goat farms. At its heart lies a remarkable abbey. The group of buildings that make up the centre of the provincial village of Pontlevoy include a fine abbey dating back to 1034, with a notorious legend, and the curious Musée du Poids Lourd (Lorry Museum), in which some 50 vintage lorries built between

There is an easy grandness about Pontlevoy's abbey buildings that belies the history of conflict which threatened destruction in the Hundred Years' War; a unity of purpose overrides the differences of style

The altar in the abbey of Pontlevoy, richly hued in tones of brown and gold, has been a focus of faith for a town which has the abbey buildings at its heart

1910 and 1950 are on permanent display in a 19th-century *manège*. The abbey, though, is far and away the village's main claim to fame, and the fact that it was destroyed in part during the Hundred Years War and has been only partially renovated has left it in a permanent state of architectural ambiguity.

For centuries the village has been dominated by agricultural life, with its feudal share-cropping system and traditional seasonal rituals, and much of that culture lingered in Pontlevoy until the 20th century. Note the engraved sun in the wall over the door at 40 rue du Colonel Filloux, the main road in the oldest part of the village.

Of historical note in the village's Municipal Museum is the material on Auguste Poulain, France's most famous chocolate maker, who was born in Pontlevoy in 1825. Also in the museum is a collection of photographs taken at the turn of the century by the village clock maker. Thanks to his efforts,

The Walk

Park at the place du Collège and visit the abbey and the Lorry Museum. The tourist office is located in the Passage du Salut.

Walk along rue du Colonel Filloux, making sure to note the medieval houses there. Turn right at the place du Marché and continue on to the main road.

Turn right at the main road and continue to the place de la Poste. Here, turn right and follow the road round the square to the right where you will enter the quaint but historically revealing rue de la Juiverie (Jewish Ghetto Street).

On the left follow rue de Cure, taking note of the wooden doors. Turn right at the end of the road, to arrive back at the place du Collège.

later generations have an authentic picture of Pontlevoy's rich heritage.

Pontlevoy's charm is of the subtle variety: you need to wander the small streets, linger in a small café and sample the goats' cheese to savour the pleasures of local life.

Poncé-sur-le-Loir
(Sarthe)

Twelfth-century Poncé-sur-le-Loir, once dominated by watermills that were converted to papermills, is one of the most prolific and authentic arts-and-crafts centres in the region. Potters, glassblowers, weavers, cabinet-makers, ceramic workers, wooden furniture painters, antique restorers, water- colourists – all work in abundance in and around this small village of 500 inhabitants. The Centre Artisanal 'Les Grés du Loir' in the Paillard Mill, at the gateway into the village, is a major focus with organised programmes and exhibitions; recent shows have included 'Tiles and Roofing Accessories in France'. The green meadows, wooded hillsides and vine-clad slopes, rock-carved cellars and age-old public washing places on the river banks – all have inspired creative souls to live and work here, and their products are shipped to galleries and shops all over the world.

The château, with its celebrated Renaissance staircase, considered one of the most remarkable of its kind in the whole of France,

The pretty yet impressive château at Montsoreau, built by Charles VII's steward, was turned into a prison by Napoleon and remained so until 1963

extends out into the garden through the *loge* with its exquisite carvings. The symmetrical gardens are planted with a labyrinth of trees and also feature an unusually pretty dove-cote equipped with ladder-like crossbeams and nearly 2,000 pigeonholes.

Not far from Poncé are the famed vineyards of Ruillé-sur-Loir, Beaumont-sur-Dême, Lhomme, Marçon, and Chahaignes, although none are quite so celebrated as the Janières and Coteaux du Loir *appellations d'origine contrôlée* (AOC) which date from the 1930s and '40s. In the nearby village of Lhomme there is a very informative museum devoted to wine.

Montsoreau
(Maine-et-Loire)

Located on the D947, this quiet and panoramic village tucked into a bend of the Loire nearly at the point where it meets the Vienne, is, like most villages of the region, best known for its well-situated château, in this case on the right bank of the river, and for the nobility that occupied it in the 15th century. Inside the elegant castle is a museum devoted to the *goums*, the calvary units recruited in Morocco. The best museum pieces were returned to the Rabat government in 1956, but the Musée des Goums is

still worth seeing. Only 1.5km south on the V3 (V roads are the smallest local routes and provide intrepid motorists with the most authentic scenes of local life and culture), the visitor stumbles upon the now reconstructed and thoroughly delightful Moulin de la Herpinière (1514), a windmill nestling in the midst of a group of troglodyte cave dwellings. When the wind is blowing and the mill is turning, stone-ground grain can be bought from the miller.

An unusual souvenir: hand-blown glass will recall a visit to Poncé-sur-le-Loir's craft centre

Troo

(Loir-et-Cher)

TROO IS A SURPRISING LITTLE VILLAGE RISING DRAMATICALLY FROM THE RIGHT BANK OF THE LAZY RIVER LOIR AND AFFORDING AN INSPIRING PANORAMIC VIEW OF THE VALLEY, HALFWAY BETWEEN THE TOWNS OF VENDÔME AND LA CHARTRE.

A fortified city during the Roman era, Troo served as a strategic spot just off the main route between Tours and Paris. Today the village can easily be overlooked by any traveller who does not make a conscious decision to stop and explore. Plan to spend at least an hour or two meandering through the winding lanes of the village, up the steep hill, past the numerous cave dwellings, and finally to La Butte, the dramatic viewpoint just in front of the massive collegiate church, and a deep medieval well named the Puits qui Parle ('The Talking Well') for its haunting echo.

From the 12th century onwards, Troo was the stage of constant battles between the French and the English. Today, of course, no animosity remains and the British are openly welcomed

Built up a slope in tiers linked by narrow alleys, passages and stairways, Troo has a labyrinth of underground galleries used as a refuge in times of war. Below left, a ruined chapel is now a private home

HEAD FOR THE HILLS

In the summer months, the best moments to stroll up the hillside from Le Cheval Blanc are after breakfast and in the late afternoon. The rough and sometimes steep path along the limestone hill leads hikers past fig trees, cave houses, and finally a Grottes Troglodytiques exhibition maintained by the Friends of Troo Association. Other main attractions include the hilltop summit look-out, La Butte, with its spectacular panorama of the bucolic valley, including the châteaux of Ranay, Lavardin and Challay as well as the tiny church of St-Jacques-des-Guérets, near by on the other side of the river, which contains Byzantine murals. The villagers speak of the few English families who have settled here and set up

although, in fact, practically no one in this somewhat forgotten village speaks English. After its long history of ruinous wars, Troo was given new vitality by the artists and craftspeople who settled in the village, attracted by its natural calm and beauty.

Commercial life in the village revolves round Le Cheval Blanc, a two-star hotel-restaurant renowned for its superb fare and excellent value, which sits on the bank of the Loir at the base of the village.

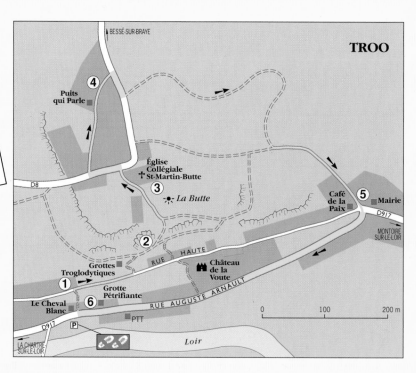

The Walk

Park in front of Le Cheval Blanc on rue Auguste Arnault/D917 and walk up the stairs to the right of the hotel. Continue to the Grottes Troglodytiques and stop in for a visit.

Keep climbing up the hillside and veer right; there are lovely cave houses on the left. When the path breaks, bear left on the unpaved side, then turn left into the paved road towards the church. This is La Butte, marked by a World War I memorial. Follow the 'Panorama' sign and climb up the circular path to the look-out.

Coming down from La Butte, visit the Église Collégiale St-Martin-Butte immediately in front of you. Upon leaving, head towards the left but take the first right before reaching the broken fortifications of the ancient wall. The Puits qui Parle is straight ahead on your left.

Continue past the well and turn right at the stop sign. About 20m before the church, turn left down a footpath (which displays an outdated speed limit sign for tanks). Follow the path along a wall past fields of wild flowers and discreet cave houses, arriving at a narrow paved road which leads you to the town hall and a café.

Turn right on the main road through town and you willl pass the steep turn up to the Château de la Voûte, which displays an assortment of regional antiques. Continue to the Grotte Pétrifiante.

6

From the cave, turn right along the main road to return to the car park.

▷ Length of walk: 2.5km
▷ Approximate time: 2 hours, including visits
▷ Terrain: Steep, unpaved sections and climbs; not suitable for wheelchairs and pushchairs
▷ Parking: In front of Le Cheval Blanc
▷ Open: Cave houses: daily mid-Jul to mid-Aug
▷ Refreshments: Restaurants and a café

Not what it seems? At first glance this house in Troo looks ordinary enough, yet like many here it is a troglodyte dwelling carved out of the hillside

farmhouses: the late Mrs Crickson, supposedly a famous food critic, and Mr John, who innocently named his country house 'Le Cabinet', a colloquialism for 'loo' that raised a few smiles on local faces.

The village church, the Église Collégiale St-Martin-Butte, captures the spirit of the place with its 12th-century square tower, Gothic windows, sloping vaulted ceiling and Roman capitals atop the columns. Protected on the plateau behind it, small farms and houses are dotted over the land, surrounded by fields of wild flowers.

ECHOES DOWN THE CENTURIES

For those who have heard of the Puits qui Parle, the covered well may initially seem disappointing, too ordinary-looking to be worth all the commotion. But the first syllable breathed over the stone hole and carried down the dark 50m shaft produces an echo of such resonance and acoustic perfection that one can understand all the lore that has built up round it. A small farm a few steps away sells pots of honey, and the owner still talks about the unfortunate man who was thrown down the well – a misadventure which took place in the 15th century!

Opposite the village post office, on the main road, is the curious Grotte Pétrifiante, a 4th-century cave of exquisite stalactites located in Madame Jeanne Tran-Duc's back garden. In the 12th century, this hauntingly beautiful geological wonder belonged to the English Crown. From the 16th century, religious burnings took place here until Prussian aggressors arrived in 1815. In 1886 the site was officially classified by the French government, and today the present owner opens up the door with a heavy latchkey to let in visitors willing to pay the small entrance fee.

THE LOIRE REGION IS IDENTIFIED IN MOST PEOPLE'S MINDS WITH ITS EXQUISITE CHÂTEAUX AND ITS SUPERB WINES, A LAND AS RICH IN HISTORY AS IT IS IN CUISINE, WITH A NETWORK OF COUNTRYSIDE TOURS THAT LEAD TO EXCEPTIONAL CASTLES AND WORLD-CLASS VINEYARDS. BUT IT WOULD BE A SHAME IF VISITORS LOOKED FOR NOTHING MORE THAN THE OBVIOUS, THE EXPECTED, FOR THE LOIRE HAS A FEW SURPRISES UP ITS SLEEVE. BENEATH THE SURFACE OF ITS FERTILE SOIL, FOR INSTANCE, LIE ANCIENT DWELLING PLACES – TROGLODYTE CAVES AND PASSAGES CARVED OUT OF THE ROCK HUNDREDS OF YEARS AGO TO PROVIDE STONE FOR BUILDING. SOME ARE NOW DECAYING AND GIVE NO IDEA OF THEIR FORMER USE, SOME STILL FUNCTION AS PRIVATE DWELLINGS OR WORKPLACES, AND OTHERS ARE OPEN TO THE PUBLIC. WITH A BIT OF PLANNING, YOU COULD EAT OR EVEN SLEEP IN ONE!

Many first-time visitors to the Loire Valley are confused when they come across the different spellings 'Loire' and 'Loir'. In fact, these are not variants or typographical errors, but completely different rivers with quite distinct geographical features and cultures. The Loire with an 'e' is France's longest

Caves of the Loire

river, at over 1,000km, running from Mont Gerbier-de-Jonc all the way to Nantes, where it spills into the Atlantic Ocean. The Loir – without the 'e' – is but a third the length of the Loire; it begins in the hills of the Perche south of the Paris area and empties into the River Sarthe near Angers.

Villaines-les-Rochers, famous for wickerwork baskets, is the site of a troglodyte village, left, where caves are still used for work. The cosy room at Dénezé-sous-Doué, above, has every creature comfort, while another cave is filled with carved 16th-century figures, right

No guide to the Loire would be complete without a tour of the strange, magical and beautiful geological phenomenon of cave dwellings, better known in the region as troglodyte dwellings. Derived from the ancient Latin and Greek word for cave dweller, these *grottes troglodytiques* in France refer to the limestone caves characteristic of the banks of the River Loire, many dating from the 11th-century. Centuries of mining the silica-rich, easy-to-work building material have left the area with about 960km of intricate passages and chambers beneath vineyards and fields on the Anjou plateau – in fact, the quality of Loire wines owes much to this tufa-rich earth.

The River Loire has the highest concentration of these cave dwellings in Europe. Indeed, it is estimated that in the 19th century nearly half the population in the region lived in these rock homes, scooped out of tufaceous limestone formed 90 million years ago. Although today many of the dwellings are crumbling, others have been carefully preserved and can be visited. (For the truly adventurous, it was recently reported that a raw cave can be bought for about £10,000.) The road that is tucked in along the riverbank between Montsoreau and Saumur is dotted with eroding remnants of troglodyte dwellings.

Hitting the Cave Trail

The redevelopment of abandoned cave dwellings was not a common practice until the 1960s. A special sightseeing circuit has subsequently developed, with troglodytic centres like Rochemenier and La Fosse in the Saumur area leading the way. Here, cave guides can be engaged by those inspired to follow the cave trail and visit houses, art galleries, restaurants, *ateliers* and museums.

The route between St Michel-sur-Loire and Vouvray along the River Loire affords motorists the chance to visit scores of cave houses, as well as storage facilities for mushrooms and wine. Other key routes include the Loir from Vendôme to Troo and south of Saumur near Doué-la-Fontaine. In Hautes-Roches in Rochcorbon, motorists can stay in the region's only cave hotel, once a monks' dormitory.

One 250km touring route corresponds closely to the Loire wine route and runs principally through the Layon Valley from Anjou to Saumur. Stops in Cunault, Fontevraud, Montreuil-Bellay and, of course, Saumur are highly recommended.

For troglodyte information, contact the tourist offices at Saumur, Montsoreau and Doué-la-Fontaine (the last has a cave tour hotline). There are several underground restaurants in the area, such as Rochemenier and Rou-Marson, serving *fouaces*, warm doughy loaves baked with a variety of stuffings.

Enter Notre-Dame-de-Cléry, above, and leave the 20th century. Its chapel of St-Jacques is dedicated to the Apostle James, left, buried in Santiago

Cléry-St-André
(LOIRET)

Only a short drive from the River Loire and the old bridge at Meung-sur-Loire, Cléry-St-André makes an enjoyable stop for those inspired by religious history and medieval relics. The village, with its 2,500 inhabitants, does not charm instantly, and might not even entice motorists to slow down, but the massive and stern basilica of Notre-Dame-de-Cléry, and to a lesser extent the 15th-century church, located prominently on the busy D951, are definitely worth a stop.

Only the basilica's square tower dating from the 14th century escaped destruction by the English; the rest was rebuilt in the 15th century. Enter the dark and haunting edifice by the transept and the centuries melt away. After taking in the statues and windows, descend into the crypt by the marble ceno-taph near the nave, where the bones of Louis XI and his wife, Charlotte de Savoie, still rest. The heart of Charles VIII is kept in an urn beneath a stone slab to the right of the nave, and the inscription on the urn has been copied on the closest pillar.

A feast for the eyes is provided by the Gothic decor of the chapel of St-Jacques, at the lower right side of the edifice. This chapel, in fact, is on the route of the famous

1

Park behind the basilica in rue Louis XI to visit the Notre-Dame-de-Cléry (allow about 30 minutes).

2

Follow rue Louis XI and turn left into the narrow rue des Soupirs, which is near the cemetery.

3

At the end of the basilica, veer to the right and continue to rue de la Gare, then turn left and continue walking to the place Charles de Gaulle.

4

Bear left at the stop sign and follow rue des Ruelles, which leads back to the D951. The basilica is to your left.

A whimsical Calder sculpture stands guard over parked cars in Saché, where the artist once lived

pilgrimage to Santiago de Compostela, which starts from the Tour St-Jacques in the centre of Paris and terminates in the north of Spain, 800km to the south.

Béhuard
(MAINE-ET-LOIRE)

Located in the Angers area of the Loire Valley, this tiny island village of a hundred inhabitants perches mid-stream on a picturesque rock cluster. The settlement of Béhuard has its origins in the 5th century as a pagan sailors' shrine, where local people prayed for the safety of those who travelled by river. In the 15th century Louis XI, believing himself saved from a shipwreck by the Blessed Virgin, erected the Église Notre-Dame in gratitude. To visit this quaint church, which is built into the rock and sheltered by tall trees, take the steps opposite the sou-

venir stand, which once housed the king during his visits. The monarch's image is incorporated into the stained-glass window to the left of the Crucifixion scene. One can imagine how this curious spot, which became a pilgrimage site, continues to provide spiritual sustenance and inspire solemn ceremonies.

The local culture of Béhuard has clearly been shaped by the ubiquitous river and its unfortunate habit of chronic flooding. The villagers are well accustomed to rising water, and each has his or her own recollection of memorable high-water moments. Assuming the river is calm and the sun is shining, visi-

tors may opt for lunch in a restaurant with a scenic view, enjoy a pastoral picnic or go for a swim at Béhuard's expansive sandy beach.

Saché
(INDRE-ET-LOIRE)

For lovers of art and literature, a stop at Saché is a must. In the 1970s American sculptor Alexander Calder settled in this peaceful grey village, and today, among the 15th-century wood-and-stone houses, a playful Calder mobile adds movement and colour to the otherwise sedate village square. But Saché's pride and honour arise from its contribution to French letter-writing. Honoré de Balzac spent much of his life in this village of fewer than a thousand inhabitants. Located on the D17 6km east of Azay-le-Rideau (known for its spectacular 14th-century moat-encircled château), Saché is proud of its own 16th-century château, set in verdant oak-wooded grounds. In the 19th century it belonged to a Monsieur de Margonne, who offered his quiet country home to Balzac whenever he needed to retreat from the attentions of Paris bill collectors. Here Balzac wrote his classic *Le Père Goriot* and several chapters of *Le Lys dans la Vallée* (which takes place in the Indre Valley). Tourists can visit Balzac's writing room – which remains practically undisturbed, complete with his quill pen on the desk and the coffee pot in place – and see manuscripts, first editions and a collection of historically valuable photographs from the writer's life in Saché.

Other Villages

ASNIÈRES-SUR-VÈGRE

Located on the D190, Asnières-sur-Vègre is the very picture of charm. Tucked into the lush valley of the River Vègre, this village of fewer than 350 inhabitants boasts a medieval bridge and a 17th-century mill. Inside the Gothic church are murals that date back to the 13th century; the best-known is the image of Hell to be found on the back of the *pignon* (gable). Also visit the massive Gothic Cour d'Asnières and the Château de Verdelles with its four strange towers, both located about 3km away on the D190.

BELLEGARDE

Up until 1645, when the Duke of Bellegarde bought it, this village was called Choisy-aux-Loges. Situated on the N60 in the midst of wheat fields and masses of red roses, the village is notable for its old, rough-plastered houses, and above all its picturesque 14th-century château with dungeons and torture chambers, riding stables, flowering bushes and remarkable Romanesque church. The château with its surrounding lake belonged to the mistress of Louis XIV, Madame de Montespan (mother of the Duke d'Antin), whose involvement with the legendary witch Madame Lavoisin brought notoriety to both her and the château.

CHAMPIGNY-SUR-VEUDE

The magnificence of Champigny's 16th-century château, the property of the Bourbon-Montpensier family, was also its undoing. Cardinal Richelieu, jealous of the building which overshadowed his own town near by, bought the château, only to destroy it. Fortunately, the Renaissance-style Chapelle St-Louis remains, with its magnificent emblems and escutcheons and vivid stained-glass windows, the colours as intense as they were 400 years ago.

DURTAL

A busy crossroads in Roman times, Durtal today is a large village seductively positioned at the gateway to Anjou. Its imposing 11th-century castle, aside from being an architectural treasure, once controlled the crossing of the Loir – and thus access into Anjou, centre of river trade – near the spot where the Loir meets the Sarthe.

The waters of the Vègre lazily pass centuries-old structures in quaint Asnières

The castle gardens were once graced by orange groves that supplied fruit for the Château de Versailles and trees to adorn the palace grounds.

Things have changed. Between 1857 and 1994, the castle was used as a hospital and rest home, but its historic significance remains as a château. Its six-storey dungeon, its two pepperpot turrets and its magnificent view of the nearby 520-hectare Forêt de Chambiers, make a visit wholly worthwhile. The old bridge over the river, affording a pleasant view of the mills of former years and the sharply angled roofs of the village houses, certainly merits a stop.

A centre of brick manufacture, Durtal is rich in a particular clay and is known for its fine Rairies earthenware. The region offers unique terracotta shops and *ateliers* and is dotted with kilns and special barns for drying pottery. At the Maison de la Terre Cuite, visitors can watch potters work and fire their latest creations.

A particularly good time to arrive in Durtal is the last Sunday in September, when it hosts one of the most elaborate antique fairs in

the region. Durtal also holds a lively market on Tuesday mornings. From February to December, racing fans can enjoy themselves at the La Carrière track.

MALICORNE-SUR-SARTHE

At the bend of a wide meander in the Sarthe, Malicorne sits on the left bank overlooking a mill and the poplar-wooded banks. On the eastern edge of the village an old earthenware *atelier*, Fäience d'Art, is still operational, producing the local *ajourés* tiles. The mansard-roofed château, dating from the 17th century, sits back from the river and sets itself apart by a moat that is crossed via a humpback bridge. The 11th-century church is partnered by a lovely 16th-century swimming pool.

MENNETOU-SUR-CHER

Mennetou is a delightful place, full of steep and twisting streets set within 800-year-old walls which still stand over 12m high. Joan of Arc stopped here in 1492 en route to Chinon to visit the Dauphin, and the Port d'en Bas is often called the Porte Jeanne d'Arc. The Grande-Rue is a narrow lane lined with ancient houses, and includes the tourist office, housed in a half-timbered building topped with red tiles next to another massive gate.

LES MONTILS

This small, little-visited village is easy to miss, but all the more enjoyable for that. Just before the village, the D764 bends sharply to the right, affording an inviting view of a dramatic ruin. At the top of the climb, there is a sharp left turn into rue du Vieux Porche. Fifty metres ahead on the left, next to the post office and almost hidden between village houses, lurk the 12th-century ruins of a tower and dungeon. Built in 1144 by Thibault IV le Grand, the Count of Blois, this tower overlooking the valley served as part of the country residence of Louis XI and Louis XII.

What is so enchanting here is the way that medieval history is constantly present, imposing and yet nonchalant.

Further down the main road in Les Montils, a 12th-century porch, frozen as an elegant ruin, frames the end of the old village. A more modern church sits on the other side of the stone entranceway. Not far away is the magnificent Château de Chéverny, one of the most stunning on the Loire circuit.

Paris & the Île-de-France

This is probably the region most visited by French and foreigners alike. Yet the Île-de-France has managed to keep secret a surprising number of treasures, both natural and man-made, from Gallo-Roman ruins to Impressionist landscapes.

La Roche-Guyon (Val d'Oise)

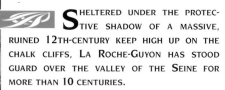

SHELTERED UNDER THE PROTEC-TIVE SHADOW OF A MASSIVE, RUINED 12TH-CENTURY KEEP HIGH UP ON THE CHALK CLIFFS, LA ROCHE-GUYON HAS STOOD GUARD OVER THE VALLEY OF THE SEINE FOR MORE THAN 10 CENTURIES.

La Roche-Guyon, 14km east of Vernon on the D913, stands on a strategic crossroads between the Île-de-France and Normandy. Throughout the Middle Ages, the village belonged to one realm or the other, depending on the vagaries of the constant warfare between England and France. It was strategically important for two reasons: the keep commanded a view over the Vexin plateau, while the lords controlled all traffic along the river. Indeed, most of their revenue came from a *droit de passage*, or toll, which they demanded of all boats.

CASTLE ATOP CAVES

A Renaissance château was constructed when relative peace returned to the region in the 16th century. French Kings Henri II and

The main road of this riverside village, above right, is seen against the hills rising from the Seine Valley; passers-by can enjoy a fine windowbox, below

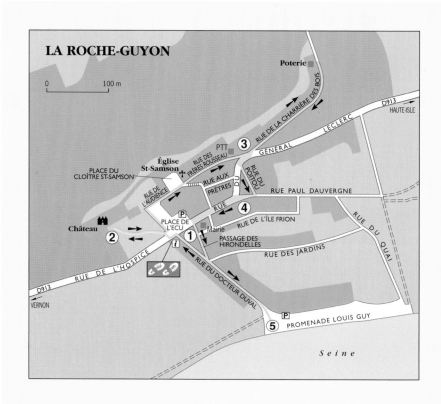

François I often stayed here when they visited the Vexin on hunting expeditions. Since the 18th century, the castle has belonged to the Rochefoucauld family. Most of the current buildings date from that period.

The château has only recently opened its doors to the public. Several itineraries lead through it, but what makes La Roche-Guyon unique is the labyrinthine network of tunnels and caves dug out of the hillside. The corridors seem to lead in and out of the stone,

from one architectural period to another. One of the earliest-known structures at the site is the 'Chapel in the Rock', little more than a grotto in the hillside. According to tradition, several local Christians were martyred here in the 3rd century.

Extensive restoration is under way throughout the château, and new rooms are opened to the public as the work progresses. An ambitious project for the grounds will return the gardens to their original 18th-

The Walk

1

Start in front of the tourist office, located in a building known as 'La Gabelle', formerly the salt warehouse. Walk across the street to the entrance of the château.

2

Turn left after leaving the château and follow rue de l'Audience to the Église St-Samson. Follow along the right side of the church (rue des Frères Rousseau). From here, rue de la Charrière des Bois leads 250m up a rather steep hill to a pottery (this section can be bypassed if too steep).

3

Return to rue des Frères Rousseau and follow rue du Général Leclerc down the hill. After about 30m, take the narrow alleyway to the left past several pretty half-timbered houses.

4

Turn right on rue Paul-Dauvergne to reach the town hall (formerly the marketplace, constructed over the former wheat market; all that remains are the stone columns).

5

Just past this building, turn left into the Passage des Hirondelles and follow the road to the riverfront (this is a perfect picnic site). Tour boats run up and down the Seine. Retrace your steps back to the tourist office.

> **i**

▷ Length of walk: 1.5km
▷ Approximate time: 2 hours, including visit to château
▷ Terrain: Level, except for rue de la Charrière des Bois
▷ Parking: At tourist office
▷ Open: Château: daily mid-April to 1 November. Pottery: weekend afternoons only
▷ Refreshments: Restaurants and cafés

A chalk-cut passage once linked the 12th-century keep, seen above the château, with the lower residence

century design. In the 17th century, La Roche-Guyon had a famous kitchen garden, an aristocratic fashion that began in the 16th century. Carefully planned, with not a branch or bud out of place, these gardens were certainly useful, but above all were meant to be an ornamental backdrop.

WARTIME OCCUPATION

After centuries of peace, the old fortress finally fell to the occupying forces of the German army. In 1944, the château became the headquarters for the German high command, led by Field Marshal Rommel, who was known for being a poor shot. The impressive series of caverns cut into the hillside were used by the Germans as bunkers and storerooms. During the time of the heavy bombardments of Mantes and Meulun, the château received a number of hits.

Rommel was injured when his car was machine-gunned from the air and was taken to hospital. Never a member of the Nazi party, he was subsequently arrested for complicity in the attempted assassination of Hitler. In fact, many secret meetings among German conspirators took place within the walls of the château.

Visitors can tour the medieval section, the 18th- and 19th-century reception rooms, the chapel and the network of tunnels in the cliff. The former stables have been restored, but to a new purpose: changing exhibits of contemporary art are held here in the summer. Concerts and conferences also take place in the château (programme information is available at the château and at the tourist office).

AROUND LA ROCHE-GUYON

Several kilometres east of La Roche-Guyon (along the D913) lies Haute-Isle, inhabited at least from Merovingian times. Until the 18th century, all the homes were cut into the rock and rose some five storeys from the base of the plateau. The 17th-century church is unique in France: it was entirely dug out of the rock, the only element visible from the outside being the small bell tower that emerges from the stone.

A short loop by car round La Roche-Guyon (4km) provides a stunning view over the Seine and the castle keep. Drive up the Route de Gasny leading west out of town; it climbs steeply up the hill, past caves (called *bouves* here) dug out of the chalky hillside. Turn right on the D100, the 'Route des Crêtes', to reach a viewpoint high above the river. Turn right at the first road, the 'Charrière des Bois', to return to the village.

Mauperthuis was made famous by the 19th-century writer Alexandre Dumas in *The Three Musketeers*. Local historians have in fact managed to trace five musketeers associated with Mauperthuis; the last of these, Anne-Pierre de Montesquiou, was Marquis of Mauperthuis and Coulommiers up to the Revolution. Indeed, a rue des Mousquetaires still exists in the village.

The town itself, on the D402, lies in the heart of the green hills overlooking the Aubetin Valley. The château, constructed for this same musketeer by Claude-Nicolas Ledoux, has since disappeared, but the

St-Sulpice's west portal: Christ with Mary, John and two angels and the Last Judgement

St-Sulpice-de-Favières
(ESSONNE)

Lying on a hill in the midst of a forest, this hamlet has a soaring Gothic gem of a church, a glorious sight in this delightful river-crossed countryside. In the days before Christianity, the site now occupied by the beautiful St-Sulpice was sacred to the early Gauls. The church, like the cathedral at Chartres, was built over a well that had been a place of pagan worship (now within the Chapelle des Miracles, off the north aisle). The Chapelle is the oldest existing structure (1180), and a well uncovered in this section dates back to that time. Traces of several 14th-century frescoes remain above the door, depicting the life and miracles of St Sulpice, a 7th-century bishop said to have resuscitated a child drowned in the River Renarde.

The luminous and much larger main structure (it can hold 2,000) is one of the most beautiful Gothic churches in the Île-de-France, with its towering vault, beautiful stone and exquisite tracery. St Louis himself is supposed to have financed part of the church. Begun in 1260 and finished in about 1320, it was an important place of pilgrimage. During the Revolution, however, the relics of St Sulpice, which had been credited

The Walk

Visitors are asked to leave their cars in the car park outside the village. Walk into the village to the Église St-Sulpice.

After visiting the church, take the small road directly opposite, called ruelle de l'Hôtel Dieu. A beautiful arch covers the entrance to the street. Walk through and follow round; the road will bring you back to the church.

Walk round to the back of the church, noting the light stonework and three tiers of windows. Take rue Alphonse Lavallée, which leads away from the church. Walk down this lane for 150–200m for a splendid view of the church's choir and windows.

with so many miracles, were stripped from the church along with the rest of its treasures, and his statue in the west portal stands armless and decapitated. Among the noteworthy furniture are a monumental churchwarden's seat and a fine set of stalls.

Église St-Nicholas and the ruins of a small pyramid still exist. Several lovely 18th- and 19th-century homes line the main street.

Rochefort-en-Yvelines
(YVELINES)

Rochefort, 15km south-east of Rambouillet on the D27, is best explored on foot. The centre of the village has hardly changed for several centuries, and many interesting details remain on the old houses, including medallions carved in stone over the doorways. Some were family arms, others indicated the occupation of the inhabitants. One of these, at number 27 rue Guy-le-Rouge, displays three cockle shells, the sign of an inn for pilgrims on the way to Santiago de Compostela in northern Spain.

The Église St-Gilles overlooks the village from the top of a flight of ancient steps; the mayor's office below is housed in a small 17th-century building that was once a courthouse and prison.

Three wells once existed in different parts of the village. The most interesting was the Puits Salé ('Salty Well'), so named because villagers lowered their salt into the well whenever the tax collector was spotted coming into town. The *gabelle*, or salt tax, was despised throughout France, and every village developed ingenious ways to avoid it.

A rare stone structure stands at the corner of rue de la Glacière and rue Guy-le-Rouge: the ancient ice house or *glacière*, squat and thick-walled. Blocks of ice packed into the building in winter kept food cold well into the hot months of summer.

Below, a bird's-eye view of village rooftops seen from the Église St-Gilles at Rochefort-en-Yvelines; right, even the side streets are full of architectural detail

Auvers-sur-Oise (Val-d'Oise)

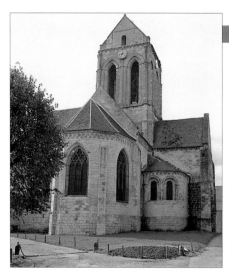

'AUVERS IS SERIOUSLY BEAUTI-FUL,' WROTE VINCENT VAN GOGH. A CENTURY LATER, IT STILL OFFERS THE SIMPLICITY THAT LURED SOME OF THE WORLD'S MOST REMARKABLE PAINTERS.

Visitors from all over the world come to Auvers-sur-Oise to discover the village where Van Gogh spent his last days. His presence still haunts the village. Almost every corner, every street looks tantalisingly familiar: he painted an incredible 70 canvases in the 70 days he spent in Auvers..

Panels reproducing paintings made in Auvers – by Van Gogh, of course, but also by other painters, including Cézanne, Corot, Pissarro and Daubigny – have been placed throughout the village on the very spot where the canvasses were originally created.

Although Van Gogh is the heart and soul of Auvers, he was far from being the first artist to discover the beauty of the village. Charles-François Daubigny was drawn to Auvers in the 1850s. He and Corot regularly explored the area, and he later built a studio in the village, which became a meeting place for many artists. He generously supported Cézanne, Renoir, Monet and Pissarro.

It was Pissarro who suggested that Van Gogh go to Auvers to escape the stresses of Paris and place himself under the care of a certain Dr Gachet. The doctor, a homeo-pathic specialist, occasional painter and keen art collector, was an early supporter of the Impressionists. Van Gogh improved greatly during his first few weeks, but his 'illness', soon returned. In one of his last letters to

Théo, his brother, Van Gogh wrote: 'I am risking my life for my work, and my reason has half-foundered because of it.' And later: 'The outlook grows dark, I see no happy future.' On Sunday, 27 July 1890, Van Gogh shot himself near the church. He died three days later in the Auberge Ravoux.

THE IMPRESSIONIST HERITAGE

Auvers seems entirely devoted to its artistic heritage. The château houses a 90-minute multimedia (and multilingual) exhibition retracing the late 19th century through the eyes of the Impressionists. The new Musée d'Absinthe recounts the story of this famous drink, known as the 'green muse', and its huge influence before it was banned in 1915.

The Walk

❶
Park by the town hall. Opposite is the Auberge Ravoux, also known as Van Gogh's House, where the painter stayed. Turn right along rue du Général de Gaulle and follow the road past the *gare* (train station).

❷
Turn left at the third street, which leads to rue E Bernard and the *église*. Follow this street to the right, past the church, to reach the cemetery where Van Gogh and his brother are buried. Retrace your steps to the church.

❸
Follow rue Daubigny round to the right to reach Maison-Atelier de Daubigny (now a museum). Return along rue Daubigny and take rue de Léry to the right, past the Musée d'Absinthe. Continue along rue de Léry to the Château d'Auvers.

❹
Turn sharp left into rue de Zundert, which becomes rue du Général de Gaulle. Just before the Auberge Ravoux, turn left into rue de la Sansonne (not named on map). Then return to the car park.

❺
An additional walk further explores the artistic link. Start at Dr Gachet's house in rue du Dr Gachet, then follow rue François-Coppée, which becomes chemin des Meulières. Along this route are panels which reproduce paintings created at each site: Cézanne's *La Maison du Pendu* and *Carrefour de la rue Rémy*, Van Gogh's *Maisons à Auvers* and Corot's *Rue de Village*.

ℹ
▷ Length of walk: 3km
▷ Approximate time: 2 hours
▷ Terrain: Fairly easy, but steep climb to point
▷ Refreshments: Cafés and restaurants

The church, seen through the eyes of a camera, above, and a genius, right. Van Gogh and his brother are buried side by side, below

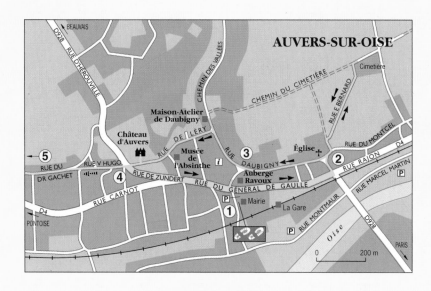

Montlhéry
(Essonne)

Lying just 20km south of Paris, the fortress of Montlhéry guarded the approach road to Paris from the year 991 until 1591, when the war-weary inhabitants of the *bourg* petitioned for its demolition. It is hard to imagine just how important Montlhéry was in medieval times. Today the N20, lined with car dealerships, fast-food restaurants and petrol stations, bypasses the town's centre, but it is worth turning off this busy thoroughfare to explore the history of what was once one of the most important fortresses round Paris.

The road leads up to the main square of Montlhéry. Although the square is now the town centre, this has not always been the case. The real soul of Montlhéry lies further up the hill. Unlike many other medieval villages in France, the oldest part lies some distance from the present-day centre. At the top of a hill stands ancient Montlhéry, the fortified and fearsome tower that guarded the Orléans–Paris road. Only the tower (the keep) and a few intriguing ruins remain. But with a

The Walk

1

Drive through the town centre up to the parking area at the base of the tower (currently under restoration). Follow rue de la Poterne down the hill for 150m. Take rue Gauché-Lauré to the left, which leads to the Grande Rue, an ancient Gallo-Roman route, which for centuries was the main Paris–Orléans road. To the left is the Porte Baudry (dated 1015), the only remaining gate in the town's fortifications.

2

Turn round and follow the Grande Rue to the Église de la Trinité (13th century). Opposite the church, take rue Notre-Dame, then turn left on rue aux Chats. This is the oldest part of the city.

3

Take rue Desgouillons to the right to the place du Marché. Return to the church via rue Stain and then follow rue de la Poterne back to the tower.

town was built below. Even in ruins, the tower retains a solemn and remote majesty, untouched by the noisy 'new' town – this is no small feat for a place so close to the suburbs of Paris.

By the 11th century, a feudal château had been constructed on this hilltop overlooking the main road, and ramparts surrounded the town. The Count of Montlhéry, a powerful, intractable brigand, was only marginally loyal to the king. Known as 'the Highwayman', he controlled the Paris–Orléans road, exacting heavy tributes from – and often terrorising – the travellers passing through his domain.

On his deathbed in 1108, Philippe I advised his son to keep a tight rein on the Montlhéry tower, saying: 'It has made me old before my time.' The château was finally dismantled on the orders of Henri IV in 1591, after a successful petition by villagers fed up with the conflicts it magnetised to the area. Only the tower was saved.

Blandy
(SEINE-ET-MARNE)

In a region where most villages are clustered round the church, Blandy comes as a surprise. Five towers – which look as if they should be festooned with colourful banners and flags – rise into view from the D47 leading to the town from the south. It is an unusual sight in the Île-de-France, and with reason: this is the only remaining medieval fortress in the whole region.

The enormous structure was built in the 14th century on the orders of Charles V. France was embroiled in the Hundred Years' War against England (and against the Burgundy Counts, allied with the English), when the king decided to increase the fortifications round Paris. The small château at Blandy, which belonged to the loyal Viscount of Melun, was transformed into an impregnable fortress.

By the 16th century, a relative peace reigned throughout France, and the menacing fortress was transformed into a superb Renaissance dwelling, complete with formal gardens and a chapel. It was, perhaps, too beautiful. Maréchal Villars, who had already acquired the nearby Vaux-le-Vicomte château, purchased Blandy, but was afraid that the king would wonder just how he (Villars) could afford two such beautiful châteaux (after all, the previous owner of the château Vaux-le-Vicomte, Fouquet, had been imprisoned for embezzlement. He therefore decided to demolish the château and use the building materials to restore Vaux-le-Vicomte. The ruined château then became a farm for the next century or so before the town purchased it in the late 19th century. In 1992 it was bought by the Seine-et-Marne *département*.

Extensive renovation work is now under way and will continue for several years. However, it remains open to the public and, despite the scaffolding and construction work, visitors can get an idea of just how a château was once built: stonemasons work in the courtyard skilfully and faithfully re-creating 14th-century sculptures, painters duplicate old frescoes, and the original moat is being partially renewed. Upon completion (which is expected to be in about 1998) the château will again reflect the majesty of the 14th century.

Door detail in Barbizon, a village that earned its place in art history with its simple country charm

Barbizon
(SEINE-ET-MARNE)

Although tiny, Barbizon is renown as the 'village of painters'. Nestled at the edge of the Fontainebleau forest, it became home to a colony of 19th-century painters and writers who arrived to explore the subtle light and landscapes round the town and to escape the constraints of the art world which snubbed their work. These artists and intellectuals – including Jean-François Millet, Daubigny, Corot and even Trotsky for a time – were precursors of the Impressionists.

The first to arrive in what was a modest village of woodcutters was, in fact, Théodore Rousseau in 1847, followed soon after by Millet. The Ganne family, who owned an inn, were instrumental in Barbizon's transformation, welcoming artists and writers with open arms. This inn, along with the homes of Rousseau and Millet, is now a museum.

Above, the towers of Blandy's fortress – the first sight of the village from afar – proclaim its history. Left, flowers frame an exit from the main square in the hilltop bourg of Montlhéry. Below, the importance of medieval Montlhéry is highlighted by the coat of arms set into the pavement by the town hall

little effort, visitors can easily imagine the power of the site in its heyday as one of the most highly prized possessions in the domain. From the top, the strategic importance of Montlhéry is instantly apparent; on a clear day, the views stretch for 30km in every direction. And from this vantage point, one can see why the more modern, commercial

Other Villages

COURANCES

The beautiful château at Courances is approached down a long, straight drive set between a pair of canals lined with two double avenues of ancient plane trees. Initially a medieval castle, it was transformed into a superb Renaissance palace in the 17th century. The flowing staircase set against the façade was copied from nearby Fontainebleau, and Le Nôtre himself designed the gardens. Throughout most of the 19th century the château was abandoned, then the ancestors of the present owners purchased it and returned the gardens to their former grandeur. After more destruction in World War II, the owners painstakingly restored the grounds, but have aimed for a more economically viable estate. The result is a creative, yet perfectly classical design. Concerts take place in the château and the church throughout June.

DAMPIERRE-EN-YVELINES

The gardens of Dampierre, 20km north-east of Rambouillet, are one of Le Nôtre's great creations, with long perspectives accentuating the dignified château. Its façades are in the homely local tradition, with warm red brick complementing honey-coloured stone. One of the most interesting rooms is the vast reception hall. Ingres was commissioned to paint two murals representing the Golden Age and the Iron Age. He began the first, then

secretly painted for other clients. Upon discovering this, the Duke de Luynes dismissed him.

The Luynes family have owned the château from the beginning; well-liked locally, they survived the Revolution and their estates were not confiscated. The slope opposite the entrance affords a view down into the complex of courtyards and gardens. Horticultural events are held in the gardens in summer.

FLAGY

Flagy, 10km south of Montereau-faut-Yonne, was considered a 'new town' when it was constructed in the 12th century by order of Louis VII. Set on the edge of the royal domain, Flagy was laid out in a grid pattern, which is evident in the seven parallel streets, all of which lead to the river. Seven bridges then cross a branch of the River Orvanne. The river was diverted in order to power a mill. This 13th-century structure still exists and is a rare example of traditional regional architecture.

GALLARDON

Like many villages in France, the church comes into view long before the rest of the town. Double flying buttresses support high clerestory windows, and the rather

However you look at it, Flagy is focused on the river, a delightful spot for idle chatter or happy solitude

plain nave gives way to a superb elevated choir and apse. All the old houses here have been restored and the streets paved carefully with cobblestones. The ruins of a top-heavy tower, known as 'Gallardon's Shoulder', are all that remain of the 12th-century keep. The tower was destroyed by order of the king in 1443; the French, worried that the English might recapture the town, did not want this menacing tower in enemy hands.

GRISY-LES-PLÂTRES

As its name suggests, Grisy-les-Plâtres, 18km north-west of Pontoise on the D22, has been an important source of gypsum for centuries. Indeed, plaster from this region was produced here from the Middle Ages. In spite of being the capital of the *département*, it has remained a quiet country village built round the tree-lined place de l'Église, dominated by the 13th-century church of St-Caprais.

GUIRY-EN-VEXIN

In an area riddled with Gallo-Roman ruins, Guiry is home to the very well-arranged Archaeological Museum of the Val-d'Oise, with a remarkable number of treasures, starting with palaeozoic fossils and extending through a period of some 3,000 centuries. Stone tools unearthed near by date from the palaeolithic age, and a large number of sculptures, tools, glass and ceramic pieces also come from the region. Guiry was a sanctuary during the Gallo-Roman period, and excavations have revealed several temples as well as wall paintings and carvings. Three Merovingian cemeteries were discovered in Guiry itself, and the Allée Couverte du Bois-Couturier was a neolithic sepulchre.

NESLES-LA-VALLÉE

Nesles, 12km north-east of Pontoise, lies on the D79 in the lush Sausseron Valley north of Paris. The 12th-century church of St-Symphorian is built in the fashion of the early Gothic cathedrals but with less structural success (note the iron tie rods supporting the roof). Directly opposite the church on the main square stands a lovely 16th-century farmhouse, the Ferme de Bereuil, an unusual element in a village of this size. Half farmhouse, half manor, it is still a working farm.

RAMPILLON

Rampillon, 18km west of Provins, has a remarkable 13th-century Gothic church on a promontory originally dedicated to the Gallic god Ram, the town's namesake. Although the exterior is severe, the 14th-century portal, representing an animated and joyful Last Judgement, is a masterpiece of medieval sculpture. Below, bas-reliefs depict the labours of the seasons – killing the pig, harvesting, beating down the acorns, treading the grapes. Statues include an exquisite 14th-century Virgin and Child set in a retable, and a scalped Thomas à Becket.

ST-LOUP-DE-NAUD

Few have heard about the well-preserved treasure here: the oldest Romanesque church in the Île-de-France, wonderfully luminous, with ancient pews lining an uneven patchwork floor. It was begun as a Benedictine chapel in the late 10th century, and work resumed in 1167, hence the distinct Romanesque and Gothic styles.

The 12th-century statues in the portal are magnificent and rival those at Chartres. St Loup is in the centre; to his right are Peter, Solomon and Isaiah; to his left are Paul, the Queen of Sheba and Jeremiah. Above are Mary and eight Apostles. The tympanum presents Christ in Majesty with the Evangelists, symbolised by the angel, lion, ox and eagle.

A small path to the left leads to the Fontaines aux Saints, a pilgrimage site with a miraculous spring, welling up from a 12th-century retable embedded in the rock, formed of sculpted panels that recount the life of St Loup.

VÉTHEUIL

Dominating Vétheuil, nestled in a loop of the Seine on the D147, is Notre-Dame-de-Grâce, with its great stepped buttresses. The late 12th-century choir and apse reflect the transition from Romanesque to Gothic. The church, with some 30 statues from the 14th, 15th and 16th centuries, was not completed until nearly 400 years later.

Vétheuil is perhaps best known for the Impressionists who worked here. The most famous of these was Claude Monet, whose paintings made the church of Vétheuil familiar the world over. He lived here for three years, producing more than 150 paintings. Camille, his first wife, is buried in the old village cemetery.

Burgundy

Paris et Île-de-France

Alsace et Lorraine

0   20   40   60   80 km
0   10   20   30   40   50 miles

Champagne

Loire

Vallery
Sens
Yonne
Joigny
St-Florentin
Migennes
Armançon
Tonnerre
Châtillon-sur-Seine
Auxerre
Chablis
Seine
Noyers
Cravant
Montbard
Courson-les-Carrières
Druyes-les-Belles-Fontaines
Montréal
St-Amand-en-Puisaye
Avallon
Époisses
Flavigny-sur-Ozerain
Clamecy
Vézelay
St-Père
Salmaise
Cosne-Cours-sur-Loire
Donzy
Yonne
Tannay
St-Brisson
Saulieu
Pouilly-en-Auxois
Dijon
Châteauneuf
Auxonne
Bourgogne
La Charité-sur-Loire
Nuits-St-Georges
Saône
Châtillon-en-Bazois
Château-Chinon
MONTS DU MORVAN
Arnay-le-Duc
Volnay
Nevers
Moulins-Engilbert
Autun
La Rochepot
Beaune
Seurre
Berry et Limousin
Loire
Uchon
Chagny
Decize
Le Creusot
Chalon-sur-Saône
St-Pierre-le-Moûtier
Luzy
Canal du Centre
Montceau-les-Mines
Mont-St-Vincent
Louhans
Arroux
Bourbon-Lancy
Gueugnon
Brancion
Cuisery
Franche-Comté
Digoin
Charolles
Blanot
Tournus
St-Amour
Paray-le-Monial
MONTS DU CHAROLAIS
Berzé-la-Ville
Anzy-le-Duc
Solutré-Pouilly
Mâcon
Marcigny
Semur-en-Brionnais

Auvergne

Vallée du Rhône

Alpes

*H*ome to some of the country's finest food and wines, Burgundy is an under-explored region rich in history.

Châteauneuf

(Côte d'Or)

FOR CENTURIES, CHÂTEAUNEUF REIGNED OVER THE VANDENESSE VALLEY AS AN IMPREGNABLE FORTRESS AND PROSPEROUS VILLAGE. WITH BOTH CASTLE AND VILLAGE CLASSED AS A HISTORICAL MONUMENT, IT IS STILL A SURPRISINGLY INTACT, ISOLATED SITE.

The remarkable château of Châteauneuf, sitting high on a hill above the Autoroute du Soleil in northern Burgundy, has seen countless people speeding past on their way to points south. Few, though, stop to explore this extraordinary structure, and the architectural integrity of its village.

The château of Châteauneuf is one of the most interesting examples of medieval military architecture in the Côte d'Or. It was almost unconquerable: rising directly over the plain, the castle was separated from the mountain by a large moat dug into the rock. Only three gates allowed access to the fortified village that lay in the shadow of the fortress, overlooking the fertile lands of the Vandenesse Valley.

Hurrying to the Mediterranean sun, most motorway drivers miss out on Châteauneuf, whose proud, austere castle, above, overlooks the Autoroute du Soleil. Those who stop will find a refreshing simplicity and a chance to gaze at leisure over fertile farmland, below

FLOURISHING TRADE

The architecture of Châteauneuf reflects the prosperity of the town's past. Many of the stone houses, dating from as early as the

14th century, belonged to wealthy Burgundy merchants and other nobles in the entourage of Philippe Pot, Seneschal of Burgundy. The place names also testify to the town's commercial importance: besides the place du Marché, there is a place aux Porcs, place aux Bœufs, place aux Moutons and so on, all within a few steps of each other.

As in other towns, towers in private homes symbolised a certain social status and conferred a *droit de défense*, or right to defence, on the property owner. Reserved for noblemen, this right entitled them to bear arms. In exchange, they were required to defend their lord and vassals. Châteauneuf was unique in that the lord of the village, Jean III de Châteauneuf, declared the residents freemen in 1267. They subsequently organised their own defence, which during the Wars of Religion was powerful enough to force the surrender of the Catholic League army that had taken refuge in the town (for which Châteauneuf received a generous reward from King Henry IV).

The castle was begun in the 12th century. The oldest remaining section is the 12th-century keep to the north; the fortified gate and thick walls date from the 13th and 14th centuries. It belonged to the Châteauneuf family until the mid-15th century, when the family name died out with Catherine de Châteauneuf. This noblewoman was burnt alive in a public square after plotting – successfully – to poison her husband, with her lover as accomplice. She personally baked the poisoned cake, and her bothersome husband, having eaten it, promptly died. Unfortunately, a servant also tasted the delicacy and suffered a similar fate. The unlikely coincidence raised suspicions, and Catherine was soon arrested and sentenced to a grisly public death. That was the end for both Catherine and the Châteauneuf family. Over the following centuries the castle changed hands many times through a series of legacies, marriages and a royal decree, finally becoming government property in 1936.

RURAL EXODUS

The population of Châteauneuf reached an all-time high in the Middle Ages, with an estimated 500 residents. Numbers declined over the years to fall to the current population of only 63. Although it is quiet now, Châteauneuf was an important agricultural centre at the turn of the century, with several annual fairs, a weekly market and pharmacies, greengrocers, a notary and doctors.

A curious superstition still reigned over the village in the early years of this century. According to custom, the first person met on New Year's Day had to be a man; otherwise, the coming year would bring catastrophe and misfortune. Everyone therefore stayed behind shuttered doors and windows until a man walked by – the sight of whom assured 365 days of good fortune.

The Walk

Start in front of the château (guided tour available). Turn right and follow rue de l'Église to place Blondeau. Head back towards the château, turning right at rue du Centre, on to La Grange aux Ânes.

Turn left to the place aux Bœufs. Note the 16th-century half-timbered house and Maison Bichot, an interesting mixture of 14th- to 16th-century styles. Several old merchants' homes line the western side of this square. From here, turn right into the Grande Rue to place aux Moutons, then left to the Belvédère de la Croix.

The Belvédère offers a spectacular view of the valley below. A panoramic table indicates towns and mountains in the distance. Return to place aux Moutons (see step 5).

Turn right along Grande Rue towards the château. Just before the Mairie (Town Hall) are several interesting houses, most dating from the 14th and 15th centuries. Pass in front of the Mairie; formerly the market, it faces the place du Marché. Return to place aux Porcs in front of the castle.

From place aux Moutons an additional longer walk (about 2km) can be made along a former Roman road, now known as Le Grand Chemin, which leads north. This goes through the forest to the ruins of L'Hermitage de St-Julien, founded in 1301.

i

▷ Length of walk: About 1km
▷ Approximate time: 45 minutes
▷ Terrain: Fairly level and accessible
▷ Open: Castle: 10–noon, 2–6.30, except Tuesday (and Wednesday off season)
▷ Refreshments: Restaurants near castle

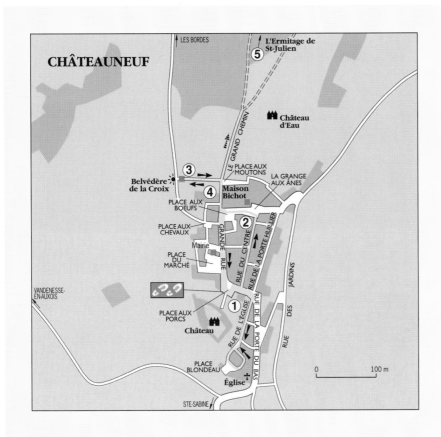

Burgundy

Flavigny-sur-Ozerain *(Côte d'Or)*

SOME TWO THOUSAND YEARS OF HISTORY LIE WITHIN THE WALLS OF FLAVIGNY, A SECLUDED WALLED VILLAGE THAT WAS A MEDIEVAL REFUGE AND, IN ANTIQUITY, A SIGNIFICANT GALLO-ROMAN SITE

The small fortified town of Flavigny sits on a hilltop at the end of the D9, 17km east of Semur-en-Auxois. Its isolation doubtless explains the unique architectural unity of the site, and may also account for the many religious communities that were established here. At one time there was a Dominican monastery (now a seminary), an Ursuline convent and a Benedictine monastery (which still exists).

Like many hilltop towns, Flavigny was a refuge in times of war and conflict during the Middle Ages. Yet its past goes back much further, to one of the most celebrated events in French history. Julius Caesar established one of his three camps near this site, while his legions laid siege to Alesia several kilometres away. The Gallic leader Vercingetorix rallied the various tribes together on this hill in a last stand against the Romans before surrendering to the unstoppable general. The Gallo-Roman excavations at the top of the hill are open to the public.

CITY OF GOD

The first religious community, a Benedictine abbey, was established in Flavigny in the 7th century and was later dedicated to St Peter (Abbaye St-Pierre de Flavigny), although no architectural trace remains of this period. The oldest visible elements date from the late 9th century. The most glorious period in the abbey's history was the 13th century, when the illuminated manuscripts painstakingly produced by the monks made this one of the greatest abbeys of its time; some of these works are now in the Vatican. Ironically, most of the original church was destroyed after

Sunlight cutting through the crooked streets and narrow passages of Flavigny draws the eye to pleasing details – faded half-timbering, blood-red blossom, cone-topped turrets and the texture of ancient walls

the Revolution; at the same time the nearby Église St-Genest (dedicated to the patron saint of actors) was declared a national monument. The pre-Romanesque ruins of the abbey include an unusual Carolingian crypt and hexagonal chapel.

The current abbot is a former *gendarme*, a widower who raised six children before taking his vows. A confectionery factory now occupies the former Ursuline convent. It is the sole remaining producer of the famous *anis de Flavigny*, a liquorice-flavoured sweet once produced and sold throughout Europe by the Ursulines.

By the mid-13th century, many residents of Flavigny began to acquire the status of freemen. This was partly because of the extensive rebuilding contracted by the abbey: needing to raise money, the abbot sold the inhabitants certain entitlement rights he held over them. The impressive bailiff's residence next to the Porte du Val was built during this period.

The Walk

Park in the Esplanade des Fossés outside the town walls and enter through the Porte Ste-Barbe to rue de l'Abbaye. Turn right past the *anis* factory to see the ruins of the Abbaye St-Pierre de Flavigny and the Cryptes Carolingiennes. Return to rue de l'Abbaye and turn right. Turn left into rue Voltaire, right into rue Lacordaire and left into the small street leading to the Porte du Val.

Note the two fortified gates of different periods. Turn back up the street and take rue de Four opposite. Turn right into rue Crébillon, then left down the first small alley to rue du Centre. Turn right.

Notice the beautiful 16th-century turret and two Renaissance houses; one of these is the tourist office. Turn left up rue de l'Église and continue along the left side of the 13th-century Église St-Genest (rarely open). Follow rue de la Poterne behind the church to the town wall.

There is a beautiful view south from Les Remparts (the ramparts). Turn right and follow the path to the end. Turn right into Petite Ruelle des Remparts.

The watchtower on the corner, too small to guard against enemies, was used to warn of fires or disturbances within the town walls. Opposite is a 13th-century building, divided in two in the 15th century. Turn left into rue de l'Ancienne Curé. Turn left into the Grande Rue.

Go past the Monastère Bénédictin on the left. Pass through the 15th-century Porte du Bourg to reach the car park.

i

▷ Length of walk: about 1km
▷ Approximate time: 1 hour
▷ Terrain: Fairly level and paved, except between points 4 and 5 (can be bypassed)
▷ Open: Crypt: 9–noon, 2–6
▷ Refreshments: La Grange, opposite St-Genest church (local products and meals available in summer). Also a small café/restaurant in rue Voltaire

IN ENEMY HANDS – BRIEFLY

For six weeks during the Hundred Years' War Flavigny was held by the English. After the war the town improved its defences; this explains the unique double fortifications at the Porte du Val, which reflect changes in mil-

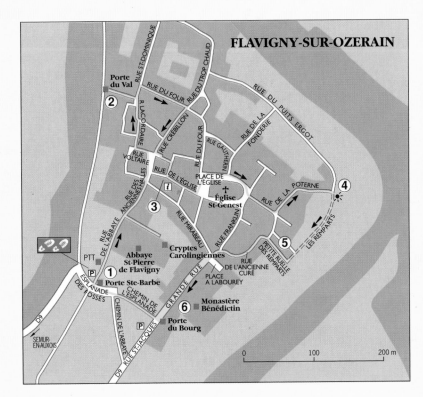

itary weaponry. The earlier inner gate, built in the 13th century, has vertical openings (*meurtrières*) for archers; in the newer 16th-century gate these were replaced by small round holes for firearms. Both were further protected by a drawbridge and a moat.

The early 16th century was a prosperous time for Flavigny. Many of the houses near the Porte de Val which have staircase towers were built during this period – an architectural innovation, as stairs were rarely constructed inside homes. Staircase towers were a highly visible statement of the wealth and rank of the residents.

Flavigny's church, top, forms part of an architectural unity that is rarely seen in the villages of France

A SPIRIT UNCHANGED

Flavigny suffered from the rural exodus common in so many French villages, and by the late 19th century it had become a quiet *village de province*. Yet even now, although many of the houses are renovated second homes for city dwellers, the medieval character of this town immunè to time enchants all who become acquainted with it.

Burgundy

The Walk

 1

Cars are not allowed in the village, so park in the designated area and walk to the gate.

 2

The entrance to the château is just inside the gate (open daily March to November; Sundays all year round). Visit the 14th-century house and tower of Beaufort, the original foundations, the keep and watchtower.

 3

Opposite the château entrance is the Auberge du Vieux Brancion. To the left is the covered market. Next to the château is the Benedictine convent.

 4

From here, take the path that leads past many 15th-century houses up to the church and its frescoes.

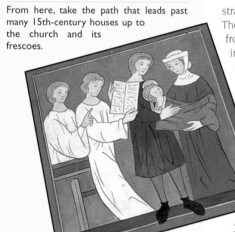

Left, the costume drawings in Brancion's castle are stylised and simple, yet convey dignity in their lines

Brancion
(Saône-et-Loire)

A feudal castle occupied this rocky outcrop as early as the 10th century. Commanding the entrance to the Saône and Grosne valleys, it was once the most important lordship in the region. All questions about the medieval village of Brancion, 15km west of Tournus, are referred to the innkeeper at the 15th-century Auberge du Vieux Brancion – and with good reason. Not only does she run the inn, her family also happen to own the château. She is one of 12 permanent residents in the village (six of whom are Benedictine nuns). There are no shops here, and no farming; tourism is Brancion's one and only activity.

Brancion's castle commanded an enviable strategic position at the head of two valleys. The Duke of Burgundy acquired the château from the Earl of Brancion, who had spent his immense fortune on financing armies sent to the Holy Land on Crusades. The château was enlarged, then destroyed and rebuilt; and finally, in 1860 – dismantled and crumbling – it was purchased by the Earl of Murard and his family. His heirs have continued his restoration work, a seemingly endless task of repairing collapsing walls and towers.

Much of the village, including several ivy-covered houses and a

Like figures in a line dance, ladies, gentlemen and their canine companions, above, present a picture of celebration in a costume drawing at Brancion castle

covered market built in the 15th century, has stood unchanged for some 500 years. The 12th-century Romanesque church at the upper end of the village is striking in its simplicity. Inside are several surprising 14th-century frescoes (unfortunately in poor condition), including a strange rendering of the Resurrection of the Dead, with figures rising from their coffins. Outside, the site commands a fine view over the Grosne Valley.

La Rochepot
(Côte-d'Or)

There is something magical about the castle of La Rochepot, south-west of Beaune. After crossing the drawbridge, visitors must knock three times before a guard pulls open the door and allows entry into the enclosed, flower-filled inner courtyard. Inside the furnished château is a fine collection of armour and medieval weaponry, and a kitchen renovated and equipped in the 19th century.

The Rochepot castle owes its name as well as its existence to two lords, Regnier and Philippe Pot, powerful vassals of the Dukes of Burgundy and members of the élite Order of the Golden Fleece, defenders of King and Church. The Pot family made an impregnable fortress of the rocky peak, which bravely resisted the assaults of the Hundred Years' War. It was not so fortunate during the Revolution, however; parts of the castle were demolished and dismantled, and the stones sold off as building material. This beautiful structure and the past it represented seemed doomed to oblivion, as was the case with so many other monuments at the time; but fate, in the figure of Madame Carnot, decided otherwise. In 1893 Madame Carnot, wife of

The village of La Rochepot with its fairy-tale castle, left, peeping over the leafy trees which surround it

the French President Sadi Carnot, purchased the ruins of Rochepot and gave the property to her son. He decided to restore and reconstruct the château to its original 15th-century style, a task that took more than 25 years.

The work involved in one of the most ambitious building projects, the well, is almost invisible. When restoration work began in 1894, the first chore was to empty the well of all the stones that filled it up. The original structure, at 72m deep, had cost as much to build as the château itself; it was dug in a single year, 1228, through extremely hard stone using only hammers and chisels, as gunpowder was then still unknown in Europe. This was no extravagance, since water would be essential if the château were put to siege. But the well also served another purpose. Some 25m down from the top of it, underground galleries connecting the castle to surrounding caves provided a final emergency exit if the besieged castle should fall to the enemy. The castle's square keep used

to stand where the terrace is now. It was destroyed during the Revolution and never rebuilt. To the left was the communal oven, a sophisticated arrangement when it was first built. The lord of La Rochepot paid for it, then charged a tax on the peasants who baked their bread here.

Montréal
(YONNE)

Only two gates – the Porte d'En Bas (Lower Gate) and the Porte d'En Haut (Upper Gate) – remain of the great ramparts that once surrounded this fortified village situated 12km north-east of Avallon. The Lower Gate leads up to the 15th- and 16th-century houses that line the little streets winding up to the church at the top of the village.

The illustrious Brunhilde, Visigoth Queen of Austrasia (the eastern dominions of the Merovingian Franks), made Montréal her home in the 6th century. This was also the

The curve of Montréal's Porte d'En Bas beckons the curious visitor through its high arch to discover a heritage of 15th- and 16th-century houses

birthplace of the powerful family of Anséric de Montréal, who ruled the town until the Burgundy dukes wrested control from them in the mid-13th century.

The 12th-century chapel was built on the site of a Roman oratory and contains a remarkable Burgundian Virgin in polychrome painted stone. The chapel was part of a primitive castle – destroyed by fire – erected around 1180 by Alexander of Burgundy.

The collegiate Church of Notre-Dame at the top of the village was constructed in 1170 and restored by Viollet-le-Duc in the 19th century. Its stark simplicity is a fine example of early Gothic architecture. Inside, an exceptional group of oak stalls is carved with scenes from the Bible and from peasant life. Outside the church there is an impressive view stretching over the Auxois Valley.

Noyers

(Yonne)

SIXTEEN TOWERS AND STRONG RAMPARTS STILL SURROUND THIS EXCEPTIONAL VILLAGE, WHICH LIES WITHIN A LOOP OF THE RIVER SEREIN. WALK THROUGH ITS ANCIENT PORTE D'AVALLON, AND ENTER THE 16TH CENTURY.

Quiet, picturesque Noyers, a perfectly preserved medieval town near Nitry in northern Burgundy, was an important stronghold in the Middle Ages. Somehow it has managed to survive intact through the centuries, untouched by the widespread destruction of the Wars of Religion, the Revolution and 20th-century urban development.

IN THE SHADOW OF RUINS

Noyers itself has survived, but the original castle that once loomed over the town lies in ruins. It was begun in the 11th century by the powerful family of Miles de Noyers, which ruled here for 10 generations. Although the castle was once considered one of the finest in Burgundy, Henry IV ordered it to be dismantled in 1599 to punish the fearsome Baron of Vitteaux. More pirate than nobleman, he was greatly feared in the region – and with reason: when angered, he regularly tossed his enemies from the top of the parade ground, called the Saut Parabin (Parabin's Leap), to the riverbank below. During the Wars of Religion enemy prisoners were thrown over these same walls.

Although Noyers was a small town, distinct neighbourhoods divided it into even smaller villages. The wealthy bourgeois lived in the half-timbered homes round the place du Marché au Blé and in the elegant 18th-century houses in the place du Grenier à Sel.

Wine-growers and farmers lived in the more modest homes along the rue Paul-Bonnetat, and several of these houses still exist. The cellar doors on the street were wide enough to accommodate large casks of wine, while the families lived on the floor above. For centuries, local wine-growers hung green, unripe grapes round the stone sculpture of the Blessed Virgin in the Porte de Tonnerre to protect the coming harvest. The Virgin apparently also received frequent offerings from young girls seeking husbands.

Noyers was once the chief administrative centre of the region. As such, it held control over the salt supplies. At one time, the salt warehouse in Noyers (in the place du Grenier à Sel) stocked enough salt for 33 parishes. Efforts to evade the hated salt tax (*gabelle*) were common, but the tax was none the less an important source of royal income, as

Gaze upwards to see Madonna and Child sheltering in a niche, and a butterfly above a bookshop

demonstrated by the sumptuous residence belonging to the tax collector, built pointedly beside the warehouse.

MEDIEVAL MEETS MODERN

Past and present have reached a happy compromise in Noyers. It is such an authentic picture of a medieval village that many French film-makers have used Noyers as a ready-made movie set (*La Grande Vadrouille*, *Chevalier de Pardaillon*, *Mon Oncle Benjamin* and *L'Enfant des Loups* were filmed here).

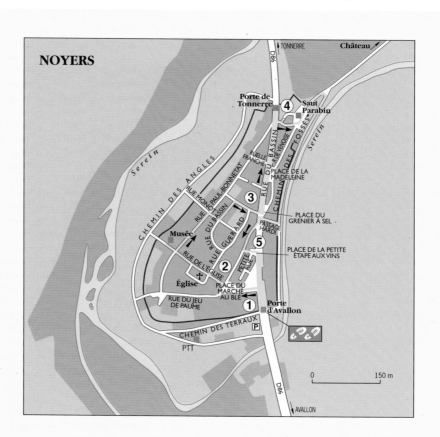

A medieval fair takes place here every two years, and the town hosts various summer music events in conjunction with the Burgundy Wine Festival, performed in the 15th-century (late Gothic) church. Just past the church is a museum that contains a permanent collection of nave paintings, donated to the town in 1990. The museum also organises temporary exhibits throughout the summer.

Every year on Bastille Day Noyers celebrates a municipal decree dating back to 1231, when a generous 13th-century lord decided to offer some of the residents a tax exemption. An arbitrary dividing line along the street was determined by the lady of the castle, who rolled an iron ball from the parade grounds; the spot where it stopped marked the boundary between the non-taxpayers and the others. The street still bears the name ruelle Franche (Free Street).

Around the place du Marché au Blé, site of the old grain market, stand the half-timbered homes of the wealthy bourgeois

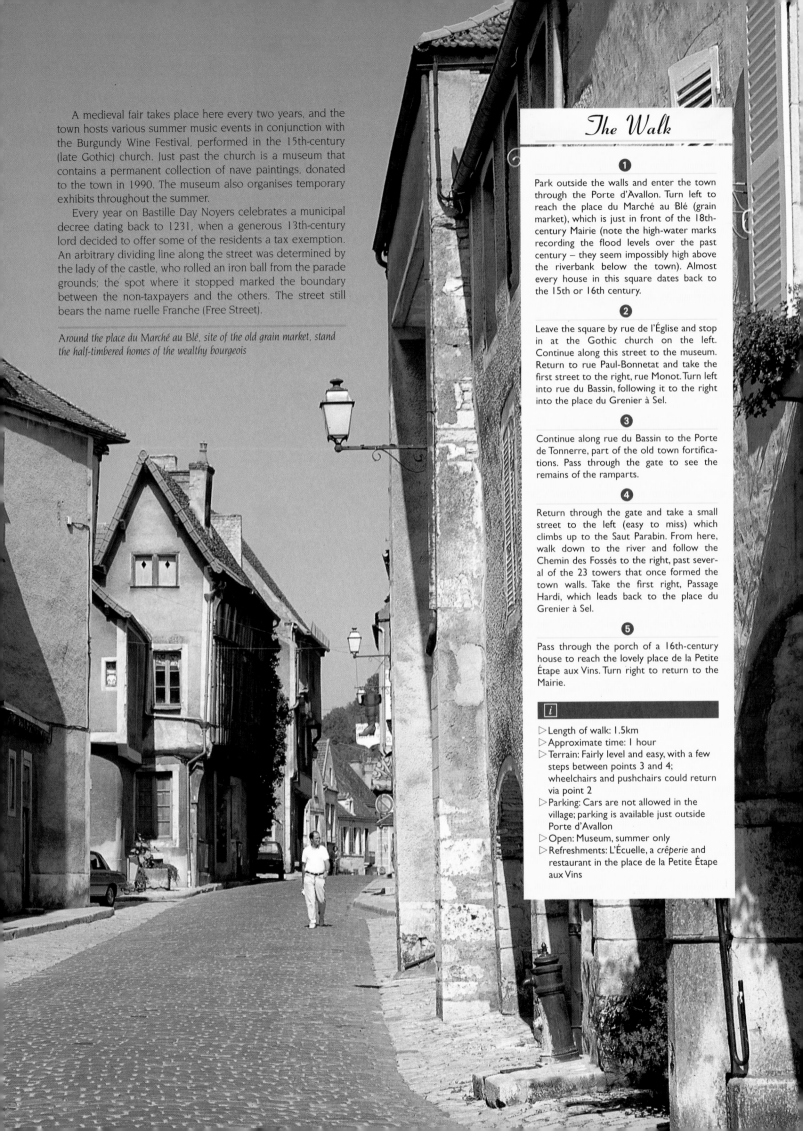

The Walk

①

Park outside the walls and enter the town through the Porte d'Avallon. Turn left to reach the place du Marché au Blé (grain market), which is just in front of the 18th-century Mairie (note the high-water marks recording the flood levels over the past century – they seem impossibly high above the riverbank below the town). Almost every house in this square dates back to the 15th or 16th century.

②

Leave the square by rue de l'Église and stop in at the Gothic church on the left. Continue along this street to the museum. Return to rue Paul-Bonnetat and take the first street to the right, rue Monot. Turn left into rue du Bassin, following it to the right into the place du Grenier à Sel.

③

Continue along rue du Bassin to the Porte de Tonnerre, part of the old town fortifications. Pass through the gate to see the remains of the ramparts.

④

Return through the gate and take a small street to the left (easy to miss) which climbs up to the Saut Parabin. From here, walk down to the river and follow the Chemin des Fossés to the right, past several of the 23 towers that once formed the town walls. Take the first right, Passage Hardi, which leads back to the place du Grenier à Sel.

⑤

Pass through the porch of a 16th-century house to reach the lovely place de la Petite Étape aux Vins. Turn right to return to the Mairie.

i

▷ Length of walk: 1.5km
▷ Approximate time: 1 hour
▷ Terrain: Fairly level and easy, with a few steps between points 3 and 4; wheelchairs and pushchairs could return via point 2
▷ Parking: Cars are not allowed in the village; parking is available just outside Porte d'Avallon
▷ Open: Museum, summer only
▷ Refreshments: L'Écuelle, a *crêperie* and restaurant in the place de la Petite Étape aux Vins

Donzy
(Nièvre)

Lying in a river valley near Cosne-Cours-sur-Loire, Donzy – a former monastic centre with a great castle – traces its origins back to the days of the Roman Empire. Driving beneath a sea-green canopy of trees along the eastern D33 approach into Donzy, the visitor feels an air of enchantment about the village and its surrounding forests.

The present-day town is situated at the confluence of the Nohain and Talvanne rivers, but traces of the first settlement are to be found a kilometre to the west, in Donzy-le-Pré, where ruins of a Gallo-Roman villa were uncovered in 1845. It is worth taking time to visit the earlier site. The ancient church lies in ruins, but the portal, which still remains, is a magnificent example of 12th-century Romanesque sculpture.

Donzy was an early centre of Christianity. The first church was built in the late 6th century, and by the 12th century it had become an important Benedictine monastery under the rule of Cluny. There was once a vast, powerful 12th-century château on the hill overlooking the town, but it fell into disrepair; the ruins stand, unseen and unvisited, behind high walls. Much of Donzy inside the town walls was destroyed during the Wars of Religion. The solid, half-timbered 16th- and 17th-century houses opposite the church date from just after these wars.

St-Caraduec church is, oddly enough, dedicated to a 12th-century Welsh saint who never set foot in France. The church itself was damaged, dismantled and rebuilt several times, most recently in 1881, which explains the distinctly Republican inscription 'Liberté, Égalité, Fraternité' on its façade.

Two watermills are still in service in Donzy. One, the Moulin de Mauperthuis, is part of the newly opened Éco-Musée, which features exhibitions about the traditional milling trade. The lovely Maison Pradelier-Rameau, the mill house in the middle of the River Nohain, produces various fine culinary oils, including walnut oil.

The Walk

Park in place de l'Hôtel de Ville, then follow signs to the tourist office in rue Audinot. Stop at the large waterwheel, which marks the entrance to the Éco-Musée (open afternoons, June to September). Continue to rue du Pont-Notre Dame and turn right, crossing the river. Note the mill house and *lavoir*.

Go straight to rue de l'Étape, following it round to the left. Opposite the church are two half-timbered 16th- and 17th-century houses. Walk round this group of houses (note the sundial at 4 rue Franc-Nohain), then take Grande Rue to place Gambetta.

3

Follow the circular rue des Remparts to the right; at rue des Forges, turn right and then left into rue de l'Étape to return to the tourist office.

Tranquil back street in the riverside village of Donzy

Solutré-Pouilly
(Saône-et-Loire)

Once described as 'a sphinx with its claws planted in the vines', Solutré is a 'pilgrimage' site for archaeologists – and at least one politician: every year, the late French President Mitterrand used to climb to the top of its hill. Once you are here, it is easy to understand his fascination with this spot.

In addition to its natural beauty, Solutré is

one of the most important prehistoric sites in France. Archaeologists have unearthed layer after layer of bones: Solutré, it seems, was a 'killing site' for well over 25,000 years. According to this ancient practice, animals were ambushed and slaughtered at the base of the cliff, which lay along a natural migration route. The remains of over 100,000 horses were found in a single hectare. The excavations are not open to the public, but a new museum, carved out of the cliff, offers impressive displays depicting prehistoric life on the site and a reconstruction of the techniques used to hunt such enormous herds of horses and reindeer.

Balancing the past with the present, Solutré, just west of Mâcon, is on the famous wine route that includes Pouilly and Fuissé. Several of the beautifully restored stone houses in the village offer wine-tastings.

Solutré's sphinx-shaped backdrop was the prehistoric site of mass animal slaughter; today grapes provide the villagers' livelihood

Époisses
(CÔTE D'OR)

Époisses, 12km west of Semur-en-Auxois, is an interesting example of a fortress constructed in the middle of a plain. Although the village is now best known for its cheese, for centuries it was an important stronghold of royal power, occupied as early as the 6th century by Queen Brunhilda. Attacked many times, Époisses was captured only once, without bloodshed, during the Wars of Religion: Catholic League soldiers, who wanted to capture the castle intact, bribed the guards at the door and walked in.

The château was originally surrounded by a double set of walls. The first enclosed the castle itself, while the second contained a large forecourt, where the inhabitants of Époisses took refuge whenever war raged. They were also allowed to build houses within the first set of walls; in exchange, they helped with the maintenance of the property. The 13th-century church (now being restored) is also inside this first line of defence.

The original castle had seven towers linked by a wall and a parapet walk, which completely encircled the inner court. During the Revolution the towers were demolished as symbols of feudal power. Inside are portraits of the many famous figures who stayed here, including the prolific letter writer Madame de Sévigné and the Grand Condé (Louis II, 4th Prince de Bourbon). The castle, still inhabited and fully furnished, has been in the hands of the same family since the 17th century. The dovecote in the forecourt is remarkable, and its 3,000 nesting holes were a sign of Époisses' importance – one hole for every *arpent* (roughly half-hectare) of property.

Époisses castle, surrounded by a now-dry moat, was captured undamaged thanks to a bribable guard

Other Villages

BLANOT

A Merovingian cemetery formed the foundations of Blanot, whose single street starts near the 11th-century Romanesque church and 14th-century priory and winds up a gentle hill. The restored church and priory were once part of the vast holdings of nearby Cluny. Locally crafted pottery is exhibited in a shop at the end of the street.

The Blanot caves, north along the D446, are the largest network of grottoes and subterranean passages in Burgundy. Discovered in the 18th century, the 21 chambers can be visited in a 1km hour-long tour (closed in winter). The path is well maintained but steep, with some 650 steps.

CHÂTILLON-EN-BAZOIS

The most memorable way to enter Châtillon is by boat, along the tree-lined Nivernais Canal, which, too narrow for commercial traffic, weaves all through this rural region plied by pleasure boats. Looming over the village is its 13th/14th-century château (open afternoons mid-July to September). The River Aron originally formed a natural moat round the fortress.

About 8km to the north, along the D945, is the Poterie de la Tuilerie, housed in an immense dome-shaped 18th-century kiln – one of the few remaining from an era when tile-making was an important local industry.

DRUYES-LES-BELLES-FONTAINES

Pervading the small quiet square in front of Druyes' 12th-century Romanesque church is the gentle murmur of running water – a reminder of its location at the source of the River Andryes, 20km north-west of Clamecy. Standing at the top of the cliff which overlooks the village are the imposing ruins of a once-great 12th-century château (open weekends in summer). For the best view of the castle, approach the village from the south along the D148.

ST-AMAND-EN-PUISAYE

The façade of the 16th-century château, designed in pink and white local brick, points proudly to the focus of activity here. Thanks to the fine clay of Myennes, St-Amand, 13km south of St-Fargeau, is the centre of a stoneware industry that dates from the 14th century and is still active today (some families claim up to 10

successive generations of potters). There are several pottery shops in the village, and a number of studios are open to visitors. Some 19km to the north-east is St-Sauveur, birthplace of the celebrated novelist Colette.

ST-BRISSON

Here in the Morvan region, nature reigns supreme, with lush forests dotted with lakes and interlaced with fish-filled rivers. The village of St-Brisson, about 13km west of Saulieu, lies at the heart of a regional park whose main information centre is located here.

The nearby Lac des Settons is a popular tourist destination. During World War II this region was a hotbed of Resistance activities, and today St-Brisson has a museum dedicated to those determined opponents of Nazi occupation.

ST-PÈRE

Overshadowed by neighbouring Vézelay, the picturesque village of St-Père lies at the foot of a hill. In addition to the marvellous 13th- to 15th-century Gothic church, Gallo-Roman baths were discovered at the nearby Fontaines Salées (open daily April to October). Many of the discoveries from the excavations are on display in the archaeological museum.

SALMAISE

The tiny 13th-century Halles of Salmaise, 15km west of St-Seine-l'Abbaye, were for hundreds of years the centre of all village activity: livestock auctions, fruit and vegetable markets and even local political gatherings were held here (the council met at 6am to discourage any opposition). Now restored, the Halles are once again the scene of a colourful Saturday afternoon market.

Further up the hillside is an 11th-century château. From here, a tiny road leads north-east to the source of the Seine, a small piece of Burgundy that now belongs to the city of Paris. This spring was venerated by the Gauls for its curative powers.

SEMUR-EN-BRIONNAIS

Lying 30km south of Paray-le-Monial, Semur produced a famous son, St Hugues, in 1024. Abbot of Cluny, he was responsible for the light, soaring Gothic design of the third Cluny church. His childhood

home here, however, was totally different: the massive, windowless walls of the St-Hugues château. One of the eeriest places in the castle is the *oubliette*, or keep. Originally a defensive tower, it was used as a prison during the Revolution. The only way in was a small hole in the upper floor; prisoners were simply dropped into the 6m pit and forgotten.

Other notable sites in Semur include the 12th-century church of St-Hilaire and the ramparts.

TANNAY

The tree-lined D119 leads from the west into Tannay, south of Clamecy. Of its 14th-century fortifications only one gate, some ruined walls and part of a moat remain. Among the 15th- and 16th-century houses is the impressive chapter house, the Maison des Chanoines.

Viticulture began here in the 13th century, and by the 18th century Tannay's white wine was considered one of the finest. Today, with phylloxera-resistant hybrids, it again ranks as one of Burgundy's good yet underrated wines.

Across the street from the church in Tannay, a pause for reflection on the steps of a village house

VÉZELAY

This is a veritable hillside gem, overlooking the Morvan regional park and surmounted by the Basilique Ste-Madeleine. One of the great pilgrimage churches of France since the Middle Ages, Ste-Madeleine is still the focus of an annual pilgrimage on 22 July, when the faithful walk the steep and winding pilgrims' route along the Grande Rue. The 12th-century basilica fell into ruin after the Revolution but was restored some 50 years later by the architect and archaeologist Eugène Viollet-le-Duc, controversial restorer of many of Burgundy's medieval buildings.

VOLNAY

The short stretch of road north and south of Beaune boasts more famous names than any other route in France. Volnay, one of the many great wine-producing villages in the Côte de Beaune, is a charming example. The 'noble' wines are separated from the rest by the D973. The great vintages come from a surprisingly narrow span of land on the uphill side of the road: higher up, the slope is too steep, lower it is not steep enough. An excellent exposure (morning sun is best), ideal altitude and perfect growing climate all contribute to the superb quality of these Burgundy wines.

Franche-Comté

Map labels

Champagne

Alsace et Lorraine

Luxeuil-les-Bains
Lure
Belfort
Vesoul
St-Julien-lès-Montbéliard
Héricourt
Delle
Champlitte
Ray-sur-Saône
Fondremand
Montbéliard
Audincourt
Gray
Belvoir
Pont-de-Roide
Pesmes
Marnay
Baume-les-Dames
Besançon
Chenecey-Buillon
Ornans
Lods
Morteau
Dole
Grand'Combe-Châteleu
Mouthier-Haute-Pierre
Arbois
Salins-les-Bains
Nans-sous-Ste-Anne
Poligny
Nozeroy
Château-Chalon
Arlay
Champagnole
Baume-les-Messieurs
Lons-le-Saunier
Orgelet
Morez
Lac de Vouglans
Les Rousses
St-Amour
St-Claude

Bourgogne

Doubs

Saône

Ognon

Doubs

Ain

CH

Vallée du Rhône

Alpes

0   20   40   60   80 km
0   10   20   30   40   50 miles

$\mathcal{F}$rom rugged mountains to rolling
farmland, this region boasts a rich culture
and spectacular scenery.

Arbois

(Jura)

THIS SIZEABLE AND PLEASANT VILLAGE, FORMER HOME OF LOUIS PASTEUR (1822–95), LIES AT THE FOOT OF A STEEP-SIDED VALLEY IN THE HEART OF WINE COUNTRY, 45KM SOUTH OF BESANÇON.

Arbois' harmonious ensemble of warm-toned stone towers, castles and old houses on the banks of the River Cuisance marks the start of the Jura wine route, running through gently rolling vine-clad hills to Belfort. Perhaps the finest part of the village is its splendid old houses along the river, best viewed from the ancient bridge (Pont des Capucins) or from the town square. The latter is flanked by elegant arcades and well-preserved 18th-century houses, many with their original wrought-iron balconies. The

Above, sellers of garlic and shallots make a reliable living out of the onion family, the sine qua non of French cuisine. Left, the River Cuisance flows along its steep valley past the handsome buildings of Arbois

Église St-Just is a gem of Romanesque and early Gothic architecture. Its ochre belfry, 64m high and crowned with an unusual bulbous dome, can be seen across the vineyards for miles around.

Arbois boasts two châteaux. Château Bontemps was built in the early 16th century for Pierre Bontemps, dean of the Église Notre-Dame, round the façade of a 12th-century fortress belonging to the Counts of Bourgogne, who also founded the nearby church in the 14th century. The medieval Château Pécauld is integrated into the ramparts of a 12th-century fortress and contains the Institute for Jura Wines and the Museum of Wine and Wine Growing, which reveals some of the wine secrets of the region.

WINE MECCA OF THE JURA

Arbois has been at the heart of wine production here for over a thousand years, and its fine wines have been much appreciated throughout history by such distinguished figures as Charles V of Spain and Napoleon. Using grape varieties not encountered elsewhere in France, they have a distinctly local character and acquire their special bouquet while ageing in oak casks.

The wines of Arbois are not only white, red and sparkling, but also rosé (described by the locals as 'onion-peel colour'), amber and grey! The amber-coloured *vin jaune*, with its nutty-sherry bouquet, is particularly celebrated here; made from the rare Savagnin grape, it is bottled only after six years of fermentation in oak casks. It is sold in a *clavelin*, a special bottle holding 62cl, a quantity unique in Europe. Try a glass with the local Comté cheese, or with a regional fondue cooked with blue cheese.

Look out also for a brandy called Marc du Jura, and the liqueur wine Macvin du Jura, a blend of grape juice and Marc du Jura aged in oak. Round every corner and down every alleyway, there are wine cellars offering a chance to try these delicious local specialities – perhaps best sampled at the shop of Henri Maire, the most famous of the Jura wine producers.

The village's annual wine festival takes place in September and is always a jovial event. More unusual, however, is the Fête Patronale, a festival honouring the town's patron saint every September, which reaches its climax with the offering of *biou* – a giant bunch of grapes – to St-Just.

Arbois' vine-growing area covers over 700ha and is full of attractive walking trails. Perhaps the best-known vines are to be found 2km north of Arbois, bought in 1874 by the scientist world-renowned for his research on the fermentation of alcohol – Louis Pasteur .

Public health owes a massive debt to Louis Pasteur, the father of modern bacteriology

A GIANT OF SCIENCE

Louis Pasteur spent his childhood and youth in Arbois and returned for all his holidays to his beloved home town. After his father died, he bought the family's tannery in 1875 and transformed it into his home and laboratory, where he would work for months at a stretch. A chemist and microbiologist, he revolutionised medicine with his studies of bacterial diseases, creating vaccines against rabies and anthrax amongst other great and varied discoveries. The house, Maison de Pasteur, which now belongs to the Academy of Sciences, has been converted into a museum. Its fine 19th-century interior and research laboratory remain as a memorial to this great man. Arbois has many other reminders of its most famous resident, including a daily guided tour taking in his school, his family grave and his vines.

The Walk

1

Start at the place de la Liberté and walk westwards down Grande-Rue, lined with wine cellars on both sides. Turn left into rue Notre-Dame and right past the clog-maker on the corner, alongside the church and past the Louis Pasteur memorial.

2

Go left down the little rue de l'Abreuvoir and left at the river, round to Château Bontemps. Bear left up the side of the castle, along the rampart walls, and turn right into rue du Vieux Château.

3

Cross the main road (rue de l'Hôtel de Ville) and enter rue Mercière on the right. Branch to the right at the fountain and go across the bridge. Turn left, then left again at place de Faramand, back across a tiny stone bridge and up rue de la Tour past the Tour Gloriette.

4

Go straight across at the next junction into rue Bousson de Mairet, and across again at the next junction, following signs to Château Pécauld.

5

Opposite the entrance to the Wine Museum, continue along rue des Fossés to the main road, the Grande-Rue. Turn right (the road becomes rue de Courcelles) and continue down to Maison de Pasteur. Alternatively, turn left to return to the main square.

▷ Length of walk: 2km
▷ Approximate time: 45 minutes
▷ Terrain: All surfaced; suitable for pushchairs and wheelchairs
▷ Parking: Free parking near the Pasteur memorial
▷ Open: Museum of Wine and Wine-Growing: 10–noon, 2–6; closed Tuesdays. La Maison Pasteur: 9:30–5:30
▷ Refreshments: Wine cellars, restaurants and cafés

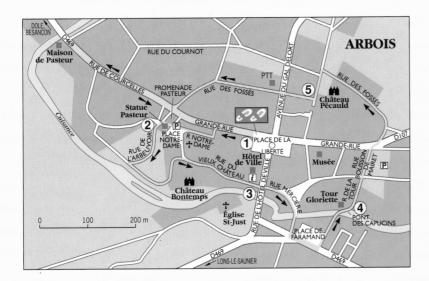

Mouthier-Haute-Pierre
(DOUBS)

The Loue Valley offers some of the most spectacular scenery in Franche-Comté, and Mouthier-Haute-Pierre is undoubtedly one of the most delightful villages in the valley. Originally two villages – Mouthier and Haute Pierre – today's village is still divided into two parts: Mouthier-Haut, with its narrow streets clustered round the church and winding up the hillside, and Mouthier-Bas, tumbling downhill towards the river.

The village owes it name and very existence to the Benedictine monastery founded here in the 9th century. It was destroyed at the time of the Revolution, but traces still remain, including the grand entrance and the arches of three naves. The nearby magnificent Gothic church has fine wooden statues dating from the 13th and 14th centuries, and the ancient houses which line the surrounding narrow streets have medieval carved door lintels, handsome arches and sculpted figures. The most interesting façades date from the 16th century.

As you explore the narrow streets, try a Marsotte kirsch for which the village is noted, with over 4,000 litres of this delicious cherry liqueur produced each year. In April 200ha of riverside cherry orchards are in full bloom – a rare sight recalled by a popular souvenir of the village, a large basket or *ruche* used for gathering the fruit. You can buy one at the boulangerie in the Grande Rue.

The cosily clustered buildings of Mouthier-Haute-Pierre, which nestles in the Loue Valley, look unexceptional from afar, yet contain treasures great and small

Mouthier-Haute-Pierre marks the start of many walks in the valley, the most spectacular being to the source of the Loue. There is also the viewpoint from the Roche de Hautepierre (882m) across village and valley to the Jura mountains, the Vosges and, on a clear day, the silhouette of Mont Blanc.

Baume-les-Messieurs
(JURA)

This tiny village, famous for its monastery, shelters in the deep Cirque de Baume, where three valleys meet. It is overlooked by the rocky edge of an eroded plateau in countryside that resonates with cascades and babbling streams. The name Baume is actually derived from *balma*, meaning cavern, and the vast caves higher up the valley are well worth exploring.

The first abbey was established in the 6th century by the Irish monk St Colomb, and in 910 a dozen of its monks set forth to found the world-famous abbey of Cluny in Burgundy. A monk of the Cluny order, Bienheureux Bernonen, in turn founded a splendid monastery here. The golden stone buildings are now mostly ruined but the grand church remains, containing some beautiful 15th- and 16th-century sculptures.

The Walk

Start at the Mairie in Mouthier-Haute. Follow rue Pavée to the right into rue Robert-Dame, past the *lavoir*, then turn left after the stone cross. Turn right at the crossroads down Grande Rue, curving left past the fountain; and then branch right down to the main road.

Cross into Mouthier-Bas and descend steeply. Turn left at the first junction into rue de la Marsotte, past the *lavoir* and on to the bridge.

❸

Back at the *lavoir*, turn right into rue des Guenbart; climb a grassy slope just before a campsite back to the road.

❹

Turn left into rue Ernest-Reyer, back up to the main road, then cross into rue de Chapite back up to the Mairie.

The original name of this village was Baume-les-Moines, simple 'monks' defining the purpose of the place. However, during the latter half of the 16th century, monastic life became less ascetic and only men of noble blood were accepted as monks. For this reason, it was renamed Baume-les-Messieurs. Of all the *messieurs* at the monastery, the most colourful was undoubtedly Jean de Watteville. During the 17th century, he became a monk in remorse at having killed an opponent in a duel, but did not enjoy the cloistered life. One night his superior found him climbing over the wall, so de Watteville shot him too and fled to Spain. There, he joined the army of the Grand Turk, became a Muslim and had a large harem. Following some double-dealing and the promise of papal absolution, he returned once more to Baume, to the position of Abbot, and here he spent the rest of his life.

Grand' Combe-Chateleu
(DOUBS)

This farming community is set in lush meadowland lying between two small valleys (*combes*) close to the Swiss border. The bells of the Montbéliard cows grazing peacefully only emphasise the serenity of the village, whose

history dates back to the 12th century. At one point, following an outbreak of the plague, it was deserted, but today it is a working village known for its taxidermy and woodwork and a method of curing ham in timber oasthouses called *fermes à tuyé*.

These famous Franche-Comté-style farmhouses combine living quarters with cattle byres, grain storage and giant *tuyé* chimneys – a massive fireplace and large stone-and-wood chimney where cured meats are dried and smoked. The local delicacies here include *jambon de*

In the agricultural village of Grand' Combe-Chateleu, the traditional architecture reflects the rural activities of the inhabitants

In the 10th century, monks from the tiny village of Baume founded Cluny, whose monks in turn built this glorious abbey

tuyé (smoked ham), Jesus sausages from the neighbouring village of Morteau, and delicious wafer-thin slices of dried beef called *brèsi* – with a loaf of bread, some fruit and a bottle of wine, they make a handsome picnic.

The Farm Museum of Beugnon, in a traditional 17th-century farmhouse in the village, gives fascinating insights into the harsh life of the local *montagnard* people, with rare blacksmiths', wheelwrights' and foresters' tools on display, alongside country crafts typical of the region.

Alternatively, visitors can also watch artist Frédérique Perrin at work in his studio, painting fine watercolours of the local scenery. The beautiful rolling countryside here is popular for walking, cycling, canoeing and, in winter, cross-country skiing.

Ornans

(Doubs)

A SMALL TOWN WITH A VILLAGE ATMOSPHERE SET IN THE PICTURESQUE LOUE VALLEY, ORNANS WAS ARTIST GUSTAVE COURBET'S HOME TOWN. ROCKY CLIFFS MAKE A MAGNIFICENT BACKDROP TO THIS 'LITTLE VENICE OF FRANCHE-COMTÉ'.

Behind the unpretentious streets of Ornans, above, the land rises up in a ridge of cliffs. Narrow byways make serendipitous frames for buildings of character

Ornans stretches beside the banks of the River Loue. Its multicoloured balconied houses, dating from the 15th to the 18th century, are set on stilts to overhang the water – a photographer's dream, particularly when illuminated at night. Another splendid sight is the Miroir d'Ornans (also known here as the Miroir de la Loue), where the rugged cliffs, church and ancient dwellings are reflected in the clear, still water of the river.

Among the usual bars and cafés which punctuate the main road are many artists' studios; you may even see artists working at their easels along the pavement. This is also the road in which to find the place to taste the local delicacy, Ornan's *saucisse*, made from pork with 'trumpets of death' mushrooms: at Boucherie Pernet, near the beautifully arcaded Hôtel de Ville (Town Hall).

High above the village, on the Rocher du Château, lies the ruined Châteauvieux (Old Castle), an ancient fortress of the Counts of Bourgogne, together with a tiny 13th-century chapel. The views from here over Ornans and the valley and across to the 700-year-old Châteauneuf are breathtaking. These are some of the oldest buildings in the region. Indeed, the history of Ornans dates back to the Middle Ages. Since then, the town has produced several celebrities, including the mathematician Pierre Vernier, inventor of the vernier scale, and the painter Gustave Courbet, the founder of Realism.

Following in the footsteps of giants: artists are still drawn to the village of Ornans, Courbet's home town

LIFE THROUGH A REALIST'S EYES

Courbet, the influential 19th-century artist, was born in Ornans in 1819 in a house on the edge of the river near the Grand Pont. His tomb can be visited in the town's cemetery. A controversial and progressive artist for this period, he started the Realist Movement; on one occasion, when asked to paint angels, he responded: 'I have never seen an angel. Show me one and I will paint it.'

Courbet's photographs represent a dossier on life in the valley during the last century. In fact, he was one of the first artists in France to depict rural poverty in his work. His home and studio have been converted into a splendid museum containing over 60 of his works and other mementoes. The rugged valley was one of his chief influences, and inspired such famous paintings as *Le Château d'Ornans* and *Source de la Loue*.

RIVER OF RENOWN

The River Loue has been officially classified as 'one of the loveliest rivers of Europe'. Flowing swiftly through a steep, winding gorge, it passes dramatic overhangs of limestone rock that tower above the lush flower-strewn valley. The region is rich in wildlife, with kingfishers, kestrels and kites all common sights. Canoeing and rafting are popular, and walkers are spoilt for choice here, with one stunning panorama after another.

The source of the Loue, a short distance away at Ouhans, is a must. This cascading spring shoots forcefully out of a cave at the foot of the cliffs. The river links underground here with the River Doubs, a fact that was discovered in 1901 when absinthe barrels were

The Walk

1

Start in the place Courbet. With the statue behind you, proceed along the main shopping street past the Hôtel de Ville, the first bridge and the riverside terrace of the place Humblot to the place du Jura, marked by a fine statue.

2

Follow the road round to the right into rue Jacques Gervais. Just after the post office there is access to a small shingle beach – a good picnic place.

3

Continue round to the main street and turn right. Ahead is the Couvent de la Visitation. Turn right again and cross the river at the ancient Pont de Nahin.

4

Turn right again and cling to the left bank of the river, behind the attractive riverside houses, to reach place Robert Fernier and the Musée Courbet.

5

Continue straight on, past the Grand Pont and the Maison de l'Eau et de la Pêche (fishing museum) into rue St-Laurent, which curves round the side of the church of the same name. Take the right fork after the church into rue du Champliman.

6

Turn right at the next bridge. Cross the river past the Miroir d'Ornans and bear right along avenue du Président Wilson, past the hospital and back into place Courbet.

---

i

▷ Length of walk: 4km
▷ Approximate time: 1 hour
▷ Terrain: All surfaced; suitable for pushchairs and wheelchairs
▷ Parking: Free parking in place Courbet
▷ Open: Maison de l'Eau et de la Pêche and Musée Courbet: 10–noon, 2–6
▷ Refreshments: Cafés, riverside terraces

emptied into the Doubs by the Pernod factory in Pontarlier. For several days, people drinking the water found that the Loue had turned into a huge free aperitif.

The river is also a fisherman's paradise. Enthusiasts will enjoy the National Fishing and Water Habitat Centre at Ornans, a fascinating exhibition on the principal techniques used in freshwater fishing, past and present. One such method is illustrated in the shady main square, named after Gustave Courbet. That artist's sculpture of a young fisherboy – *Le Pêcheur de Chavots* – shows him poised with a *chavot* fork, which is used to capture small fish in the river.

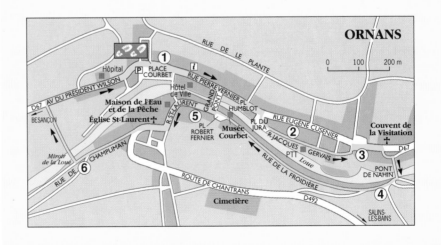

A *curving back street of Champlitte kindly offers the weary walker a seat with a view*

Champlitte
(HAUTE-SAÔNE)

Near the borders of the regions of Franche-Comté, Burgundy and Champagne, this ancient fortified village on the regional Route des Vins rests in a rich valley on the banks of the River Salon.

The history of Champlitte dates back to the minting of Roman coins in the 3rd century, and every period since has left its traces. This is especially notable in its architectural heritage, which includes remains of the original fortifications, attractive Renaissance houses in the place des Halles and an unusual Gothic belfry in the place de l'Église.

The château with its Renaissance façade and 18th-century wings is home to the Museum of Arts and Popular Traditions. This folklore museum helps preserve local customs and evokes the atmosphere of days

gone by through re-created village scenes combined with the use of sound and video. Another fascinating place is the Musée 1900 des Arts et Techniques. Here you will find two entire streets re-created, complete with cheese- and clog-makers, baker, glass-blower and wheelwright, illustrating as well the technological developments of the 20th century and the various effects they have had on these traditional crafts.

Champlitte's narrow streets and cobbled alleyways are lined with the large 18th-century residences of wealthy wine merchants as well as simple wine-growers' houses; together they cluster round elegant squares crowned with obelisk fountains, typical of the Haute-Saône region. Taste the local wines at the Musée des Pressoirs, an open-air museum with a collection of ancient wine presses, cooperage and distillery. The village comes to life every winter on 22 January, when it hosts a wine festival dedicated to St Vincent, the patron saint of *vignerons* (wine-growers), celebrated since 1719.

Nans-sous-Ste-Anne
(DOUBS)

The remote hamlet of Nans-sous-Ste-Anne is set in a wooded landscape cut by deep gorges, near a spectacular tributary of the River Lison. Its location is unique, surrounded by the sources of five rivers: running along their valleys, these create a giant star formation of cliffs with Nans in the middle. Once an important stronghold, the village lies on an ancient salt route and still has vestiges of a castle, dismantled in the 17th century.

The chapel of Ste-Anne, erected in the 15th century, contains a striking statue of the Virgin Mary made of Nans-sous-Ste-Anne earthenware. The village *faïencerie* thrived from 1840 until 1929, producing unusual pieces of flower-patterned china, trinkets and fine statues which are collectors' pieces today. The Taillanderie Museum, an original 19th-century agricultural toolworks, remains in full working order – a system now unique in Europe, with waterwheels and solid-oak bellows, powered by the River Archange, a tributary of the Lison.

The source of the River Lison is one of the great natural sights of Franche-Comté, a thundering roar of water blasting out from the base of a vertical rock face. The whole area is full of geological curiosities. Upstream from the source is the Creux Billard, a cylindrical abyss formed in the cliffs. The magnificent Grotte Sarrazine and the caves at the source of the Verneau – popular with potholers and geologists – are also worth visiting.

Nozeroy
(JURA)

Although very much a village, Nozeroy prides itself on being the smallest town in France. Dominating the ancient Miège Valley, it was the feudal capital of the Counts of Chalon, who in the Middle Ages controlled the salt route from Franche-Comté towards Switzerland and Italy. An appealing walled village, it still has the old ramparts and ruins of a medieval castle and an important Gothic church as proof of its rich history.

There has been a fortress on this site since the early 13th century. The present castle was constructed by Louis II of Chalon-Arlay in 1424. One year, the north-west tower collapsed and the lord of the manor allowed the villagers to use the materials for their homes. Thanks to his generosity, it is still possible to see the odd carving, statue or piece of stonework embedded in the walls and doorways of ordinary houses. The most impressive façades, embellished with Gothic niches, sculptures and portals, date from the 16th century.

In the main square there is an imposing clock tower, formerly the main entrance to the village and an excellent example of the region's military architecture. Perhaps the most unusual sight in Nozeroy is inside the beautiful Gothic church: the altarfront of *orfroi* (orphrey) embroideries made here by the Annonciades nuns in 1650. The fine designs are embroidered with very thin strands of straw, plaited in seven different ways – a local craft called straw embroidery. The central design of the Good Shepherd is of pearl.

Set in verdant woodland, Nans-sous-Ste-Anne makes a fine centre for exploring the area's caves and river sources. Timber, inset, is a valued natural resource

Other Villages

ARLAY

Arlay, situated 15km north of Lons-le-Saunier, is well known for its fine castle. Built in 1774 by the Countess of Lauraguais, it was altered in the 19th century by Prince d'Arenberg and contains some fine period furniture and a superb library and dolls' room. The park offers a pleasant walk up to the medieval ruins of the fortress of the Counts of Chalon-Arlay (former Princes of Orange) and affords good views of the surrounding countryside and the château vineyards. The ruins form a romantic setting for over 40 species of birds of prey, which attract a large number of visitors.

The simple village beyond straddles the river with its ramshackle Jurassien farmhouses. A short avenue of chestnut trees leads to the church, its tile roof varnished so that it gleams.

Arlay is an important wine producer; one family has been working in the vineyards here for over 200 years, and the present *vigneron* has a collection of wines dating from before the Revolution.

CHÂTEAU-CHALON

Renowned for its ancient abbey and its wines, this small village sits majestically on the crest of a rocky spur. The ruins of a medieval castle, built here to protect a Benedictine abbey founded in the 8th century, offer broad views from the old ramparts over the surrounding vineyards, among the best known of the Jura.

Château-Chalon produces the very best of the region's *vin jaune*, an amber nutty-flavoured wine, bottled only after six years of fermentation in oak – delicious in the local speciality, *coq au vin jaune*. If you are lucky, you may also find another unusual regional wine, *vin de paille* (straw wine), made by keeping grapes for several months before pressing and not bottling the wine for over a decade.

CHENECEY-BUILLON

Arriving at the peaceful hamlet of Chenecey-Buillon is like winding the clock back a few hundred years. Lying by an ancient stone bridge that crosses a gently flowing trout stream (reputedly one of the best in France), this serene place is named after the Chenecey family castle, round which the village developed in the 12th century. A former abbey, once a thriving community founded by the Cistercians in 1133, now also lies in ruins here.

The square 14th-century chapel is worth a visit, as is the old forge, which operated from 1500 until as recently as 1950. There is only one hotel, on the bank of the river; popular with fishermen, it promises guests a stay of total tranquillity.

FONDREMAND

It is hard to believe that this little village of traditional Franche-Comté houses, peacefully basking in the Romaine Valley, was once an important fortified town. The imposing Romanesque keep, built by the former Dukes of Burgundy, dominates a medieval château at the top of the village; today it houses a curious museum of local history, set up by the village curé, containing a bizarre mixture of puppets, lace and old farm tools. Visitors can also climb down steps inside the fort wall to explore the dank and musty dungeons.

The most striking feature of the village is undoubtedly the source of the River Romaine. Emerging from under the keep, the bubbling spring is channelled into a stone basin, *lavoir* and ornamental lake.

Locally Fondremand is noted for its three-day arts and crafts festival every July, when the village comes alive with music and folkloric events.

LODS

Lods, a sleepy old wine-makers' village climbing steeply up the banks of the River Loue, fully deserves its reputation as one of the prettiest villages in France. Although it no longer produces wine, Lods still has numerous wine-growers' houses, some from the 16th century. One contains the Musée de la Vigne et du Vin (Museum of Wine and Wine-Growing), where you can visit the cellars.

At the top of the village, there is a belvedere with fine views along the valley. Even from here the river can be heard as it rushes down a series of small weirs.

PESMES

Built on the borders of Burgundy and Franche-Comté, and perched above the River Ognon, this attractive village has kept its charm despite a turbulent history. A settlement has existed on this site since Roman times, but Pesmes has been razed to the ground on more than one occasion and was decimated by the plague.

Enclosed within the walls are many vestiges of the past, hidden in a labyrinth of narrow lanes bursting with flowers. The main shopping street runs from the castle to one of the two remaining gates, the Porte St-Hilaire. The 12th-century church by the gate is crowned by a glistening dome of russet, green and yellow, typical of churches in the region. In the choir is a magnificent painting by local artist Jacques Prévost, a pupil of Raphael. A walk along the ramparts by the castle affords pleasant views of the river, the setting for frequent *son et lumières* in summer.

RAY-SUR-SAÔNE

Ray's russet-tiled ochre houses cling to a hill on the banks of the majestic River Saône. Its castle, the former fortress of the Baron of Ray, dates from the 13th century, with splendid views over the Langres Plateau to the Jura and Vosges mountains. Rebuilt in the 17th and 18th centuries, it retains its original Romanesque tower and also has a magnificent symmetrical courtyard and immaculately manicured gardens.

The scenery is exquisite, with terracotta-coloured soil and fields of sunflowers. The river makes an ideal place for picnics, swimming and walking, and you can even hire a houseboat for a trip downstream to explore neighbouring villages.

LES ROUSSES

Close to the Swiss border in the Jura mountains, Les Rousses is one of the Jura's loveliest holiday resorts, offering a wide range of activities including horse-riding and windsurfing. Delightful walks lead through forests and across wide plateaux to take in views over Lake Geneva to the Alps. In winter, when the lush green pastures and dark forests are blanketed with snow, Les Rousses is transformed into a ski resort, with ice skating on the frozen lake. The challenge of the Transjurassienne cross-country race is taken up by 3,000 skiers every year.

The village itself, with its pretty chalets and fine dairy products, is deeply rooted in tradition. The local timber is valued by makers of musical instruments, who appreciate its special resonance.

An old wine press in Lods recalls the days when grapes were cultivated here

The *Atlantic Coast*

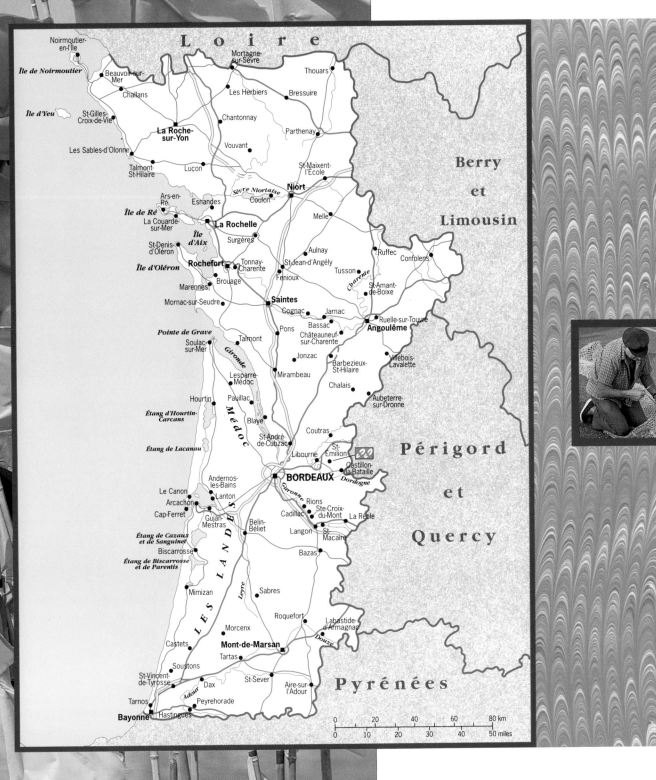

LOIRE

Noirmoutier-en-l'Île
Île de Noirmoutier
Beauvoir-sur-Mer
Challans
Île d'Yeu
St-Gilles-Croix-de-Vie
La Roche-sur-Yon
Les Sables-d'Olonne
Talmont-St-Hilaire
Luçon
Ars-en-Ré
Esnandes
Île de Ré
La Couarde-sur-Mer
La Rochelle
Île d'Aix
Surgères
St-Denis-d'Oléron
Île d'Oléron
Rochefort
Tonnay-Charente
Marennes
Brouage
Mornac-sur-Seudre
Saintes
Pointe de Grave
Talmont
Soulac-sur-Mer
Gironde
Lesparre-Médoc
Hourtin
Pauillac
Médoc
Étang d'Hourtin-Carcans
Blaye
St-André-de-Cubzac
Étang de Lacanau
Coutras
Libourne
St-Émilion
Castillon-la-Bataille
Dordogne
Andernos-les-Bains
Le Canon
Lanton
BORDEAUX
Arcachon
Garonne
Rions
Cap-Ferret
Gujan-Mestras
Cadillac
Ste-Croix-du-Mont
La Réole
Belin-Béliet
Langon
St-Macaire
Étang de Cazaux et de Sanguinet
Bazas
Biscarrosse
Étang de Biscarrosse et de Parentis
Leyre
Sabres
Mimizan
Roquefort
Morcenx
Labastide-d'Armagnac
Castets
Mont-de-Marsan
Douze
Tartas
Soustons
St-Vincent-de-Tyrosse
Dax
St-Sever
Aire-sur-l'Adour
Adour
Tarnos
Peyrehorade
Bayonne
Hastingues

Mortagne-sur-Sèvre
Thouars
Les Herbiers
Bressuire
Chantonnay
Parthenay
Vouvant
St-Maixent-l'Ecole
Sèvre Niortaise
Niort
Coulon
Melle
Aulnay
St-Jean-d'Angély
Ruffec
Confolens
Fenioux
Tusson
Charente
St-Amant-de-Boixe
Cognac
Jarnac
Bassac
Pons
Châteauneuf-sur-Charente
Ruelle-sur-Touvre
Angoulême
Jonzac
Barbezieux-St-Hilaire
Villebois-Lavalette
Mirambeau
Chalais
Aubeterre-sur-Dronne

Berry et Limousin

Périgord et Quercy

Pyrénées

0 20 40 60 80 km
0 10 20 30 40 50 miles

St-Émilion

(Gironde)

THE EPITOME OF A PRESTIGIOUS WINE VILLAGE, ST-ÉMILION BOASTS IMPECCABLE GOLDEN HOUSES BASKING AMIDST TIGHT GREEN LINES OF NOBLE VINES. VISITORS FIND A WARM, EFFICIENT WELCOME HERE, AND ADD TO THE ANIMATED ATMOSPHERE.

With vineyards stretching as far as the eye can see beyond the ancient city walls, pink pantiled roofs undulating down the two hills on which the village is built, and plenty of vantage points from which to enjoy the undeniably pretty views, St-Émilion can hardly fail to please even the most jaded eye.

Forming part of the large vineyard region of Bordeaux, the large village exudes prosperity – brought not only by its world-class wines, but also by the large number of visitors who use it as a base for vineyard tours, or who come simply to see the sights and enjoy a coffee or meal in one of the many restaurants and cafés dotted along the narrow lanes. The stylishness of the attractive shops clearly reflects the tastes and purses of its discerning international clientèle.

CHURCHES, CLOISTERS AND CATACOMBS

St-Émilion has a few particularly interesting sights connected with its origins as the spot chosen by an 8th-century hermit named Aemilianus. The porous limestone on which the village sits provided the Breton monk with the perfect material from which to fashion a grotto, hewn out of the rock, in which he spent his latter years – not in total solitude, but with many devoted followers who came to visit the holy man. St-Émilion's 'hermitage' can still be visited, as can nearby catacombs, ancient burial grounds likewise carved out of the rock.

As word of Aemilianus's deeds spread, the village became a popular destination for

Enjoy an alfresco meal at a terrace restaurant, above, then walk in the cool cloisters of the collegiate church

pilgrimages. As a result, the hermit's followers began work on an extraordinary underground sanctuary known as the Église Monolithe (Monolithic Church), carved out of a single block of rock between the 8th and 12th centuries. The simple interior is extremely impressive for its size, and three 16th-century windows provide light.

Outside, the 14th-century porch has a fine tympanum. The belfry rises from the little square above the church; it combines elements from the 12th, 14th and 15th centuries, and offers excellent views over the town from the spire.

Almost flanking the Église Monolithe is the tiny 13th-century Holy Trinity chapel, built by Benedictine monks, with slender ribbed vaulting. In contrast, the Romanesque and Gothic collegiate church, near the Porte du Chapitre, is huge. Its 14th-century porch, with a tympanum portraying the Last Judgement, is particularly impressive.

The remains of several monasteries can be found in St-Émilion. The cloisters of the

Order of the Cordeliers, though in a ruinous state, are nevertheless evocative; visits are free and wine-tasting is available. Those of the collegiate church are at the back of the tourist office; the slender twinned columns are very elegant. The former collegiate refectory and monks' dormitory now contain the tourist office and can be freely visited.

OF VINEYARDS AND WINE

There have been vines growing in this region since Gallo-Roman times. The Roman poet Ausonius owned vineyards here, and the present-day Château Ausone, said to have been built upon the remaining foundations of his villa, is still ranked among the very best of the St-Émilion *grands crus*.

The wines of St-Émilion are subject to a strict quality control and evaluation by a panel of experts, a system established in the Middle Ages and continued to the present day. The committee of judges was appointed

A wine capital of world class, St-Émilion nevertheless keeps its village character intact, with the grand spire of the Église Monolithe reigning over all

by the town council, and they were known (and still are) as *jurats*. The guild of the *jurats* (known as the *Jaurade*), attired in red robes and ermine, celebrates the spring fair and the grape harvest in colourful ceremonies which involve ascending to the roof of the Tour du Roi (King's Tower); the harvest is declared open by the sounding of a trumpet.

You can become acquainted with the vineyards of St-Émilion by taking a 'little train' tour from the collegiate church, during which a 35-minute commentary gives the background to some of the commune's famous wines. To sample individual wines or get more information about a particular vineyard, enquire at the Maison du Vin.

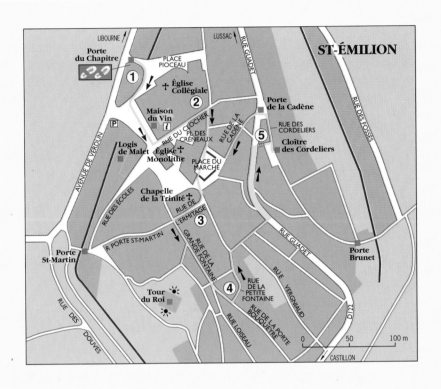

The Walk

❶

Start by the Porte du Chapitre at the collegiate church. Beyond the neighbouring Maison du Vin, turn left into the rue du Clocher. In the place des Créneaux just to the right is the belfry of the Église Monolithe and views over place du Marché.

❷

Continue along rue du Clocher for a few steps, then take the alley (Tertre de la Tente) to the right, down to the place du Marché. Here is the entrance to the Église Monolithe, the Trinity Chapel, St Émilion's hermitage and the catacombs.

❸

Take rue de l'Hermitage, then turn left into rue de la Grande Fontaine. A little lane leads right to the Tour du Roi (fine views).

❹

From rue de la Grande Fontaine, take rue de la Port Bouqueyre; turn left into rue de la Petite Fontaine, then take the right fork and steep steps to reach rue Guadet. Turn left, follow the road round the bend, then follow a sign to the right to the cloisters of Les Cordeliers (more steps).

❺

Upon leaving the cloisters, turn right into rue des Cordeliers back down to rue Guadet; cross to the left, through the Porte de la Cadène into rue de la Cadène, returning to the place du Marché.

---

i

▷ Length of walk: 1 km
▷ Approximate time: 2 hours (including visits)
▷ Terrain: Some very steep lanes, heavily cobbled, and steps
▷ Parking: Near the Porte du Chapitre
▷ Open: Tourist office: daily 9:30–12:30 and 1:45–6/6:30. 'Little train' tour: Jun–Oct
▷ Refreshments: Many restaurants (some very pricey) and cafés

The Walk

Start at the tourist office in the place Trarieux, where you can purchase a combined entrance ticket for the Église Monolithe, which is open daily, and a small museum depicting a typical 19th-century village classroom.

Take rue St-Jean leading down to the Église Monolithe. You can walk along the lighted galleries which surround the nave.

Retrace your steps back to the square, then follow rue St-Jacques up past several fine buildings (some of which used to house convents) to the School Museum. An explanatory leaflet (available in English) outlines the principles of education under the Third Republic, while the classroom evokes the conditions of the time. A little further on is the Église St-Jacques, with its splendid façade.

Balconied houses in the old style adorn Aubeterre, which lies on an ancient pilgrimage route

Aubeterre-sur-Dronne
(CHARENTE)

Near the leafy banks of the River Dronne, and ranged alongside the steep white cliffs which gave this town its name, Aubeterre has a prosperous air and is keen to show off its sights. Its long history stretches back to neolithic times; remains have also been found of a Gallo-Roman *oppidum* or stronghold (the Romans named this place *Alba Terra* after its white cliffs). The neat, rectangular main square is named after, and presided over by the bust of, Ludovic Trarieux, who founded the League for the Defence of the Rights of Man. Cafés overlook a plane tree-fringed *boules* pitch in the square, while the remains of Aubeterre's ancient castle survey pleasant scenes.

The church of St-Jacques is a former Benedictine abbey church; its finely sculpted façade, incorporating signs of the zodiac, is the only part which remains from the original 12th-century building. Geometric motifs of Spanish-Arabic influence are a legacy of the village's position on the popular pilgrimage route to Santiago de Compostela.

Aubeterre's past has rarely been peaceful. It was the scene of civil war between Catholics and Protestants and of fierce resistance against its English overlords during the Hundred Years' War. The English-built keep, known as the Donjon de Swyllyngton, was razed by Cardinal Richelieu. In the 16th century, Aubeterre's inhabitants revolted against the salt tax and threw the tax collectors into the river.

Several convents existed at Aubeterre. Indeed, in the times of medieval pilgrimages, convents were said to outnumber hostelries, a fact which angered many male pilgrims and soldiers alike. Remains of these buildings are now incorporated into private houses; although none can be visited, fine doorways and other features can be distinguished along the narrow streets.

Another remarkable structure here is the unusual 12th-century Église Monolithe hewn out of the rock underneath the castle, on the site of an earlier chapel. The dim interior gives an impression of immense height, although the nave measures only 27m by 16m. Galleries link the church to the castle.

on top of the fortifications (with a perimeter of about 1.5km); punctuated by seven bastions topped with bartizan turrets, it looks out over the totally unspoilt rural surroundings and towards the islands of Aix and Oléron. There are two access gateways into the village, but very little traffic disturbs the calm of the little streets and unpaved paths, which are laid out on a grid pattern. Several of Brouage's military buildings have survived the ravages of time, in particular the forges and the coopers' workshop.

Restoration of the 17th-century church was financed by the people of Quebec, Canada, to honour their city's founder, Samuel de Champlain, who was born here. An exhibition inside illustrates his exploits, and the site of his birthplace can be visited.

A bartizan turret projects from the top of Brouage's fortifications, with views of salt marshes and islands

Some of the best views of Ste-Radegonde can be had from across the mud flats just to the south-east of the village, where fishermen still use the picturesque *carrelets* – nets suspended from a pulley, which sway above the water when at rest.

Just across the little bay to the north-west of Talmont, the small port and resort of Meschers-sur-Gironde is built partly on a cliff site, on top of a warren of troglodyte dwellings. Used since prehistoric times, these caves have given shelter to various outlaws over the centuries, including pirates, contraband merchants and Protestants. Nowadays they can be viewed only by taking refreshment in one of the restaurants which occupy the cliff site – or better still from a boat, for an overall appreciation of the cliffs.

Brouage
(CHARENTE-MARITIME)

It is hard to believe that this picturesque, sleepy and isolated community, peacefully sited amongst windswept marshes and now looking out over placid oyster beds, was once a major medieval port and capital of the salt trade. At the edge of some 8,000ha of salt marshes, with the seafront just beyond its north walls, Brouage's strategic position near the other great port of La Rochelle was to influence much of its history.

Allied to the Catholic cause, Brouage became involved in Cardinal Richelieu's siege of the Protestant haven of La Rochelle in 1628, when it became the royal army's arsenal. Richelieu then proceeded to rebuild its fortifications, creating what was considered to be an impregnable stronghold maintained by a large garrison.

The expansion of the ports of Rochefort and La Rochelle, combined with the silting up of the salt marshes, accounted more than any military endeavour for Brouage's decline; her role in the Revolution amounted to the provision of a prison for priests. Today's visitor can wander along the grassy watchpath

Talmont
(CHARENTE-MARITIME)

Clinging to a tiny rocky peninsula to the north of the River Gironde, the minute village of Talmont is surprisingly airy, with gardens and an abundance of hollyhocks cheerfully rambling over the pale grey stone of the cottages and the cobbled lanes. Parking is at the entrance to the village, and once this busy part has been negotiated, the village is surprisingly unspoilt.

At the top of the village lies the Romanesque church of Ste-Radegonde, perched on a promontory surrounded by a little cemetery and exposed to the elements. One part of the nave of this beautiful church was lost to the sea in the 15th century. The foundations have been shored up repeatedly, but it remains under constant threat. Indeed, erosion was responsible for the destruction of much of the original fortified town in Roman times.

Leave your car just outside Talmont and stroll through its little streets unbothered by engine fumes and noise

MANY CULINARY SPECIALITIES OF THE WESTERN FRINGE OF FRANCE ARE, QUITE NATURALLY, ASSOCIATED WITH THE SEA, WHERE THE OYSTER REIGNS SUPREME, AND WITH THE GREAT VINEYARDS OF BORDEAUX, WHERE THE SOIL CONDITIONS AND MILD CLIMATE HAVE FOR CENTURIES PRODUCED THE SUPERB GRAPES THAT ARE TRANSFORMED INTO WINES CONSIDERED BY CONNOISSEUR AND NOVICE ALIKE TO BE THE WORLD'S FINEST. THE DISHES AND SAUCES ENHANCED BY THAT NOBLE INGREDIENT SET THE STANDARD FOR THE REST OF THE CULINARY WORLD.

WHETHER CONSIDERING WINES OR SEAFOOD, OR ANY OTHER SPECIALITIES OF THE ATLANTIC REGION, THE CHOICES IS ENORMOUS AND IT IS BEST TO BE INFORMED, HOWEVER SLIGHTLY. AND AT THE END OF A MAGNIFICENT MEAL, YOU MAY FIND THAT A HEALTHY BANK BALANCE IS JUST AS IMPORTANT!

Bon Appétit

The food and drink of France, in all their diversity, have long been ranked among the best in the world (Francophiles would say they are the best), and within France itself each region has its favoured specialities. Here by the Atlantic coast, the ingredients supplied by land and sea have the advantage of being complemented by the area's world-class wines.

Gifts of the Sea

Shellfish dishes centre on oysters and mussels. For oysters, only a few simple facts need to be taken on board. There are two basic types: the *plate* and the *creuse*. The former, a native European oyster with a flattish, smooth shell, has long been considered a delicacy but is now relatively rare. It can be found in the Marennes, one of the most important oyster-farming regions in France, which lies between the Charente and the Gironde estuaries, where it acquires a greenish tinge from algae in the oyster basins. More common are the longer and fleshier *creuses*, an imported variety, which can be either *fines* (*de claires*) or the larger *spéciales*, which have spent longer being fattened up. Oysters are most likely to be served raw, but may also come stuffed with butter and garlic, deep-fried, or *à la bordelaise*, which means accompanied – improbable though it might seem – by

Fresh seafood, with a baguette and a bottle of wine, makes a meal fit for a king

rather spicy sausages. Mussels are another local speciality, with their production centred round Brouage and the island of Oléron. A speciality of the Charente is *mouclade*, in which mussels are cooked in a sauce of wine, egg yolks and cream (sometimes a drop of Pineau des Charentes is added).

Freshwater fish is plentiful and includes shad, barbel and salmon. A particular Bordeaux delicacy is the eel-like lamprey from the Gironde estuary; it is usually served with leeks, red wine and garlic. (Lamprey requires care in preparation because it possesses a poisonous thread which needs to be extracted.) Baby eels, called *pibales*, come from the same area and are usually served grilled. There are several varieties of fish ragoût: in Poitou, a *chaudrée* might include conger eel and white fish cooked in white wine, shallots and butter; in Charente, the ingredients of a *migourée* will be similar, although they might not include eel.

The Rest of the Menu

The various areas of salt marsh, particularly that near Pauillac in the Médoc, produce fine lamb (*agneau de pré-salé*). Charente snails are known as *cagouilles* and are smaller than their Burgundy cousins. Goat and hare may also appear on menus, usually in a sauce which includes liberal quantities of red wine or Pineau. Game includes wood pigeon and guinea fowl; and *foie gras* is classically served with a glass of sweet white Sauternes.

The Charente is known for the excellent quality of its vegetables, particularly broad beans and the fine white haricot beans known as *mojettes*, often served with butter and cream. Melons, greengages and plums are plentiful here; further south, in the Landes, can be found the *pruneau d'Agen*, a venerable variety of plum grown since the Crusades. A speciality of a small area near Coulon is angelica, used in cakes and creams and also in liqueurs.

Cheeses made from the milk of goats and sheep are produced throughout the region; the sharp *chabichou* from Poitou is justifiably famous. Cream cheeses such as the Caillebote d'Aunis, or the Jonchée from the Stonge area, are often served with sugar and cream.

The Supreme Complement

The vineyards of Bordeaux produce all types of wine: red, dry white and sweet white. They include five great wine areas: the Médoc, the largest area, where the greatest wine châteaux are situated, produces deep red, rich and silky wines redolent of blackcurrants and oak; Graves produces some distinguished white wines; and St-Émilion and Pomerol, attractive settlements on the banks of the Dordogne, produce robust and plummy reds, some with a stature comparable to the best of the Médoc; and Sauternes, famous for its powerful sweet white wines. All around are other wine districts, which offer less famous names but often better value. Here one can spend many pleasurable hours seeking

Take your choice from the two types of creuse *oysters. Above right, enough wine for the keenest thirst*

out small communes in which to taste and buy.

The finest wines are accorded a status of *Appellation d'Origine Contrôlée* (AOC), which covers the area of their origin; there are around 50 in the Bordeaux area. As a rule of thumb, the smaller the area covered by the AOC, the finer the wine. Thus the AOC Margaux (one of the top wine villages) will generally indicate a superior wine to an AOC Médoc (in which area Margaux is situated), which in turn will be more interesting than a basic AOC Bordeaux (which covers the entire region). As with all generalisations, discovering the exceptions makes for happy hunting.

The finest wines have a category of *crus classés* (from *premier* to *cinquième*); below the *crus classés* come the *crus bourgeois*, which can be very high in quality. Information on wine production and vineyards is freely given at the various Maisons du Vin throughout the region. The larger ones such as in Bordeaux or St-Émilion organise wine tours and visits to châteaux.

The classic red-wine grape is the Cabernet Sauvignon, from which the greatest *crus classés* are made. A greater volume of wine, however, is made from the humbler Merlot, which nevertheless attains great heights in the area of Pomerol. The honey-sweet dessert wine of the Sauternes area, quite unlike other sweet white wines, is produced by a kind of rot which attacks grapes grown only in certain areas, producing a highly concentrated juice and wine of incomparable character.

The white wines of the Charente area go largely towards the production of that other great French drink, cognac. The distillation of wine was first practised in the area in the 16th century, and Cognac's early trade was largely sustained by the English and the Dutch, who called the drink *brandewijn*, from which we derive the term 'brandy'. The classification of cognac is according to the length of time it has spent in the cask: from 3-star through VO (Very Old) and VSOP (Very Special Old Pale) to various 'Reserves', which have spent 20 to 40 years maturing. Pineau des Charentes is a fruity fortified aperitif wine, either red or white, which is served very cold. It is also added to sauces and stews.

The Walk

①
To the right of the church as you face it in the place Royale is the former grain market; its stone measure is at the corner of the square. Opposite you will find the 16th-century timbered Maison Malartic, where Henri IV stayed.

②
Near by, in the rue du Café Chantant, is the former Café du Peuple, evoking livelier times in the village's history.

③
Take rue de la Chaussée to the side of the Maison Malartic. The house at number 11, on the corner of an alley, is the oldest house in the village and retains signs of fortifications.

④
At the foot of rue de la Chaussée, turn right into the Route de Betbezer; on the right is the former wash-house.

Above left, the 16th-century house that hosted King Henri IV when he stayed in Labastide

Labastide-d'Armagnac
(LANDES)

The expansive arcades of Labastide's market square so impressed King Henri IV that he resolved to copy them. His son Louis XIII fulfilled the plan in Paris

Despite Labastide's many fine buildings, the village has largely escaped the tourist itinerary, and visitors will probably be able to appreciate its timeless appeal in near solitude. South-west France enjoys a wealth of bastide villages, medieval 'new towns' whose regular grid design incorporated early ideas of town planning. Many are much altered, and many finer examples have had their charms exploited to a degree which leaves little room for any medieval atmosphere.

A rare exception is Labastide-d'Armagnac, which possesses many fine buildings and a remarkable arcaded market square of noble proportions. However, a large number of its houses await restoration, and there are few facilities to divert visitors unless they happen to arrive during one of the annual local festivities.

Brought under English ownership through the dowry of Eleanor of Aquitaine to Henri Plantagenet (the future King Henry II of England), the fortified village was founded in 1291 and its square (place Royale) named in honour of the king. Some time later Henri IV, while staying in the 16th-century timbered building that occupies a corner of the square, resolved to copy the harmonious arcades and despatched his architects to study the design. While Henri's plans were not to come to fruition during his reign, they were realised by his son, Louis XIII. Thus the little village of Labastide became the model for France's most famous and arguably most beautiful square, the place des Vosges in Paris.

Several typical features of a bastide town can be appreciated here, such as the grain measure cut into the stone wall of the former grain market, a covered wash-house, and the practice of leaving a space between buildings at the corners of a square to enable rainwater to drain from roofs to ground-level gutters. In addition, there is a severely harmonious classical château designed by the the architect of the Grand-Théâtre at Bordeaux, a church (16th- to 18th-century) with a particularly impressive *trompe l'oeil*, and a house (still named Café du Peuple) which used to serve as a *café chantant*, featuring songs and music, and whose preserved interior can be glimpsed through the windows.

Coulon
(DEUX-SÈVRES)

Coulon is the capital of the huge area of marshland known as the Marais Poitevin, situated on what was once a large gulf which over the centuries became silted up. Successful attempts at taming the resulting salt-marsh wilderness were made as far back as the 11th century, when drainage channels and canals were created, and continued over the years despite the interruption of wars – most drastically during the conflict between Catholic and Protestants. Under Henri IV the region saw the creation of Dutch-style polders and dykes.

Now the area is enjoying a new prosperity as its subtle charms are sought out by tourists. Shimmering glades of poplar and willow, ash and alder, cut with canals and lazy rivers green with duckweed, characterise the region known as La Venise Verte (Green Venice). Further west is an area of 'dry' marshland, with salt pastures and vegetable crops including the local speciality, plump white haricot beans known as *mojettes*. Near Coulon another relatively rare crop, angelica, is grown for culinary and medicinal use.

The large handsome riverside village of Coulon itself has plenty of boat trips on offer (with or without a guide), pedalo and bicycle hire, a museum covering the history, ecology and customs of the marshlands and its people, and smart cafés and restaurants. It also has many attractive old houses, almost all impeccably restored. The interesting Romanesque church is notable for a rare outside pulpit, from which the preacher would deliver his sermon to boatmen on the canal.

With the help of a guide, the dream-like tranquillity of Coulon's canals can be savoured from a hired punt

In *charcuteries* in the main square, the place de la Coutume (the name recalls the customs taxes levied on passing merchants), you can still find a pâté made from coypu, a large member of the beaver family found in abundance along the waterways. At the museum shop special wicker eel-catching baskets sell for a fairly modest sum.

Tusson
(CHARENTE)

This tiny village does not feature in guide books, and is well off the tourist track as a result. With barely 300 inhabitants, no monument or site of major historic importance, and no feature such as a perched castle or riverside setting to provide a focal point, Tusson would seem to have little appeal for visitors. Yet anyone interested in rural life and architecture, and in restoration techniques, will find this modest hamlet to be an open workshop, where well-informed guides take visitors round the restoration works.

Tusson is, in fact, one of the main workshop sites of the Charente area operated by the Club Marpen, which teaches various restoration techniques through a variety of projects to international groups of students, including many would-be architects. Traditional woodworking, stone-cutting and roofing techniques are practised, in styles appropriate to the age of a particular building, under the direction of master craftsmen. All the workshop sites can be visited, and methods are explained.

In medieval times, Tusson was an important community, with an abbey frequented by the sister of François I. Over the years the village grew in importance, and many fine Renaissance houses bear witness to Tusson's prosperity. In the 19th century, it was a major market centre for the Poitou donkey, a particularly large local variety with a long-haired reddish coat, and became famous for its fairs. At the turn of the century there were some 1,200 inhabitants.

The advent of motor transport and rural depopulation produced an inevitable decline. However, an enterprising council has contributed to a spirit of new optimism. Several houses have already been expertly restored, a number can be rented as *gîtes*, and young site workers inhabit a couple of houses, creating a lively atmosphere. Of two museums, one is devoted to rural life and skills, the other (a 16th-century house used by François I's sister) is furnished in period style and has a medieval garden. Other sights include the remains of the abbey, stained-glass window workshops and 1950 frescoes of the Buffet school in the church.

Other Villages

ARS-EN-RÉ

Just beyond an isthmus at the western end of the populous Île de Ré – its lanes busy with campers and cyclists throughout the summer – lies the attractive port and resort of Ars-en-Ré. At the edge of an area of salt marshes, the village became a salt port, receiving Dutch and Scandinavian ships. Evidence of Ars-en-Ré's former prosperity includes a fine Renaissance town house, but more typical are the neat white cottages with green shutters and specially reduced corners which enabled carriages to negotiate the tight bends of the narrow lanes. In the central square is a fascinating church, whose slender black and white spire served as a landmark for mariners; since 1840, when

The car-free river port of Mornac is an artisans' mecca, with many sorts of crafts

lightning struck it, the spire has leant at a slight angle.

CADILLAC

Cadillac, in the Gironde *département*, forms part of the vineyard region of Côtes de Bordeaux, an area that specialises in sweet dessert wines. The rather sombre medieval bastide town, with houses of creamy white stone, is still partly contained within its 14th-century fortifications. At the heart lies the austerely elegant late 16th-century château of the Duke d'Epernon, who razed the former outdated medieval castle in order to build a luxury dwelling to rival those of the king. The sumptuous edifice took 30 years to complete. Much was destroyed during the Revolution, and the rest fell into disrepair. However, following recent restoration, the remaining building displays rooms of immense grandeur, with exceptionally rich marble fireplaces, and a fine set of 17th-century tapestries woven on site.

FENIOUX

Barely a hamlet, the tiny cluster of buildings which make up this rural village comprises an extraordinarily pretty cream-stone Mairie in a restored private house, a couple of dwellings and, in particular, a fine church and a notable Romanesque Lantern of the Dead – a hollow stone column at the top of which a beacon was lit, its flames symbolising eternal life. The ascent is somewhat claustrophobic, and the 38 steps are steep.

The church dates in part from the 9th century and is remarkable for its exceedingly slim spire. The west front is sculpted in the rich Saintonge style typical of the area.

MORNAC-SUR-SEUDRE

A lively seaside resort atmosphere permeates this tiny little river port at the southern end of the Seudre oyster farms. The narrow little lanes between freshly painted white cottages, bright with flowers and painted shutters, are traffic-free (parking is at the entrance to the village). Summer visitors come to purchase wares from the many artisans who have set up homes and shops in the village, adding to the interest and colour. Studios and shops with silk paintings, fishing-net knits, jewellery or pottery contribute to an enjoyable couple of hours' stroll, complemented by an ample supply of cafés and ice-cream parlours.

SABRES

This small Landes settlement is the access point for the excellent Éco-musée de la Grande Lande, which is reached from here by a former resin-tappers' train. The museum, which covers many hectares, re-creates the life of a rural Landes community of the 19th century in original houses, many of which used to occupy the current site. The aim of the museum is to show how the inhabitants provided for their daily needs, how they adapted to local ecological conditions, and their cultural traditions.

Following the drainage and afforestation of the moors and swamps of the Landes in the 19th century, sheep-breeding gave way to forestry. Inhabitants of the area – landlords, tenant farmers and servants – lived in clearings in the forest. An exhibition building explains the food production chains, while all round are the livestock of the time – including bees, sheep, pigs and hens – and the crops and trees that contributed to the community's self-sufficiency.

Extensions of the museum, covering the resin industry and popular customs and beliefs, are situated in the neighbouring villages of Luxey and Moustey.

ST-AMANT-DE-BOIXE

This very quiet village, with neat suburban villas aligned in quiet tree-lined hillside streets, boasts a very impressive former abbey church 69m long. Having been built and altered over several centuries (mainly 12th to 15th), the interior effectively illustrates the transition of vaulting styles through the years, displaying a domed, early barrel vault, followed by groined and rib vaulting. There are many other points of interest, including capitals and restored 14th-century frescoes which originated in the crypt. A broad flight of steps leads down into the church, which was built on sloping land. Outside are scant remains of the former cloister.

VILLEBOIS-LAVALETTE

This large hilltop village south of Angoulême offers views over pale terracotta roof tiles towards the surrounding countryside, and the remains of its ancient castle – including ramparts, and seven 13th-century towers – built on the site of an *oppidum* (Gallo-Roman stronghold). In the heart of the village is the very fine 17th-century covered market, built on 13th-century foundations. A market is held on Saturday mornings.

VOUVANT

A substantial but quiet village surrounded by woods and farmland, Vouvant looks down over a loop of the River Mère in the Vendée. Of its medieval fortress, all that remains is a ruined 13th-century keep, in front of which lies a broad esplanade shaded by chestnut trees – an excellent spot for a picnic. The village also has a very attractive Romanesque church. The rich sculpture round its main doorway features mythological animals, a semicircle of supporting atlantes, the Last Supper, and a pair of less well-defined sculptures incorporating Samson overcoming a lion and with Delilah.

Berry & Limousin

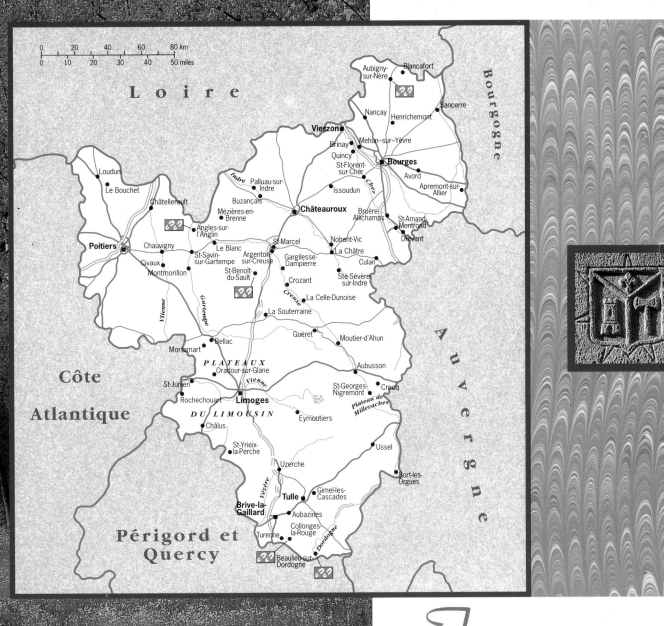

Loire

| Scale |
| 0 20 40 60 80 km |
| 0 10 20 30 40 50 miles |

Bourgogne

Aubigny-sur-Nère
Blancafort
Nançay
Henrichemont
Sancerre
Vierzon
Brinay
Mehun-sur-Yèvre
Quincy
St-Florent-sur-Cher
Bourges
Avord
Apremont-sur-Allier

Loudun
Le Bouchet
Châtellerault
Palluau-sur-Indre
Issoudun
Buzançais
Mézières-en-Brenne
Châteauroux
Bruère-Allichamps
St-Amand-Montrond
Angles-sur-l'Anglin
St-Marcel
Nohant-Vic
Drevant
Poitiers
Chauvigny
Le Blanc
Argenton-sur-Creuse
La Châtre
St-Savin-sur-Gartempe
Gargilesse-Dampierre
Culan
Civaux
St-Benoît-du-Sault
Crozant
Ste-Sévère-sur-Indre
Montmorillon
La Celle-Dunoise
La Souterraine

Côte
Guéret
Moutier-d'Ahun

Atlantique
PLATEAUX
Bellac
Mortemart
Oradour-sur-Glane
Aubusson
St-Junien
St-Georges-Nigremont
Crocq
Rochechouart
Limoges
Plateau de Millevaches
DU LIMOUSIN
Châlus
Eymoutiers
St-Yrieix-la-Perche
Ussel
Uzerche
Bort-les-Orgues
Gimel-les-Cascades
Tulle
Brive-la-Gaillard
Aubazines

Périgord et Quercy
Turenne
Collonges-la-Rouge
Beaulieu-sur-Dordogne

Auvergne

Dordogne
Creuse
Indre
Cher
Vienne
Gartempe
Vézère

France's heartland offers historic
and literary associations and the stillness
appreciated by cyclists and ornithologists.

Aubigny-sur-Nère

(Cher)

A LIVELY MARKET TOWN WITH MANY SPLENDID HALF-TIMBERED HOUSES, AUBIGNY TAKES PRIDE IN ITS CONNECTION WITH THE STUART CLAN. JUDGING FROM THE HIGH STREET, YOU COULD BE IN SCOTLAND.

This delightful and bustling little market town, still much contained within the boundaries of its former ramparts, is of particular interest for its connections with the Scottish House of Stuart, which owned the town for some 200 years. A source of some pride for the local community, this link has resulted in a recent twinning with a Scottish town, the display of Stuart flags and tartans in the summer, and a Franco-Scottish Festival in July.

The earliest traces of Aubigny date back to Gallo-Roman times, when the settlement was called *Albiniacum*. Little more is known until the 12th century, when the town belonged to a chapter of the Abbey of St Martin of Tours. The inhabitants appealed to the king for better protection against neighbouring landowners, and in 1198 his son granted the town Royal Burgh status. He then organised its restructuring, with ramparts, four gateways with drawbridges, round towers about 50m apart, and finally a hilltop castle. All this, however, did not prevent the English from sacking and burning the town twice during the Hundred Years' War.

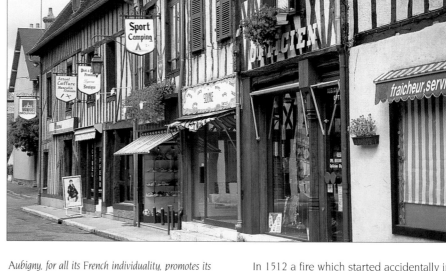

Aubigny, for all its French individuality, promotes its cross-Channel links – look out for a recently acquired British pillar box and traditional telephone box

help in the war against the mutually hated English. Thus began a long period of Scottish involvement in the area, as many other Scots came to settle in Aubigny, setting up important glass and cloth industries. The present-day rue des Foulons (Fullers' Street) refers to these early years, when people trod wool in the river to start the process of 'fulling' it.

In 1512 a fire which started accidentally in the communal baking oven destroyed every house in the village except one. The *seigneur*, Robert Stuart, let the inhabitants use trees from his estates to rebuild their houses, hence many of the half-timbered houses date from this time. The Stuart arms can still be seen on a keystone in the lodge porch of the Stuart castle and on a vault in the church.

In 1672, the town returned back to royal ownership, then was given to the Duchess of Portsmouth, favourite of England's Charles II.

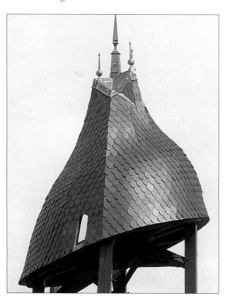

CROSS-CHANNEL CONNECTIONS

In 1423, six years before Joan of Arc started her campaigns, Charles VII gave Aubigny and the surrounding countryside to John Stewart (later Stuart), the Constable of the Scottish army, as an expression of gratitude for his

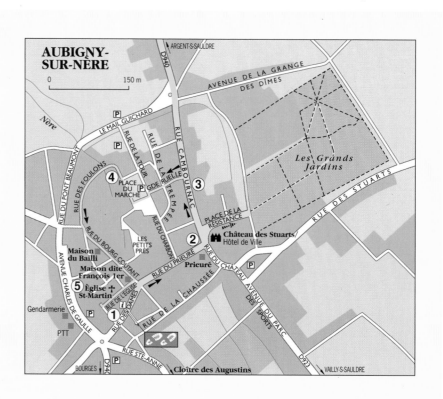

AUBIGNY-SUR-NÈRE

0   150 m

The Walk

❶

Start at the tourist office in rue des Dames. Opposite are 15th- and 16th-century houses with characteristic timbering. Go down the main street, rue du Prieuré.

❷

At the end is a former priory rebuilt in 1758. Just ahead is the Château des Stuarts, with a museum and extensive gardens.

❸

Leaving the castle, cross to the left and take rue Cambournac, Several houses here are imposing mansions with wide coaching doorways. Turn left into Grande Ruelle, leading to place du Marché.

❹

Take rue des Foulons in the corner of place du Marché, which crosses the River Nère. Number 10, just to the right, is a fine 15th-century house, sole survivor of the fire of 1512; the slate pattern of the gable identifies the trade of a former owner. Opposite is Maison du Bailli; carved decoration here includes the initials of Robert and Anne Stuart.

❺

Ahead, at the corner of rue du Bourg Coutant and rue de l'Église, is one of Aubigny's finest houses, the recently restored early 16th-century Maison dite François 1er. To the right is the Église St-Martin.

ⓘ

▷ Length of walk: About 800m (plus castle gardens)
▷ Approximate time: 1 hour
▷ Terrain: Flat, generally on pavements
▷ Parking: Near church, or several other places, including place du Marché (except Saturday)
▷ Open: Tourist office, rue des Dames (May to September); other months in Hôtel de Ville: hours 9–noon, 2–6
▷ Refreshments: Cafés, restaurants

Fit for a duchess: Aubigny was given to the Duchess of Portsmouth by Louis XVI

Thus Aubigny became the possession of the English Richmond family until 1841, when the Duke of Richmond sold all the remaining lands and the pretty summer castle of La Verrerie, 10km away.

AUBIGNY TODAY

Many of Aubigny's slate-roofed houses display their timber construction, and in various patterns: square, barred (like a rural gate) or, on the most luxurious houses, lozenge (diamond shaped). The most common pattern combines vertical, horizontal and diagonal struts (St Andrew's cross). In a little alley linking rue de la Trempée and rue Cambournac, there is an example of straw-and-clay cob, which was plastered on to wooden laths.

The Solonge's architectural style can also be seen in the Cloître des Augustins, a former monastery founded by the so-called Black Augustinians, 400m south of the town centre. This 17th-century building (used for concerts and other events) features the characteristic blend of stone and rosy pink brick.

Little remains of the Château des Stuarts, which now houses municipal offices and two museums, one celebrating 'The Auld Alliance' between France and Scotland. Exhibits trace the town's development and the family trees of the Stuarts and Richmonds, and there is a collection of tartans. Behind the castle are pleasant formal gardens and an arboretum.

Angles-sur-l'Anglin *(Vienne)*

WITH ALL THE INGREDIENTS FOR A PICTURE POSTCARD – BOLD CASTLE RUINS OVERLOOKING A MEANDERING RIVER THICK WITH REEDS AND WATER LILIES, MILL WHEEL, DOVECOTES, ROWS OF POPLARS – ANGLES CANNOT FAIL TO PLEASE.

Angles-sur-l'Anglin occupies a splendid position on and around cliffs along the little River Anglin. Creamy-brown houses, their steep roofs covered with flat brown tiles, present a harmonious aspect when seen from across the stone bridge leading to the village.

Angles proudly proclaims itself a 'Village Fleuri' and is duly filled with flowers – in window boxes, tubs, and adorning the lawns edging the castle. Steep cobbled lanes link the two parts of the village, the Ville Basse

Green and golden: leaf and stone contrast to create Angles' appeal, while cliffs and river add drama

and the Ville Haute, while the road takes a more sweeping approach. It is barely provided with pavements along the lower part, as houses huddle alongside. The rocks leading to the former bastion of La Huche-Corne are carved with rough boot-shaped steps to facilitate the climb, but there is also a gentler path leading down from ramparts to the river. With views at every turn and pleasing old houses all round, Angles is well worth a stroll and provides several shady picnic spots, including the ramparts at the edge of the Champ de Foire or along the riverside.

THE FIRST ANGLAIS

To the south of Angles, there is evidence of prehistoric occupation, and Magdalenian rock paintings have been found in a cavern. The village itself was first settled by a branch of the Germanic Angles tribe who, along with the Saxons and the Jutes, arrived in England (Angleterre) around the 5th century. Those who came to this part of France probably took up residence on the banks of the Anglin, a tributary of the Gartempe, in the 9th century, and gave the settlement their name. To this day the inhabitants are called 'les Anglais' ('the English').

The ample remains of Angles' medieval stronghold, high on a rocky outcrop above the river, bear witness to the domination of the château over the surrounding territory. Towers, high walls and the flight of stairs carved out of the rock from the riverside during the Hundred Years War evoke more troubled times, and a guided tour includes tales of a long siege. Yet, in common with other fortresses of the time, the stronghold was abandoned in the 18th century and used as a stone quarry. There are fine views of it from the bridge over the River Anglin, from the Jardin de la Poste near the church of St-Martin, and from the former bastion known as La Huche-Corne at the edge of the Champ de Foire, now a large grassy space fringed by horse-chestnut trees.

On the other side of the river from the château is the Chapelle Ste-Croix, the remains of an 11th-century monastery, surrounded by ancient houses built on the site of the former abbey buildings.

Angles was the birthplace, in 1421, of one of France's most infamous characters, Cardinal Balue. This ambitious man rose from a modest background to become Chaplain to the King, Secretary of State, and finally Cardinal. To him are attributed the cruel wood-and-iron cages, barely bigger than a

man, in which prisoners were kept in dungeons like the one at the castle of Loches. As fate would have it, the Cardinal himself was incarcerated in one for eight years, on the orders of Louis XI. He was eventually set free, and continued his life in Rome. A house at the junction of rue du Château and La Cueille is presumed to be Balue's birthplace.

LOCAL CRAFT REVIVED

Angles has a very special local craft: drawn-thread embroidery, known as *les jours d'angles*. With its origins in the 19th century, the technique involves using tiny, finely pointed scissors to cut and draw out regular patterns of thread from an even-weave textile, and then very precise embroidery on and around the gaps created. The continuity of this labour-intensive and highly skilled activity is being encouraged by the help of an association devoted to education and promotion.

A workshop where you can watch the intricate processs being carried out and buy the finished items, made from silk, linen and cotton, is situated in a house on rue du Pont (in winter the location changes to the Groupe Scolaire building in rue Blancoise). Plainly the prices reflect the woman-hours devoted to this specialised craft; a single item on display here represents as much as 537 hours of intricate work.

The village organises several events throughout the summer, including craft and book fairs, and a firework display.

The gentle pace of village life means there is always time for conversation with a friend

The Walk

Start at the Champ de Foire. From the belvedere there are views over the river and towards the château. Take the narrow rue de l'Église to the left, passing the church.

A short way past the church, turn right into the narrow, steep and stony La Cueille. Turn right at the bottom, into rue du Pont. Halfway down on the right is the Atelier des Jours d'Angles (embroidery workshop).

Continue down to the bridge and cross the river to the Chapelle Ste-Croix.

4

Retrace your steps back over the bridge and up rue du Pont. Take rue du Château to the right, past the château; then turn left into rue du Four, which climbs back up to the upper town. At the top, go into the square (la Place), turn left and take the little alley that cuts under the second storey of some houses (l'Arceau). Go to the right of the church, into rue St-Jean, which passes the Mairie. Then turn left to return to the Champ de Foire.

> **i**

> ▷ Length of walk: about 1km
> ▷ Approximate time: 1 hour, plus visit to workshop
> ▷ Terrain: Some steep streets; one (La Cueille) is stony and cobbled
> ▷ Parking: In the Champ de Foire (free)
> ▷ Open: Tourist office: July to September daily, 10–12:30 and 2:30–6
> ▷ Refreshments: Café and hotel/restaurant near tourist office

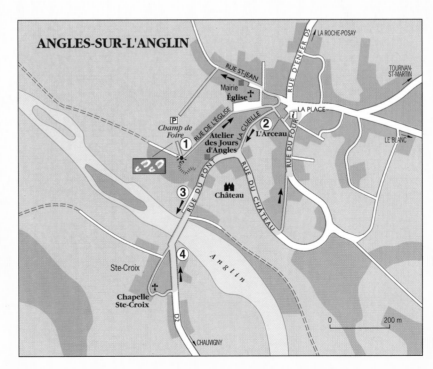

Beaulieu-sur-Dordogne *(Corrèze)*

NAMED **B**ELLUS **L**OCUS (**B**EAUTIFUL **P**LACE) BY **A**RCH-BISHOP **R**ODOLPHE OF **T**URENNE BECAUSE OF ITS EXCEPTIONAL LOCATION ON THE **R**IVER **D**ORDOGNE, THIS MEDIEVAL TOWN HAS A SPLEN-DID ABBEY AND FINE **R**ENAISSANCE HOUSES.

It was in the 9th century that Archbishop Rodolphe of Turenne became enchanted with this 'beautiful place', at a gracious curve in the river where the two regions of Quercy and Corrèze meet. Deciding that it would make a perfect setting for monastic life, he founded an abbey, which became the home of Benedictine monks. The monks managed to survive the Wars of Religion but they were driven out during the Revolution, leaving only a few crumbling walls of their monastery.

A 'beautiful place' indeed: the riverbank, above, magnetises those with time for a book, a stroll or a picnic. Church carvings, left, flow with movement

However, the beautiful abbey remains and today serves as Beaulieu's parish church (Église St-Pierre), focal point of the village and the finest example of Romanesque ecclesiastical architecture in Corrèze.

LESSONS IN STONE

The original monastery was built in 850 by monks from Cluny to shelter pilgrims, and soon developed into an important centre of pilgrimage. The existing building, however, bears witness to the wealth and splendour of the 12th century. Its most notable feature is the magnificent tympanum (porch carving), which boasts some of the finest sculptures in south-west France, carried out in 1125 by craftsmen of the Toulouse School.

Above the doorway, the Last Judgement is represented in great detail. On the pillars below are a series of demonic characters including the seven-headed Beast of the Apocalypse, the grotesqueness of its appearance further enhanced by the weathering of the stone. Other carved scenes, such as the Temptation of Christ and Daniel in the Lions' Den, can be clearly identified.

The interior of the abbey is equally impressive, with its lofty nave, barrel vaulting and precious medieval carved figure of the Virgin overlaid with silver. Although Beaulieu is no longer an important pilgrimage destination, it still celebrates the Feast of Holy Relics during the first weekend of September.

The town itself is carefully designed. Despite lying on the main road between Tulle and Bretenoux, the route actually skirts the town centre, passing a line of shops, cafés and restaurants, following what was once part of the inner defensive wall. This wall is today marked by a boulevard which encircles the attractive old town, with a spider's-web pattern of little lanes and alleys leading to the medieval heart of the town and the great Benedictine abbey.

Many of the finest houses in Beaulieu are in the immediate vicinity of the abbey and date from the Renaissance, constructed in mellow pink and grey granite and decorated with ornamental windows and turrets. Perhaps the most decorative is the Maison d'Adam et Ève. Once a rest house closely associated with the monastery, its façade is finely adorned with columns, medallions and magnificent statues representing the king and queen, the sun and the moon and, of course, Adam and Ève at the moment of temptation. Another gem of the town, the pretty 12th-century Chapelle des Pénitents right on the river's edge, has been converted into a quaint local museum.

RIVER OF CHANGE

Down by the river, it is easy to understand the Archbishop's enthusiasm for the surrounding countryside. It is here at the border between the *départements* of Corrèze and Lot that the Dordogne changes character. Following 60km of fast-flowing torrents through narrow gorges, the river widens at Beaulieu and becomes calmer.

Although Beaulieu is more of a town than a village, the river gives it a serene atmosphere more typical of the small villages in Corrèze. Often referred to as 'the Limousin Riviera' owing to its mild climate and rich vegetation of darkly wooded rolling hills,

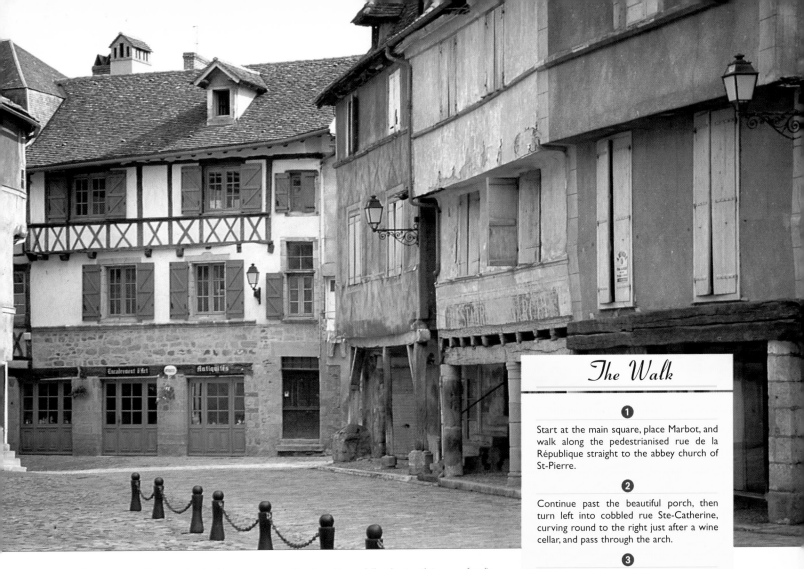

1

Start at the main square, place Marbot, and walk along the pedestrianised rue de la République straight to the abbey church of St-Pierre.

2

Continue past the beautiful porch, then turn left into cobbled rue Ste-Catherine, curving round to the right just after a wine cellar, and pass through the arch.

3

Turn left and follow the boulevard Rodolphe de Turenne round, entering a small alleyway on the right. Follow 'Passerelle des Aubarèdes', between two high walls, and at rue des Estrémouillères fork right into rue des Aubarèdes alongside the cemetery. Continue until you reach the river and turn left along the riverside path. Go past the chapel and slipway, and continue a short distance along the quai Faugères.

4

Turn left up a narrow side alley next to the road sign, then left again behind the riverside houses. Return towards the chapel.

5

Go right at the road junction and fork right into rue de la Chapelle. Continue straight on through an arch and bear right round past the Maison d'Adam et Ève and a statue of the Virgin Mary to the abbey entrance. Return past the statue to the main road and turn left back towards place Marbot.

Beaulieu is a popular spot for bathing, camping and sightseeing.

Beaulieu was once a major inland port, and many of the riverside buildings, graced with wooden balconies, are particularly splendid. The goods unloaded along the ancient quayside were then ferried to the surrounding uplands by gaily decorated pack

Growing old gracefully, showing their age or benefiting from a facelift – Beaulieu's ancient buildings have their own personalities, and authentic character

ponies. Strolling along the riverbank on a sunny tranquil afternoon, one can imagine their hooves clattering over the cobbles and through the nearby woodlands.

| i |

▷ Length of walk: 1.5km
▷ Approximate time: 45 minutes
▷ Terrain: All surfaced and suitable for wheelchairs and pushchairs
▷ Parking: Free at the main square
▷ Refreshments: Cafés, bars and restaurants

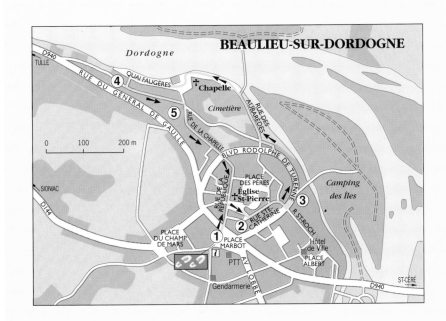

BEAULIEU-SUR-DORDOGNE

Apremont-sur-Allier
(CHER)

Apremont, just west of Nevers, possesses exceptional beauty: golden-stone houses capped with russet roofs, flowers rambling up walls and along lanes, a willow-fringed river and, surveying the scene, a turreted castle. Despite the beauty of this village and its surroundings, Apremont remains unspoilt and uncrowded – like a film set waiting to be discovered – and its shady riverside benches,

quiet even in the high season, offer an ideal location for a picnic.

The château, on the site of an ancient fortress, was already somewhat delapidated by the 15th century, according to a charter dated 1467; it was rebuilt and five of its towers, with ramparts and machicolations, were restored. In 1722 the château was acquired by Louis de Béthune, whose descendants occupy it to this day. Some parts – notably the stables, in which there is a fine carriage museum – can be visited during the afternoon in high season.

One of the more recent members of the family was responsible for much of the restoration work undertaken in the village. In 1894, after marrying one of the descendants of Béthune (Antoinette de Rafelis-St-Sauveur), Eugène Schneider devoted his life to improving and renovating the buildings and the estate. His wife continued this work until her death in 1969.

In the 1930s the couple took on the task of restoring the village houses. They demolished any that did not fit in with the site, and in their place built new ones in the traditional

The Walk

1

Park at the church and walk towards the centre and castle.

2

In the village on the right is the entrance to Parc Floral. Take a flower-covered path to the right; at the top, curve left and go uphill for views over the village and towards the castle. Follow paths along the waterfall, wander round the lakes and finally descend to a small café.

3

Next to the café, outside Parc Floral, is a former covered wash-house. Take the road down towards the river, past Maison des Mariniers, and turn left along the river road, which has plenty of parking areas and willow-shaded benches.

4

The river road joins the main village street just north of the church. Turn left to return to the church car park.

medieval Berry style, in harmony with the others. Carved door lintels testify to the age of many of the buildings; the oldest is the 15th-century Maison des Mariniers, which guarded the entrance to the old river port.

The glory of Apremont, however, lies not only in its wonderfully picturesque houses but in its Parc Floral, created since 1970 in the 'English' style, inspired by Vita Sackville-West's gardens at Sissinghurst in Kent. In a glorious setting of ponds, waterfalls, fine trees, arbours and lush lawns (which, visitors are reminded, are there to be walked on), are herbaceous borders in subtle hues, rambling roses and wisteria, and decorative follies including a 'Chinese' bridge and a 'Turkish' pavilion in the centre of a lake. This wonderful park is well worth a leisurely visit.

Sun-baked walls and rich red roofs: Apremont's cottages are fringed with fragrant, multicoloured borders, climbing roses and tumbling windowbox blooms, a combination of exceptional beauty

Gallo-Roman era, the museum examines early settlers' influence on this area. There are good collections of objects found during the excavations; one item, a domestic altar unique in Gaul, was found at the site in 1986.

Part of St-Marcel's later history can be gleaned from the church. Begun in the 11th century and finished in the 15th, it once formed part of a Benedictine priory. The exterior culminates in a substantial shingle-

Left, cyclists take a kerbside break by a Sancerre pâtisserie. Below, the ancient church at St-Marcel

Sancerre
(CHER)

This well-preserved (if somewhat over-gentrified) and peaceful village perched at the top of the highest hill in the region has earned much of its reputation from the quality of its dry white wines and its steep limestone-and-clay-based vineyards. The village, which borders on the Burgundy region north of Nevers, also produces a delicious and creamy goats' cheese, called Crottin de Chèvre, to accompany its wine.

The village has not always been so tranquil. In 1534, during the Hundred Years' War, Sancerre was a Huguenot stronghold which surrendered to the attacking Catholics only after seven months of siege, when driven to near starvation. Local lore has it that the villagers were reduced to eating leather and pulverised slate to survive.

Today the tradition of wine-making dominates the culture of Sancerre, whose wealth is clearly connected to its oenological success. Wine-tasting and direct purchasing from the growers are prevalent in Sancerre, and the smaller growers are particularly pleased to present the fruits of their more intimate vineyards to international visitors.

Apart from the wine tour, the town needs exploring on foot to negotiate the steep, narrow streets where parking space is scarce. The tall red-roofed house, formerly owned by the public notary and now occupied at weekends by Parisians, is a prime example of the village's lasting appeal. The Tour de Fiefs, visible for miles, is the last remaining vestige of Sancerre's château. The unforgettable

view from the top of the village, from the blind back side of the hill out over the meandering Loire Valley, makes this fashionable hideout a rare delight.

St-Marcel
(INDRE)

This unpretentious village, now virtually a suburb of the lower town of Argenton-sur-Creuse, was once the main settlement from which the latter grew. For this was the site of the Gallo-Roman *Argentomagus*, a name which may have come from 'silver market'.

St-Marcel has been the subject of very extensive archaeological excavations, and some of this famed site can be seen by wandering round the hillside next to the large car park. Explanatory display panels identify the various parts of the town and give background information.

It is well worth visiting the large new museum, whose popularity has seemingly not affected the quiet little community. As well as giving substantial information on the

covered bell tower. Inside are some very fine early 16th-century choir stalls, and the crypt houses remnants of the tomb of St Marcellinus. The few remains of St-Marcel's ramparts have been incorporated into houses (look for signs of arrow slits).

St-Benoît-du-Sault *(Indre)*

ST-BENOÎT-DU-SAULT SEEMS TO AWAIT A FAIRY GODMOTHER TO WAKEN IT FROM A LONG SLUMBER. THOSE WHO PREFER THE PICTURESQUE DECAY OF TIME-RAVAGED VILLAGES TO PRISTINE RESTORATION SHOULD HASTEN TO VISIT IT NOW.

Situated in unremarkable countryside between the plunging gorges of the multi-dammed Creuse and the flat marshes and lakes of the Brenne, St-Benoît-du-Sault lies in the very centre of France, undiscovered and unspoilt. In many ways it is typical of those deeply rural areas which are well off the tourist track, far from the major conurbations and efficiently bypassed by main roads and motorways – in this case the A20, which lies a mere 8km away.

The area round St-Benoît is mainly devoted to agriculture. It is neither rich in sights nor particularly scenic, and it has little industry to offer employment opportunities. Economic decline has inevitably resulted, and regeneration can be achieved only by attracting new inhabitants and new investment. In the local tourist

The face of St-Benoît tells simply of the centuries it has seen, while the local population, like the farmer below left, get on with their traditional rural lives

brochure, the council affirms its ambition to welcome more visitors, and announces tentatively that it hopes some will come to live.

A GRACEFUL DECLINE

Yet St-Benoît-du-Sault lags behind many of its less well-endowed rival communities, who have made more aggressive attempts to attract both tourists and new residents with thoughtful restoration and conservation projects. The village is still in a state of crum-

bling disrepair: many of its ancient houses are little more than piles of stones, its gardens are overgrown, and no cheerful window-boxes or pots of red flowers brighten up the browny-grey walls of the houses or adorn the squares.

For many, this state of affairs is a positive attraction. Here one can escape the tourist hordes, see a piece of rural France as it has looked unchanged for centuries, and contemplate the purchase of some appealing ruin at an affordable price. Some will see the lack of

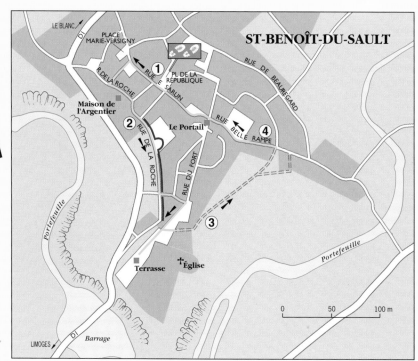

ST-BENOÎT-DU-SAULT

The Walk

1

Start in the place de la République in the heart of the village. Go up rue Émile Sarun to the tiny place Marie-Versigny, then turn left and left again into the rue de la Roche, with the 15th-century Maison de l'Argentier on the right.

2

Continue down rue de la Roche (also called rue des Guichets) towards the church at the southern end of the village, finally taking an alleyway to the left up to rue du Fort. There is fine view from the *terrasse* in front of the Romanesque church.

3

To the north side of the church, a little path skirts the outside of the former ramparts, offering views of the Roman bridge lying to the east.

4

At the end of the path, take the steep rue Bellerampe to the left. Go up past the old gateway, le Portail, back into rue Émile Sarun, which leads to place de la République. The lane through the Portail, rue du Fort, is lined with many old houses and leads down to the church.

ℹ

▷ Length of walk: About 700
▷ Approximate time: 45 minutes
▷ Terrain: Gently hilly lanes leading up into the village centre. No rough sections
▷ Parking: Relatively easy within the village centre
▷ Refreshments: Basic cafés only

tourist paraphernalia, even the absence of flowers, as a refreshing change from the often too-pretty similar perched villages, which rather unnecessarily proclaim themselves *Villages Fleuris*.

Some signs of new life are nevertheless appearing in St-Benoît. A couple of artisans have taken up residence and display their wares; one, a silk painter, offers bed-and-breakfast (*chambres d'hôtes*) in the tower above one of the ancient gateways. Meanwhile, despite its size, St-Benoît manages to support three *boulangeries/pâtisseries*, a shop selling hand-made chocolates, two butchers and a *charcuterie*. Surely evidence enough that all is not lost in rural France.

FROM BENEDICTINES TO BARONS

High on a granite promontory within a loop of the River Portefeuille, St-Benoît-du-Sault grew on the site of the Gallo-Roman settlement of Salis, round the Benedictine abbey which was founded here in the 10th century. By then, the Benedictine order had established itself throughout the land and began to have a profound influence on the society of the Dark Ages.

Medieval abbeys tended to be very wealthy institutions: taking in monks of aristocratic birth, they were generally lavishly endowed by noble patrons. The disciplined and literate monks played a pioneering role in agriculture, clearing forests, draining marshes, converting brushwood into arable land, creating hedges, banks and ditches,

and planting vines. They managed large estates, developed markets for their surplus produce, and earned tithes and income from tenants. St Benedict had declared that 'idleness is the enemy of the soul' and – in the early days at least – the monks were indeed rarely idle.

The gradual decline of the monasteries after the 14th century tilted the balance of power towards the feudal barons. St-Benoît was a fiefdom of the lords of Brosse (whose ruined castle, destroyed by the English during the Hundred Years War, lies about 10km to the south-west). Protected by a double set of ramparts pierced by five fortified gateways, St-Benoît became a prosperous little town, as can be seen from the remains of its richly ornamented houses built during the 15th and 16th centuries.

AN AGREEABLE AMBLE

Today, St-Benoît repays a quiet amble round its cobbled lanes and alleys, down to the so-called Roman bridge over the Portefeuille, or over the dam built just below the former priory. There are fine views of the village from the far side of the lake which has been formed by the dam and, conversely, good views of the lake from the priory terrace by the largely Romanesque church. From the rampart walk you look over rambling gardens filled with hollyhocks and untamed vines, down to the meandering Creuse.

For the present at least, St-Benoît is keeping its age-old identity unadorned – the essence of its appeal

Collonges-la-Rouge *(Corrèze)*

IN ALL OF FRANCE THERE IS NO OTHER VILLAGE QUITE THE COLOUR OF THIS ONE. BUILT ALMOST ENTIRELY OF DEEP PURPLE-RED SANDSTONE, THIS SMALL VILLAGE POSITIVELY GLOWS IN THE SUNLIGHT.

There is no denying that the 'Ruby of Bas-Limousin' is a real gem, fully deserving its classification as a historic site and one of the most beautiful villages in France. The tranquil lanes of this enchanting village reveal that little has changed over the centuries. Tucked round every corner are miniature châteaux and manor houses adorned with wisteria and climbing vines, each one set in immaculately tended gardens, with attractive courtyards and terraces shaded by stately walnut and chestnut trees.

Rouge and rose colour a covered passageway, left, through one of the little streets that curve and dip between delightful houses like the one above. Though small, Collonges has long welcomed strangers, as it was on a pilgrimage route to Santiago de Compostela

Many of the officers of the Viscounty of Corrèze had their summer residences in Collonges. One of the most exquisite is the 16th-century home of Gédéon de Vassignac, lord of Collonges: straight out of a fairy tale, it is laden with gables, towers and miniature pepper-pot turrets.

At the lower end of the village stands the Château de Benge – a twin-turreted manor house with a striking Renaissance window, set against a backdrop of poplars and walnuts – which once belonged to an influential *vigneron* in Corrèze.

The architecture of Collonges reflects building styles from all three surrounding areas: the flat grey-tiled roofs are typical of Limoges; the *pigeonniers* are Quercynois; and some houses have *bolets*, small roofed galleries typical of the Périgord region, used for drying chestnuts, maize and tobacco.

The most dominant feature of the village is a Romanesque church, built on the site of a Benedictine priory, with a handsome Limousin belfry and a powerful battlemented keep which towers proudly over the village.

PAST TIMES, PRESENT PLEASURES

'Collonges the Red' has managed to remain relatively unspoilt by tourism thanks to its distance from the Dordogne, and has retained a unique traditional atmosphere.

The communal oven is near the market square, together with the long-handled paddle used in the baking process. Some of the villagers still remember bringing their loaves and pastries here on baking day.

Another ancient feature, prominent on many of the arched doorways and entrances, is the carving of symbols on the keystones, sometimes a heart, a star or simply some initials and a date. Le Vieux Porche, a most interesting and original shop, reproduces these arched red sandstone doorways in miniature as ornaments.

The entrance to the Castel de Maussac in the village has a particularly splendid embellishment: a scallop shell or *coquille St-Jacques* which, together with the Hôtel de St-Jacques-de-Compostelle, recalls the fact that Collonges-la-Rouge was once a stopping place for pilgrims travelling along the famous route to the hugely popular shrine of St James the Apostle at Santiago de Compostela in northern Spain.

The Walk

 1

Start at the tourist office situated on the D38. Go down rue de la Barrière past the Musée des Arts et Traditions Populaires at the Maison de la Sirène (Mermaid's House) and the Hôtel St-Jacques de Compostelle and under an arch.

 2

Fork right and continue downhill past the *crêperie* to the 16th-century Château de Benge. Go back through the arch, turn right at the twin-towered Maison des Ramade de Friac, through a series of arches and under the wooden covered Halle to the church.

 3

Continue past the church, leaving it to your left, down past Castel de Vassinhac in the rue de la Garde and straight on to the Musée Vivant de l'Oie.

 4

With the entrance to the museum behind you, go straight ahead up a narrow lane to the Castel de Maussac. Turn immediately left, continuing to the Manoir de Beauvirie. Turn left again and wind through the oldest part of Collonges.

 5

Turn left at the sign to the Galerie Vigreyos towards the former Chapelle des Pénitents (today a museum) and the main square.

 6

Turn right and leave the square through the arch by the *auberge*. Turn right and return uphill to the tourist office.

ℹ

▷ Length of walk: 1.5km.
▷ Approximate time: 1 hour
▷ Terrain: All surfaced and suitable for wheelchairs and pushchairs
▷ Parking: Free at the tourist office
▷ Open: Goose Museum: Easter to Oct
▷ Refreshments: Cafés, bars and restaurants

GEESE AND GOOD FOOD

Collonges is the unlikely venue for a rather unusual museum. The Musée Vivant de l'Oie at the Ferme de la Veyrie is home to over 70 species of geese from round the world, waddling about in open grassy paddocks. The small museum documents the creatures since prehistoric times, while the shop displays ancient culinary traditions and sells goose-liver pâté and other delectations

The village has several of its own specialities too: violet mustard, made from an ancient recipe using black mustard seeds and unfermented; *vin de noix* (walnut wine), tasting like a nutty port wine, drunk cold with a slice of frozen orange; and wafer-thin walnut biscuits, called *les lauzes aux noix*, made with nuts, egg whites and walnut liqueur.

The roofscape, right, is full of interest; below, geese galore greet you at a rather surprising museum

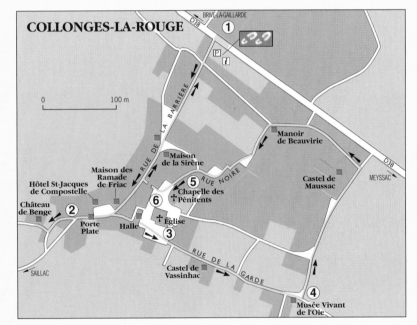

The Walk

❶

A pleasant short walk can be enjoyed by taking a path to the right of the castle/tourist office (as you face it), which curves round behind the little lake.

❷

The lakeside path joins a small road which leads down to the church. After visiting it, turn left into the road leading back to the village centre.

❸

Turn right into the village square, and then turn left at the far end. A little street to the left leads back to the castle.

Mortemart's small covered market, above, and the old refectory with its grazing sheep, right. Opposite, George Sand entertained a cultural galaxy, including Chopin, Flaubert and Balzac, at her house in Nohant

Mortemart
(HAUTE-VIENNE)

This pretty little community is situated on the Monts de Blond, one of the well-watered Limousin plateaux, lush with pastures, hedges and forests of oak, beech and chestnut. The village of Mortemart grew up round a castle first built in 995, and for centuries the home of the Mortemart family. Its most famous member was probably Madame de Montespan, a favourite of Louis XIV, the Sun King. In 1330, no fewer than three religious establishments were founded here by a native of the village, Cardinal Pierre Gauvain: a hospital administered by the Carmelite order, a college directed by Augustinians, and a Carthusian monastery. A few of the former monastery buildings survive, austere and harmonious in creeper-covered pale grey stone. The part next to the chapel houses an exhibition hall and administrative offices surrounding an internal garden.

The 14th-century monastery chapel, topped by a strange bell-shaped belfry covered in slate, now serves as the parish church. It has a very fine set of 15th-century oak choir stalls, with splendid misericords depicting strange animals, demons and various vices. There are also a baroque retable and a gilt lectern from the same period.

There are very few remains of the former fortress castle, which was dismantled by Cardinal Richelieu. The little that still stood was roofed and restored, and now houses the tourist office. It enjoys a picturesque site beside a little lake in the heart of the village.

The village square is a large, partly cobbled area with a café and a particularly fine 17th-century covered market. All is spruce and neat, and bright with flowers.

Moutier d'Ahun
(CREUSE)

On the upper stretch of the River Creuse, before its turbulent descent through the tight gorges between Fresselines and Argenton, this delightful and peaceful little village enjoys a beautiful setting amidst wooded hills. The ivy-covered browny-grey houses, roofed with brown tiles, merge into the background, and the gentle sweep of the river is enhanced by a fine old bridge.

Dominating the village is the beautiful church, which includes the remains of a former abbey church (virtually destroyed by the English during the Hundred Years' War) and of a subsequent church which was also badly damaged during the Wars of Religion. What remains is partly Romanesque – including the elegant rectangular belfry – and partly Gothic. The west doorway is particularly decorative, carved with lively characters.

The glory of Moutier's church, however, is to be found inside. Monks in the late 17th century commissioned an Auvergnat sculptor by the name of Simon Bauer to produce a set of carved stalls and panelling, and the result is a supreme example of the woodcarver's artistry, which completely covers the walls of the chancel and apse. The carvings are extraordinarily rich in detail: animals and lush vegetation, cherubs and monsters, twisting columns and branches of trees, and lions supporting the lectern with their paws.

Outside the church the village square is shaded by venerable plane trees. There are almost no shops in Moutier, and only a solitary artisan's exhibition diverts visitors from quiet contemplation.

Left, a fine example of intricate woodcarving in the church of Moutier d'Ahun, by the 17th-century sculptor Simon Bauer

Nohant-Vic
(INDRE)

Few places evoke the past as atmospherically as the hamlet of Nohant-Vic, the home of Aurore Dupin Amandine, better known as the writer George Sand. Here, in her grandmother's house, the young Aurore spent most of her childhood and adolescence. Throughout her active career, she continued to return in times of trouble to the quiet Berry countryside that she loved so dearly. Finally she left Paris altogether and came to live again at Nohant, spending the last 30 years of her life in good works, thus earning the title 'The Good Woman of Nohant'.

The Château de Nohant, maintained as a museum devoted to George Sand, remains as it was in her day. You can see her study, desk, and bedroom full of memorabilia, and the dining table set ready to receive her guests – Chopin, Liszt, Balzac, Flaubert, Delacroix , Dumas, Turgenev – who would all gather here and entertain each other. You can also visit the little theatre where she enacted her plays, and the puppet theatre created by her son Maurice.

Nohant still stages versions of George Sand's novels and plays, as well as hosting Chopin recitals. The annual end-of-July fair, with traditional local musicians, would have met with her approval, for Sand bemoaned the vanishing rural customs and decline of medieval ceremonies that were still flourishing at the time of her childhood.

In front of the château is the musty, tiny grey 11th-century church, with its rustic brown-tiled porch, which George Sand attended. In need of restoration, it is still full of charm. Her grave is in the village cemetery.

There are only a few other houses and a small café arranged round the grassy elm-shaded clearing which serves as the village square. If you can manage to arrive here before the hordes of literary pilgrims, you will be able to savour the peaceful atmosphere that more genuinely evokes the spirit of her writing.

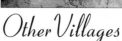

Other Villages

BLANCAFORT

This tiny village of nearly a thousand people rests on the banks of the Sauldre on the Route Jacques-Coeur 23km from Gien. Blancafort possesses a highly original bell tower and a pink-brick château which is fully furnished and inhabited. But its most fascinating attraction is situated on the D8, heading towards Concressault. The Musée de la Sorcellerie specialises in the supernatural, magic and the imaginary life of human fantasy. Be prepared to meet Merlin, dragons and strange forms without heads or hands called *birettes* (typical of Berry, a region known for witchcraft and mysticism).

LE BOUCHET

In the heart of the Brenne marshland – an area of swamp, peat bog, heathland and over a thousand lakes – lies Le Bouchet, headquarters of the Brenne Regional Park. Its 166,000ha provide a home for more than 250 species of bird, 30 species of dragonfly, thousands of European pond tortoises and wild boar, and 35 species of orchids. The lakes are rich in carp, tench, roach, pike and zander, and are fished from October to March.

Le Bouchet's well-restored houses are mostly built of red sandstone quarried from local hillocks. One serves as the Regional Park Centre, an exhibi-

Classic country life: living close to the soil and enjoying its fruits

tion centre with craft displays and excellent videos on the flora, fauna and culture of the area (English available). A little medieval fortress peeps through trees across the Mer Rouge.

CROCQ

On the vast granite Plateau de Millevaches, from which rise several major rivers (including the Creuse, the Vienne, and the Vézère), Crocq is a pleasant and substantial village gathered at the foot of the remaining towers of its medieval fortress. You can follow the path of its former ramparts (Chemin de Ronde) and trace the sites of its former gateways (marked on a display map). Next to the tourist office, in the Chapelle de la Visitation in rue de la Chapelle, is displayed a particularly interesting early 16th-century triptych, painted in rich colours on oak and walnut wood, depicting the life of St Eloi.

CROZANT

The medieval castle of Crozant was one of the largest and most powerful fortresses in central France, its ramparts, interspersed with 10 tall towers, extending to more than a kilometre. Today only the ruins enjoy the spectacular situation high on a rocky promontory above the confluence of the Creuse and Sedelle. You can scramble over the ruins (entrance tickets from the Hôtel des Ruines at their foot) or search for the best viewpoint from the river below. Boat trips are available on the reservoir to the north side of the fortress.

Crozant village, high to the south of the site, is a modest and old-fashioned little walking resort. An early Touring Club de France sign on the corner of the church warns motorists of the 'Descente Rapide/Tournants Brusques' before the road descends – not that alarmingly – to the castle and river.

DREVANT

On the southern outskirts of the market town of St-Amand-Montrond, the little community of Drevant is determined to make the most of its possessions, and the few streets – not particularly ancient or with houses of architectural note – are smartened up by lines of bright marigolds. But Drevant's houses are not what you come to see. Instead, turn right

towards the canal to discover some fine Gallo-Roman ruins: of a theatre, a forum, public baths and temple. On high season afternoons (except Monday and Tuesday) you can go round them for free; at other times, you will have to be content with looking at them from behind a fence. A path has been created along the Canal du Berry, which was dug between 1810 and 1840, and extends for 271km.

GARGILESSE-DAMPIERRE

The charms of the very scenic stretch of the leafy River Creuse upstream from Argenton-sur-Creuse were famously discovered in the last century by George Sand and a coterie of writers and artists, including Théodore Rousseau and Claude Monet, and Gargilesse is one of its most delightful villages. Gargilesse is hardly less attractive than when George Sand came to stay in the little cottage, now owned by her granddaughter, in the heart of the village. The brown-tiled roofs and creamy-brown houses, the small 18th-century castle (the original building was destroyed in 1650), the Romanesque church with fine frescoes in the large crypt, and walks in the surrounding woods and vales are much the same as when she described them in her book *Promenade Autour d'un Village*. Gargilesse has a Sunday market in season and, at the end of August, a music festival featuring the harp.

GIMEL-LES-CASCADES

This small village, lying 12km north-east of Tulle, boasts the highest waterfalls in the Limousin. The three falls have a total drop of nearly 153m into a gorge aptly named the Inferno. Perched high above them in a dramatic setting is the ruined Romanesque church of St-Étienne-de-Braguse. Other sights in the village include the ruined château and a 15th-century church built in typical Limousin style. Nearby Lac Ruffaud offers a refreshing dip and a shady retreat for picnics.

NANÇAY

Set in the flat, wooded marshland of the Sologne, sparkling with ponds and lakes and dotted with low brick cottages, Nançay is a typical village of the area, with a pretty hotel, a couple of cafés and antique shops, and an excellent

bakery selling the local *sablés* biscuits. Much of it is built in the characteristic and appealing pink brick and timber in criss-cross patterns. Nançay also has the archetypal little château of one's dreams, in similar style but with additional pointed turrets and decorative machicolations. Unfortunately this is closed to visitors, who must content themselves with peering through the fence. However, some restored stables and farm buildings near by serve as a striking modern art gallery with changing exhibitions, open to the public at weekends.

PALLUAU-SUR-INDRE

Sleepy Palluau is a large but very quiet village set above the right bank of the gentle poplar- and willow-lined Indre. It is dominated by its large castle set in a fine park, whichr sits on top of ancient tufa quarries that have long been colonised by bats. The keep dates from the 11th century. The village church, a former collegiate church, is currently closed for restoration. A small Romanesque church, which has been incorporated into a group of private houses, can be visited in rue Basse (the tourist office has the key). The shops are few, and there is little to do here except wander by the river or go fishing (apply to the Café-Tabac in rue Basse).

STE-SÉVÈRE-SUR-INDRE

This little town has a large, attractive, partly cobbled market square, with a fine 17th-century market hall. It is well worth visiting on market day (Wednesday morning), when the cafés fill and there is a lively bustle. A ruined keep looks down over tree-covered slopes to the River Indre below.

TURENNE

This 'small town with a great past' is named after the Turenne family, who for many generations remained independent of the Crown. The 'Great Turenne', born in 1611, was the first member of this family to regard himself as French. An earlier family celebrity was Maria, one of the best-known troubadours of the 13th century. The Tour de César, the oldest building, and a red-stone clock tower are all that remain of a once mighty castle destroyed in the Revolution. The rest of the village tumbles down the hillside, creamy stone houses hidden behind Virginia creeper and geraniums, with steep grey-slate roofs and turrets.

The Auvergne

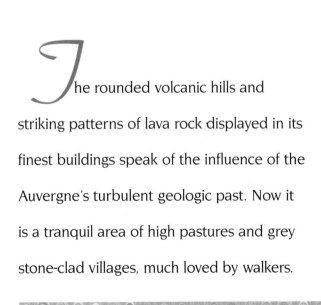

The rounded volcanic hills and striking patterns of lava rock displayed in its finest buildings speak of the influence of the Auvergne's turbulent geologic past. Now it is a tranquil area of high pastures and grey stone-clad villages, much loved by walkers.

Salers

(Cantal)

BUILT OF DARK GREY LAVA BUT FAR FROM BLEAK, THE PIC-TURESQUE HOUSES AND STEEP-ROOFED MAN-SIONS OF THIS LITTLE HILL TOWN DRAW LARGE NUMBERS OF APPRECIATIVE VISITORS BOTH IN AND OUT OF SEASON.

A perfect fortified hilltop village of tall, sombre grey and black volcanic-stone mansions with pepper-pot turrets and steep stone roofs, Salers draws summer visitors like bees to a honey pot. But despite the certain lack of solitude in any walk round the village, the place is well worth a tourist pilgrimage.

Salers drew visitors as early as the 18th century, when the town's annual festival understandably gained notoriety after a generous but misguided benefactor inaugurated

A carving of extraordinary expressiveness, showing the Entombment, graces the church at Salers

the custom of dispensing free wine from the village fountains. The number of merry-makers multiplied, but so – predictably – did public disorder, and the custom was finally discontinued. Today's visitors may be more sober, but are no less appreciative of Salers' more enduring charms.

FAME AND FORTUNE

Salers' period of prosperity began at the end of the 15th century, when it became the seat of the regional bailiwick. Prestigious families, who provided the judges, settled here and built their turreted mansions, several of which remain to this day.

Buildings to visit include the former Bailiff's Court (Bailliage), with a splendid Renaissance fireplace; the 15th-century Maison des Templiers, housing a small museum of typical interiors and traditional cheese-making techniques; and the Maison des Bargues, with two 17th-century wood-panelled bedrooms and a fine courtyard.

Other mansions and houses whose exteriors merit a look include the house of President Pierre Lizet just inside the Belfry Gate (Porte du Beffroi); the Hôtel de Ville and the Maison de Flojeac, in the Grande-Place; the Maison Lacombe, just off the Grande-Place in rue de la Martille; the Hôtel de la Ronade in rue des Nobles, off the Grande-Place; and the Maison Bertrandy in the Avenue de Barrouze.

Roof tiles of hand-hewn stone mottled with lichen have an almost lifelike quality as they cover, fish-scale fashion, the slopes and angles of Salers' housetops

A MODERN MOUNTAIN INDUSTRY

In the 19th century a man by the name of Tyssandier d'Escous, immortalised by a monument in the main square, devoted himself to improving the local cattle stock, and the resulting 'Salers' breed was a great success. To this day its milk is the basis for much of the area's cheese. A sturdy beast with a curly reddish coat, the Salers has hooves well suited to long, wet treks at high altitude, and a constitution that adapts to wide variations in temperature. In addition, Salers cows produce an average of one calf a year.

In days gone by, cheese was made by individual cowherds in low stone-roofed huts high up on the summer pastures. But today the life of a cowherd, isolated with his herd for up to five months at a time, is increasingly a thing of the past. Changed, too, are the age-old implements and homely setting of cheese-making. Tight regulations now limit or prohibit the use of wood, for instance, or the presence of an uncovered earth floor. Modern production methods for 'farmhouse' cheeses still incorporate many of the old processes and designs, but the implements are more likely to be stainless steel.

Despite the almost total decline of individual cheese makers up on the summer pastures, small-scale producers are still numerous, and their cheeses are highly regarded. A Salers de Fermier cheese is well worth seeking out if you like the taste of the more commonly found Cantal.

ROOFSCAPES OF CHARACTER

The appeal of French village roofscapes is undeniable, whether they be the rosy ridges of terracotta pantiles glowing in a southern sun, or the hand-hewn stone slabs, glistening in the rain, which signal a mountain location.

Salers is an excellent place in which to study the latter kind of roof in all its glory, for every one has been beautifully restored using the rough stone tiles known as *lauzes*. Extra interest is provided by the marriage of decorative architecture, more common to Renaissance châteaux with Salers' essentially simple, rural style of roofing. Thus, dainty turrets and dormer windows are topped with chunky slices of rock, hand-tailored to fit curve or point.

The Salers *lauzes* are made of schist and arranged like fish scales, diminishing in size towards the top ridge. The weight of a *lauzes* roof requires a strong support structure, usually made of oak. In former times, the *lauzes* were secured with wooden pegs; now these are more likely to be zinc. *Lauzes* are still hewn by hand, and continuing restoration work throughout the Auvergne has provided this ancient craft with a welcome boost.

Looking down on life: a couple of men are amused by what they see going on below in the place Tyssandier

The Walk

 1

Park just off the D680, then take rue Notre Dame to Église St-Matthieu (mainly 15th-century, with a 12th-century porch). Take rue du Beffroi which climbs gently to the Tour de l'Horloge. Turn left after the gate into the Grande-Place, otherwise known as place Tyssandier-d'Escous.

 2

In the square are the Bailliage (bailiwick, guided visits) and several fine mansions.

 3

South of the square, take rue des Nobles; on the right is the interesting Hôtel de la Ronade, with a five-storey tower.

 4

Return to the square and turn left into rue des Templiers; the Maison des Templiers can be visited.

 5

At the end of rue des Templiers, turn left along Avenue de Barrouze. From a shady esplanade at the end you can view the Maronne Valley across to Puy Violent.

 6

Go back along Avenue de Barrouze towards Porte de la Martille. On the right, at the junction with rue de la Martille, is the Maison Bertrandy. Follow rue de la Martille back to Grande-Place.

i

▷ Length of walk: about 1km
▷ Approximate time: 1 hour (plus visits)
▷ Terrain: Fairly gentle with some cobbled streets
▷ Parking: Behind the church, off the D35 and D680
▷ Open: Tourist office: daily from May to mid-October; Bailliage; Maison des Templiers; Maison des Bargues

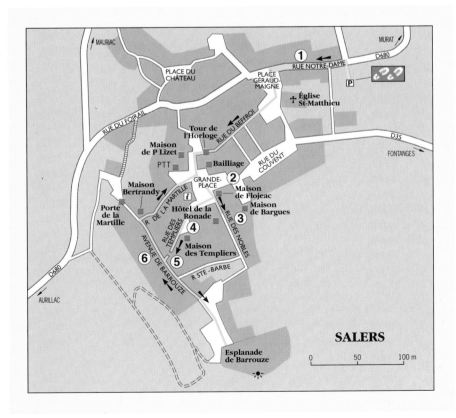

SALERS

0   50   100 m

Usson

(Puy-de-Dôme)

THIS SMALL HAMLET OF LAVA-STONE HOUSES AND ARTISTS' WORKSHOPS, MEMORABLY SET ON A BEAUTIFUL HILL AMIDST LUSH GARDENS AND GENTLE PATHS, IS A FAR CRY FROM THE RUGGED TERRAIN FURTHER SOUTH AND WEST

High on a solitary volcanic mound which looks out over the fertile Limagne plain to the west of the Monts du Livradois, Usson betrays little of its past. The few rough grey and black basalt houses, surprisingly roofed with rosy pantiles which evoke more southern climes, hardly constitute a village. Indeed, the community is scattered over the hillside amidst grassy paths, trees and rocks.

A PAGE FROM HISTORY

The history of Usson is inextricably linked with that of one person: Marguerite de Valois, otherwise known as La Reine Margot, a tragic figure born in the middle of the 16th century. For 60 years she was intimately involved in many of the religious and power struggles of the age, yet her place in most history books is generally confined to a footnote, emphasising her role as a pawn in the hands of more powerful players.

Marguerite was the sixth surviving child of Henri II and Catherine de Médicis. Her father, with whom she had almost no contact, died when she was six. Her brother, François II, became king and died barely a year later. Another brother, Charles IX, ascended the throne at the age of 10 and died at 23.

The young princess, attended by typical pomp and circumstance, moved constantly between the châteaux of Blois, Amboise, Chenonceaux, Montceaux, Fontainebleau, St-Germain-en-Laye and Orléans. At 11, she embarked with her mother and brother Charles on a two-year 5,000km tour round the country, accompanied by several thousand courtiers, servants, guards, government ministers, doctors, scribes and animals.

The 16th century was a very troubled time for France, with religious wars between Huguenots (Protestants) and Catholics, political intrigues and the problems of succession. In an attempt to stem the tide of continuing civil wars, the scheming Catherine de Médicis arranged for the 19-year-old Marguerite to marry the Huguenot figurehead, Henri of Navarre. However, just after the nuptial ceremony, 2,000 Huguenots were killed in Paris.

A prominent hill behind Usson, where tourists can follow the salamander, below, on a self-guiding walk

Civil war flared again and Marguerite was caught in the middle, mistrusted by both Catholics and Huguenots.

OBJECT OF CONTEMPT

Throughout her whole life, Marguerite remained in awe and fear of her power-hungry and intrigue-addicted mother, whose final gesture was to disinherit her daughter. Neither was Marguerite's marriage a success: her husband showed little inclination for fidelity and treated her with contempt. Marguerite meanwhile became the object of hate and suspicion for her brother, Henri III. After a succession of so-called scandals, he imprisoned her in 1587 in the impregnable fortress of Usson.

Marguerite, whose husband became Henri IV after she had been at Usson for three years, created a veritable court at her Auvergnat outpost, attracting writers, poets and musicians. She amassed a substantial library, wrote her memoirs and other works, and led a generally happy life here – despite having to limit her servants to a mere 90, owing to dire straits following decades of high spending. She did not leave her prison until 1605, following protracted negotiations, on the annulment of her marriage.

With a reasonable settlement agreed, Marguerite and Henri achieved a state of reconciliation. Eventually she returned to Paris and had a busy old age acting as a friendly 'aunt' to the young Dauphin, Henri's child by his new queen, Marie de Médicis.

Below, the Queen of Heaven and the Infant Jesus, Who blesses and provides for the world, watch over the village, below right, from the peak of the hill

Usson's formidable fortress existed for only a little longer than its former royal 'captive'. In 1633 it was demolished by Cardinal Richelieu, as were almost all the other fortified castles in the area. Nothing remains.

VILLAGE OF ARTISANS

Today, Usson is a beautiful and peaceful haven which has attracted a number of artisans. The small 15th- and 16th-century church and the few houses have been restored, the paths cleared and flowers planted. A suggested walk through the village and up the hill is plotted on a map at the village entrance; made of enamel on volcanic stone, this is the work of a village craftsman whose studio can be visited. The walk is way-marked by enamalled signs depicting a salamander, the emblem of François I, Marguerite's grandfather, and Marguerite herself. While climbing the hill, note the striking columns of basalt rock called *orgues*, formed millions of years ago by lava flows.

Crowning the summit is a large statue of the Virgin, over a hundred years old. More enamel orientation tables set out the various peaks and mountain ranges visible in the distance, including the Monts Dore, the Puy de Sancy, the Monts du Forez and the Livradois. On the plain below, the former vineyards (destroyed by phylloxera in the last century) have given way to a gentle green and gold patchwork of pastures and crops.

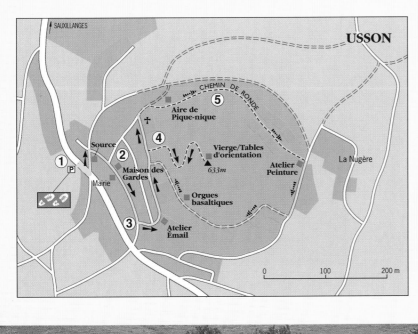

The Walk

1

From the foot of the village, by the little parking area, take the road uphill on the left, passing the *source* (village spring) which served the community until 1970. The road then curves to the right.

2

Pass the Maison des Gardes on the left (probably built with stones from the ruined château). Continue along, curving left.

3

Bear left at the junction; on the right is the Atelier Émail (enamel workshop). Continue uphill to the church.

4

At the church turn right, passing the war memorial, then take the path up the hill to reach a couple of viewpoints, with benches, and orientation tables at the top.

5

An alternative path (mostly gentle and grassy) at the church encircles the hill, following the former ramparts (Chemin de Ronde) and passing an Atelier Peinture (artist's studio). Once round the hill, the path passes a picnic area and car park, returning to the church.

i

▷ Length of walk: About 1.5km, plus 800m for Chemin de Ronde
▷ Approximate time: 1½ hours, including stops, plus another hour for Chemin de Ronde
▷ Terrain: Reasonable paths but quite steep in places
▷ Parking: At the foot of the village or behind the church
▷ Open: Church: afternoons only
▷ Refreshments: Cafés, picnic area

THE STUNNING LANDSCAPE THAT IS NOW THE AUVERGNE WAS FASHIONED BY TUMULTUOUS UPHEAVALS WHICH TOOK PLACE MILLIONS OF YEARS AGO, WHEN HUNDREDS OF VOLCANOES ERUPTED, SPEWING OUT ROCKS, LAVA AND ASH. RIVERS WERE BLOCKED, DAMMED OR DIVERTED, VALLEYS AND, CAVES CARVED OUT AND THE EARTH PUSHED INTO PRECIPICES OR SLOPES. THE AUVERGNE, STILL ERUPTING WHEN MAN FIRST SETTLED IN THE ROCK SHELTERS OF THE DORDOGNE, NEVERTHELESS PROVED HOSPITABLE: BAMBOO GREW ON THE VOLCANIC ASH, AND RHINOCEROS, ELEPHANTS AND TIGERS ROAMED THE SLOPES. THE ICE AGE LATER ADDED ITS OWN CREATIVE IMPULSE TO THE CONTOURS OF THE LAND. LATER STILL, WHEN ALL HAD CALMED AND PEOPLE BEGAN TO SETTLE IN THE AUVERGNE, THEY FOUND THE LANDSCAPE MUCH AS WE SEE IT TODAY.

A Land Before Time

The volcanoes of the Auvergne, all long extinct, fall into four groups. The youngest in geological terms (a mere 2 million years old) are the Monts Dômes, a series of over a hundred little cones rising less than 600m above a rock plateau scarred with long black lava flows. To the south are the Monts Dore, the remnants of three mighty volcanic cones, whose turbulent career of glaciation and erosion has resulted in a dramatic landscape of craters, lakes, great boulders, rock prisms and steep escarpments. To the south-east, Montgerbier-de-Jonc, in the Monts du Vivarais, includes every variety of volcanic shape and various types of lava – bluish-black basalt, black labradorite and pale grey phonolith.

The gentler Monts du Cantal, by contrast, are not in fact separate volcanoes but part of a single whole: the enormous Cantal volcano, which in its time reached a height of over 3,000m and whose lava spread out over an area of almost 4,000sq km. Because this area suffered a greater degree of erosion than the others, the result was a series of sloping plateaux with valleys radiating from the volcanic centre.

The volcanic matter thrown up by the explosive eruptions has contributed to the productivity of the Auvergne soil. For instance, the basalt lava on the Cantal plateaux (called *planèzes*) has produced a high-quality pasture, which in turn is converted by grazing

animals into the area's long-famous mountain cheeses. On the lower plains, known as *limagnes*, decomposed lava and volcanic ash formed a fertile dark brown soil on which tobacco, wheat, fruit and sugar beet were grown with success. In the bottom of some of the volcanic craters there are peat bogs, while the Mézenc massif boasts a wonderfully rich flora, including some species unique to the Massif Central.

Vistas Vast and Various

For the visitor, the volcanoes of the Auvergne offer some superb walking, with the opportunity of reaching mountain summits without too much equipment or difficulty (most are under 2,000m). Some heights are accessible – or nearly so – by car, and offer wide panoramas over a fascinating cratered landscape quite unlike any other.

The most popular peak is the Puy de Dôme, at 1,465m. Reached by a toll road, it has the remains of a Roman temple, a television transmitter, an information centre and a shuttle bus to the summit. Clearly, this is not the place to come for undisturbed contemplation of the fine views, as shown by the illustration here.

Two other worthy sites are less visited. The first is the beautiful, extraordinary Puy de Pariou, with restricted access because it lies within a military training zone. It is, in fact, two volcanoes with concentric craters. The second is the Puy de la Vache, reached by way of a path along the boulder-strewn lava flow (the Cheire d'Aydat) whose action created the Lac d'Aydat by closing off the Veyre Valley. There are two main areas where this type of black and rocky lava flow – now covered by juniper and pine trees – can be seen: here (south of the Puy de la Vache), and north-west of the Puy de Côme (the Chaire de Côme).

Bizarre Shapes, Beautiful Lakes

The highest peak in the Monts Dore range is the Puy de Sancy at a height of 1,885m, reached by a cable car. In the north of this range can be seen some other typical volcanic phenomena formed by the contrac-

Above, poppy fields in the Puy de Dôme against a backdrop of lush hillside. Left, tourists line the route on the popular and leisurely climb up the Puy de Sancy

tion of lava as it cools – in particular the spectacular Roche de Tuilière, once the chimney of a volcano, which displays a superb arrangement of pale grey trachite rock gathered in column prisms. A similar contraction in basalt lava results in tight linen-fold columns called *orgues*; this is found particularly at Bort-les-Orgues, where the columns stretch over 1.5km, and in Murat. Smaller outcrops can be found in many other places in the region, including Usson (see pages 136–7).

The mountains of the Cantal volcano are beautiful and various in shape. The highest is the Plomb du Cantal at 1,855m, accessible by cable car or by path from Super-Lioran. There are several fine drives in this area, over high passes, in particular the Pas de Peyrol, and along splendid narrow valleys split by gorges. One of the finest peaks is the Puy Mary, looking out over high pastures scattered with shepherds' huts, in which until very recently the inhabitants made cheese by hand every day.

The massif of the Mézenc is more rural than the other three areas, and figures less frequently on the tourist itinerary. Mont Mézenc itself is an extremely beautiful mountain, reached by either of two reasonably easy footpaths (from the access roads, about an hour there and back). The massif is particularly attractive in June, when narcissi carpet the ground. A feature of the Auvergne volcano country is its many lakes, sometimes set in craters, sometimes created by lava flows damming upstream waters or blocking valleys. Another characteristic is the abundance of thermal or mineral-rich springs, their purity enhanced by filtration through deep layers of volcanic rock. Some waters are bottled, some form the basis of curative treatments in the many spas that dot the area – mainly developed since the 19th century, although some go back to Roman times.

The hard volcanic rock of the Auvergne has long been valued as a building material, lending the man-made structures here a unique richness of colour. Golden arkose (a kind of sandstone) or pale grey granite is mixed with black basalt in Romanesque churches throughout the region to memorable effect. Large chunks of lava stone went into the building of formidable medieval castles, which after their demolition served in turn as quarries for humbler abodes. The solidity of the lava and its ability to take enamelling at high temperatures have resulted in a local industry of plaque- and sign-making, for both practical and decorative use. In the latter form, enamelled lava can be seen enhancing many resort streets. Sometimes, the crafted lava takes the form of orientation tables on mountain-tops – a fitting destiny.

The village of Le Puy, below, is dwarfed by the imposing basalt tower in its midst, one of several in the Auvergne region. Inset right, dramatic orgues, *or organ pipes, basalt lava formations, seen here on a path to the summit at Usson in the Puy de Dôme*

Blesle
(HAUTE-LOIRE)

In a narrow, wooded valley south-west of the Alagnon gorges, this large stone-built village was once the site of a powerful Benedictine abbey run by wealthy noblewomen. The Benedictine abbey at Blesle was an entirely independent institution, reporting directly to the pope. The nuns, who were not confined to the cloister, all occupied their own houses round the central courtyard, and the abbess was, in effect, the ruler of the village.

Blesle's abbesses were finally obliged to surrender power to the Barons of Mercoeur, who occupied the neighbouring fortress, of which only the square keep remains. Of the abbey buildings, only the church of St-Pierre, a 14th-century house and the house of the last abbess (now the town hall) escaped destruction, although the church lost its belfry in the Revolution, and the nearby former parish church lost all except its belfry. Blesle has consequently become known as 'the village with a church without a belfry, and a belfry without church'.

The Walk

From place de l'Église, take the path through the abbey building to the left of the church doorway, which leads into place de la Mairie.

Turn right out of the square, through place du Vallat, into Avenue du Vallat, which skirts the remains of the ramparts. Turn right and follow the road down to the junction with the D8 (about 100m).

Turn right into rue du Portail Neuf (a sign indicates 'Bourg Ancien'). Number 10 has a very old door edged with a vine. Go into place du Breuil, turn left into rue du Puits St-Joseph, then immediately turn right. Cross rue des Houlles and go into rue de la Vachonne. A house at the end has a fine Romanesque window.

Take rue des Houlles left, then turn left into rue du Portail Neuf with a keep on the left and the Musée de la Coiffe further on.

Turn back and go left into place des 4 Chemins, then place aux Sabots, which follows the ramparts past timbered houses being restored. Cross the bridge, then turn right into tiny rue St-Esprit, leading to a 14th-century belfry. Rejoin rue du Portail Neuf and go left back to place de l'Église.

The splendid, sturdy-looking Maison de Madame Borange in the village of Blesle, where abbesses once ruled the community

The rough, dark volcanic stone of the village buildings is enlivened with a weath of interesting detail. There are 15th- and 16th-century houses with carved timbers and doorways, a house with a Romanesque window, remains of the former ramparts and towers, the 17th-century turret and doorway of an old hospice (part of which now houses a hat and bonnet museum), as well as the Barons' keep and the 14th-century belfry of St-Martin. The Romanesque abbey church has a beautiful wooden door and sumptuous carvings on capitals and window arches.

The streets and little squares within the former ramparts are huddled close together, and houses are still being restored. The place has a bustling atmosphere, with some busy shops and a couple of modest hotels and cafés. The tourist office can suggest 2- to 3-hour walks in the vicinity, taking in the woods around Blesle or the volcanic basalt columns known as *orgues* to the east of the village.

In Montpeyroux, Madonna and Child surmount a double arch, left. Above, village coat of arms

Lavaudieu
(HAUTE-LOIRE)

In this rural hamlet, houses crumble gently, barns are open to the elements, hens roam in the bumpy square and dogs sleep in the sun. The single café and neighbouring restaurant do good business in the absence of competition, and all the sights are closed at lunch.

And sights there are, of particular interest to those whose taste is for Romanesque architecture. Lavaudieu was the site of a Benedictine abbey, founded in the 11th century. While relatively little of the original complex still stands, what remains is very fine and has been well restored. There is a golden-pink abbey church with 14th-century frescoes depicting New Testament scenes, including Christ carrying the Cross, the Crucifixion and a fascinating allegory of the Black Death. The cloisters have single and double columns in a variety of shapes with richly carved capitals. The refectory has a large 12th-century mural of the Virgin Mary in Majesty.

Near the abbey buildings, a former baker's house is now a museum of local crafts and traditions. Displays include clog-making and lace-making.

In high season, all the sights are covered on a guided tour. Out of season, the guide may be located at the house next to the abbey – except, of course, at lunchtime.

Montpeyroux
(PUY-DE-DÔME)

This small fortified village, just off the Clermont-Ferrand/Issoire motorway, sits on a high mound of golden sandstone from which it derives its name (mont pierreux) and from whose quarries it was built. For centuries Montpeyroux belonged to the powerful Auvergne family of La Tour, from which Queen Catherine de Médicis was descended.

The village was surrounded by oval-shaped fortifications; much of the 40m keep remains today. Note the small holes in its wall, set in a spiral pattern. These held the wooden scaffolding which grew with the tower itself; on completion, the empty holes provided light for the internal stairway.

Over the centuries, the villagers' main livelihood, apart from quarrying, was wine-making – until phylloxera ravaged their vineyards. Most of the houses were of a design known as 'vine-growers' houses'; sadly, only one example remains intact today. Built close together, sometimes linked by an arch, they had an exterior staircase shaded by an extension of the roof, under whose tiles cheeses were matured, and a ground-floor fermentation room with an arched fretwork door for air circulation.

With the demise of the wine industry and the closure of the quarries in 1935, Montpeyroux suffered typical rural decline, with a serious loss of population (down to 262 in 1982) and dilapidation of its dwellings. Thankfully, the 1950s saw the arrival of an architect determined to tackle restoration projects. Since then, much excellent renovation has been achieved.

The village of Montpeyroux is well worth a visit. In addition to the original keep, there is a fine 14th-century gate, several small towers and many beautiful old houses. All is spruce and well cared for, with newly cobbled alleyways and an abundance of flowers.

houses (one housing the local museum); two medieval gateways, one (the Porte d'Orient) a bastion, the other serving as a watchtower and belfry; an 18th-century covered market and a fine stone well 27m deep. In the centre of the village is a remarkable circular courtyard surrounded by curving houses, generally dating from the 13th to the 15th century, whose history is something of a mystery This so-called Cour des Dames may once have been the site of a wooden keep.

X marks the spot on a crumbling Charroux façade, left. Below, a 17th-century bas-relief of St John the Baptist at the moment of martyrdom and a statue of St Anne and the young Virgin Mary stand out from the shadows in Tournemire's Romanesque church

Charroux
(ALLIER)

The ancient fortified town of Charroux flourished in the Middle Ages. Two orders of knights contributed to its wealth, administering large tracts of land comprising pastures, vineyards and woodlands. In the Middle Ages, Charroux formed part of the territory of the Bourbon family, one of the most powerful in the land, which was to produce no fewer than eight Kings of France. The city flourished under wise administration and was occupied by two orders of knights, including the important Knights Templar. A population of some 3,000 people included merchants, artisans, soldiers and lawyers.

Despite the incorporation of the Bourbon principality into the French state in 1531, and the later dissolution of the monastic orders, Charroux fought against decline. In 1831 there were still 1,731 inhabitants, but other factors took their toll, and the former town is now no more than a large village, which was in a ruinous state only 30 years ago. Since the early 1970s, however, substantial restoration work has revitalised the village, and the residents are determined to protect and preserve their heritage (unlike the local council of 1959, who set about destroying all the buildings of the former convent and sold off the Renaissance fireplaces).

Today a walk round the village takes in the fortified 12th-century church, which once formed part of the town walls; a fine 15th-century timbered house in the corner of which was placed a lantern (an early form of public lighting); several beautiful stone

The Walk

1

From the church of St-Jean Baptiste, turn right, then right again into rue de l'Horloge, passing a fine example of a timbered house on your right.

2

Turn left into rue de la Poulaillerie; pass the public well. On the right are the Musée de Charroux, a shop selling local mustards and nut oils, and a fine house said to have been inhabited by the Prince de Condé. At the foot of this street is another interesting house facing you, just to the right, in rue de l'Auditoire.

3

To your right is the Porte d'Orient, from which inhabitants dropped rocks, boiling water and oil on to invaders. Turn up rue de l'Auditoire, then take one of the alleys left towards rue de l'Ancienne Mairie, then take another alley into the Cour des Dames.

4

To the south of the Cour, take a covered passageway past the Maison des Consuls back to rue de l'Horloge. On your right is the Porte d'Occident and belfry.

5

From the south side of the church, you can take a circular route round what was the dry moat. Take rue Moirnat and then rue Grande, pass the place d'Armes and follow rue des Fosses and finally rue du Pavillon back to your starting point.

The Auvergne

Tournemire
(CANTAL)

In the glaciated landscape of rocks and boulders which typifies the western edge of the Cantal volcano, near the spectacular crest road that links Salers with Aurillac, the little village of Tournemire is inseparable from its neighbour, the Château d'Anjony, which shares the promontory surveying the Doire Valley below. Yet the two families who owned them, Anjony and Tournemire, were far from neighbourly. Fierce rivalry over the centuries resulted in a bloody vendetta, which ceased only when the Tournemires left their territory in the 17th century.

The Anjony family is still in residence, and their château is one of the finest in the area. Built in the 15th century by one of Joan of Arc's companions on the instructions of Charles VII, its deep-red exterior has a central keep and four immensely tall flanking towers. A wing was added in the 18th century to provide a more comfortable standard of living. A guided tour reveals several points of interest, in particular some vivid 16th-century frescoes in the Knights' Hall depicting members of the Anjony family and romantic legends. There is some fine furniture, tapestries and objets d'art.

The village of Tournemire itself now offers little competition to its former rival, apart from a small Romanesque church and grey volcanic-stone houses with steep slate or *lauzes* roofs. There are a couple of cafés, gardens tumbling down the hill, and the sound of scrabbling hens to punctuate the silence. The local tourist office (in neighbouring St-Cernin) can suggest some waymarked walks; one encircling Tournemire is 10km long and takes about 3 hours.

Orcival
(PUY-DE-DÔME)

Tightly huddled in a narrow wooded valley, the utterly grey village of Orcival – built of volcanic stone and covered with roofs of slate – is totally dominated by its extraordinary Romanesque basilica, at once grey and forbidding, but also of beautiful, harmonious lines, a result of the fact that it was built almost without interruption. Only the spire no longer has its original aspect, having been partly destroyed during the Revolution.

Inside the basilica are tall and slender pillars, a wealth of carved capitals depicting strange beasts and demons, and a variety of styles of vaulting. Near the entrance is a collection of prisoners' shackles, offered to the Virgin as thanksgiving on their release. At first the church seems dark inside, but on approaching the chancel, one is aware of more light suffusing the interior. In the crypt there is a modern altar and a 14th-century wooden statue.

Orcival is one of the Auvergne's pilgrimage centres. On Ascension Thursday, which falls 40 days after Easter, large crowds gather

The verdant valley enclosing Orcival sets off the beautiful basilica and the white cross on the hillside

to venerate the Virgin Enthroned, her statue decorated with silver and gilt. At other times, Orcival is hardly less busy, with cars vying for the few spaces in the cramped car park beside the church.

Just north of Orcival lies the delightful restored Château de Cordes, a fortified manor house with gardens designed by Le Nôtre.

Other Villages

ARLEMPDES

This tiny village occupies a quite extraordinary site on a rocky spur overlooking the young Loire, as it winds and carves its way north towards Le Puy. Surrounded by basalt lava flows and built of volcanic rock, the ruined castle (guided tours only) at the very top of the village commands exceptional views. In the cobbled village itself there are a couple of cafés and a simple *auberge*, but little else. Parking is available in fields outside the village, and a lane leads down to a pleasant riverside picnic and swimming spot from which you can enjoy even more views of the perched castle.

CARLAT

This village offers yet another ruined castle on a basalt lava flow, but there the similarities with Arlempdes end. There is free access to the flat, wide rock high above the village (up a small rock stairway known as the Escalier de la Reine), where once a vast castle stronghold existed. Inhabited by a series of rebellious counts – and also, for a short while, by the pleasure-loving Marguerite de Valois, estranged wife of Henri IV, who entertained lavishly here (see Usson) – the fortress of Carlat was finally razed by Henri in 1604, and almost nothing remains.

The short walk up to the castle-rock through the small and very sleepy village offers views over the gentle wooded hills of the Carladès, above grey lava-stone houses roofed with rough stone tiles (*lauzes*) and their garden plots of vegetables and flowers. At the top the views extend over the neighbouring valley.

CHEYLADE

This unremarkable mountain village serves as a resort for anglers and walkers, and enjoys a fine position in the Cheylade Valley, not far from the Peyrol Pass on the side of the Puy Mary (1,787m). The valley road towards the pass cuts through fine scenery, woods and pastures. While there is little of obvious interest in the village itself, it is well worth a halt in order to visit the rough little stone-roofed church, which has a feature of unique interest: a 17th-century coffered oak ceiling made up of 1,350 painted-wood pictures – of strange animals, flowers, plants, angels' heads and coats of arms, all in a naïve style. Illumination is available by coin meter.

HÉRISSON

A substantial village above the pretty River Aumance, Hérisson is overlooked by the russet stones of its ruined castle high on the hill at the top of the village. Hérrison offers some pleasant walks, such as one to the nearby Romanesque Châteloy church (2km, along a marked path), which has fine views over the valley, or to the oak forest of Tronçais (11km, about 3 hours), whose wood is used to make barrels for Cognac and claret. The best views of Hérisson itself can be enjoyed from the bridges over the river, to the south of the village.

MARCOLÈS

Attached to a priory founded by a 10th-century count, this village was known as Pagus Marculiscus and was fortified in the 13th century. Still largely contained within its medieval walls, the village – once a prosperous market town on a pilgrimage route to Santiago de Compostela in northern Spain – retains some fine old houses, many with vaulted cellars which were used as stores for wine and cheese. There is a 15th-century gateway, an early Gothic church and little cobbled alleys known locally as *carrierons*.

Marcolès is in the heart of the gentle rural area of the Châtaigneraie (Chestnut Groves), and dishes using chestnuts can be savoured in local restaurants, especially at festival times.

ST-FLORET

This village huddles in the steep-sided valley of the River Couze de Pavin, in an area riddled with gorges and precipitous winding roads which link the valley villages. Most of its rough stone houses have been restored, and St-Floret presents a picturesque ensemble, colourful with curving terracotta pantiles and pots of flowers. To one side of the narrow village are the substantial remains of a medieval castle, approached by a rough rock stairway; in a large chamber there are some interesting 14th-century frescoes.

ST-NECTAIRE

Divided into two distinct halves, St-Nectaire-le-Bas and St-Nectaire-le-Haut, this village is noted for its cheese, its church and its spa. The magnificent Romanesque church dominates the upper village and includes a treasury containing several 12th-century artefacts. The spa is in the lower village, where the feature is the 'Petrifying Fountain' or Falls, an extraordinary water source whose incredibly rapid lime deposition rate turns objects to stone and creates beautiful natural sculptures.

ST-SATURNIN

This village is very attractive, not least for its large and striking Romanesque church built of a mixture of pale arkose (a kind of sandstone) and black volcanic stone, arranged in alternating patterns on its exterior arches. In the little tree-shaded square by the church is another, earlier, fortified chapel and several fine houses, in particular the Villot house, with a stained-glass mullioned window.

St-Saturnin belonged to the powerful family of La Tour d'Auvergne, famous for one of the last of their line, Queen Catherine de Médicis, wife of Henri II and mother of three French kings including the unfortunate François II, who was married briefly to Mary Queen of Scots.

St-Saturnin's medieval fortress is sited at the edge of the village above a ravine; it is currently undergoing extensive restoration and serves mainly as a venue for exhibitions and conferences. Nearby, in the place de l'Ormeau, is a 15th-century fountain decorated with entwined branches. The market square is the site of a pig market during the two big cattle fairs which still take place in May and October.

Père et fils cycling along the deserted rue Principale in St-Saturnin, where in the background can be seen the village's towering church, built of sandstone and black lava from the region

The Rhône Valley

It is said that the region round Lyon is irrigated by three rivers: the Rhône, the Saône and Beaujolais.

Le Crozet

(Loire)

THIS MODEST MEDIEVAL BOUR-GADE 27KM NORTH-WEST OF ROANNE OVERLOOKS THE ROANNAIS VALLEY, SITTING ON THE FIRST OF THE GENTLE SPURS WHICH LEAD TO THE MONTS DE LA MADELEINE LYING TO THE SOUTH.

The name of Le Crozet is thought to have derived from the French word *croix*, signifying its location near a major crossing of ancient Roman roads. Isolated to the north and south-west by two ravines (called *corze* or *craze* in Old French, other possible namesakes) and protected by hills, the village enjoys fine natural defences. Known in the 10th century as a *nid d'aigles* (eagle's nest or eyrie), the village of Le Crozet was the haven to which the Viscounts of Mâcon repaired upon returning from their escapades.

SECURE AND PROSPEROUS

In 1220, Le Crozet became the property of the Counts of Forez, who reinforced its security by enclosing it within a second wall 2.5m thick. This new fortification – which made Le Crozet accessible to outsiders only via two drawbridges – included nine towers, of which only the imposing granite Tour à Bec stands today. Though partially masked by houses, vestiges of this wall and its towers flank the Grande Porte, which was once decorated with a sundial and a sheep; it now bears

the renovated coats of arms of the Dukes of Bourbon and the Counts of Forez and is still the main entryway to the old village.

Ceded in the late 14th century to Louis II, Duke of Bourbon, Le Crozet became a prosperous *châtellenie*, with a communal oven, a *grenier à sel* (salt warehouse), three markets, a cobbler, a butcher and numerous artisans. The village remained under the Bourbon family until 1527, when the king confiscated it as punishment for their support of his enemy. In 1531 Le Crozet passed into the royal hands of King François I. By the late 17th century, it had lost much of its importance, as well as its judicial seat, to the better-situated neighbouring village of La Pacaudière.

TREASURE TROVE OF HOUSES

The primary interest of Le Crozet is a series of unusually well-preserved (and lovingly restored) examples of medieval and Renaissance architecture. The fine half-timbered Maison des Bois, now the town hall, dates from the late 15th century and belonged to an officer of Charles III of Bourbon, High Constable of France. The 16th-century Renaissance-style Maison Dauphin, built of yellow limestone known as *pierre de Charlieu*, is decorated with asymmetrical moulded Gothic windows and formerly

The elegant Maison Dauphin (detail below left), formerly a boucherie, *now sells antiques*

served as a butcher's shop. Renovated by its present occupants, the Maison Dauphin now houses an antiques shop and features a majestic original fireplace decorated with grape vines, while a lovely little courtyard hugs the far end of the house.

Across the main street from the Maison Dauphin are the ruins of the old church, a primitive chapel reconstructed in 1659 on foundations dating to the 12th century. The church remained in use until 1860, and is now the site of a diminutive courtyard which is dramatically illuminated by night.

When standing at the place du Terrail, at the foot of the hill where the present-day church is located, one's eyes are drawn to the marvellous polished brick façade of the 15th-century Maison Papon, built by the father of Jean Papon, celebrated barrister, author and royal favourite. Over the 16th-century main entry is a coat of arms bearing the inscription: 'Sileto et spera 1535' (Remain silent and hope). Among the fascinating details are the coats of arms and inscriptions emblazoned between the four mullioned windows of its principal Renaissance façade. There is also a bas-relief between the two main windows which reflect a superstitious practice of the time: in it, two people are washing their feet in a fountain, the belief being that the washing of hands and feet would keep death at bay. The Latin inscription reads: 'Lavaluant pedes et manus ne forte moriantus.' The façade at the far end of the courtyard, with a small spiral staircase, is the oldest.

The Walk

Park outside the ramparts and enter the old village through Grande Porte which leads on to La Grande Charrière and place Mario Meunier. Maison des Bois is on the left facing the square.

Head downhill from Maison des Bois, ducking inside a marked passage on the left leading to a little courtyard with an ancient well and a monolithic coping. At the far corner is Tour à Bec. Back at Maison des Bois, continue towards La Petite Porte. On the right is Maison Dauphin; on the left are ruins of La Vielle Église. At the bottom of the street on the left is Maison du Cadran (15th century) inscribed: 'Carpe Horam'.

Turn right into rue de la Poternel, leading towards the church. Bear right, following signs for Maison des Amis du Vieux Crozet, to emerge at place du Terrail.

Head left up hill to visit the church and *donjon* (keep) just behind it.

5

From the church, return down the path towards place du Terrail and bear left past Maison Papon to emerge at place Mario Meunier.

---

i

▷ Length of walk: 1km
▷ Approximate time: 30–45 minutes
▷ Terrain: Well-paved, gentle slopes accessible to wheelchairs and pushchairs
▷ Parking: Outside castle ramparts
▷ Open: Museum: daily Jun–Sep, 3–6:30
▷ Refreshments: *Auberge* by Grande Porte

Above right, the view through the Grande Porte, or Porte Ogival, takes in the Mairie up the staircase

Opposite this house is an ivy-covered museum, the Maison des Amis du Vieux Crozet (16th century). Inside, there are exhibitions on traditional crafts and furnishings. Look for the sheep gargoyle on the cornice.

In 1862, the remains of Le Crozet's fortified castle were razed and the substructure used as a foundation for the present-day neo-Gothic church. The castle's 12th-century keep still stands, however, though stripped of the turret that once served as the ancient chapel's bell tower. Formerly, a drawbridge from the castle provided the sole access to the keep, but today visitors can climb to the top for an exceptional view of the Beaujolais region, the Monts de la Madeleine and the Charolais Mountains to the east.

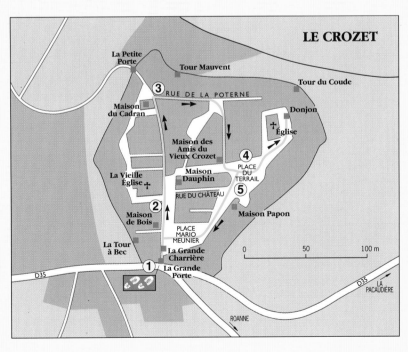

Labastide-de-Virac

(Ardèche)

PROUDLY SITTING AT AN ELEVATION OF 275M, LABASTIDE HAS LONG BEEN A STRATEGIC LANDMARK, WITH ITS TOWERS PRESIDING OVER THE SURROUNDING VINEYARDS AND THE CASTLE AT ITS HEART.

The village of Labastide-de-Virac, located 12km south of Vallon-Pont-d'Arc, holds an important position in many ways: as a link along the road from Barjac to Vallon-Pont-d'Arc; as a stopover for kayakers who have navigated down the River Ardèche; and as a resting place for hikers along the well-known GR (Grande Randonnée) 4 from Pont St-Esprit to Le Vans.

The castle, with its imposing circular towers, has been at the core of Labastide's development from the 15th century. Today it pays homage to silk-making, which flourished in the region until relatively recently, with displays of the complete life cycle of silkworms and of traditional methods and tools used in the fabric's creation.

The advantageous site of Labastide-de-Virac has a history dating from the Roman Empire (a *bastide* is a small fortress, while *Virac* is the Roman name – the 'ac' ending being characteristic of Roman settlements).

The north-south road, best seen from the ramparts of the castle, is called *la voie royale* and is one of the oldest in Europe. The Romans and Gauls used the road to cross over the nearby Pont d'Arc in the grottoes of the Ardèche, as the river was too tempestuous to cross by boat. Later, during the Crusades, the Kings of France passed by Labastide on their way to the Camargue, where they embarked for the Holy Land – the soldiers stationed in the *bastide* ensuring a safe royal passage.

BASTION OF PROTESTANTISM

The last revolt of the Camisards, or Protestants from the Cévennes, against the royal aegis just before the French Revolution took place beneath the castle walls. More than 400 perished, and weapons and bones can still be found today in the Plaine Sous La Veille. When Louis XIII and Richelieu threatened to raze the château because it was Protestant, the seigneur – who himself resided in nearby Barjac – allowed the machicolations and other defensive devices of the castle to be dismantled. As a result, this was the only castle of its kind to survive in the region. You can see the room in which slept the Duc de Roure, who led the Huguenot uprising against royal authority. In it can be seen a hasty letter appealing for

The tall spire, visible from a narrow lane, points to the church, above. Hungry caterpillars make a meal of mulberry leaves: silkworms are exotic residents of Labastide, right

help when the castle was besieged, as well as the *meurtrières* (loopholes) from which harquebuses and other small arms were fired.

TREASURES OF ART AND NATURE

Parts of the castle are very elegant and fine examples of the Languedoc Renaissance, being the work of masons brought from Italy. The interior provides solid proof that the Renaissance was brought to France via the south. The spiral staircase is the most beautiful and well-preserved in the Languedoc

region, and is classified as a historical monument in and of itself. Note the original door of the castle, from the 15th to 16th century, and the French-style ceilings. Upstairs there is a huge fireplace in a room filled with old documents and books, including one of the oldest Bibles in Europe, printed in Geneva in 1678 and translated by the 16th-century poet Clément Marot. It also contains items belonging to the Pradier family, who once owned the castle (Jean-Jacques Pradier sculpted the statues now round the obelisk at the place de la Concorde in Paris).

LABASTIDE-DE-VIRAC

The Walk

1

Start at place de la Fontaine. Walk up rue Centrale, following the signs to the château. At the end of the street on the right is a large white stone house with suns and moons on the shutters and a large sundial dating from the Revolution, inscribed '*Soyez Bon Citoyen*' (Be a Good Citizen).

2

Follow a sign to the left, down an incline towards the Bouquinerie and the tower of the 15th-century Catholic church. Continue towards the main road and turn right, retracing the town's former ramparts.

3

Take a steep concrete stairway leading up to right past cypress trees towards the château. Bear right and go uphill, circling the old ramparts of the castle.

4

On the left is a lantern for Au Vieux Porche restaurant. Walk through an arcaded cobbled passageway and turn right. Pass through a second arcade to emerge at a street leading up to the left. At the top of street, you are at the foot of the château.

5

After visiting the château, head towards a grilled gateway and back down to place de la Fontaine.

ℹ️

▷ Length of walk: 600m
▷ Approximate time: 30 minutes
▷ Terrain: Relatively rough, requiring good walking shoes. Not accessible to wheelchairs and pushchairs except for former ramparts
▷ Parking: Outside town hall
▷ Open: Castle: Easter to September 10–noon, 2–7. Catholic church: fourth Saturday of the month
▷ Refreshments: La Petite Auberge (regional specialities and open-air terrace)

Here also is a display of traditional methods of silk-making, on which the area's wealth was based until the beginning of this century. Olivier de Serres, a famous Ardéchois and minister under Henri IV, brought back the mulberry tree and silkworm from China (a mulberry tree planted by him still stands at the rear of the castle). Silkworms were, and still are, raised in the castle. Once the women who worked here acted as incubators, keeping pocketfuls of silkworm eggs warm in special aprons they wore under their skirts.

The town's former ramparts are flush with chestnut and fig and passion fruit trees, cypress, Virginia creeper, thyme, wisteria and oleander, and the panorama from here is outstanding, with a view over the Cévennes from Mont Lozère to Mont Gerbier de Jonc and the lower Vivarais. You can see both the Protestant temple and the Catholic church, as

The Romans, with their unfailing eye for a strategic location, appreciated Labastide's road and river links

well as the neighbouring hamlet of Crottes, annihilated by an SS division in 1943 (the maquis or Resistance took refuge in the grottoes during World War II). Here you can gaze over rooftops of clay tiles moulded, so locals claim, on women's thighs.

From the heights of the ramparts you can survey the wilderness, ideal for walks and picnics, which draws as many tourists each year as le Mont-St-Michel. The fight to preserve this rugged territory is led by Michel Pivert, a local whose exhaustive map of the region's nature walks may be found in the château shop. Select a goat's cheese to accompany a Vin de Pays des Coteaux de l'Ardèche and vintages like Cabernet Sauvignon or Syrah red wine. Try the farm shop by the entrance to the village; ring the bell for service.

Chamelet
(RHÔNE)

The polished-tile roof of its church and, behind that, an imposing keep dating from its feudal past dominate the once-fortified village of Chamelet and its narrow, twisting streets. Like many other little villages along the region's *Route des Vins*, this village in the Azergues Valley has a predominantly agricultural heritage. Though it is widely considered one of the oldest former *châtellenies* in France, the exact origins of Chamelet are not known, nor is the derivation of its name – it might come from the Roman colony known as Camilliacum, or possibly from *mallarium*, a storage vase for honey. In this region long prized as a plentiful hunting ground, wild thyme blankets the uncultivated hills, and bee-keeping is still a common business. The dialect here is thought to be seasoned with a mix of vulgar Latin and old Celtic words, resulting in such variations as *vindîme* for *vendange* (grape harvest) and *vint* for *vent* (wind); as recent as less than a century ago, locals still spoke of harvesting *tsevenie* instead of *chanvre* (hemp).

Historically, Chamelet is first mentioned in a title ceding the *châtellenie* and château to Guichard III, Sire de Beaujeu. It is thought that his son, Guichard IV, then passed it as a peace offering to the bellicose Archbishop Reynaud in the 11th century. In 1312, Philippe the Fair, King of France, deposed the Archbishop of Lyon, and Chamelet became the property of the Crown.

Chamelet's ancient covered market, below, offers a shady spot to sit and survey the ivy-clad houses

The Walk

From the main road, follow signs for Le Bourg (parking is limited, so try alongside the church and in front of the town hall). As you ascend, look for vestiges of the village ramparts.

After visiting the church, walk downhill along rue Principale towards place du Marché. At the end of the first street on the right is the keep, once a dungeon.

Pass through the marketplace and follow Chemin de la Concorde up a long, gradual slope. The road curves sharply right, leading to La Chapelle, a hamlet named after the ruined Romanesque church which stands down the right fork of the road from the crest of the hill. Retrace your steps down to Les Halles. To your right a road leads to the *route nationale*. Now walk back towards the church.

In the heart of the old town stands Les Halles, a covered marketplace built of massive oak beams. The original 16th-century structure was restored early this century. The road which passes along the arcades of Les Halles leads to the ruins of a Romanesque chapel and an ancient cemetery in the hamlet called La Chapelle. The church, which is presumed to have been the place of worship for local peasants, was still in use at the end of the last century.

At the crest of the hill stands the recently built town hall and the renovated Gothic

Below, the narrow streets of Chamelet zigzag round corners, inviting skid marks from swerving cycles. In Ambierle, right, an intricately patterned roof glistening in the sunlight is just one of the glories of the village's 15th-century church, on the site of an earlier abbey destroyed in the Hundred Years' War

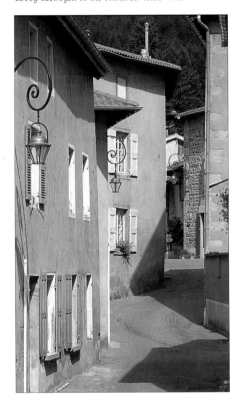

Chapelle des Pénitents, which was restored this century. In the choir are two very interesting 15th-century stained-glass windows: on the right is Ste Claude in episcopal garb; on the left, St Sebastien dressed as a wealthy 15th-century bourgeois. Two bay windows and Gothic arches remain intact.

As you leave the church, lean over the stairwell and you may glimpse the ancient keep, now privately owned, which is all that remains of the château. It is generally presumed that several houses in Chamelet rose from the castle's rubble. Though copious historic documentation of the Middle Ages is available on this area, the power behind the construction of the original castle remains a mystery, as does the reason for its demise.

Ambierle
(LOIRE)

Lovely old homes are scattered throughout Ambierle, a village set on a 460m crest 17km north-west of Roanne and a favourite spot for artists in summer. A magnificent church is the crowning glory of the old bourg.

Ambierle's history is interwoven with that of the Benedictine abbey founded here in the Middle Ages. Originally part of the Order of Cluny during the 10th century, it became a priory in 1101, but the abbey was torched at the end of the Hundred Years War in 1441. The church which currently stands was built between 1470 and 1491 by Antoine de Balzac d'Entraygues, the Bishop of Valence and Die, in yellow stone on top of the remains of the 14th-century transept. In the nave, Christ's Passion is presented in beautiful stained-glass windows; in the choir are oak stalls carved with näive figures. But the church is most famous, and deservedly so, for its triptych retable, attributed to Roger van der Weyden or one of his pupils.

The Musée Forezïen offers a glimpse into the arts and popular traditions of the region: the *auberge*, the bourgeois salon, the couturier's workshop, the surgeon's quarters, and so on. Peasant life and customs serve as themes for three annual festivals: on 22 January the feast of St Vincent, patron saint of the vineyard (a *brioche* the size and shape of a human being is blessed); on the last Sunday in August, a large procession and historical festival; and on 11 November the feast of the patron saint of the parish, St Martin.

Cervières
(LOIRE)

This village, founded just over 800 years ago, has since gone through a series of transformations – from a fortress to a key merchant town noted for its black wool sheets, woollen serge and fabrics, to the small village where tourists come to stroll past Renaissance dwellings, visit the Flamboyant Gothic church in the medieval bourg or enjoy a picnic overlooking the scenic plain.

Cervières lies at an altitude of 880m. As you approach, notice the *pierres branlantes*, huge rocking stones said to be vestiges of Druidic priests who sought refuge from Roman invasions in the high ground. The village provided an excellent vantage point from which to control the Roman road, (Grand Chemin), from Lyon to the Auvergne.

In 1180, the Count of Forez ordered a *château fort* to be constructed to protect his county while he was away at the Crusades. Originally, the castle was ringed by a crenellated rampart. Now only a few ruins survive – Richelieu ordered the castle razed in 1637.

Take a stroll round the Chemin de Ronde, especially in the wider area towards the north. The parish church dates from the 15th and 16th centuries and features a 15th-century näive wooden pietà, a series of curious small sculpted heads with medieval coiffes, and the processional cross used by the Pénitents Blancs, a religious brotherhood founded in 1655 whose members marched through the village draped in white cloaks and hoods, with only their eyes visible.

Pérouges

(Ain)

ON A PROMONTORY OF THE DOMBES PLATEAU, OVERLOOKING THE AIN AND RHÔNE RIVER VALLEYS, THIS DOUBLY FORTIFIED MEDIEVAL VILLAGE HAS BEEN CLASSIFIED AS ONE OF THE COUNTRY'S MOST BEAUTIFUL VILLAGES.

Pérouges stands out as one of the best-preserved examples of medieval architecture in the whole of France, the majority of dwellings being transitional in style with Italianate influences, and dating from 1500–1600. Pérouges has been lovingly and faithfully restored: only five of its 120 houses are modern, which explains its use as a location for such films as The Three Musketeers and Monsieur Vincent. Not a single electrical installation clutters the exteriors of these houses, which are set along narrow, winding streets paved with brown *galets* (cobbles).

At its height, Pérouges was a bustling producer of hemp. Local industry now thrives more on tourism than on craftsmanship. Begin your exploration under the enormous lime tree in the central square – Pérouges merits a whole leisurely day.

THE ITALIAN CONNECTION

Pérouges is said to have been founded by a Gallic tribe returning from Perugia in Italy (the old spelling and coats of arms of Perugia

All but abandoned by 1900, Pérouges has a wealth of details, like this astronomical sundial

and Pérouges are identical, both towns thrived on the weaving trade, and the local dialect has remained strikingly close to Italian). Two centuries later, in 58 BC, the Romans invaded the region and built a tower to serve as a beacon along the road leading from the Rhône Valley and to help in defending Lugdunum (now Lyon), 35km to the north-east. A presbytery now stands on the site of the ancient tower.

Located strategically on the frontier of France and the former Duchy of Savoie, Pérouges also bordered Dombes, Lyon and Bresse – making it prey for many a besieging army. By the middle of the 14th century, Pérouges was the peaceful and prosperous fiefdom of the Counts of Savoie, and a centre for several important trade fairs to do with weaving. Other local specialities were Rousette wine, sausage and *ypocras* (hippocras), a heady elixir of traditional Maury wine and spices including, cloves, ginger, saffron, cinnamon and honey (Pérouges lay on the spice route from the Middle East).

PÉROUGES

CHEMIN DE DERRIÈRE LA TOUR

RUE DE LA TOUR

Puits de la Tour

Ostellerie

Église Ste-Marie Madeleine

PL DE L'ÉGLISE

Maison Cazin

Maison du Vieux St-Georges

CHEMIN DE LA FONTAINE

RUE DES RONDES

Maison Carrière

RUE DU PRINCE

PLACE DE LA HALLE

RUE DU SOUTERRAIN

Grenier à Sel

Musée

La Porte d'en Haut

Maison du Prince

Vieux Pressoir à l'Écureuil

Maison Herriot

RUE DES CONTREFORTS

AU FOUR

RUE DE LA HALLE

RUE DE LA BRUNE

RUE DU TAMBOUR

La Porte d'en Bas

Maison des Dîmes

RUE DU FOUR

RUE DES RONDES

PROMENADE DES TERREAUX

0   50   100 m

The Walk

Park outside the village ramparts, then pass through the Porte d'en Haut to the church; if the weather is fine, climb up the adjacent tower.

The first *ruelle* on your right leads to place de la Halle (also called place du Tilleul). Note the façade of Maison du Vieux St-Georges, with its 15th-century wooden equestrian statue. Next to the Ostellerie is a façade with a sundial inscribed in old French: '*Je ne marquerois que les beaux jours*' ('I will mark only the fine days'); behind is rue des Rondes. Continue down rue des Rondes.

On the left is a traditional weavers' *atelier* Mireile Closiez; on the right is Maison Cazin, with grilled semicircular windows. Further down is Maison Herriot, with bay windows and *crochets* (hooks) for drying hemp. The old *grenier à sel* stands opposite. On the left near the junction of rue des Souterrains is an interesting house which features Romanesque, Gothic and Renaissance windows.

There is a superb view from Porte d'en-Bas, and from here the Chemin de la Fontaine circles outside the ramparts. Continue up rue des Rondes.

Turn right up rue des Contreforts to see an old *pressoir à l'écureuil*. Return to rue des Rondes; on the near right-hand corner is Maison des Dîmes (tithes). Continue uphill.

At place de l'Église, turn right into rue du Prince, once the main commercial street, noting Maison Carrière (now the town hall) on the corner. At the elbow of the street is Maison des Princes, former administrative seat of the Princes of Savoie, now a museum with amedieval medicinal garden. Continue round to emerge back at place de la Halle.

▷ Length of walk: 1.5km
▷ Approximate time: 45 minutes
▷ Terrain: Cobblestones, occasionally steep
▷ Parking: Outside ramparts, near Église Ste-Marie Madeleine
▷ Refreshments: L'Ostellerie du Vieux-Pérouges; numerous cafés, bars and restaurants

A restaurant in the main square offers a chance to enjoy a drink or a meal in good company. A unique taste of Pérouges is to be found in ypocras, a spicy drink whose recipe is hundreds of years old

In 1468 the Duke of Savoy and the Duke of Burgundy combined forces to ward off the troops of King Louis XI. The Pérougiens built a wall behind the Porte d'en Bas (Lower Gate) to fend off the king's men who, having broken down the door, found the village impenetrable and retreated. An old inscription over the door reads: '...To old Pérouges, impregnable town! The Dauphinois wanted to take the town but could not; so they took the door, the hinges and the locks. The Devil take them.' Pérouges was restored to France with the signing of the Treaty of Lyon in 1601. The local men were enlisted as soldiers, and the town remained independent – and more importantly, exempt from taxation.

A DESERTED VILLAGE REVIVED

Pérouges's prosperity, long reliant on hemp, began to decline when linen became more popular. By 1900 the village had suffered two further blows: most of the surrounding vineyards had been wiped out by phylloxera, and the population had plummeted to six people as families moved to cities to take jobs in factories and the railway industry. Pérouges seemed destined for the wrecker's ball, but for the timely founding of the Comité de France de Conservation du Patrimoine by future President Edouard Herriot and Anthelme Thibaut, whose grandson now runs the Ostellerie du Vieux Pérouges.

The half-timbered main building of the Ostellerie, like the museum opposite, dates from the 14th century and is an excellent example of a popular architectural ploy: the ground floor, whose area was the basis for taxation, is overhung by larger (untaxed) upper storeys. Built of very light materials, these houses were easily dismantled so that important visitors could gain access to the main square, and were able to be quickly rebuilt again afterwards.

Just inside the machicolated Porte d'en-Haut (Upper Gate) is the simple 15th-century Église Ste-Marie Madeleine, built on Roman foundations and with its western wall formed by the village ramparts. The central vault bears the coat of arms of Savoie as well as symbols of the Four Evangelists. The circular oculi are quite striking. To the right of the choir is a 17th-century painted wooden statue of St George, patron saint of Pérouges, slaying the dragon. The retable sustained heavy damage during the Revolution, but the Gothic baptistery remains, as well as the sculpted hand pulling vines.

Le Poët-Laval
(Drôme)

Virtually abandoned after World War I, when it served as a mere stone quarry, the labyrinthine village of Le Poët-Laval now offers open-air concerts, exhibitions and well-crafted pottery. Le Poët-Laval is a triangular-shaped medieval village located 24km from Montélimar. In bright sunshine, the blanched stone of its houses and terraces might remind one of the Holy Land itself, rather than a simple sanctuary commanded by the Knights Hospitaller for those embarking on the Crusades. After a period of near total neglect, Le Poët-Laval witnessed a resurgence of interest and activity from the 1950s.

There have been several renovation projects, and a new arts centre complete with open-air concerts and exhibits was inaugurated in 1995. The village, adorned with Gothic flourishes and lying on a gentle slope, is classified as one of the most beautiful in France, and is particularly lovely when the oleanders bloom and the cicadas hum. The surrounding land is marked by contrasts, blending dark and formal cypress, wild mountain terrain and the subtle undulations of the valleys.

The origins of Le Poët-Laval are Roman, but it reached its peak of prosperity as a great agricultural, weaving and pottery centre during the 14th and 15th centuries. The Knights Hospitaller, founded in 1113 by Pope Pascal II, constructed the village over 800 years ago. The fortified site, ringed by ramparts, served as a resting place for those heading south towards the Camargue to embark on the Crusades.

Built in the 12th century, then modified during the 13th and 15th centuries, the castle was ransacked during the Revolution, and afterwards deemed national property. Individuals bought it, then sold off its wood, tiles and stones. But the massive keep remained relatively intact, given its girth, and still looms over the village. A commandery for the Knights was later added in the lower section of the village.

Near the castle stands the 12th-century Chapelle St-Jean des Commandeurs; all that remains today is part of the nave and the choir with a semicircular apse. Originally Catholic, the village was under Protestant control from 1574 to 1587. The Musée du

Lush dark hillside behind the triangular village of Le Poët-Laval

Protestantisme Dauphinois is housed in what was both a *maison commune* of the Hospitallers from the 15th century onwards and, in the 17th and 19th centuries, a Protestant temple; this double function saved it from destruction after the Edict of Nantes was revoked. The museum recounts the history of the village and of Protestantism from their beginnings to World War II.

The Walk

1

Park in Cour des Commandeurs at the foot of the château. Go down the steps to the village; Chapelle St-Jean is on the right. After visiting the chapel, continue down a ramp and turn right into rue Neuve for a view over the village and its ruins.

2

Retrace your steps, continue down rue du Château through the Grand Portal and down a series of shallow steps. Ruins of old houses are on the left.

3

Turn left into rue de l'Ancien Temple. The Musée du Protestantisme is on the left; note the coat of arms over the door. Further along is the 14th-century Tour Sud des Remparts.

4

Return to rue du Château, turn left to pass through the Grand Portal and walk along rue des Remparts to see the exterior of the village. The *commanderie*, now a boutique, is down the street to the right.

5

Return through the Grand Portal, up rue du Château. Turn into rue Couverte de la Tournelle, past the Dit-Elle tea salon, under an arcade and up a cobbled street.

6

Turn right up some steps towards the Arts Centre, then right into rue de la Chalanque. Take the next left and climb a series of steps opposite the portal back to the château.

Canoeists enjoying the calm waters of the River Ardèche at Vogüé

Vogüé
(ARDÈCHE)

Shaped like an amphitheatre, this medieval village some 11km south of Aubenas is tucked into an alcove formed by a high cliff and the River Ardèche. This village makes a picturesque point of departure for those visiting the region, and particularly for anyone embarking on rafting expeditions.

One of the most impressive features of Vogüé is its proud Château des Seigneurs de Vogüé, with its four towers, Romanesque chapel with stained-glass windows by Manessier, sculpted retable and relics of St Bartholomew. The castle was first built in the 12th century and was renovated in the 15th and 17th centuries. Note the embossed door surmounted by a pediment and also the

hanging gardens. Exhibits in the castle include engravings by Jean Chièze, an artist from the Ardèche.

The winding stone streets are arcaded in places. In summer, you can swim, canoe or kayak in the river, or go rock-climbing. The ancient fortifications of the village are visible from the river's edge.

Oingt
(RHÔNE)

In the heart of the *pierres dorées* (golden stones) region, this lovely medieval *village fleuri*, located 20km south-west of Villefranche-sur-Saône, deserves a leisurely visit. Though several relics dating to Roman times (58 BC), such as pottery and coins, have been unearthed here, the Romans left behind a far more important legacy: the first Beaujolais vineyards, a name familiar to wine-lovers all around the world.

In 1093 the territory was ceded to Umfred d'Oingt, whose powerful family reigned peaceably and prosperously for three centuries until the line of descent ended for lack of an heir.

Streets lined with beautiful houses meander up from the main Porte de Nizy (the only gate remaining of the original three) to the 14th-century parish church, which wa once the Château de Prosny's private chapel. On the *culs-de-lampe* supporting the choir arcade are sculpted the faces of the Oingt family, among them that of the celebrated French mystic Marguerite d'Oingt, the first author to pen a work in Franco-Provençal.

A litte further down the D39 is the pretty little *bourg* of St-Laurent-d'Oingt, which is also recommended for anyone in the area and in need of refreshment . Here the Guillard family runs a cosy and affordable *ferme auberge*. A very *bonne table* accompanies the house peach-leaf and nut wines.

Other Villages

CHARNAY

The golden stone making up this fortified village – set in the land of the *pierres dorées* 13km south of Villefranche-sur-Saône – glistens impressively as you enter Charnay, particularly on a sunny day. Be sure to visit the church, construction of which was begun in the 12th century and not completed until the 19th. Its semilune apse of white limestone is a fine example of 12th-century Romanesque architecture. Worthy of note is the church's Gothic polychrome stone statue of St Christopher, which is believed to date from the 13th century and is said to be the only one in Europe to feature the saint with the Christ Child astride his left shoulder, Syro-Palestinian style.

The town hall, in the main square, is housed in what used to be a 17th-century castle called La Mansarde. It is now surrounded by lovely 15th- and 16th-century houses of *pierre dorée*.

A fine wrought-iron gate leads to one of the golden stone houses in Charnay's main street

LA GARDE-ADHÉMAR

Offically one of France's most beautiful villages, the view from here of the western part of the Tricastin is similarly outstanding: the plain of Pierrelatte sliced by an ancient Roman road, the Donzère-Mondragon Canal, a pair of rather jarring nuclear power plants, and the mountains of Ardèche in the background. Out of season the winding narrow stone streets of this tidy village are picture-perfect. A stroll reveals art galleries, craft shops and, by the church, a garden containing hundreds of species of aromatic and medicinal plants, all labelled as to their effects.

The Romanesque church is one of the loveliest in the region, dating from the second half of the 12th century. Its high nave and western apse are exceptional in their simplicity and splendour. There is also an interesting stone altar once used for pagan rituals. The Chapelle des Pénitents, once integrated into the feudal castle, was

later converted into a place of worship for the Confrérie des Pénitents Blancs. A fresco on the rear wall depicts two kneeling Penitents in their white hoods.

MALLEVAL

As you head south to Malleval along the D30, the soothing sound of rushing water greets your ears and the overall beauty of the village is at its most striking. Its sheltered location at the confluence of the Eparvier and Batalon rivers made Malleval a key vantage point from which to observe the route from the Rhône Valley to the Vivarais. Malleval prospered from the Middle Ages to the 16th century; at its height it counted 300 houses, two judicial courts, a garrison and a large market. In 1574, during the Wars of Religion, the Protestant Seigneur de Reynaud set fire to the village. Catholic soldiers recaptured the town, but razed its *château fort* in order to avert further skirmishes. Of its ramparts, only the privately owned north-east section stands today. The renovated parish church features an 11th-century choir.

MIRABEL

An impressive 13th-century keep and ruins overlook Mirabel, a lovely village built into the ledge of a basalt cliff on the edge of a volcanic massif, 16km east of Aubenas. Mirabel was once an important fortified town which controlled the route from the Rhône to the Cévennes and played a strategic role in the Wars of Religion.

Many of the houses, dating from the 15th and 16th centuries and built of striking yellow-limestone and dark volcanic rock, are set into the ramparts. Note the covered rue de la Tour and the arcaded stone streets. Mirabel offers a stunning view of the Cévennes mountains and the Bas (lower) Vivarais, particularly in springtime when the almond trees are in full blossom.

RIVERIE

Once a major thoroughfare, Riverie is situated on a promontory high above the Mornant plateau, between the forests of Chatelard and Chantolais. Riverie's importance as a medieval *péage* (tollhouse) was based on its proximity to the watershed at the Col de Ste-Catherine: from here the

River Coise flows towards the Loire and the Atlantic, while the Bozançon bears towards the Rhône and the Mediterranean.

Now a sparsely populated enclave, Riverie was the setting for one of the bloodiest chapters in local history. In 1570, after the village seigneur allied himself with Henri de Bourbon, heir to the French throne, soldiers besieged Riverie and slaughtered 400 men. Their blood, it is said, flowed all the way down the mountain to the neighbouring town of St-Didier, a kilometre below. To commemorate the return of peace and the end of the Wars of Religion, Henri IV ordered a lime tree to be planted in 1595 in the square behind the church. From here, a stroll round the Chemin de Ronde traces the outer ramparts of the 11th-century fortified castle.

ST-MONTANT

Bordered by a stream and situated at the mouth of a gorge in the ancient province of the Vivarois lies one of the region's picture-postcard villages. But unlike other small villages which hibernate out of season, St-Montant has a year-round vibrancy.

The medieval *bourg* that grew up at the foot of the château (in ruins since the 16th-century) has been contained by triple fortifications, leaving its 11th- and 15th-century façades, miniature staircases and vaulted passageways largely intact.

Park the car and follow rue Principale past the town hall to the 12th-century Église San Samonta, a classified monument with a 10th-century chapel and a sanctuary dating from the 5th century. Fragrant paths lined with oak, olive and fruit trees wend their way up into the surrounding hills. The Fête de La St-Jean, is at the end of June.

SCEAUTRES

A striking block of basaltic cliff, said to be unique in Europe, looms over the Sceautres. Perhaps it foreshadows the fate of this tiny hamlet, which seems on the brink of extinction in a generation's time, judging by the uninhabited limestone and volcanic rock houses.

Life is found at the foot of the village in a makeshift café and, further down the road, a beautiful *auberge*. At dusk you can watch the cows come home – right down the main road. For hiking enthusiasts, a trail leads to the top of the volcanic cone, which offers a tremendous view of the Teoumale Valley and the surrounding plain.

The Alps

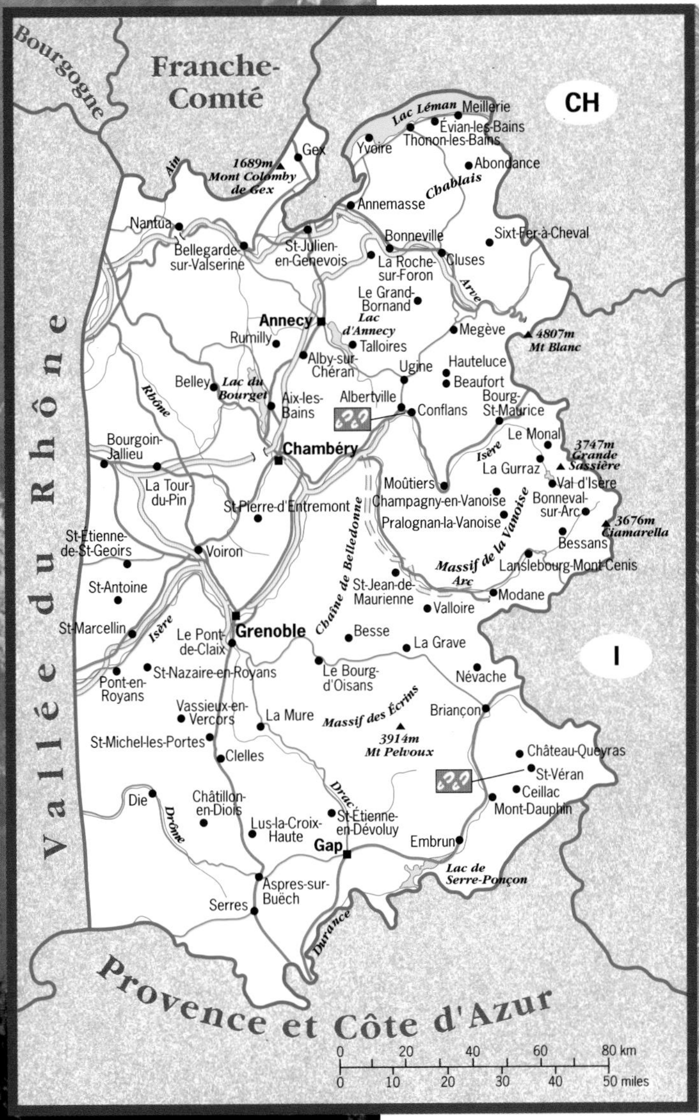

Bourgogne
Franche-Comté
CH
Lac Léman
Meillerie
Évian-les-Bains
Thonon-les-Bains
Yvoire
Abondance
Gex
1689m Mont Colomby de Gex
Ain
Chablais
Annemasse
Nantua
Bellegarde-sur-Valserine
St-Julien-en-Genevois
Bonneville
Sixt-Fer-à-Cheval
La Roche-sur-Foron
Cluses
Arve
Le Grand-Bornand
Annecy
Lac d'Annecy
Talloires
Megève
4807m Mt Blanc
Rumilly
Alby-sur-Chéran
Ugine
Hauteluce
Beaufort
Belley
Lac du Bourget
Rhône
Aix-les-Bains
Albertville
Conflans
Bourg-St-Maurice
Le Monal
3747m Grande Sassière
Isère
La Gurraz
Val-d'Isère
Chambéry
Bourgoin-Jallieu
La Tour-du-Pin
Moûtiers
Champagny-en-Vanoise
Pralognan-la-Vanoise
Bonneval-sur-Arc
3676m Ciamarella
Bessans
St-Pierre-d'Entremont
St-Étienne-de-St-Geoirs
Voiron
Massif de la Vanoise
Lanslebourg-Mont-Cenis
Arc
St-Jean-de-Maurienne
Modane
St-Antoine
Chaîne de Belledonne
Valloire
St-Marcellin
Isère
Le Pont-de-Claix
Grenoble
Besse
La Grave
I
St-Nazaire-en-Royans
Le Bourg-d'Oisans
Névache
Pont-en-Royans
Vassieux-en-Vercors
La Mure
Massif des Écrins
Briançon
3914m Mt Pelvoux
St-Michel-les-Portes
Clelles
Château-Queyras
St-Véran
Ceillac
Mont-Dauphin
Die
Châtillon-en-Diois
Drac
Drôme
Lus-la-Croix-Haute
St-Étienne-en-Dévoluy
Gap
Embrun
Lac de Serre-Ponçon
Aspres-sur-Buëch
Serres
Durance
Vallée du Rhône
Provence et Côte d'Azur
0 20 40 60 80 km
0 10 20 30 40 50 miles

AU BEL HABIT

The pure air and seemingly endless days of sunshine make this region a paradise for nature and sports enthusiasts. Despite tourism, many old traditions still play a part in village life.

Conflans *(Savoie)*

BUILT ON A ROCKY SPUR ABOVE THE ISÈRE AND ARLY RIVERS, THIS MEDIEVAL VILLAGE, A DISTRICT OF ALBERTVILLE IN THE TARENTAISE VALLEY, ONCE MARKED THE FRONTIER SEPARATING ITALY AND GAUL.

Historically, Conflans was a great trading hub, and merchants, pedlars and travellers relied upon the road for passage. Livestock and cheeses, cloth, leather and skins, grains and wine were bartered at the market in the main square. Its strategic location brought it prosperity until the end of the 18th century, and if it became less prosperous over time, the old section of the village has remained remarkably intact since the time of Amédée VI, the 'Green Count' of Savoie. Still standing today are vestiges of the 15th-century ram-

Above, an abundance of shop signs. Left, golden light illuminates the triple-nave St-Grat

parts (partially destroyed during Henri IV's storming of the city), the Savoie and Tarine gateways to the village, the 12th-century Tour Sarrasine from which the lords watched over the whole valley, the 15th-century Ramus Tower (once the residence of the lords of Beaufort), and the partially restored ruins of the 14th-century Château Rouge. The public gardens, in which the Tour Sarrasine stands, are lovely around sunset.

HEART OF THE VIEILLE VILLE

In the charming Grande Place, oleander blossom and pastel-toned buildings with *trompe l'oeil* effects set off the 18th-century fountain designed by the Piedmontese artist Garella. The square – best seen early in the morning, when free of tourists, or later in the evening – is the heart of the old village, where markets and fairs are held. The red-brick Maison Rouge in the Grande Place, built during the 14th century, was inspired by the architectural style of northern Italy. Wander down the narrow arcade-capped *ruelles*, and while in the rue Gabriel-Pérouse note the fine old wrought-iron shop signs, especially the peacock at number 24.

Of the ancient monuments in Conflans, the church is the most recent. Named Notre-Dame-de-l'Assomption, but better known as the Église St-Grat after the patron saint of Conflans, the fresco-covered church dates from the early 18th century. It features a pilaster doorway, three naves, six cruciform pillars, tall semicircular windows and cut stones. Note also the baroque portal and the church tower.

ANGELS OF THE ALPS

Inside, the remarkable pulpit, designed by Jacques Clerant in 1718, is surmounted by laughing cherubs and decorated with garlands and other motifs – an excellent example of the energetic baroque style of the Savoie region. Also by Clerant are the wooden panels of the six baptismal fonts, which are set on stone basins and feature similar cherubs, garlands and motifs. The fine woodworking tradition of the Alps is evident in the statues. The side altars were built after funds were raised by some of the village's prominent families. One is dedicated to St Francis de Sales, who during one of his visits advised the inhabitants of Conflans to invite the Capuchins to the village.

The Maison Rouge museum, featuring Conflans' ethnological history, is presented on three levels. Its archaeological treasures include a Roman iron scale found in Gilly; at 1.53m, it is believed to be the largest of its kind discovered in Europe and dates from the 2nd or 3rd century AD. There is also a display on the history of skiing, and a reconstruction of 14th-century living quarters, traditional tools and domestic life.

A market featuring regional products is held in the Grande Place on various Sundays, or every Thursday in neighbouring Albertville. Several festivals are scheduled throughout the year, including the Floral Festival in April, the Vintage Car Festival in June, and the yearly Bastille Day celebrations. Also in July is Albertville's International Festival of Military Marches. This is one of the most important festivals in France, with prestigious bands from round the world taking part each year.

Peering down a passageway – rue de Senat de Savoie – into the cheerful and welcoming main square

The Walk

① Park outside the Porte Tarine; on entering the village turn left up rue Frederic Bonvin. Go up towards the Site Panoramique with its view over Albertville.

② Walk round towards the Jardin Public de la Tour Sarrasine with its encircling vine-covered arbour.

③ Leave the garden and go down the stone steps. Cross the Grande Place and enter rue Gabriel Pérouse.

④ Visit the Église St-Grat, then continue down rue Gabriel-Pérouse, passing by the fountain near an arcaded passageway.

⑤ Turn left into Chemin de la Petite Roche; the Tour Ramus is on the left as you come down. Turn up the second small arcaded passageway on the left, returning to rue Gabriel Pérouse.

⑥ Turn right, then take the next set of steep steps to the left. Bear right up the steps to reach Église St-Grat. Circle behind the church, coming out on to a paved walkway overlooking rooftops and a private garden. Turn left into rue Abbé Larius-Hudry. Take the right-hand fork down: Château Rouge is before you. Circle round the château (rough, rocky path). Bear left for a good view of the ramparts through a gateway. After 50m or so, look back at the vestiges of ramparts encircling the château (steep drop). Retrace your steps down through the gateway, bear left and head back down to the centre.

ⓘ

▷ Length of walk: 2.5km
▷ Approximate time: I hour
▷ Terrain: Cobblestones, steps and arcaded passageways limit wheelchair and pushchair access
▷ Parking: Place Cassety and outside Porte Tarine
▷ Open: Museum: daily. Guided tours of Conflans, museum and nearby Château de Manuel de Locatel can be arranged
▷ Refreshments: Cafés, *crêperies* and restaurants in Grande Place

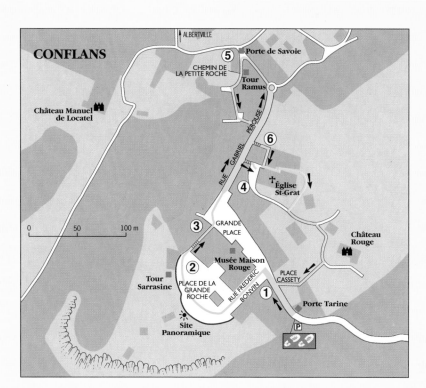

CONFLANS

Pont-en-Royans
(Isère)

Pont-en-Royans is dramatically set beside the Gorges de la Bourne, which until the 19th century were the only way in or out of the limestone massif of the Vercors. For long a cloth town and commercial centre, about 25km west of Villard-de-Lans, Pont-en-Royans has been ranked as a *site classé* for its historical beauty, lauded by the 19th-century French writer Stendhal during his travels. With its narrow serpentine streets, imposing limestone ledges and brightly coloured houses overhanging the River Bourne, Pont-en-Royans is one of the most unusual villages in the Dauphiné province.

Its origins date back to the Middle Ages, when the 11th-century feudal tower and ramparts defended the villagers and the convent below. Village life sprang up at the river, and during the 14th and 15th centuries houses were built on wooden struts to jut out over the Bourne. Later, the silk and wool trades flourished, and the bridge was built to enable muleteers to cross the river with their goods and to give access to the plain.

The original village extended from the medieval watchtower (today it houses a siren as well as a 1740 clock) to the place de la Porte de France. Outside the walls of the village, on the other side of the tower, is the place du Temple, once the Protestant section of the village. The church was demolished in 1680 upon Louis XIV's orders, and Pont-en-Royans was the object of great rivalry between Protestants and Catholics during the Wars of Religion. Legend has it that the Bourne ran red with blood.

The River Bourne flows beneath looming cliffs that shoulder right up to the village of Pont-en-Royans

Today the village has the feel of a real, functioning town, not merely a tourist haven. The underground market arcades, bombed during World War II, now house a cultural centre. Some of the cantilevered houses, damaged by large lorries passing through the village, continuously undergo renovation.

For a relaxed meal, you can picnic on the banks of the Bourne, rich with trout. Bring a bottle of the local wine made from walnuts, or some of the region's sausages and cheese. Or eat in one of the village restaurants to sample the ravioli stuffed with fresh goat's cheese or with mussels. Locals claim that lumberjacks from Piedmont introduced the cheese-stuffed delicacy after pangs of homesickness got the better of them.

On the outskirts of the village, just before the village limits sign en route to the Cirque, is the Fontaine de St-Ponce, with legendary properties particularly beneficial to the eyes, and having the same source as Evian. In June, more than 30 waterfalls spill over the Cirque du Fer-à-Cheval, whose escarpments reach 500–700m in height. The Cascade de la Méridienne is on the far left, the Cascade de la Lyre on the right. Just 5km away is the Cascade du Rouget, the 'Queen of the Alps'.

Roofs of strong colour and design in St-Antoine provide a striking change from monochrome stone

St-Antoine
(ISÈRE)

The focus of this medieval village, standing at the edge of the Chambaran nature reserve 25km north-east of Romans-sur-Isère, is an enormous abbey built between the 13th and 15th centuries to house the relics of St Anthony, 4th-century founder of Christian monasticism. A local lord, returning from the Holy Land in 1070, had brought the relics back to La Motte-aux-Bois, and the village was rechristened St-Antoine.

Notice the striking 17th-century roof of the town hall at the entrance of the tree-lined abbey: the style is borrowed from Burgundy. Inspiration for the Gothic church's remarkable façade comes from Dijon. Begun at the end of the 12th century and completed in the 17th, it is built of local sandstone. Inside, is a rich collection of frescoes, some as early as the 15th century, Aubusson tapestries and a 16th-century ivory Christ. There is a good view from outside the church over the ivy-laden rooftops of the village.

St-Antoine's streets contain many handsome old homes, as well as an apiculture centre and an old distillery. Each summer, a festival called Nuits Médiévales features concerts, recitals and exhibits.

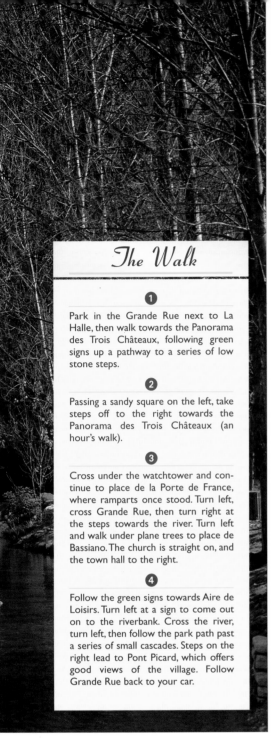

The Walk

1

Park in the Grande Rue next to La Halle, then walk towards the Panorama des Trois Châteaux, following green signs up a pathway to a series of low stone steps.

2

Passing a sandy square on the left, take steps off to the right towards the Panorama des Trois Châteaux (an hour's walk).

3

Cross under the watchtower and continue to place de la Porte de France, where ramparts once stood. Turn left, cross Grande Rue, then turn right at the steps towards the river. Turn left and walk under plane trees to place de Bassiano. The church is straight on, and the town hall to the right.

4

Follow the green signs towards Aire de Loisirs. Turn left at a sign to come out on to the riverbank. Cross the river, turn left, then follow the park path past a series of small cascades. Steps on the right lead to Pont Picard, which offers good views of the village. Follow Grande Rue back to your car.

Sixt-Fer-à-Cheval
(HAUTE-SAVOIE)

This winter sports resort, 25km south-east of Morzine, has a fine setting at the confluence of the 'high' and 'low' sections of the River Giffre. The oldest part of the village is on the right bank, where a lime tree said to be 6m across grows in the great main square. The buildings cluster round the former Augustinian monastery (now a hotel) founded in the 12th century by monks from the parent abbey in Abondance. During the Middle Ages it was one of the most important monastic communities in the Alps ('Alps' in local patois meaning 'pastures').

Snow-capped craggy heights feed the waters round Sixt-Fer-à-Cheval, an area with many waterfalls

'THE SUN,' claimed Voltaire, 'is the greatest clock in the world.' In a region of France reckoned to bask in at least **300** days of sunshine annually, it seems quite natural that the art of the sundial should flourish. Since the end of the Middle Ages, gnomonists have known how to record the hour on a flat surface (a skill known as horology). Before the mass production of clocks and watches, sundials were commissioned throughout the Hautes-Alpes to adorn chapels, cathedrals and private and public buildings – bearing images from fairy tales, fables, ancient tragedies, or caveats as to the ephemeral nature of time and matter: 'Il est plus tard que vous ne croyez' (It is later than you think) or 'Vita fugit sicut umbra' (Life flees like a shadow).

Passing the Time

Thus it was that the Hautes-Alpes region of France once possessed more than 400 sundials, some 284 of them dating back as far as the 18th century. Crusaders had brought back the angled gnomon (the Greek word for pointer or indicator) from the Orient at the end of the Middle Ages, and its construction has not evolved much since the 15th century. Its shifting shadow regulated such daily tasks as cooking, bringing in the herds and prayer. And, continuing through the 18th and 19th centuries when the use of sundials flourished, their presence on churches could not help but remind the faithful that God Himself was the author and master of time.

The Art of Timing

A 'Historical Route of Sundials' charts a path through this land of dials, whether painted on to façades or sculpted in stone. Three elements are used to establish the time: latitude, longitude and the exact orientation and angle of the façade. Each gnomon, or style, must point towards the North Star, with its axis parallel to

Eroded over time: the faded faces of St-Véran's sundials still adorn many walls in the village. A study of their details reveals the interests and beliefs of past eras, though their appeal is timeless. Above, note the 'ZGF' signature at the inner upper left corner

the north-south lines of longitude. The face of the dial is traced, then painted alfresco on to whitewashed plaster using natural pigments: black from calcinated bone, yellow ochre, red from ferrous oxide, brown from burnt sienna, green from oxidised chrome.

Sundials incorporate a virtual encyclopaedia of symbols reflecting ancestral interests and beliefs down the ages: olive branches, stars, tropical birds, fleurs-de-lis (homage to the king), the imperial eagle, the rooster (symbol of Gallic vigilance), horns of plenty, the peacock – and T-squares and compasses, instruments which reminded everyone of the Great Architect of the universe.

Sundials were used in the mountains until the departure of the Germans during World War I. There followed a period of mass production of clocks and watches and then the 'quartz revolution'. But 1960 saw a resurgence of gnomonic creativity, and nearly 130 contemporary sundials were painted. One striking example can be found in the village of St-Véran (see page 164), on the south-western façade of the 18th-century church tower. Four highly stylised birds in a sea of stars are a reminder that in St-Véran – at an altitude of 2,040m, the highest village in Europe – the '*Coqs picorent les étoiles*' (the roosters peck at the stars).

The Fine Italian Hand

There are 15 or so sundials in St-Véran, both old and contemporary, including one on the Maison Romain Mathieu executed by the eclectic artist Giovanni Francesco Zarbula, the master of gnomonic art, who worked prolifically during the middle years of the 19th century. A native of Piedmont, he was either a mason or a painter, as were many Italians who immigrated to the Queyras region. He went from Arvieux and Brunissard in 1832 to Pragelato in 1872, leaving his artistic 'ZGF' signature trademark during that period in French history which witnessed the July Monarchy (1830), the Second Republic (1848), the Second Empire (2 December 1852) and the Third Republic (1871) as well as, in Italy, the unification of the country (1859–70).

As was usual in the Italian tradition, Zarbula used very vivid colours in his designs, which were often crowned with imaginative animals, exotic birds, flowers or a rooster. He frequently received commissions to decorate the houses of the wealthy. The presence of a sundial on the façade of a house thus evolved into an external sign of affluence. One of Zarbula's most brilliant sundials, dated

1843, is in Val-des-Prés in the Clarée Valley, at the Maison J Roux. Its familiar animal themes present two ibis in rainbow colours pecking at a cluster of grapes above a *trompe l'oeil* design and against a fake marble background.

Designed and positioned with fine mathematical precision, sundials are slowly being restored

Operation Rescue

If one sees this array of sundials as a kind of open-air museum spanning valleys and mountains, the need for a 'curator' becomes obvious. Over a century ago, a man named Raphael Blanchard saw that need and decided to act to preserve the sundials in the Briançonnais region, which in general are more ancient than those, for example, in the Queyras. Each summer, while holidaying in the area, he meticulously recorded in his notebook all of the adages he ran across. Blanchard also took photographs of the sundials and had 31 dials reproduced in engravings. In 1895, he published a notice in the *Bulletin de la Société d'Études des Hautes-Alpes* to protest the decline in gnomonic art, wiped out by the availability of cheap watches and mechanical timepieces.

In 1979 the first campaign to promote sundials in the Hautes-Alpes was launched in the Briançonnais region. The first restoration efforts were undertaken in 1984 by the Club du Vieux Manoir, which has since sponsored a series of workshops and publications detailing salvage and restoration techniques. But, a century after Raphael Blanchard logged 152 sundials in the Hautes-Alpes, an inventory revealed the alarming fact that 84 had been destroyed, and those that remained often lacked a gnomon. The Club du Vieux Manoir campaign has spread over the past 10 years and hopes to encourage more active concern for these regional treasures.

St-Véran

(Hautes-Alpes)

S<small>T-VÉRAN, ON THE SLOPES OF</small> M<small>ONT</small> B<small>EAUREGARD ONLY</small> 10<small>KM</small> <small>FROM THE</small> I<small>TALIAN BORDER, HAS THE HIGHEST</small> <small>ALTITUDE OF ANY COMMUNE IN</small> E<small>UROPE.</small> S<small>UNSHINE IS THE NORM IN EVERY SEASON.</small>

St-Véran is one of eight villages in the Parc Naturel Régional du Queyras, the smallest and most mountainous of France's 24 regional parks. Winter, with up to 7m of snow, lasts five to seven months. Despite the cold, the village boasts 300 days of sunshine each year, and the temperature can vary by 30 degrees Celsius in a day. Because of its sunny inclination, St-Véran at one time had 15 sundials, 11 of which exist today (see pages 162–3).

Skiing and other snow sports are the obvious attractions for winter, and in the summer the natural beauty of the surrounding mountains and valleys, with over 2,000 species of alpine flowers, draws crowds of walking, canoeing and climbing enthusiasts.

DEATH OF A DRAGON

The village takes its name from Véran, 6th-century Bishop of Cavaillon and patron saint of shepherds. The legend of St Véran has many versions, but most agree that Véran

Above, a typically sunny sky; right, a traditional St-Véran house, with a wooden loft for drying the hay

killed a dragon, thus saving the herds that travelled from Provence to the summer grazing grounds of the Queyras. Today, only about 500 sheep, 70 cows and half a dozen farmers remain in the village, but sheep and cattle still come to the Queyras for the summer (arriving by lorry these days).

In the Middle Ages, much of the forest on the surrounding fertile slopes was cleared, which helped St-Véran's population grow to around 900. But over time, both natural and man-made disasters have taken their toll, and now there are only 260 inhabitants. In 1526 the centre of St-Véran was completely destroyed by fire; and plague, cholera, avalanches, famines and the Wars of Religion have played their part in the depopulation.

The 19th and 20th centuries saw enormous economic and social changes. In 1856, the building of the first proper road to St-Véran increased the rural exodus, but modernisation had its benefits as well: electricity arrived in 1928, the telephone in 1929 and, finally, tap water in 1950. The opening of the first hotel in 1934 and the first ski-tow in 1936 brought tourism to the Queyras and with it an influx of wealth to the village.

BUILDING A WAY OF LIFE

St-Véran's traditional-style houses, about a hundred in all, give the village a rare architectural unity. The houses were built with three purposes in mind: to shelter the people, to stable the animals and to store the harvest.

The main road in St-Véran leads past flowing water spouts that spill into an old wooden trough

The houses rest against the slope, and all have entrances on the top and bottom floors. The ground floor and the side wing (called the *caset*) were built of stone, with very thick walls and small windows to preserve the heat. The main ground floor housed the animals, but in the winter the family would share their quarters for warmth. The *caset* had a kitchen and storerooms on the ground floor, with bedrooms for summer use on the middle floor. The upper floors of the main building were made of larch wood so that circulating air could dry the hay (kept on the top floor) and help preserve the grain (stored on the middle floor).

The oldest of the houses, built in 1641, is now the Soum Museum, with local arts and crafts exhibits and re-creations of traditional village life. La Vieille Maison, just above the *boulangerie*, was the last house to be occupied in the old way. The owners moved out in 1976, and now the public can visit this completely unmodernised house and imagine the traditional lifestyle of an Alpine villager.

Religion has always played an important role in the area, and St-Véran's present church, which dates from 1683, replaced a 16th-century one destroyed during the Wars of Religion. It has a variety of wooden statues and sculptures, made patiently by villagers during the long winters. Three large wooden mission crosses, with their carved symbols of Christ's Passion, are a feature in the village. These crosses, erected by Catholic missions earlier this century, are found throughout the Queyras region.

Carpentry is a skill of long standing in this region famous for its wooden toys and furniture. A walk round the village reveals plenty of items for sale, as well as demonstrations of wood-carving and furniture-making.

The Walk

1

Start from the car park near the *boulangerie* at the bottom of the village. Follow the road uphill, passing La Vieille Maison on your left, and bear left at a fork.

2

At a mission cross, turn sharp left along the main village street, which passes through four central *quartiers* destroyed by the fire of 1526. Notice sundials on the buildings.

3

Continue past the church and tourist office on the left and, on the right further on, a *fontaine* (drinking fountain) on the corner of the road leading to the Remontées Mécaniques (ski-lifts).

4

Continue straight on, passing another drinking fountain on the right and, further on, the Soum Museum on the left. Houses thin out here; after about 100m, turn sharp left and go downhill.

5

At the bottom of the slope, where a road joins from the right, continue straight on, climbing gently to reach the car park.

ⓘ

▷ Length of walk: 2km
▷ Approximate time: 1 hour
▷ Terrain: All surfaced and suitable for pushchairs and wheelchairs
▷ Parking: At bottom of village near *boulangerie* (free)
▷ Open: Soum Museum: daily, charge
  Vieille Maison: daily in July and August; otherwise by appointment (groups only, charge)
▷ Refreshments: Cafés and restaurants

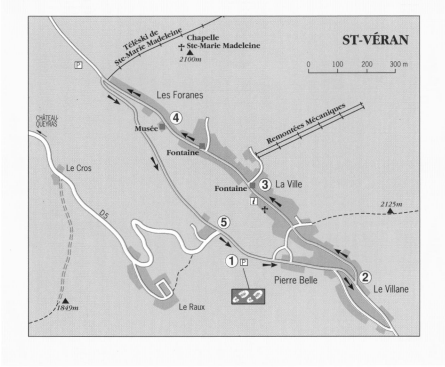

St-Véran map:
- Téléski de Ste-Marie Madeleine
- Chapelle Ste-Marie Madeleine ▲ 2100m
- ST-VÉRAN
- 0 100 200 300 m
- CHÂTEAU-QUEYRAS
- Les Foranes
- ④ Musée
- Remontées Mécaniques
- Fontaine
- Le Cros
- D5
- Fontaine ③ La Ville
- ⓘ ✝
- ⑤
- 2125m ▲
- ① Ⓟ
- Pierre Belle
- ② Le Villane
- ▲ 1849m
- Le Raux

The Walk

1

Start from the car park by the place de la Mairie. Walk down the steps towards the lake and follow the path to the small square by the fishing port.

2

Turn left, passing the church, then right into place du Thay. Take rue de la Maison Carrée towards the château to rue du Lac.

3

Turn left up rue du Lac, passing Le Jardin des Cinq Sens on your left, until you reach the crossroads in front of the Porte de Génève. Turn right down rue du Port.

4

Turn left along the quay. Follow the gravel path on your left uphill and turn left at the surfaced road to re-enter the village through Porte de Génève.

5

At the crossroads turn right down the Grand' Rue. Just before the Porte de Rovorée, turn left down rue de l'Église . The Vivarium is on the left and straight ahead is place du Thay. Take the same route back to the car park beside the lake.

Yvoire
(HAUTE-SAVOIE)

Set on a strategic promontory beside western Europe's largest lake, Yvoire occupies a position that was for centuries a natural crossroads for merchants and pilgrims, just 12km north-east of Geneva. The promontory occupied by Yvoire marks the dividing line between the Petit Lac and the Grand Lac of Lac Léman, the largest lake in western Europe. In 1308, Count Amédée V of Savoie, who wanted to control the lucrative Alpine passes to Italy, fortified the village and rebuilt the old château. By the 15th century the Savoie extended from Berne to Nice and from the Saône Valley to Turin, but it lost most of its territory 150 years later.

Although the layout of the village has hardly changed since the 14th century, today only two gateways and a section of the fortifications are still in place, while the château, which was attacked in the 16th century, has been reduced to a keep. It is not possible to visit the château, but the old kitchen garden has been turned into Le Jardin des Cinq Sens, and includes a maze as well as medicinal and aromatic plants, fruit trees, roses and lilies. For a closer look at the 14th-century ramparts, you can visit the Vivarium; as well as housing over 200 different species of reptile, it has a good view of the interior of the walls.

Yvoire is one of the ports-of-call for the pleasure boats that cruise round Lac Léman from May to September, and high summer sees the village's narrow streets packed with souvenirs and tourists. But calm returns out

Europe's largest lake, Léman, laps the edge of Yvoire, which grew up at a strategic site near the Alpine passes to Italy. Today its harbour, left, is a regular port-of-call for the lake's pleasure boats. Yvoire's elegant church tower, above, is topped with tiles of black onyx

of season, and as the lake gently laps against the shore and the mist nearly obscures the old keep, Yvoire's medieval past seems not so long ago.

Abondance
(HAUTE-SAVOIE)

The village of Abondance lies in an isolated valley 28km south-east of Évian-les-Bains. Despite its lonely position, the valley has been inhabited for nearly 4,000 years.

Abondance boasts the Haute-Savoie's only complete surviving abbey. Augustinian monks arrived in the valley in 1080, and the abbey church was built in 1275. Although the church's original nave was destroyed in 1643, the Romanesque ambulatory and apsidal chapels are still standing. The latter are decorated with bas-reliefs and 15th-century murals, while *trompe-l'oeil* statues were added to the choir and transept in the 19th century. The cloisters, built around 1350, are joined to the church by the ornate Porte de la Vierge; in the 15th century the Piedmontese painter Jacquerio Giacomo decorated them with a series of murals depicting the Virgin Mary's life. In the museum attached to the abbey, there is a permanent exhibition of religious artefacts.

The main part of the village, on the other side of the River Dranse, was developed only in the 19th century. The village market takes place on Sunday mornings, and it is worth trying some of the locally made Abondance cheese, which is something between a Gruyère and a creamy Reblochon. In the summer the area is perfect for exploring on foot, and in the winter the valley is well known for its cross-country skiing.

Bonneval-sur-Arc
(SAVOIE)

Bonneval-sur-Arc is 30km south of Val d'Isère at the foot of the Col de l'Iséran. The village takes its name from the River Arc, which flows through this high valley, and is situated within the Parc National de la Vanoise. The Vanoise covers 28 communes as well as forests, pastures, lakes, rocks and glaciers and lies between the Maurienne and the Tarentaise valleys.

Bonneval-sur-Arc, at 1,835m above sea level, is the highest village in the Maurienne and also the best-preserved. All the houses are built in the local style, with rough stone walls nearly a metre thick and gently sloping, paving-stone roofs. Wood is a precious commodity at this altitude, so although the houses have solid wooden beams and balconies, fuel comes in the form of dried manure. With electricity, telephone and television cables installed underground, the narrow streets look much as they did when the first tourists arrived in 1880.

Tourism is a major source of revenue for Bonneval-sur-Arc. Ten ski-lifts climb up to 3,000m, and even in the summer there is skiing on the Pissaillas glacier on the Col de l'Iséran. The surrounding glaciers and mountains offer plenty of summer hiking and sporting opportunities, as well as the chance to see rare Alpine fauna such as ibex, chamois and marmot.

Originally, the village was a farming community, with most of the villagers raising cattle and cultivating barley, and even today agriculture plays a part in the local economy. On the edge of the village a modern *fromagerie*, housed in a traditionally built chalet, produces and sells regional cheeses such as Beaufort, Emmental and Tomme. Local arts and crafts are also on show at the Grande Maison in the centre of the village.

Other Villages

ALBY-SUR-CHÉRAN

There is a steep drop down into this medieval village, once owned by the Counts of Geneva. The old section of this quiet *village fleuri* is crowned by the chapel of St-Maurice (now a concert hall), whose 13th-century choir used to be the keep of the former castle. The old section extends from the former keep down to the Pont-Vieux spanning the Chéran; the triangular ochre- and rose-toned place du Trophée, with its fountain and arcades, is at the centre.

Until this century, Alby was known for leather-making, and there are plans to erect a cobbler's stand in the place du Trophée. Along with the Cobbler's Museum, it will demonstrate how footwear was once made.

BEAUFORT

This sizeable village, 20km north-east of Albertville, is a prosperous commercial centre that has given its name to the region. The 19th-century Morens bridge, which crosses the River Doron, leads to the baroque church of St-Maxime and the old part of the village, whose winding streets are shaded by overhanging roofs.

Beaufort's fine cheese, known as 'the prince of Gruyères', takes at least six months to mature. The dairy cooperative (open to the public) makes over 800 tonnes of cheese a year, traditionally from the milk of Tarine cows grazed on summer pastures. For centuries, Alpine farmers have kept several chalets in the mountains where they graze their cattle. As the snow melts, they move to higher chalets, returning to the village in winter.

CHÂTEAU-QUEYRAS

As you cut through the Combe du Queyras on the D947, the impressive fortress at Château-Queyras (meaning 'large crag') looms into sight, and the view is breathtaking. The château dates from the 13th century, when the mountain republic extended into Italy. The keep displays a richly detailed history of the castle.

The village, about 40km southeast of Briançon, is located in the heart of the Queyras regional park, a wildlife haven which has carpeted with globeflowers, yellow gentians (used to make the aperitif Suze), anemones and cornflowers. The village slopes down towards green fields, and the houses are decorated with lively sundials, evidence of the region's abundant sunshine. As

you leave the village, stop at the Maison de l'Artisanat in nearby Château Ville-Vieille; there you can see an unusual *armoire* with eight keyholes.

CHÂTILLON-EN-DIOIS

Châtillon is set between Mont Glandasse and the River Bez 14km south-east of Die. Renowned for its little winding *ruelles*, called *viols*, Châtillon was named a *ville botanique* in 1993, with a specific theme – climbing plants and fountains.

From the bridge can be seen the base of ancient ramparts, now forming the foundation of houses, along the viol du Fossé. Their construction took 104 years and, predictably, caused numerous disputes between taxpayers and seigneurs. The walls were demolished by the Governor in 1573 to prevent the Protestants from transforming their town into a fortress. The first Protestant chapel, built in 1610, was destroyed after the Edict

Sun and shade in the yard of a house in Châtillon-en-Diois

of Nantes was repealed. It was rebuilt on the same site during the Revolution.

LA GURRAZ

The surfaced road ends at this small hamlet south-east of Bourg-St-Maurice, but rough roads lead up to the huge waterfalls (frozen in winter) that spring from the La Gurra glacier.

Villagers here still use the hay-lofts in the old stone houses and grow produce on the steep slopes. The church, with its baroque interior and tall bell tower, has recently been restored, and the communal bread oven is still fired up on special occasions. A small restaurant, Le Fenil, serves fondue and fresh salad from its garden.

HAUTELUCE

The Hauteluce Valley, overlooked by Mont Blanc, is reputedly the most beautiful in the area. In the village, 28km from Albertville, stone houses cling to the slope. Summer concerts are held in the 16th-century church, with its ex-

quisite altarpiece and interior. Outside, the walls are decorated with 19th-century *trompe-l'oeil* murals.

The small *éco-musée* organises exhibits on life in the mountains as well as projects for safeguarding the region's future.

MEILLERIE

This tiny fishing port, not being on Lac Léman's pleasure boat route, is a restful spot in high summer. Steep steps and narrow streets winding between gardens connect the different levels of the village. The priory church has its 13th-century choir and square bell tower. Towards the quay is the house where Jean-Jacques Rousseau stayed in the 18th century. The cave in his novel *La Nouvelle Héloïse* was supposed to be at Meillerie, but no longer exists. Byron and Lamartine, the poet-politician, also visited here.

NÉVACHE

Névache spreads along the River Clarée at the foot of the Col de l'Échelle, the lowest mountain pass between France and Italy. As well as the Ville-Basse and Ville-Haute, the *commune* includes the hamlets of Plampinet, Le Cros and Salé. The church in the Ville-Haute was founded by Charles VIII in 1490; the Byzantine-inspired portal is striking, as are the structure, vaulted nave and baroque altar-piece. The hospitable Joie de Vivre *auberge*, in Salé, has an organic food shop and a small ski school.

ST-MICHEL-LES-PORTES

St-Michel-les-Portes, tucked away north-east of Chatillon-en-Diois, offers some of the region's best vistas, whether of the snow-capped peaks of the Écrins and the Oisans or the gentle plains of the Trièves. The lush greens combine well with the brightly coloured houses. An ancient oven still functions occasionally, and there is a mill where walnut oil was once produced.

TALLOIRES

This popular village on the shores of Lac d'Annecy exudes affluence and and offers the best in outdoor activities, including paragliding, sailing, diving and water-skiing. The Benedictine priory, which was established here in 1031 and served as a centre of daily monastic activities until the Revolution, is now a centre for academic studies and international conferences.

Périgord & Quercy

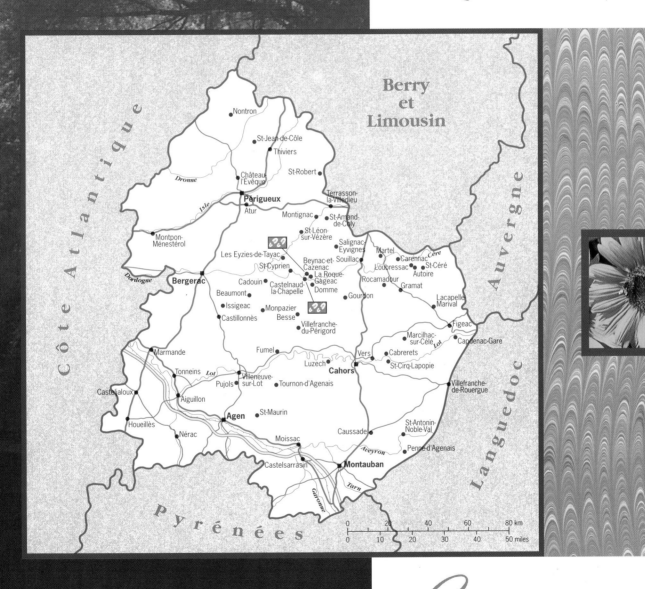

Berry et Limousin

Nontron
St-Jean-de-Côle
Thiviers
St-Robert
Château l'Évêque
Dronne
Isle
Périgueux
Terrasson-la-Villedieu
Atur
Montignac
St-Amand-de-Coly
St-Léon-sur-Vézère
Salignac-Eyvignes
Martel
Cère
Carennac
St-Céré
Les Eyzies-de-Tayac
Souillac
L'Oubressac
Autoire
St-Cyprien
Beynac-et-Cazenac
La Roque-Gageac
Rocamadour
Gramat
Montpon-Ménestérol
Dordogne
Bergerac
Cadouin
Castelnaud-la-Chapelle
Domme
Gourdon
Lacapelle-Marival
Beaumont
Issigeac
Monpazier
Besse
Castillonnès
Villefranche-du-Périgord
Figeac
Fumel
Marcilhac-sur-Célé
Lot
Capdenac-Gare
Luzech
Vers
Cabrerets
Marmande
St-Cirq-Lapopie
Cahors
Tonneins
Lot
Villeneuve-sur-Lot
Villefranche-de-Rouergue
Pujols
Tournon-d'Agenais
Casteljaloux
Aiguillon
Houeillès
Agen
St-Maurin
St-Antonin-Noble-Val
Nérac
Caussade
Penne-d'Agenais
Moissac
Aveyron
Castelsarrasin
Montauban
Garonne
Tarn

Côte Atlantique

Auvergne

Languedoc

P y r é n é e s

0   20   40   60   80 km
0   10   20   30   40   50 miles

*G*olden cliffs and majestic rivers complement castles and famed sites in this region of gastronomic renown.

Beynac-et-Cazenac (Dordogne)

BEYNAC-ET-CAZENAC, WITH ITS DRAMATIC FORTRESS RISING SHEER FROM THE CLIFF FACE, SITS BESIDE ONE OF THE MOST HISTORIC AND SCENIC SECTIONS OF THE RIVER DORDOGNE, ENHANCING THE RIVER'S REPUTATION AS ONE OF FRANCE'S LOVELIEST.

Houses scrabble up the hillside that leads to the fortress, owned by the Beynac family until the 1950s

The village of Beynac consists of a cluster of golden-stone houses lining the river beneath a 150m cliff. Perched at the top is a formidable medieval fortress, once one of the four great Périgord strongholds. The stark eastern face of the castle is particularly striking, seeming more a work of nature than a man-made structure.

HISTORY DRENCHED IN BLOOD

Over the centuries Beynac has been served a generous measure of misery and violence. In the 12th century it was held by the wicked Mercadier, whose men terrorised the local countryside. The village was dismantled by Simon de Montfort and the anti-Cathar 'crusaders' in the early 13th century, then rebuilt by the Barons of Beynac, fortified with double ramparts to safeguard it against further sieges. The Lord of Beynac, however, was a notorious robber baron, and the dreaded castle, dominating a strategic bend in the river, became known as l'Arche de Satan (Satan's Arc).

A stony-faced lion obligingly spouts water for passersby, handy for removing travel grime

The village eventually became a French military stronghold during the Hundred Years' War, rivalling the English fortress at Castelnaud on the other bank of the Dordogne, which acted as a roughly defined front line. You can see the awesome profile of Castelnaud and the neighbouring fortresses of Fayrac and Marqueyssac from the castle terrace, in a spectacular panorama stretching as far as the *bastide* of Domme (see page 173). For a closer view, take a boat trip from the quay. The castle remained in the Beynac family until as recently as the 1950s. Since then it has been declared a historic site, and been carefully restored and opened to the public. The main building dates from the 13th century and was extended in the 15th century. The great Hall of State, where the Périgord barons would discuss affairs of state, still has its original magnificent barrel vaulting. Beynac was one of four Périgord baronies, and the baronial flags can still be seen. Just off the hall is a small oratory decorated with Gothic frescoes; one depicting the Last Supper is particularly striking for its naïve style and perspective.

A second chapel is anchored on to the cliff between the two surrounding walls. It was between these walls that invaders were trapped and stoned. You can still see the pulley used for hauling rocks back up to the fortress ready to bombard the next prisoner.

ANCIENT CRAFTS …

The village beneath the fortress consists of rows of elegant 15th- and 17th-century houses and tiny squares scattered down a steep footpath called the Caminal del Panieraires (Basketmakers' Path). Although today no basketmakers remain, there are several artisans' workshops near the castle entrance, and a small museum of folklore in the 14th-century tower.

Close by, on the slopes behind the village, is the open-air Archaeological Park. Located in a setting of extraordinary reconstructed Neolithic dwellings whose design was based on recent local research, the museum demonstrates the ancient crafts of flint-stone carving, the making and firing of Gallic earthenware, bone sculpture and other centuries-old crafts.

… AND CLASSIC CUISINE

Périgord is, of course, a great gastronomic centre famous for its truffles, walnuts, *foie gras* and many other delicious *confits* or conserves. Beynac is an ideal place to experience some of these delicacies. Maison Lembert, on the edge of the village, offers guided tours of their workshops to see the various conserves being produced, followed by a *dégustation*. Alternatively, every evening at the Ferme de

The Walk

Start at the car park down by the river and climb the gentle hill between the post office and the Hôtel-Restaurant du Château. Take the first turning to the right, following a pedestrian sign to the castle. After the Hôtel de la Poste, curve round to the left past a small stone cross and continue to climb.

②

Turn right at the next junction, up several steps, past the tower and through an arch, and continue to climb up to the Taverne des Remparts. Turn sharp right and follow the castle wall round to the chapel. Return to the Taverne and on up to the entrance to the Château de Beynac. Having visited the château, head back down the same path until you reach the cross.

③

Turn left just below the stone cross along a path which descends gently past a row of vine-clad cottages down to the main road.

④

Turn right at the Hôtel Bonnet (with a riverside terrace) and return to the car park along the riverbank.

_i_

▷ Length of walk: 2.5km
▷ Approximate time: 1 hour (plus castle)
▷ Terrain: All surfaced, but too steep for wheelchairs
▷ Parking: Free riverside parking
▷ Open: Château, daily, Mar–mid-Nov
▷ Refreshments: Bars and terraces

Now owned by the state, Beynac's impressive fortress has been well restored and is open to the public. From the riverside, its forbidding walls seem to have risen out of the very cliff that supports it

la Porte behind the castle, you can see ducks and geese being fattened up by the traditional _gavage_ method to increase the weight of their livers.

The village of Beynac makes an ideal touring centre for visiting the many splendid villages along this stretch of the river, including Domme, La Roque-Gageac and Castelnaud – not forgetting the neighbouring hilltop hamlet of Cazenac, worth a detour for its Gothic church and exceptional views. Beynac and Cazenac were arch-enemies for centuries, and their names remain inextricably linked.

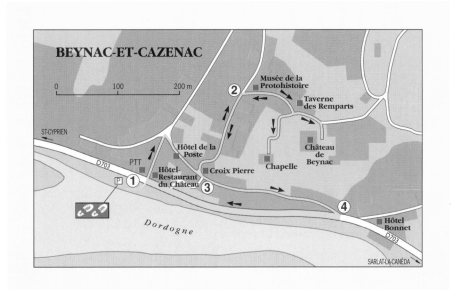

BEYNAC-ET-CAZENAC

0   100   200 m

ST-CYPRIEN

Musée de la Protohistoire

Taverne des Remparts

Hôtel de la Poste

D703

PTT

Hôtel-Restaurant du Château

Croix Pierre

Chapelle

Château de Beynac

Hôtel Bonnet

Dordogne

D703

SARLAT-LA-CANÉDA

Carennac
(LOT)

Carennac, a lovingly restored, romantic picture-postcard village of golden stone and turreted rooftops, ranks among the prettiest villages on the banks of the Dordogne.

The buildings of Carennac, restored to their original beauty by local artists and craftsmen, are huddled round a 10th-century priory, renowned for its 12th-century carved doorway and Flamboyant cloisters. The priory owes its fame to the prelate and author François de Salignac de la Mothe-Fénelon, the prior here from 1681 to 1685 before he became Archbishop of Cambrai. At Carennac it is possible to hire small boats to explore tiny Calypso Island, which so enchanted Fénelon that he described it in *Télémaque*, his celebrated literary achievement. His castle, attached to the priory, contains the Maison de la Dordogne, a superb museum which concentrates on all aspects of this fascinating 500km-long river – from flora, fauna and fishing to modern river management. The somewhat eccentric Museum of Aromas with its intriguing sign – 'The smells are free' – is worth a visit if only for its originality.

The Walk

Start at the priory entrance. Turn left out of the courtyard, cross the bridge and immediately turn left again. Take the first turning to the right and follow the road round until a T-junction and the Roman path.

Turn left and left again across the stream until coming to the priory. Bear right at the cemetery, then left at the main road, past the Mairie and the *auberge*.

A small path immediately after the *auberge* zigzags back towards the centre of the village. Where the path forks, bear left and then left again at the road, round to the Romanesque chapel and Musée des Arômes et du Parfum.

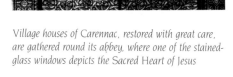

Head back towards the path, but stay on the road until you reach the post office. Now turn left at the main road and return to the priory.

Village houses of Carennac, restored with great care, are gathered round its abbey, where one of the stained-glass windows depicts the Sacred Heart of Jesus

Domme
(DORDOGNE)

The village of Domme, overlooking the River Dordogne from a high rocky crag, is one of the best-preserved *bastides* of the Périgord region. Its position is particularly unusual as bastides were usually built on flat ground to facilitate greater symmetry.

The *bastide* was founded in 1280 by Philip the Bold of France, and it took decades to construct because of Domme's situation. The usual rectangular plan proved impossible to realise, so the layout of the village is trapezoidal, with the main square at the top rather than the centre of the town.

The northern side of the village was never fortified because the inhabitants believed that the sheer cliff drop was sufficient protection from the enemy. Nevertheless, in the 16th century, the invincible Protestant Geoffroi de Vivans scaled the rocks with 30 of his men and seized the *bastide* without a fight. Subsequently the village changed hands repeatedly, especially during the Hundred Years War. Today, this rock face is called the Barre and offers one of the most magnificent of all Dordogne views.

The Promenade des Remparts takes you past the three remaining gateways to the bastide. From 1307 to 1318, the well-preserved 13th-century Towers gateway was used as a prison for the Knights Templar, who left their drawings on the walls for posterity.

Roses and vines decorate the honey-coloured gabled cottages clinging to the sloping streets. The oldest house, the Hôtel du Batteur de Monnaie dating from 1282, was the home of Philip the Bold's master coiner. The main street, lined with specialist shops selling wine, pâtés and potted goose, is a gourmet's paradise.

Beneath the village is a network of underground passages and caves with striking stalactites and stalagmites. The villagers hid in these caves during the Hundred Years' War and the Wars of Religion, and during the German Occupation Resistance workers used them as a refuge until they were exposed by collaborators and shot. The entrance is beneath the 16th-century covered market.

St-Cirq-Lapopie
(Lot)

The golden timber-framed houses with their typical Quercynois tiled roofs, beautifully restored by local artists and craftsmen, make this one of the most appealing villages in France. The ancient houses are staggered up a steep hill, crowned by the rugged ruins of a castle with spectacular views across the River Lot. The names of the cobbled streets leading down to the towpath honour the traditional craftsmen whose skills were once the wealth of the village, including metalworkers in the rue Payrolerie and hide merchants in the rue de la Pélissaria.

The village has been well known for its wood-turning since the Middle Ages, and has attracted painters for centuries, including Post-Impressionist Henri Martin, as well as the Surrealist poet André Breton, who remarked: 'Every morning when I get up, I have the impression of contemplating through my window the very best of Art, Nature and Life.'

Above, hilly St-Cirq. Below, the 13th-century bastide of Domme stretches back from the curving banks of the Dordogne, perched on a rocky crag which for centuries seemed to guarantee impregnability. Once breached, the town changed hands a number of times

Castelnaud-la-Chapelle (Dordogne)

THE IMPRESSIVE CASTLE OF CASTELNAUD-LA-CHAPELLE, BUILT DEFIANTLY ON TOP OF A HIGH CRAG ABOVE THE DORDOGNE, COMMANDS ONE OF THE REGION'S BEST VIEWS, PUNCTUATED BY CHÂTEAUX AND RIVERSIDE VILLAGES.

The village of Castelnaud nestles peacefully in a majestic loop or *cingle* in the river, surrounded by a patchwork of meadows and fields. The flower-decked golden-stone houses cling to the hillside on slim terraces leading up to the château which, although ruined during the Revolution, has been restored to much of its former glory.

In many respects the castle is typical of the Middle Ages, with its machicolated keep, curtain wall and bailey. Later additions such

On its elevated vantage point, Castelnaud occupies an enviable position above the River Dordogne

as the artillery tower demonstrate the development of fortress architecture and weaponry.

Castelnaud castle prides itself on being the most visited château in the region – quite an achievement when you consider that it lies on the Route des Mille et Un Châteaux du Périgord (Route of the Thousand and One Castles of Périgord), ranging from rather austere medieval fortresses to the rich exuberance of Renaissance châteaux. Inside the castle, the Museum of Medieval Siege Warfare has working models including a primitive cannon and catapults. There are several reconstructed battle scenes in the towers, and on summer evenings you can relive the castle's chequered past in a *son et lumière*.

FAIR MAIDEN OF CASTELNAUD

The château of Castelnaud (or rather Castel-nau, meaning 'new castle') dates originally from the 13th century. It changed hands constantly over the centuries and is said to have been destroyed and rebuilt more than 10 times. For most of the Hundred Years' War it was garrisoned by a band of English knights, in permanent battle with the French-controlled garrison downstream at Beynac.

In 1572 the fortress was inherited by seven-year-old Anne de Caumont following the death of her father. Her scheming guardian kidnapped the poor girl and forced her to marry his son. Five years later the latter was killed in a duel, and the girl-widow was kidnapped once more and married to a nine-year-old. Anne was aged 18 for her third and equally unhappy marriage to François d'Orléans, who took control of her estate. It is hardly surprising that she ran away and entered a convent.

A 'WALNUT STORY'

This region thrives on truffles, *foie gras*, wine and walnuts. In fact, the Périgord region produces two-thirds of all nuts consumed in France. Périgord walnuts have been used over the centuries for a variety of purposes and in particular for oil, gâteaux and liqueurs. Walnut wood is highly coveted for its rich colour and mottled texture. At the excellent Musée de la Noix you can see the traditional methods of nut-cracking, still used today, with a *tricot* or small mallet and a flat stone. To crack the shells without damaging the kernels is still considered an art.

Walnut lore is common. They say that King Louis XI used to have his beard shaved with heated walnut shells, and the French equivalent of a tall story is *une histoire à la noix* – literally, a walnut story!

The nut harvest takes place throughout the month of September. However, only walnuts which are sold before 15 September are entitled to be called 'fresh walnuts'. After this

The Walk

Start at the car park near the bridge at the foot of the village. Go up the steep path beyond the post office, signposted 'Château Piétons' and zigzag up to the tiny chapel.

Continue along winding lanes and alleyways, following a series of red and white painted waymarks, through two splendid stone arches, and turn right just past the Mairie up to the château.

③

Having visited the château, return to Les Tilleuls bar and turn into the short, narrow lane behind the bar. Bear left up a grassy path and take the first right along a mossy wall behind the castle, up to a wooded limestone escarpment and viewpoint, marked by a wooden cross.

Shortly beyond the viewpoint, turn left, then right at the house drive and left again on to a surfaced road. At the next junction, turn right, going over the brow of a hill, and descend steeply, following the road as it goes round past the Ramonets farm down into the valley.

Bear left alongside the Walnut Museum's orchards and continue straight on at the junction down a small grassy track which runs parallel to the road. Follow the lane into the village, past the chapel and down the original path to the car park.

▷ Length of walk: 3km
▷ Approximate time: 1½ hours (excluding visits to castle and Walnut Museum)
▷ Terrain: Largely unsurfaced; unsuitable for wheelchairs or pushchairs
▷ Parking: Free parking near the bridge
▷ Open: Château, daily
▷ Refreshments: Café bars

Come to Castelnaud in September for the walnut harvest and nut-cracking sessions

date they are dried, either in the sun or artificially, and sold as 'dried walnuts'. Should you visit the region in the latter half of September, you could join in the nut-cracking (a good *e'noiseur* or shell-breaker cracks about 25kg of walnuts a day) or simply relax by the river and enjoy a slice of *gâteau aux noix* in one of Castelnaud's cafés.

Castelnaud is undoubtedly one of the most charming and attractive villages of the Périgord. Not only is it a perfect base for touring the region, but it is also a popular base for activity holidays, especially riding, canoeing and rock-climbing.

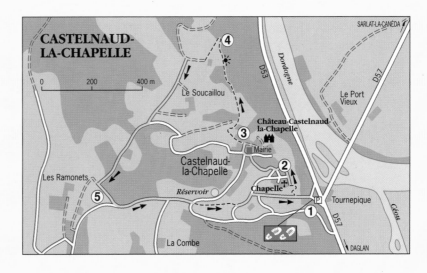

1

Start at the village bar. Go up the steep lane beside the bar past the manor house. The road curves round to a small green with well-placed benches.

2

Fork left and slowly descend. On the second curve follow a narrow gravel path to the left and then immediately right, under the arch to the main road, and turn left.

3

Take the first right which leads round to the church. Continue past the Mairie back to the main road opposite a fountain.

4

Turn right, then right again by the car park, along the Chemin de la Cascade, a long, steep climb well-rewarded by a breathtaking view. Return the same way to the car park.

Autoire
(Lot)

Surely no other village in the region boasts as many towers and turrets as Autoire, which cascades down the valley slopes. Its gables and red-tiled roofs represent authentic Quercynois style.

Lying in a deep gorge leading to the River Dordogne at the heart of the old province of Quercy, Autoire is without doubt one of the prettiest villages in France. This was once an important wine-growing region, and hence the village boasts a large number of magnificent Renaissance manor houses built by wealthy *vignerons* in the style of miniature châteaux. Even the farm buildings, with their tower-like dovecotes, resemble castles. These charming dwellings are clustered round tiny squares and fountains.

At the top of the village is the Château de Limargue, an attractive *gentilhommière* dating from the 16th century. At the lower end there is a finely sculpted Romanesque church offering views of the impressive limestone amphitheatre at the end of the valley, where a waterfall plunges 30m down the surrounding cliffs. Clinging to a ledge near the cliff top are the ruins of a folly-like fortress dating from the Hundred Years War called the 'Château des Anglais', the name given to many ancient ruins of uncertain history in the region.

Although the village no longer produces wine, it is famous for its Reine-Claude plums. If you are fortunate enough to visit in the second half of July, you can take advantage of the annual plum market.

Sheltered in a steep gorge which leads to the River Dordogne, Autoire is known for its fine plums

Above, magical Rocamadour, seemingly notched into a sheer cliff face, draws countless visitors and pilgrims. Right, La Roque-Gageac stands flush with the cliff

Rocamadour
(LOT)

The fascinating village of Rocamadour, with its enchanting jumble of stone-built medieval houses hanging from a dizzying near-vertical cliff, is dramatically sited in the gorge of the River Alzou – the second most important tourist centre in France.

Its fame dates back to the 12th century when the body of St Amadour – identified as Zacchaeus, a disciple of Jesus – was discovered beneath the chapel of the Virgin. According to tradition, Zacchaeus's wife Veronica had wiped the face of Jesus on His way to Calvary, and because of this they had to flee Palestine. Miracles occurred from the time the body was discovered, and Rocamadour remains one of Europe's most important pilgrimage destinations to this day.

The village is built along two very narrow ledges on a sheer limestone cliff face. From the main street pilgrims used to climb on their knees up the 233 steps of the Via Sancta to the seven churches grouped together on one of the ridges, to pay homage to the 12th-century Vierge Noire (Black Madonna) carved out of walnut wood, and to visit the Chapelle Miraculeuse, containing a bell which is said to toll by itself before a miracle occurs. Some people still make the steep ascent, kneeling to pray at every step.

The village offers numerous other attractions, including the Grotte des Merveilles with its cave-paintings over 18,000 years old, a 14th-century fort, a butterfly garden with species from all over the world, and a unique model railway. Although the majority of the village is pedestrianised, there are lifts and a small tourist train to help you on your visit.

La Roque-Gageac
(DORDOGNE)

The most surprising aspect of La Roque-Gageac is that, despite giving the impression of great antiquity, many of the buildings date from the latter half of this century, following destruction during the German Occupation. Nevertheless, they have been lovingly reconstructed and blend in perfectly with the original medieval buildings. As a result, the village remains something of a tourist honey-pot, with its neat rows of golden houses squashed against the steep golden cliff on a bank of the Dordogne. Here the thriving farming community specialises in tobacco, walnuts, maize, asparagus and strawberries. Like the neighbouring village of Domme (see page 173), La Roque-Gageac, with its fine manors, picturesque houses and exotic vegetation, is classified as among the most beautiful and most-visited villages of France.

The main sights include the ruined 12th-century fort, disguised against the cliff face, and the early Renaissance Manoir de Tarde with its pepper-pot roof. Former home of Jean Tarde, 16th-century astronomer and friend of Galileo, the manor remained in the family for several centuries, and members of the family still live in the village.

La Roque-Gageac was once a walled township with over 1,500 inhabitants, including 300 soldiers who protected the summer palace of the Bishops of Sarlat. Before the road was built, the village was an important river port for shipping salt and wood, which was carried by traditional flat-bottomed boats called *gabarres*. You can occasionally see them tied up alongside the little quay, where larger boats modelled on the *gabarres* depart for regular sightseeing trips.

Other Villages

CABRERETS

Pressed against the foot of a sheer limestone cliff face and dominated by the 14th-century Château Gontaut-Biron, tiny Cabrerets consists of a string of pretty stone houses with multicoloured shutters, lying along the River Célé in a wild valley. Here in 1922 two 14-year-old boys were walking when their dog suddenly disappeared down a hole, which proved to be an opening in the roof of a cave containing 20,000-year-old paintings of mammoths, bison and horses. The original entrance of this remarkable underground sanctuary, the Grotte du Pech-Merle, was discovered in 1949, and the cave is now open to the public.

CADOUIN

The sleepy village of Cadouin is best known for its honey-coloured Cistercian abbey, founded in 1115, and as home to the controversial 'holy shroud' thought to have covered the dead face of Christ, brought back from Antioch by a local priest. When in 1934 it was proved to be an 11th-century fake, Cadouin ceased to attract pilgrims.

The abbey is worth a visit for its intricately carved Flamboyant Gothic cloisters, as is the craft centre demonstrating work from 24 local ateliers. The extraordinary Musée du Vélocipède traces the history of cycling, from the hobby horse to the mountain bike.

LES EYZIES-DE-TAYAC

Les Eyzies lies in the midst of a region rich in prehistoric sites, some dating back over 40,000 years. The discovery of so many caves and shelters in the area over the last century has made the village the world capital of prehistory. The Font-de-Gaume cave displays a veritable menagerie of animals painted on the cave walls, and the main museum – the Musée National de la .Préhistoire – has its home in the restored 13th-century fortress halfway up the cliff above the village.

MARTEL

Time seems to have stood still in the pedestrianised streets of 12th-century Martel, centre of the regional nut trade. The ancient grain measures can still be seen at the wooden market in the square.

The town was named after Charles Martel, who built an abbey here in 732. It later became the capital of the Viscounts of Turenne, known locally as the 'Town of Seven Towers'. Its strong fortifications bear witness to its violent past. Even the striking church of St-Maur consists of battlements and buttresses. The Hôtel de la Raymondie is just one of many fine buildings in the town, and houses a fascinating museum of old Quercy maps.

MONPAZIER

This 13th-century town, founded by Edward I of England, has over 30 buildings classified as historic monuments. Pass through one of three fortified gateways into the little streets of honey-coloured buildings, laid out grid-style. The main square, with its covered arcades, cafés and tempting shops, is an ideal place to while away a sunny afternoon. The covered market here still contains a set of 15th-century measures. It is an important market town, thriving on its local produce of tobacco, chestnuts, strawberries and mushrooms.

PENNE D'AGENAIS

This medieval hilltop settlement, 10km east of Villeneuve-sur-Lot high above the River Lot, takes its name from the Celtic word for

Well-preserved Monpazier: underneath the arches in place des Cornières

mountain crest. The ancient gateway leads into a network of narrow streets lined with restored rose-coloured houses, which climb steeply past artists' and artisans' workshops to the remains of Richard the Lionheart's 12th-century fortress. At the top, the modern basilica of Notre-Dame-de-Peyragude offers extensive views across Lot-et-Garonne.

The village is famous for its prune products, and also its *tourtières* – an apple tart speciality – celebrated during July in the merry Fête de la Tourtière.

ST-CÉRÉ

St-Céré is an old market town in the valley of the River Bave, full of attractive 15th- to 17th-century half-timbered buildings with brown-tiled roofs. The market is known today for its strawberries and plums, but you can still see the taouilé, a stone bench in the place du Mercadial where fishermen once displayed their catch. The town's museums pay tribute to their most celebrated resident, Jean Lurçat (1892–1966), famous worldwide for his work on tapestry design and technique. His brilliantly colourful tapestries are shown at the Casino Gallery. A footpath behind the gallery leads to the medieval towers of St-Laurent on a hill high above the town.

Languedoc

The sun-soaked Languedoc is a region of contrasts. Its ancient villages, whether capping stony hilltops or nestling in the meander of a quiet river valley, are as remarkable for their historical interest as for their stunning natural settings. The pig and the goose rule most menus here.

Languedoc

Conques *(Aveyron)*

LOST IN THE WILDERNESS OF A SMALL GORGE, CONQUES, WITH ITS 12TH-CENTURY ROMANESQUE CHURCH AND THOUSAND-YEAR-OLD STREETS, IS BOTH A CULTURAL MAGNET AND A SPIRITUAL CENTRE OF INTERNATIONAL IMPORTANCE.

The history of Conques is closely linked to the spiritual and artistic renaissance which took place from the 10th to the 12th centuries, marking the end of the Dark Ages. As the 8th century was drawing to a close, the hermit Dadon selected this desolate spot as a retreat. Soon a small Benedictine community developed under the protection of the Carolingian kings.

IN PURSUIT OF A SAINT

At first the abbey received little notice because of its isolation and the infertility of the region. Furthermore, the abbey was without saintly relics, objects which held great religious importance during the Middle Ages. But the monks here had long coveted the bones of Ste-Foy, a child martyr burnt and beheaded in Agen around AD 303. After many attempts to acquire the relics, one of their number, a certain Ariviscus, succeeded in appropriating them towards the end of the 9th century.

Thanks to the illicitly procured relics, Conques became a major halt on the Via Podensis from Puy-en-Velay to Moissac. This

An extraordinary depiction of the Last Judgement, above, is set over the west door of the church. Its animated figures, weathered over the centuries, still hint at the colours which originally brightened them

was one of the four major routes to Santiago de Compostela in northern Spain, the most popular pilgrimage site of the Middle Ages, where the remains of St James the Apostle are said to be buried. Catering for the masses of travelling pilgrims, with their continuous donations, brought wealth and power. Thus Conques rose to eminence in the 11th and 12th centuries, and the artistic development of the abbey and town followed.

TREASURE OF A CHURCH

The present church, begun in the 11th century, is one of the few nearly complete surviving examples of High Romanesque architecture. The ground plan was designed to serve two purposes: to hold large crowds of pilgrims and to serve as the abbey church. The large ambulatory allowed pilgrims to view the relics of Ste-Foy which were exposed in the choir. The size of the church, however, was restricted by the terrain, and strong retaining walls had to be built to the north and to the south. Depending upon

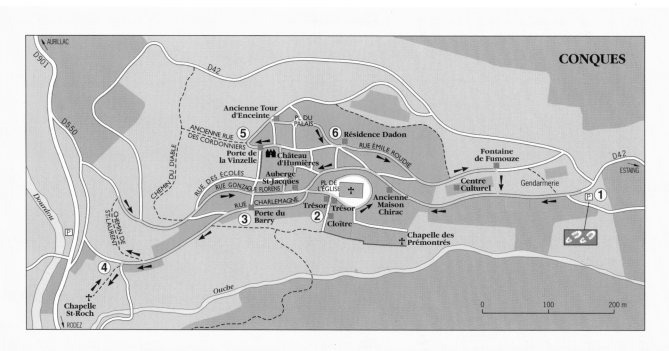

The Walk

1

Start from the car park and walk towards the church, in place de l'Église.

2

After visiting the church, walk through the cloisters to the refectory and *trésor* (abbey treasure). Circle the church completely to return to the place de l'Église. From here, take the steps on the right.

3

Walk down rue Charlemagne past the Porte du Barry. Turn left at the fork, then walk up the steps to the Chapelle St-Roch.

4

Retrace your steps up rue Charlemagne to a small footpath on the left near an iron cross. Follow the footpath to a surfaced road and turn right to return to the village. Immediately before the Auberge St-Jacques, take the steps on the left. Now turn right, then left. At the junction turn left again towards the Château d'Humières and continue uphill to the Porte de la Vinzelle.

5

Pass under the arch and turn right. Just after a tower, turn right again. Continue to the place du Palais and turn right.

6

At the Résidence Dadon, take rue Emile Roudié to the edge of town. At the Centre Culturel, take the steps on the right and return to the car park.

$\boxed{i}$

▷ Length of walk: 3km
▷ Approximate time: 3 hours
▷ Terrain: Mostly cobbled. Some steps and steep paths. Not suitable for wheelchairs or pushchairs, except points 1 and 2
▷ Parking: Free outside village; charge near cultural centre
▷ Open: Church: daily in season 7:30–7:30; off season 8–6. Treasure: daily in season 9–7
▷ Refreshments: Cafés, inns, restaurants and *pâtisseries*

---

one's vantage point, the church appears either built into the slope or perched on a rock, very tall in relation to the village.

The abbey's most famous feature is the 12th-century tympanum over the west door. Best seen in the setting sun, this masterpiece of Romanesque sculpture depicts the Last Judgement in vivid detail. Amongst the saved and the damned, there are 124 figures, some of which still retain the original polychrome.

The interior of the church is strikingly pure, with a vast and austere choir vaulting 22m upwards. The intricate relic grille in the choir is one of the most renowned wrought-iron pieces of the Middle Ages. On the walls of the sacristy, a 15th-century fresco portrays the martyrdom of Ste-Foy. The refectory, to the far side of the cloister, contains a prestigious collection of medieval religious metalwork. The golden statue of Ste-Foy, one of the oldest reliquary statues in Christianity, and the 'A' of Charlemagne are of particular interest. Another collection, near the front of the church, contains more recent objects.

FOCUS ON THE MEDIEVAL

The village of Conques is charming, with old half-timbered houses with stone roofs. Its steep cobbled streets and numerous stairways transport you back in time. In fact, the plan of the village has not changed since the 10th century. The houses, which were built at the end of the Middle Ages, frequently have two entrances, one on the first storey and another on the second. As a local adage

Stepped rooflines peek out from the wooded slopes, below. The village centre, above right, is sheer inspiration for its Medieval Art and Civilisation Centre

points out: 'At Conques, you can enter the by attic and leave by the cellar'.

Conques is also an active centre of research and study. The European Centre for Medieval Art and Civilisation offers seminars, lectures, and theatrical and film presentations. An international festival of medieval and classical music has been held every summer since 1982. There are also music courses for accomplished musicians. The Feast of Ste-Foy is celebrated each year on the Sunday following 6 October.

Estaing
(AVEYRON)

Perched on a rocky outcrop where the Coussanes flows into the sleepy waters of the Lot, Estaing reflects the subtle harmony of its position between the Languedoc and the Auvergne. Built in a northern style with heavy slate roofs, Estaing's nevertheless has a southern flavour, with vineyards covering the hillsides. Dominated by a splendid and well-preserved castle with an elegant watchtower, the little village also boasts a 15th-century church as well as many fine medieval and Renaissance buildings. The Estaing family, an illustrious old French family, held the castle until after the Revolution, when it was sold publicly. Today, it belongs to a religious order, the Sisters of St Joseph, and is open to the public.

The villagers still have great respect for their local customs and need little prompting to don traditional costumes and entertain visitors with music and dancing. The village feast day is on the first Sunday of July, when St-Fleuret, the village patron, is honoured by a solemn, 1,000-year-old procession in which the entire village takes part. The famous iron cross on the Gothic bridge has become the symbol for Estaing's expatriate communities, especially those in Louisiana and Argentina, reproduced in jewellery.

An important halt on the Via Podensis – a major pilgrims route to Santiago de Compostela, where the Apostle James is said to be buried – the village has been welcoming pilgrims since the 9th century.

Entraygues-sur-Truyère
(AVEYRON)

Entraygues means 'between the waters'. This unspoilt village, situated at the confluence of the Lot and its tributary the Truyère, retains the simple, slow-paced atmosphere of yesteryear. It is an excellent starting point from which to discover both the upper Lot Valley and the far more rugged Truyère Gorge.

The Lot, whose banks afford lovely walks, has always played an important role in village life. Until the advent of the railway, the Lot was navigable. As long ago as 1551, Entraygues possessed its own river fleet. In the 19th century, boats sailed as far as Bordeaux, transporting coal and stockfish (wind-dried cod). Vestiges of the river's history can still be seen in the village: remains of an old port, two Gothic bridges, numerous flood scales and an interesting mill. From the turn of the century until 1960, this 14th-century mill, converted into a generator, provided Entraygues with electric power. Nowadays, the river is used only for irrigation and, of course, for popular leisure activities – fishing, canoeing and swimming.

In 1903, Vidal de Lablache, one of the founders of modern geography, said of the area: 'Nowhere has France lovelier valleys, more brilliant light and more variety of vegetation.' And little has changed in villages such as these. As with all the villages along the Lot, the soil of Entraygues and its environs is cultivated wherever space allows. Medieval houses are surrounded by gardens and fruit trees, giving the visit an intimate feeling: at times it is almost like walking

The Walk

①

Park on the banks of the Lot and walk towards the Gothic bridge.

②

Take the rue François-d'Estaing. Turn left up the rue d'Oultre. Take the first street on the right and turn right again back towards the river. Turn left in front of the town hall up the rue Belières, then left again up the rue du Collège. Take the steps to the rue du Barry and continue downhill to the front of the church.

③

After visiting the church, cross the square to the castle. The keep and the terraces can be visited.

④

From the square, follow the rue du Pont to the Coussanes. Cross the bridge, go up the stairs opposite. At the cemetery, follow the river back to the banks of the Lot.

Wooden shutters and lace curtains frame a senior resident of Estaing, who obligingly pauses to pose

through someone's garden. Entraygues' own wine, called Vin du Fel, can be sampled in the cafés round the place de la République.

The village dates from about the same time as the castle, which was built between 1278 and 1290 by Henri II, the Count of Rodez. Struck by its strategic location, he constructed a magnificent edifice with ramparts, 13 towers and a drawbridge. The present structure is a mixture of several original towers and 17th-century additions. Owned by a religious order, it is used as a children's holiday centre and is closed to the public.

Entraygues is set 'between two waters', the Lot and the Truyère, a double advantage for leisure purposes

La Couvertoirade
(AVEYRON)

In the middle of the dry and desolate Larzac Plateau, this miniature fortified village with its intact ramparts and six towers still holds the allure of the Middle Ages. Pass through the North Gate and into another age.

At the top of winding, eroded steps cut into the rock itself, the fortified church helped to defend the village. In the adjoining graveyard are several unusual medieval stelae which date from the times of the Templars. Circular in shape, they are carved with the Maltese cross and formerly all faced east towards the rising sun, as a sign of the Resurrection. La Couvertoirade was long held by the Templars, then by the rival order of the Hospitallers, and served as a commandery. The château itself, built by the Templars, housed sick and aged knights, a sort of pensioners' home for knights.

The village is composed of several rural yet elegant 17th-century residences, built during a period of prosperity, as well as many smaller houses. The best of these line the narrow rue Droite. They were built to accommodate both man and beast: the vaulted lower levels were used for sheep, while the upper levels, reached by sturdy exterior stone steps, were reserved for the family.

Like many areas of the Languedoc, La Couvertoirade became depopulated in the 20th century and fell into ruin. Today, thanks to a revival of craft trades (glass-blowing, pottery, woodwork, musical instruments, leather goods and weaving) and the encouragement of local historical societies, its population is growing, and restoration continues.

Yet the village remains in harmony with nature. Not far from the South Gate, there is an excellent example of a *lavogne*, a basin used to collect precious drinking water on the rocky *causse*. Several adjoining sheep farms supply ewe's milk for the world-famous Roquefort cheese made near by.

A Maltese cross, highlighted by the sun, is featured on the distinctive stelae in La Couvertoirade

Najac

(Aveyron)

DOMINATING A SWEEPING CURVE OF THE AVEYRON GORGE, NAJAC SITS LIKE AN ISLAND ON A GRANITE SPUR, REVEALING A HIDDEN MAJESTY AS IT WINDS ALONG THIS ROCKY CREST.

The village of Najac holds a key place in French history. Many factions disputed long and hard over possession of this naturally defensive site, which was an instrument of the French Crown. The tale of Najac is one of strife and rebellion – the English Occupation, the Albigensian Crusade, the Hundred Years War and regional conflicts, including the Rebellion of the Croquants – punctuated by periods of commercial prosperity.

ROYAL COMMAND

The village, with its fine houses dating from the 14th century onwards and its numerous fountains, is a perfect example of a street village. Its long main axis stretches 1.5km along the crest of the promontory, under the shadow of the lofty castle which crowns the wooded slopes and is frequently lost in the mists rising from the valley below.

The present castle, a royal fortress of the 13th century, perches boldly 200m above the Aveyron Valley and dominates the entire region. Strategically placed on the border of the Rouergue and Quercy, it commanded an important position between Aquitaine, the

Its proud profile eroded and overgrown, the castle, below, memorably dominates Najac, above

Languedoc and the Auvergne. With its towering keep, its veritable labyrinth of passages and communicating towers, the fortress pos-

sessed the most modern military and architectural innovations of its time. The castle's construction took 10 years, with 2,000 workers coming from all over the kingdom of France to contribute their talents. The keep, which stands 38m high, affords a superb view over the stone roofs of the village and the gorges beyond.

ST-JEAN AND THE HERETICS

Between the castle and the river, near the centre of the original medieval village, is the 13th-century church of St-Jean, which the inhabitants of Najac were condemned to build as a punishment for their allegiance to the Cathar heresy of dualism. Austere and solid, it is a fine example of the southern Gothic style, the first of this type in the region. One of the most original features of the church is its quadrilobe windows, unique to 14th-century France. Also noteworthy is the 13th-century wrought-ironwork. The interior, which was restored in 1989, is controversial in its modern appearance.

The original Gallo-Roman town was situated just before the church, near La Pause (so-named because travellers would stop to catch their breath here before continuing uphill into the town). As in many medieval towns of the region, Najac is divided into three parts: the *cité*, the *bourg* and the *bastide*, or *faubourg*.

The *cité*, which developed mainly during the 13th century, covers the upper village around the castle, between the Porte de la Pique and the former drawbridge, which was not far from the Maison du Sénéchal.

The *bourg*, on the narrow promontory between the castle and the bastide, developed near the former church of St-Barthélémy, the patron of the town. The beautiful nearby monolithic fountain, built in 1344, carries the arms of Blanche de Castille, mother of St Louis, who resided here.

The *bastide*, whose present plan dates from the 15th century, developed where the promontory joins the Ségala Plateau. Here, the single, serpentine street widens into a lovely arcaded square. Unlike most *bastides*, which are rectangular, Najac's unusual trapezoidal shape is a function of the terrain. The charm of the square, with its wrought-iron balconies, timber-framed upper floors and houses resting on stone pillars, is enhanced by the double row of acacias, the potted plants and greenery. It has an open, relaxed feeling to it: the inhabitants come and go, chatting about the events of the day or just sitting out in the open air.

FROM FOOD TO FESTIVALS

The square was formerly an important market place for cloth, wine, livestock, barrels and ham (indeed, Najac has been famous for its ham since the Middle Ages: Rabelais' Pantagruel praises no other). Today, the square is still the centre of daily activities, and on more ceremonial occasions it hosts processions, concerts and summer festivities.

Regular markets take place on Sunday mornings, as well as a farmers' market on Wednesday mornings. Annually on Bastille Day (14 July) and again on the Assumption, 15 August, a flea market is held here. On the first weekend after the Assumption, the Festival of St-Barthélémy takes place, including costumed processions and children's games as well as dances featuring Occitan singing and popular bands.

A spur-of-the-moment purchase – whether an antique or just bric-a-brac – makes a unique souvenir

The Walk

Park near the *gendarmerie*. Enter the bastide and walk down the left-hand side of the square. Continue downhill past the monolithic fountain.

At a small square, opposite the Ancienne Église St-Barthélémy, there is a view of the château. Continue towards the château.

Just before the castle grounds, turn left through the arch, past the Maison du Sénéchal. Continue up rue du Château and into the Cité du Castel. Here the street becomes rather steep. At a small square, a paved footpath leads up to the castle.

After visiting the château, continue along the path past the Porte de la Pique, as far as the Église St-Jean. After visiting the church, turn left and walk past the front entrance. Continue downhill past gardens and old houses to rue Basse, which leads into a narrow footpath before veering left to rejoin the main street. Turn right.

Go past the monolithic fountain and up the main street to the *bastide*. Walk along the opposite side back to the *gendarmerie*.

i

▷ Length of walk: 2.5km
▷ Approximate time: 2½ hours
▷ Terrain: Some steep sections and steps
▷ Parking: Free near *gendarmerie*
▷ Open: Castle: Apr– Sep, daily 10–noon and 2:30–5 (Oct: Sundays only)
▷ Refreshments: Restaurants and cafés

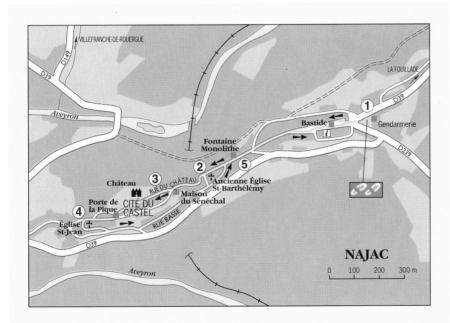

NAJAC

0 100 200 300 m

F IRE, ONE OF THE SYMBOLS OF LIFE AND PURIFICATION, IS ASSOCIATED WITH HEAVEN, EARTH AND HELL. FROM THE ANIMATED INFERNO SCENE OF THE LAST JUDGEMENT CARVED ABOVE THE CHURCH DOOR AT CONQUES, TO THE EAST-FACING, RISING-SUN STELAE IN THE GRAVEYARD AT LA COUVERTOIRADE, FIRE AND ITS 'PERSONIFICATION', THE SUN, HAVE PLAYED A CENTRAL ROLE IN IMAGERY, RELIGION AND NATURAL PHILOSOPHY DOWN THE AGES. WHETHER IN INDUSTRY OR IN ART, OUR PRESENT CIVILISATION COULD NOT EXIST WITHOUT FIRE. USED IN THE ARTS, ONE OF ITS PRIMARY FUNCTIONS IS THE TRANSFORMATION OF MATTER. IN THE LANGUEDOC, THIS IS INTIMATELY ASSOCIATED WITH PRODUCTS SUCH AS CERAMICS, METALS AND GLASS.

The Fire Trades: Past and Present

In the Languedoc, ceramics were first produced on an industrial scale during Gallo-Roman times. At Graufesenque near Millau in the Aveyron, where the archaeological site is open daily (except on major holidays), there were 500 potters in the 1st century AD. As one of the largest known ceramic centres of the Roman Empire, Graufesenque exported millions of vessels across the entire Empire, from Scotland to Arabia, even (exceptionally) as far as India. In those days the *causses* were covered with forests capable of supplying ample fuel for the great fires required by the kilns, which were used to bake tens of thousands of vessels at a single firing. The workshops at La Canourgue in the *département* of the Lozère were equally important. An excellent collection of Roman ceramics can be seen at the museum in Millau.

Here are just two examples of the diverse skills of craftsmen in the Languedoc region, past masters of the fire trades. Right, a simple but elegant ceramic vase, detail from the village of La Couvertoirade and, below, the fine bridge over the river at Albi, whose bricks match those of the town's cathedral, opposite

Clay has been a faithful and versatile servant throughout the ages. Prehistoric domestic pottery, made on a smaller scale in settlements all over the region, has been yielded up at numerous excavated sites in the Languedoc, particularly at Foissac in the *département* of the Aveyron and on the plains of the Grands Causses. Hundreds of years later, clay was used to form the very substance of Albi, which, like so many other towns in the region, was built largely of brick. Those humble blocks were arranged into Albi's finest asset, the imposing cathedral of Ste-Cécile, one of the most famous medieval brick structures in the world. On a more down-to-earth level, the varnished pottery of Anduze in the *département* of the Gard has been famous since the 17th century and is much used as gardenware. In the present day, continuing the tradition of this most ancient craft, the studios of artistic potters and ceramists can be visited at countless villages and towns throughout the Languedoc region, including Pézenas, Cordes (see page 190), Najac (pages 184–5) and La Couvertoirade (page 183).

Mined, Melted, Minted

There were also many Roman lead and silver mines, in places such as Najac, and gold mines like those in the Tarn. Iron was extracted wherever deposits were available. The Merovingian mint at La Canourgue used local ores. During the Middle Ages, Villefranche-de-Rouergue in the Aveyron was famed for its gold, silver and brass ware, and a royal mint was founded there in 1463. The medieval gold- and silverwork at Conques was at least partially produced by local masters.

Pewter, an alloy based on tin, has long been crafted in the Languedoc region, and was made even in the smaller towns such as Sauve and St-Guilhem-le-Désert. Today, handmade pewter is still crafted at Villeneuve-d'Aveyron as well as in St-Gal.

In the 6th century BC, iron was in use as an artists' medium throughout Celtic Europe. After the Iron Age, it was relegated to a more utilitarian role until renewed interest in the metal developed at the end of the 11th century. The magnificent 12th-century relic grille at Conques is one of the most remarkable examples of medieval ironwork. Other regional examples of wrought-iron can be seen at Najac and at Sérergues. Continuing in the tradition of artistic ironwork today, internationally renowned 'blacksmith' Jean Marc, who works at Cordes, has created a poetic series of characters – not without a touch of irony – ranging from the literary to the military, Don Quixote to de Gaulle.

Iron was produced near Decazeville during the Middle Ages. As a commodity, however, it was manufactured by pre-industrial methods – until Christmas Day 1828, when the first blast furnace in Decazeville produced its inaugural smelting. Nowadays, serious iron production has become a thing of the past for the Languedoc. However, amongst other forms of industrial reconversion, Decazeville recycles the tin sheeting used in the manufacture of Roquefort cheese.

The iron cross on the bridge at Estaing, the work of a local smith, inspired the small golden cross that is often worn by 'expatriate' Aveyronnais women in Paris and as far afield as Argentina and the American state of Louisiana, where large communities emigrated. Handmade bronze, silver and gold jewellery is also made in workshops at the nearby town of Montézic.

Steel is of major importance at Laguiole, a small town in the Aubrac also famous for its cheese, its bulls and one of France's most famous restaurants. The Laguiole knife, first produced in 1829 by Pierre Calmels, is internationally famous (as Asian counterfeits prove) and has achieved near cult status among the French, both young and old. Traditionally made with bone hafts and brass bolsters, these handsome handmade folding knives are definitely a more elegant alternative to the common Victorinox. An 18m facsimile blade crowns the plateau at the Forge de Laguiole. A small enterprise employing 90 craftsmen, the Forge was founded only in 1987 and makes an interesting (and free) visit.

Beautiful workmanship inside the medieval cathedral of Conques, inset. Above, the red brick wall of Albi's imposing cathedral of Ste-Cécile

Clearly an Art

Glass-making requires not only the correct sand but also vast amounts of wood for fuel. During the Roman and medieval periods, the forested Bas-Languedoc was a centre of glass production. Later, at the time of the Industrial Revolution, glassworks suffered industrial strife in the region. When over half the employees at the Carmaux factory lost their jobs in 1895, Jean Jaurès founded a workers' cooperative glassworks in Albi. This collective venture is still in existence nearly a hundred years later. Today, individual glassblowers who have elevated the skill to an art form can be seen in Cordes and La Couvertoirade.

All these fire trades require fuel on an enormous scale. The denuded *garrigues* of the Mediterranean basin and the deforested *causses* (where grazing sheep prevent the forest from returning) testify to the use of wood for this purpose. But as early as the 13th century, coal was used for fuel by monks in both the Tarn and the Gard. By the 18th century, industrial exploitation had begun, with coalfields near Decazeville, Carmaux, Albi and Alès. In the Cévennes, coal brought great prosperity to the region, employing 23,000 miners in 1947. Yet, as elsewhere in the Languedoc, the industry eventually collapsed. Today, abandoned coal tips may be seen, incongruously, amongst vineyards and umbrella pines.

On the whole, however, the Languedoc was bypassed by the Industrial Revolution. Indeed, in many ways the region is even less industrial than in the past. The area has seen a decided dwindling of its population: the 1987 figures for the Midi-Pyrénées indicate fewer inhabitants than in 1846. Such small industries as there are tend to cluster round the larger cities, leaving the original character of the market towns and villages preserved – and a major attraction to visitors. Here, in rural Languedoc, the fire arts live on in people's homes, encountered in the warmth of the hearth ... and the meals on the table!

Ste-Enimie

(Lozère)

STE-ENIMIE'S CHARM SEEMS TO TRANSCEND THE PASSAGE OF TIME. A MEDIEVAL VILLAGE AT THE HEART OF THE GORGES DU TARN, IT WAS FIRST AN IMPORTANT RELIGIOUS CENTRE, THEN A COMMERCIAL HUB.

Énimie, daughter of Clotair II and sister of King Dagobert, was a virtuous Merovingian princess sought for her incomparable beauty by many noble suitors, but she had decided to devote her life to God. King Clotair nevertheless betrothed her to a rich baron. When she implored God to remove her beauty, her prayer was granted: the pious princess was disfigured by a hideous leprosy.

Her suitors fled. All cures failed against the ailment. One day, after many months of suffering, Énimie begged for alleviation. An angel then appeared and ordered the afflicted princess to go to Gévaudan, where the waters of the Burle would restore her beauty. The king prepared a worthy escort and, after many adventures, the party was finally guided to the source by pagan shepherds.

SOURCE OF HEALING

Upon bathing in its waters, Énimie's infection was cleansed, but it reappeared when she tried to leave the gorge. Bathing once more, she was cured again. But at each attempt to leave the gorge, the mysterious malady returned. It became clear that her calling was to remain in the heathen gorge. Énimie is said to have died around AD 628 after having established a convent and a monastery – the origin of today's village. Her story was recorded by the 13th century troubadour Bertrand de Marseille.

It was round the monastery on the top of a hill that a small village grew. At the beginning of the 10th century, however, it fell into total desolation and was ceded to the Benedictines, who created a pilgrimage shrine in 987 dedicated to the patron of the village. On terraces filled with soil carried by hand, the monks established vineyards and orchards of fruit and nut trees.

The village grew into a fortified city, and commerce and trade developed, particularly the weaving of wool. In the 15th century, the monastery became an abbey. Then, during the Revolution, the monks were expelled and the abbey – including its priceless library – destroyed by fire; the archives were said to have burned for eight days. Restoration of the monastery began in 1870, but the collapse of the weaving trade, the havoc of World War I and the mechanisation of farming sent Ste-Enimie once again into decline.

Off the place du Presbytère, a little street, above, dips down within the valley of the River Tarn, right

LIVING WITHIN HISTORY TODAY

The 12th-century church is a good example of regional Romanesque style. From here the narrow Chemin des Moines allowed the monks direct access to the abbey without passing through the village. The abbey, built between the 7th and 14th centuries, received pilgrims on their way to Rome or Santiago de Compostela. Three 10th- to 11th-century rooms – the vestibule, crypt and refectory – are open to the public. They now house various exhibitions.

The place au Beurre, formerly a farmers' market, has a fine example of a medieval house with projecting upper storeys. Potters sold their wares at the nearby place des Oules. At the Halle au Blé wheat, meat and wool were bartered for wine, fruits and walnut oil. A standard measure (5 litres) carved in stone can still be seen. The partially vaulted rue de la Privadenche, with its medieval houses, was built to accommodate porters and their loads. The Vieux Logis, a folklore museum, reconstructs past village lifestyles.

The Source de Burle is a Vauclusian fountain near the village. Walk from here to the hermitage of Ste-Enimie for an unequalled view of the sunrise over the gorge.

There is a fortnightly evening arts and crafts market in July/August, and the village feast day is on the first Sunday of October.

The Walk

① Park on the banks of the Tarn near the Gothic bridge and walk up to the church.

② After visiting the church, take the footpath (Chemin des Moines) towards the *monastère* (abbey) Turn left towards the Maison du Portier for a nearby viewpoint.

③ Continue uphill past the Maison du Portier to the back of the abbey, where several medieval sections can be seen.

④ Return to the base of the abbey and turn left into the place del Plô. Take the stairs on the left to the Salle Capitulaire.

⑤ From the place del Plô a covered passage-way leads to rue de la Privadenche. At the end of the street, turn right and continue to the Halle au Blé. Walk downhill to the place au Beurre and down rue del Serre towards Le Vieux Logis Folklore Museum.

⑥ Just before the church, take the covered passage to the rue Basse, formerly the main street. Turn left, walk to the end of the street, turn right and right again and walk back along the river, past shops and restaurants, towards the bridge.

> *i*

▷ Length of walk: 1.5km
▷ Approximate time: 1½ hours
▷ Terrain: Stairs and several steep sections
▷ Parking: Free along the banks of the Tarn
▷ Open: Folklore Museum: Apr–Sep
▷ Refreshments: Restaurants and cafés

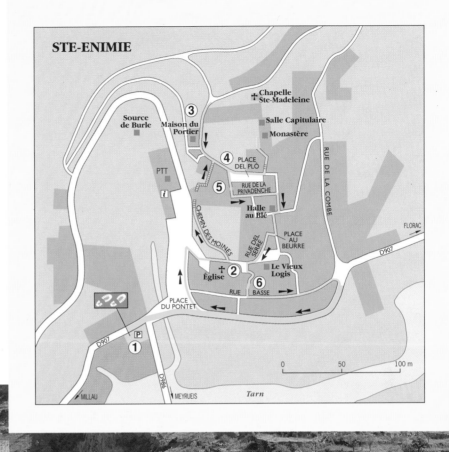

STE-ENIMIE

✝ Chapelle Ste-Madeleine
Source de Burle
Maison du Portier
Salle Capitulaire
Monastère
③
④ PLACE DEL PLÔ
PTT
⑤
RUE DE LA PRIVADENCHE
RUE DE LA COMBE
i
Halle au Blé
CHEMIN DES MOINES
RUE DEL SERRE
PLACE AU BEURRE
FLORAC
D907
✝ Église
②
⑥ Le Vieux Logis
RUE BASSE
PLACE DU PONTET
①
P
0   50   100 m
D907
D986
← MILLAU   ← MEYRUEIS   *Tarn*

BANNE

This medieval village is shaped like a horseshoe: at one end is a 12th-century church, at the other the ruins of a fortified castle atop a limestone cliff, the two connected by the curve of a single main road. Well-preserved streets wander up to the demolished stronghold, and in summer the place du Vieux Fort hosts craft fairs and open-air concerts. About 8km north-west, in Les Vans, Le Carmel, a former Carmelite convent, is an ideal and affordable place to relax in front of a fire, sip chestnut liqueur and soak up the ambience.

BRASSAC

Nestled amidst wooded hills, Brassac is a health resort with a refreshing summer climate. Once an important centre for the wool trade, the village still seeks a living in the textile industry. The enormous iron hooks visible on the 12th-century humpback bridge were used by dyers to dry material. The village has two castles, on either side of the river. One of them, with its feet in the Agout, houses a weaving museum; the other is now a hotel.

BRISSAC

Dominated by a 12th-century castle, Brissac possesses a true Mediterranean flavour. Olives and vines are cultivated in a large agricultural basin lying between gorges of the River Hérault. This verdancy contrasts refreshingly with the rocky *garrigue* of the surrounding limestone.

LA CANOURGUE

La Canourgue occupies an attractive site above the River Urugne. Pedestrianised streets are lined with old houses, some of which overhang canals, and the square has several interesting houses. The church is a mixture of Provençal style and a Romanesque choir.

The antique ceramic workshops at the nearby Gallo-Roman and Merovingian site of Banassac compare to those at Graufresenque near Millau. Branassac wares were once exported as far as Pompeii.

The 6th-century mint, supplied by local silver mines, produced one-tenth of all Merovingian coins.

CORDES

Capping an isolated outcrop of Steep, winding cobbled streets lead through Cordes' medieval arch-ways to the old town, founded in 1222 as a Cathar *bastide*. In the 14th century the textile trade flourished here, as attested by many elegant Gothic buildings, but religious conflict and the plague ended its prosperity. Cordes struggled along until the mechanisation of the textile industry struck its death blow. In 1941 the painter Yves Brayer moved to Cordes, and his artistic school brought about the village's revival. Resident sculptors, weavers, painters and ironworkers have restored many old houses.

LA GARDE GUÉRIN

Built in large blocks of local granite, the small farming community of Garde Guérin was founded in the 10th century as a fortified out-post on the most desolate part of the Lozère Plateau, and was the haunt of numerous brigands. This village served as a base for the *pariers*, 27 nobles, each owning a fortified house within the ramparts, who escorted travellers for a fee. The village was defended by an imposing castle. From the keep, there is a view of the nearby Gorge du Chassezac. The panorama extends as far as Mont Ventoux.

LAUTREC

Formerly an important medieval city, Lautrec is a veritable chess-board of narrow streets. Of its fortifications, only the Porte de la Caussade (complete with arrow slits) and the ramparts remain. Several 17th-century houses possess quiet courtyards and gardens. The market square has a splendid old well and half-timbered houses raised on wooden pillars.

The village has extensive views to the south and west: sometimes even the Pyrenees can be seen. The local speciality crop is pink garlic, and the region is known for leather goods.

LE MALZIEU-VILLE

Situated at the edge of a bleak granite plateau, this enterprising community is determined to make its charms better known to visitors. Recent restoration of its numerous old houses, fortifications and gateways has transformed the village, which can be viewed from the tower (now the town hall) at the side of the tourist office – open free to visitors, provided they can cope with heights and steep steps.

MEYRUEIS

Meyrueis, known for its clean air, is a small market town at the confluence of the Bétuzon, Brèze and Jonte rivers near the wild and unspoilt Jonte Canyon. The Maison Belon with its Renaissance windows and the Tour de l'Horloge (vestiges of ancient fortifications) are among the best buildings.

In a delightful setting 2km south of town, the 15th-century Château

To market, to market … but not a pig in sight! Fruits in their season, which is long in Languedoc, weight the tables

de Roquedols serves as the information centre for the Cévennes National Park.

STE-EULALIE-DE-CERNON

Ste-Eulalie sits in the verdant valley of the Cernon, former capital of the area. With its ramparts, parapet walk, machicolated towers and fortified gates, it exemplifies a fortified 15th-century commandery. From here the Knights Templar conquered the nearby *causses*. The village square, with its plane trees and fountain, is typically southern. The Romanesque church boasts a fine baroque door. Two kilometres south, the Pic de Cougouille affords a fine view over the Larzac Plateau.

ST-GUILHEM-LE-DÉSERT

This imposing village, at the confluence of the Verdus and Hérault, is built round an abbey founded by St Guilhem in 804 to house a relic of the Holy Cross given to him by Charlemagne, but only its 11th-century church remains. The cloisters, crypt, refectory (museum) and apse are particularly noteworthy. The village is composed of two parallel streets linked by passages. On a nearby hill castle ruins offer an excellent view of the site and the gorges of the Verdus.

SAUVE

At the foot of the Cévennes, beside the River Vidourle, sits the appealing village of Sauve, with its slim, high houses, shady squares, labyrinth of little streets and covered passageways and several fine examples of Renaissance windows.

Above the village are the ruins of the Château de Roquevaire, surrounded by cypresses. Local craftsmen specialise in the production of fire-hardened forks, fashioned from nettlewood trees grown on the rocky soil of the region.

THINES

Visitors venturing to Thines need nerves of steel to negotiate the vertiginous roads with impossibly narrow bridges leading to this magnificent tiny village perched 518m over the River Thine. From the car park, 150m downhill, steep pathways wend round brown shale houses and *clèdes* (houses used for drying chestnuts) which are roofed with stones. The church was founded in the 12th century by Byzantine monks seeking 'a universe of peace and culture'.

The Pyrenees

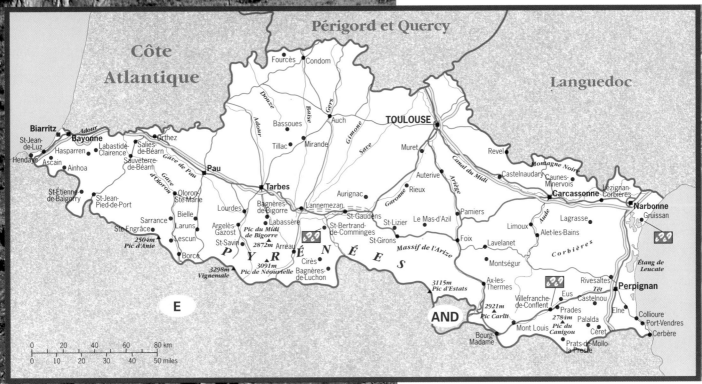

Périgord et Quercy

Côte Atlantique

Languedoc

Fourcès · Condom

Douze · Bassoues · Gers · Auch · Gimone · **TOULOUSE**

Adour · Tillac · Mirande · Save · Muret · Revel · Montagne Noire

Biarritz · Adour · Orthez · Salies-de-Béarn · Auterive · Canal du Midi · Castelnaudary · Caunes-Minervois · Lézignan-Corbières

St-Jean-de-Luz · **Bayonne** · Labastide-Clairence · Sauveterre-de-Béarn · Gave d'Oloron · **Pau** · Ariège · **Carcassonne** · **Narbonne** · Gruissan

Hendaye · Ascain · Ainhoa · Gave de Pau · Oloron-Ste-Marie · **Tarbes** · Garonne · Rieux · Pamiers · Lagrasse · Aude

St-Étienne-de-Baïgorry · St-Jean-Pied-de-Port · Lourdes · Bagnères-de-Bigorre · L'Annemezan · St-Gaudens · Le Mas-d'Azil · Limoux · Alet-les-Bains · Corbières · Étang de Leucate

Sarrance · Bielle · Labassère · St-Bertrand-de-Comminges · St-Lizier · Foix · Lavelanet

Ste-Engrâce · Laruns · Argelès-Gazost · St-Savin · Pic du Midi de Bigorre · St-Girons · Massif de l'Arize

2504m Pic d'Anie · Lescun · *2872m* · Arreau · **P Y R É N É E S**

Borce · *3298m Vignemale* · *3091m Pic de Néouvielle* · Cirès · Bagnères-de-Luchon · *3115m Pic d'Estats* · Montségur · Ax-les-Thermes · Rivesaltes · **Perpignan**

E · **AND** · *2921m Pic Carlit* · Villefranche-de-Conflent · Eus · Castelnou · Têt · Elne · Colloure · Port-Vendres

Bourg-Madame · Mont Louis · Prades · *2784m Pic du Canigou* · Palalda · Céret · Cerbère

Prats-de-Mollo-la-Preste

0 · 20 · 40 · 60 · 80 km
0 · 10 · 20 · 30 · 40 · 50 miles

The Pyrenees region offers a richness and variety of history, culture and landscape unrivalled in France, from the Catalan villages along the sparkling Mediterranean coastline, across wild and rugged snow-capped mountains, to the Pays Basque on the Atlantic coast.

Gruissan

(Aude)

THE ANCIENT ROMAN PORT OF GRUISSAN, SURROUNDED BY LAGOONS, SALT MARSHES AND FLAMINGOS 15KM FROM NARBONNE, REPRESENTS A TRULY MEDITERRANEAN MIX OF FISHERMEN AND WINE GROWERS, DESERTED OUT OF SEASON.

Surprisingly, the small fishing village of Gruissan is not actually on the coast. Over the years it has been distanced by a string of lagoons, formed by a build-up of alluvial deposits from the River Rhône along the Languedoc and Roussillon coastlines as far south as Perpignan. Gruissan is entirely surrounded by these small lagoons, each one edged with a ribbon of sand, their shimmering blue waters punctuated by pink flamingos against a backdrop of low hillsides.

The different lagoons round the village serve different purposes. The Étang de l'Ayrolle has been cultivated into salt marshes, an important industry in Gruissan, with glistening white mountains of salt just behind the village. Fishermen block the entrance to the freshwater Étang de Gruissan to catch the fish with the ebb and flow of the tides. The largest lagoon, the Étang de Bages, is popu-

lar for sailing and windsurfing, while the Étang de Campignol has many migratory birds and is surrounded by wild flowers, including orchids and rare wild tulips.

The entire lagoon region is rich not only in flora but also in fauna. Wild boar, hare and badgers are frequently spotted and there are over 8,000 species of insect, including several types of grasshopper unique to the area.

SCENTED HILLS, FAMOUS VINES

Just beyond the lagoons is a dramatic change in scenery. The hilly landscape gives way to the Massif de la Clape, a series of high limestone cliffs, canyons and valleys harbouring a wealth of Mediterranean plants. Their slopes are clad in fragrant pine, rosemary, thyme and lavender, laced with waterfalls and patched with extensive vineyards. This is one of the main growing areas for the wines of the Aude *département*, a region famous for its fine wines, most notably Fitou, Corbières and Minervois.

The wine domaines are the only properties in this wild and rugged landscape, except for the tiny chapel of Notre-Dame-des-Auzils, where Gruissan fishermen come each year on 29 June to celebrate a fishing festival in honour of their patron, St Peter.

THE ANCIENT FISHING PORT

Gruissan village has been designed on an entirely circular layout, with its labyrinth of narrow streets and alleyways resembling a giant spider's web. The traditional fishing cottages, their speckled orange, rust and golden

Traditional pots known as cônes or amphores lie safely cushioned in baskets awaiting a buyer in the market

roofs soaked in sunlight, cluster round the Barbarossa Tower, with its spectacular views of the village, lagoons and salt marshes.

The village is riddled with wine-tasting cellars, including the Cave Coopérative which offers *dégustations* every Monday evening. Gruissan bursts into life three times a week for a bustling market of fruit, vegetables and local specialities, while at the harbour, local fishermen sell the daily catch at little stalls.

Just beyond the fishing harbour, on reclaimed land, is Gruissan-Plage, a long sandy beach lined with houses or chalets on stilts, where Jean-Jacques Beneix made his cult film *Betty Blue*. The stilts were originally intended to keep the houses out of the water. Nowadays, they stand far from the water but still delight the eye. On the beach, oyster and mussel farmers offer their products.

Alternatively, you can visit the Fumeries Occitanes (fish smokehouse) at the far end of the beach every Tuesday and Friday morning to see the fish being salted, dried, then smoked over beech fires. Should you wish to join the fishermen, the Merry Fisher Club and the Gruissan Tuna Club offer regular boat trips for shark, swordfish and tuna fishing, or just a gentle voyage along the coast.

Near the village is an extensive but tasteful modern marina development called Port Gruissan. Its bustling docks are full of cafés and restaurants juxtaposed with the quiet local bars of the village, and its modern yachts and motor cruisers dwarf the tiny boats in the fishing harbour. Nevertheless it provides the village with another industry – tourism – and it provides the tourists with enough variety to please all tastes.

A pleasing street detail, left, and a bird's-eye view of the village, right, as seen from the château

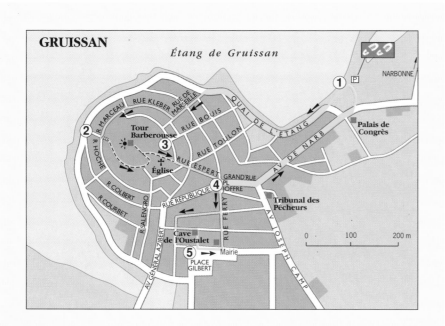

GRUISSAN

Étang de Gruissan

NARBONNE

Palais de Congrès

Tour Barberousse

Église

GRAND'RUE
PL JOFFRE

Tribunal des Pêcheurs

Cave de l'Oustalet

Mairie

PLACE GILBERT

RUE DE MARSEILLE · RUE KLEBER · R MARCEAU · R HOCHE · RUE BOUIS · QUAI DE L'ÉTANG · RUE TOULON · RUE ESPERT · R COLBERT · R COURBET · R SALENGRO · RUE REPUBLIQUE · RUE FERRY · AV DE NARB · AV JOSEPH CAMP · AV GÉNÉRAL AZIBERT

0   100   200 m

The Walk

❶

Start at the car park opposite the Palais de Congrès. Follow the road along the edge of the lake, round two bends, and turn left into rue de Marseille. Take the second turning right along rue Kléber and continue into rue Marceau.

❷

At the junction with rue Suffren and rue Hoche (not named on the map), turn left up some steps and round to the left up a dirt track. Branch right and continue round the castle to the church and some steps on the left leading up to the castle tower (Tour Barberousse) and a magnificent viewpoint.

❸

Return down the steps and continue down beside the church into the main shopping street, rue Espert.

❹

Turn right at place Joffre into rue Ferry. Bear first right, then left at the main road to reach the Cave de l'Oustalet.

❺

Go through the cave and into place Gilbert. Turn left, then left again opposite the Mairie, back to place Joffre. Go right along Grand' Rue, then first left opposite the 18th-century Tribunal des Pêcheurs (Fishermen's Law Court) back to your car near the Palais de Congrès.

---

i

▷ Length of walk: 2.5km
▷ Approximate time: I hour
▷ Terrain: Points 2 and 3 unsuitable for wheelchairs and pushchairs
▷ Parking: Choice of car parks
▷ Refreshments: Cafés in the Grand' Rue

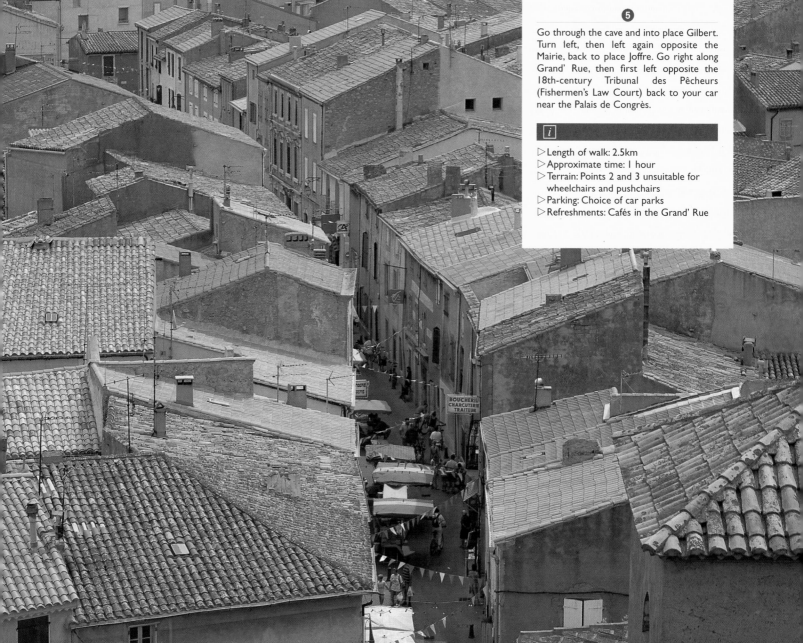

St-Bertrand-de-Comminges *(Haute-Garonne)*

THE MASSIVE CATHEDRAL OF ST-BERTRAND STANDS ON A ROCKY OUTCROP GUARDING THIS SMALL VILLAGE AND THE REMAINS OF A SUBSTANTIAL ROMAN CAPITAL CITY, TUCKED INTO THE FERTILE GARONNE BASIN.

On the 9km southbound approach to St-Bertrand-de-Comminges from Montréjeau, you are struck by the sheer size of the awesome buttressed cathedral looming up in the distance, towering above the modest red-roofed village that surrounds it. It is easy to see why this village has been voted one of the most beautiful in France, situated in the heart of the Pyrenean countryside, overlooking verdant meadows and surrounded by the foothills of distant, snow-capped mountains. It is also one of the most popular tourist

The light, tranquil cloister of the cathedral, above, contrasts with the dark wood of the choir inside, where carved panels depict scenes from the Bible, church tradition and the lives of the saints, left and opposite

destinations in the region – best visited early in the morning, in the evening or, better still, out of season.

WHERE LEGIONS MARCHED

At the foot of the rocky hump, capped by the delightful medieval village of St-Bertrand, lies the site of one of the most important cities of Roman Aquitaine: *Lugdunum Convenarum*, which at its peak had a population of 50,000 inhabitants. Strategically placed, it commanded all the routes in the Garonne basin leading to Luchon, Toulouse and Tarbes. It was to this place that Pompey's legions crossed the mountains from Spain, barely two days' march away. And it was to this important provincial capital that Herod Antipas of Galilee was reputedly exiled by the infamous Emperor Caligula, four years after the Crucifixion.

Lugdunum Convenarum is generally thought to have been founded in 72 BC, although its full history has yet to be unearthed. Excavations are in progress, but currently it is possible to see the large marketplace, several baths, the forum, a theatre and all the main elements of an efficient Roman city.

The town was largely destroyed by Barbarians during the 4th and 5th centuries, and in the 6th century it was stricken by the plague. A small remnant of the population managed to survive; dwelling at the foot of the hill, they kept the village alive until the 12th century, when it again flourished.

ENCOUNTERING ART HISTORY

In 1120 Bertrand, Bishop of Comminges, decided to build a magnificent Romanesque cathedral above the village. The cloister is particularly attractive because it is open to the valley on one side, with sweeping views of meadows, vines and cypresses playing an integral part in daily worship. A medieval episcopal city soon grew up round the cathedral, attracting pilgrims. Since then, the cathedral has been considerably enlarged and embellished by successive bishops, to

specialising in Pyrenean wool garments and fine local faïence.

Across the meadows from the upper village, shaded by cypress trees, lies the small early Romanesque basilica of St-Just, erected on the site of a Roman necropolis and built with stone from the old Roman town. After visiting the many fascinating sites in the neighbourhood, one can return to the classical theme in the extraordinary Restaurant Le Lugdunum, 2km away in the village of Valcabrère, with its unique Roman menu containing the recipes of Marcus Gavius Apicius, legendary chef of the Roman Empire.

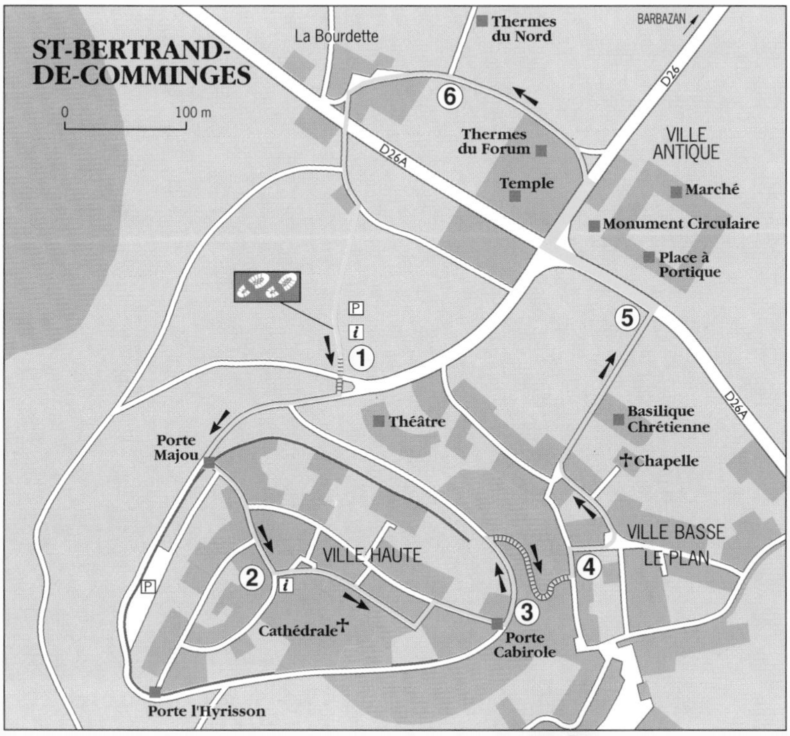

ST-BERTRAND-DE-COMMINGES

0   100 m

Map labels: La Bourdette · Thermes du Nord · BARBAZAN · D26 · Thermes du Forum · D26A · VILLE ANTIQUE · Temple · Marché · Monument Circulaire · Place à Portique · ⑥ · ⑤ · P · i · ① · Théâtre · Basilique Chrétienne · †Chapelle · D26A · Porte Majou · P · ② · i · VILLE HAUTE · ④ · VILLE BASSE LE PLAN · ③ · Porte Cabirole · Cathédrale† · Porte l'Hyrisson

---

such an extent that an observant visit is like a journey through the history of art.

Following the canonisation of Bertrand in 1218, the cathedral increased considerably in importance as a place of pilgrimage. In the 14th century, to cater for the flow of pilgrims, Bertrand de Got, Bishop of Comminges and first Pope in Avignon, added a vast Gothic nave. In the 16th century the cathedral acquired its remarkable choir and organ. The finely sculpted panelling of the choir is described as a wooden church lying inside a stone one, while the organ is considered one of the 'Three Marvels of Gascony' (the other two being the stained-glass windows at Auch and the bells at Rieux).

Today the cathedral stands encircled by a fortified village of half-timbered 15th- and 16th-century houses with steep ramparts, bustling with streetside cafés and craft shops

The Walk

❶

Start at the main car park in the lower village. Go up the steps to the right of the tourist office following signs 'Accès Ville Haute' and through the Porte Majou. Climb steeply, bearing left at the fork, up to the cathedral.

❷

Turn left alongside the cathedral buildings, pass through an arch, zigzag round to the Porte Cabirole to leave the Ville Haute.

❸

Beyond the village wall, bear left round the first corner and down the steep steps to the right to the Ville Basse le Plan.

❹

Turn left at the bottom, first right, then left again at the crossroads, past old farmhouses and barns, following the road round to the right past the chapel and remains of a 5th-century Basilique Chrétienne.

❺

Turn left at the T-junction, past further Roman remains (including the marketplace/*marché*), right at the crossroads, then first left alongside the Thermes du Forum (Roman baths).

❻

Continue along the road through a tiny hamlet, La Bourdette. Cross the main road and continue to the car park.

---

i

▷ Length of walk: 2km
   ▷ Approximate time: 1 hour
      ▷ Terrain: All surfaced. Visitors with wheelchairs and pushchairs are recommended to do the walk in two halves (upper/lower village) with car or mini-train transfers
      ▷ Parking: Free parking in lower village.
   ▷ Refreshments: Cafés and restaurants in upper village

Collioure
(PYRÉNÉES-ORIENTALES)

A glittering jewel on the Côte Vermeille, Collioure nestles inside a deep bay. Behind the Catalan village are the Albères Mountains, with their famous Banyuls wines, including an excellent Collioure rouge. Collioure exudes warmth and colour, apricot houses and orange-tiled roofs in bright contrast to the azure sea and striking vermilion cliffs. It was these colours, combined with the luminous Mediterranean light, that attracted the Fauvist painters Matisse and Derain to the village in 1905. Other generations were to follow them here, among them Picasso, Braque and Dufy. Today a 'living museum' based on reproductions of their canvases has been set up *in situ*.

Although now a relaxed resort and artists' haven, Collioure was once an important fishing port and still boasts a beautifully restored fleet of ancient Catalan fishing barques, lateen-rigged and brightly painted in primary colours, moored in the intimate harbour. At the turn of the century, this was the centre of the Roussillon anchovy and sardine industry; today, although fishing is secondary to tourism, locally caught anchovies remain a delicacy, together with the delicious Catalan dishes of *suguet* and *zarzuella* – a reminder that Spain is only 16km away.

Behind the harbour, the old quarter of Mouré is a shopper's paradise, narrow streets bursting with Catalan craft shops. The

Near the Spanish border, Collioure offers a lovely sandy beach and water sports at its busy little harbour

The Walk

1

Start at the car park at place du 8 mai. Cross the bridge and turn left down to the harbour. Continue past the church on to the sea wall to the chapel and lighthouse.

2

Return to the church and turn right up rue de la Paix. Turn left at the top of rue du Mirador, then take the third street on the left down some steps.

3

Now go right, first left, then right again into rue Pasteur, across the bridge and up rue de la République.

4

Turn left opposite the church and go along the main road and down to the promenade. Turn left and return along the promenade in front of the castle to the car park.

12th-century Templar castle stands sentinel at the harbour entrance, and is now a museum dedicated to Catalan culture. Opposite are the heavily fortified church of Notre-Dame and tiny chapel of St-Vincent, whose belfry once served as the village lighthouse.

Labastide-Clairence
(PYRÉNÉES-ATLANTIQUES)

This little-known 14th-century village lies in the delightfully named Valley of the Joyous, 23km south-east of Bayonne, and represents a veritable melting pot of cultures, embracing Basque, Gascon and French traditions.

The long principal street, cut across by numerous alleyways, is lined with half-timbered, whitewashed houses embellished with red or green shutters. From the typically Basque 17th-century church, with its attractive Romanesque porch and cloisters, the road leads down to the arcaded main square. The place des Arceaux is the heart of the village, with cafés spilling into the square and the arcaded houses hiding a museum of local history and a dozen exclusive craft shops.

Labastide-Clairence is not only 'one of the most beautiful villages in France', it is also a mecca for artisans, including an enameller, glass-maker, cabinet-maker, blacksmith and two weavers – one a specialist in mohair, the other in tweeds – who supply several of the top Paris couture houses. All their ateliers are open to the public, and a huge annual pottery fair attracts many thousands of visitors to the village each September.

Another craft here is the production of *palas* and *chisteras*, the equipment needed to play *la pelote basque*, a traditional sport resembling royal (real) tennis, involving great speed, strength and agility. It is often played at the village *fronton*, with a huge round-topped wall, usually painted peach or pink, at one end of a marked court. Hidden behind an attractive façade in the main street of Labastide is a *trinquet*, or indoor court, where the ancient game of *pelote* remains the most popular sport in the village.

Aurignac
(HAUTE-GARONNE)

The village of Aurignac, 25km north-east of St-Gaudens, lies along a high ridge rising above rolling green hills brightened by golden sunflower fields, on the borders of the Pyrenean foothills. At the end of the 19th century the village became world-famous following the discovery of prehistoric remains here, giving its name to the Aurignacian era (35,000 to 18,000 BC).

It was in 1860 that Edouard Lartet, a palaeontologist from the neighbouring Gers region, first found a prehistoric cave shelter. His excavations yielded a large collection of flints, bones and animal remains, outlining the most significant period in human pre-history, that of Cro-Magnon man, of whom present-day man is the direct descendant. Lartet's discovery and subsequent research of the site marked the official beginning of the study of prehistory as a science. Aurignac's Musée de la Préhistoire chronicles Lartet's remarkable story alongside a display of his finds. The actual shelter lies on the outskirts of the village, on the scenic D635 to Cassagnabère-Tournas.

The village, entered through the ancient Notre Dame gateway, is a cluster of sand-coloured medieval and Renaissance corbelled houses with beautiful brick and wooden façades and brilliant orange pantiles. It is particularly atmospheric at night, when the narrow streets and alleyways are lit by yellow lanterns.

Of particular note within the village walls are the ruined castle, built in 1240 by the Counts of Comminges, which affords glorious views of the central Pyrenees from the top of its keep, and the church of St-Pierre, classed as a national historic monument and reached through a fortified gateway beneath a 16th-century belfry, ornamented with striking

A detail of the arch of Aurignac's Notre Dame portal, above, and the colourful shutters of the half-timbered houses of Labastide-Clairence, below

gargoyles. The entrance to the porch is supported by four twisted pillars of exceptional rarity and a beautifully carved Romanesque doorway.

Villefranche-de-Conflent (Pyrénées-Orientales)

THIS DELIGHTFUL ROSEY-HUED VILLAGE OF JUST 250 INHABITANTS, LYING BEHIND MASSIVE RAMPARTS NEAR THE MEDITERRANEAN EDGE OF THE SPANISH BORDER, IS LISTED AS A SITE OF NATIONAL ARTISTIC AND HISTORICAL IMPORTANCE.

Six kilometres south-west of Prades, where the grand Têt Valley suddenly constricts into a dramatic, narrow gorge, and tucked round a sharp curve in the road at the confluence of the Cady and the Rotja, lies the tiny village of Villefranche, hemmed in by steep-sided mountains. The village, originally called Villa Libéra, was founded in 1090 by the powerful Guillaume Raymond, Count of Cerdagne, and constructed in local rose-coloured marble.

Enclosed behind its strongly fortified walls, Villefranche has always played a vital defensive role in the Conflent region, due to its important strategic position on the route to Spain. Initially, Villefranche belonged to the kingdom of Aragon, then to Spain and finally, by the mid-17th century, to France. Since then, the ravages of time have largely bypassed the village, leaving an outstanding ensemble of ancient buildings, some dating from as early as the 11th century. The names

The Porte d'Espagne, above, links Spain, which held the fortified site, left, to the 1600s

of the gateways – Porte de France and Porte d'Espagne – remain as testimony to its significant military past.

VAUBAN'S MILITARY MARK

The village initially grew up round an 11th-century tower, and as it grew in military, administrative and economic importance, the village walls were augmented – a witness to diverse periods of architectural history, from the Middle Ages to Napoleon III.

The unusual vaulted walkway was severely damaged by the French when Villefranche was Spanish-held, but upon being returned to the French in 1659 following the Treaty of the Pyrenees, it was rebuilt by Sébastien Vauban, Louis XIV's military engineer. In 1680 Vauban also added the Sentinel Fort Libéria, high on the mountainside, to protect the village. The climb up the thousand-step underground stairway (not recommended for the claustrophobic) is rewarded by splendid views. A minibus ferries visitors from the car park to the fort museum, which was a women's prison during the reign of Louis XIV and a POW camp in World War I.

The Walk

Start at the Porte de France and proceed up the main rue St-Jacques, past art shops and wine cellars to the church and the pink marble square.

Turn right at the end of the square just past the bar Le Vauban, then left along rue St-Jean up to the Porte d'Espagne. Turn right alongside the ramparts until you reach the next gateway.

Turn left through the gateway, under a series of arches and on to the ancient bridge of St-Pierre (and access up to Vauban's fort).

Return across the bridge, under the arches and continue straight ahead back to rue St-Jean. Turn left, past the medieval tower En Solenell on the right, down to the Porte Roussillon. Turn right here and return to the Porte de France.

▷ Length of walk: 1.5km
▷ Approximate time: 45 minutes
▷ Terrain: All surfaced. Suitable for wheelchairs and pushchairs
▷ Parking: Free parking by the Porte de France
▷ Open: Fort: daily 10–6 (summer), 9–7 (Apr–Oct). Ramparts: daily 10–7.30 (summer), 2–5 (winter)
▷ Refreshments: Cafés and restaurants

Looking along rue St-Jacques, as seen from the oft-augmented ramparts: visitors get a friendly welcome

ARTS, CRAFTS AND CATALONIA

Behind the imposing military fortifications, visitors receive a friendly welcome along the cobbled streets, where craft shops hang traditional wrought-iron signs announcing their Catalan-style pottery, glass, embroidery, art and leather. For good luck, buy seven ears of wheat in a leather pouch; as a symbol of welcome and renewal of life, buy a traditional Catalan 'sorceress' to hang from the ceiling (the sorceress gets on her broom at the end of winter to chase away the cold weather).

The village is also renowned for its gastronomic delights. Regional specialities include lamb roasted with mountain thyme, duck with honey and apples, and the delicious *crème catalane*. After Easter, Villefranche hosts a fête of flowers and gourmet delicacies, and the famous Trobada de Gayants de Catalunya – a procession of giants representing the different villages of Catalonia.

The Romanesque church of St-Jacques, with its pink-marble portals and elegant Gothic bell tower, is not to be missed. Nor are the caves within a short walk. Grande Canalettes is the most famous, with breathtaking stalactites, stalagmites and other formations beautifully illuminated. The Grottes Canalettes are for the more adventurous, with hand-held torches to light the way.

THE LITTLE YELLOW TRAIN

Villefranche marks the start of the picturesque mountain train service, Le Petit Train Jaune – known throughout the south-west of France – up to Latour de Carol on the sunny mountain plateau of the Cerdagne. With optional stops at thermal resorts, the spectacular Nyer Gorge, the ruins at Olette and the unusual Cerdagne church at Planès, the full return trip (a great day out) takes 4 hours.

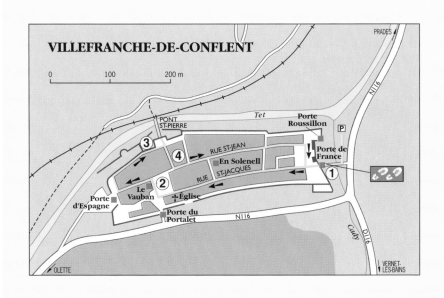

VILLEFRANCHE-DE-CONFLENT

Angels gaze down from elaborately styled ceiling of Arreau's church, announcing Religion, Faith, Hope and Charity

The Walk

Start at the car park at the marketplace. Go up the main street and round the back of the church. Turn left, right, then left again along the riverbank. Cross the first bridge.

Continue along the riverbank past the second bridge to the Église St-Exupère and the Château des Nestes.

Cross the river and the main road behind the château and climb up to a chapel. Turn right up to a viewpoint, then return to the chapel and continue straight on.

Cross the next bridge into the square, up the rue Principale, past the Maison des Lys and back to the car park.

Arreau
(HAUTES-PYRÉNÉES)

Going by a brief first impression, it would be easy to drive past Arreau as, from the main road, its sombre grey houses and grey slate roofs do not look particularly inviting. However, the heart of this charming village rewards exploration, as its overhanging half-timbered houses provide a most authentic medieval ambience, and its bustling market is renowned throughout the region. Situated in the High Pyrenees and crossed by the converging Neste du Louron and Neste d'Aure rivers, the village has an undeniably picturesque setting, enhanced by the sound of rushing water in the background.

The former ancient capital of four valleys, Arreau prospered over the centuries, largely because of its strategic position, equidistant from the Mediterranean and the Atlantic and on a main trading route with Spain. Many people have passed through the village and left their mark on the buildings, from Roman legions, pilgrims and Spanish smugglers to Republican armies fleeing from Franco and soldiers of the Wehrmacht.

The most attractive buildings in Arreau include the beautiful Renaissance Maison des Lys, covered in exquisite fleurs-de-lis timber-work, and the Romanesque church of St-Exupère, Bishop of Toulouse, who left his episcopal seat following the invasions of Toulouse to return to his humble Aurois roots. The Château des Nestes contains a fascinating museum of the Pyrenees.

Arreau has a full complement of shops selling local woollen, leather, copper, glass and wooden crafts, alongside wines and gourmet delicacies. One of the local treats worth seeking out is the *gâteau à la broche*. This is a tempting sticky cake containing vanilla, rum and almonds and nicknamed 'Pyrenean rock' or 'sweet fir tree' because of its unique appearance (like starfish piled on top of each other). Initially brought to the Pyrenees from the Balkans by Napoleon's armies, it is renown as a choice dessert for celebration days in the region.

Borce
(PYRÉNÉES-ATLANTIQUES)

The tiny village of Borce sits at the foot of the Col du Somport in the rugged Aspe Valley, 8km south of Lescun, at the start of the wild and dramatic pine-clad peaks of the Pyrenean National Park, with marvellous views over the border into Spain.

The majority of tourists who pass through Borce are hardy walkers, as the village lies along the Grande Randonnée 10 trans-Pyrenean footpath, which follows the route of an ancient Roman road. Otherwise the village remains completely unspoilt by tourism, and consists of little more than a single street of grey stone houses with a church, *épicerie*, communal *lavoir* and bar.

Because of its strategic position on the Franco-Spanish border, the village was an important stronghold in the Middle Ages. Today its slate-roofed houses are splashed with red-painted wooden doorways and shutters, and their window grilles are adorned with flowers. On closer inspection you can find elegant mullioned windows, vaulted doorways and finely engraved lintels – a living museum of medieval architecture.

This area is the last stronghold of the Pyrenean brown bear. Indeed, Borce would have remained virtually undiscovered by tourists had two young boys not returned from a picnic in 1971 carrying a tiny baby bear, its mother presumed shot by poachers. Jojo the bear cub soon became a huge tourist attraction and remained the village mascot until his death 20 years later.

It is believed that fewer than ten brown bears now remain, to be found only in the Aspe and Ossau valleys. In an attempt to preserve the bears, a project called 'Plan Ours' has been launched. An information centre at the edge of the village – Le Clos aux Ours –

explains the bears' life in the mountains and their future, and is home to two resident bears called Antoine and Ségolène.

Fourcès
(GERS)

Take time to discover Fourcès, a perfect circular bastide along the Armagnac route, 13km north-west of Condom. The inhabitants are justifiably proud of their village and its beautiful main square (actually a *place circulaire*). Surrounding it are half-timbered, flower-decked houses which date from the 12th and 13th centuries, their covered balconies resting on wooden pillars. Plane trees shading

the large green create a cool retreat in summer for a game of *boules*. With its bar, *crêperie*, high-quality craft shops and tiny museum, the green is the centre of village life.

The *bastide* is enclosed within a semicircular wall, part of which lies alongside the River Auzoue, making a pleasant walk from the 15th-century castle to the fortified mill. The river has influenced architecture in the village, with living quarters often located on the first floor in case of flooding.

One of the best times to visit Fourcès is during the last weekend in April, when the village becomes a mosaic of flowers for the Marché aux Fleurs, attracting over 20,000 visitors to its tiny squares ablaze with colour. In

the summer months there is an extensive programme of open-air concerts, theatre and folkloric *soirées*.

The lush surrounding countryside is a patchwork of vineyards splashed with sunflower fields and meadows dotted with creamy-coloured cows, all interspersed with traditional Gascony farmhouses offering tastings of the local Armagnac brandy. The village prayer tellingly reads:

'O Lord –
Give me good health, for a long time,
Love from time to time,
Work not much of the time,
And Armagnac ... all the time.'

The rugged terrain that surrounds Borce is also the home of the last of the brown bears to be found in the Pyrénées. Fourcès, inset, glows in the light of sunset

AÏNHOA

One of the most delightful of all the Basque villages, Aïnhoa exemplifies the very best of rural Basque architecture in its single street of whitewashed houses, with shutters painted blood-red to match the decora-

tive half-timbering. The village lies less than 3km from the Spanish border, on the route to the famous pilgrimage centre of Santiago de Compostela, and has had a reputation for warmth and hospitality ever since its foundation in the early 13th century. Following the Thirty Years War, it was almost entirely rebuilt to cater for muleteers on the route between Bayonne and Pamplona. Its 14th-century church is particularly notable for its wood carvings and Basque gallery. In front of the church in the village square, the *fronton* wall resonates daily to the dry crack of the *pelote* ball, a unique and skilful regional sport.

ALET-LES-BAINS

Alet-les-Bains is one of 30 thermal spa villages in the Pyrenees. Lying along the right bank of the River Aude 32km south of Carcassonne, the village was already known for its waters in Gallo-Roman times but did not really flourish until the 17th century, when Nicolas Pavillon, Bishop of Alet, converted the ancient Benedictine abbey into a majestic Gothic cathedral. Today it stands in ruins near the place de la République at the heart of the village. Six narrow lanes radiating from here in a star formation are lined with elegant Renaissance half-timbered ochre houses, their upper storeys cantilevered overhead.

BASSOUES

The bastide at Bassoues, founded in 1279, lies in the midst of Armagnac country, 35km southwest of Auch. However, the 11th-century basilica of St-Fris is witness

to an earlier settlement here. The story goes that Fris, nephew of Charles Martel, was shot by bandits, buried near

Bassoues and his grave forgotten for many years. His body, still in perfect condition, was rediscovered by a peasant, and the villagers, recognising this as a miracle, built a church in his honour.

The bastide, with its characteristic arcaded main square, covered market and fortified ramparts, is dominated by a massive machicolated keep, 43m high, which towers over the village.

CASTELNOU

The peaceful village of Castelnou nestles in a valley of rich red soil in the heart of the rolling Basses Aspres countryside of the Roussillon. Inside the 13th-century battlemented ramparts, the steep paved streets are lined with houses of rust-coloured brick and stone clothed in oleander, fig trees and ivy. The 10th-century castle, with

fine views over the bright terracotta roofs to the distant snow-peaked mountains, is well-known for its Château de Castelnou wines, on sale in the village *caves* or restaurants. In summer there is a Tuesday craft market beside the Romanesque church, and a honey festival in September.

LAGRASSE

Historic Lagrasse, set on the banks of the River Orbieu 40km southwest of Narbonne, is famous for its ruined abbey. Founded in 799 by Charlemagne and linked to the village by an 11th-century humpback bridge, the current abbey buildings include a magnificent 16th-century bell tower which dominates the village and a Romanesque chapel, as well as the grave of composer Hector Berlioz. The village itself consists of a mass of medieval houses, many hiding magnificent painted ceilings, clustered round a covered market. Surrounded by vestiges of its once impressive defences, it lies in vine-clad rolling countryside at the heart of the Corbières region.

The Three Graces, as you've never seen them before, sit down to eat in Lagrasse, an example to hungry passers-by to join them inside

MONTSÉGUR

This village, on the edge of the Pyrenees, represents one of the region's most important historic sites, its ruined castle having served as the final and tragic refuge to the Cathars in the 13th century. Following a 10-month siege by Catholic forces, 225 Cathars climbed down from the fortress, to be burnt alive on a communal pyre rather than betray their beliefs, thus marking the end of their sect. The orderly village of whitewashed houses lies below the sheer-sided rocky pinnacle crowned by the ruined fortress. The strenuous climb to the top affords fine broad views.

RIEUX

Rieux lies in a majestic loop in the River Arize, 45km south-west of Toulouse in the lush, hilly region of

the Volvestre. Dominated by its splendid 14th-century cathedral, Rieux became an episcopal city in 1317, bringing great wealth and enabling the villagers to build high defensive walls and unusually decorative, turreted houses. Four hundred years later, the bishopric was dissolved and Rieux returned to its quiet agricultural existence.

Today it remains totally unspoilt and a perfect place to escape the crowds – except on the first Sunday in May, when spectators cram the narrow streets for the village's 16th-century festival, Le Tir au Papogay, with archers dressed in medieval costume aiming at a wooden parrot perched on top of a 45m pole.

ST-ÉTIENNE-DE-BAÏGORRY

Lovers of wine and food should not miss the delightful village of St-Étienne, 11km west of St-Jean-Pied-de-Port, on the scenic route through the beautiful, broad Vallée des Aldudes. St-Étienne is a well-known gastronomic centre, with local dishes including *piperade basquaise* (like an omelette with tomatoes and peppers) and *menestra* (a spicy vegetable hotpot). It is also an ideal place to taste the Irouléguy wines, considered to be the best in the Basque country.

The finely preserved houses, grouped together along the banks of the River Aldudes, are decorated with strings of sun-dried red peppers which match the colour of the ornate half-timbering, creating a memorable Basque atmosphere. From here, a road climbs to the Col d'Ispéguy and the Spanish border, just 8km away.

ST-SAVIN

This deeply traditional village stretches along a mountainside at the heart of the High Pyrenees. Its well-known and popular festival of sacred music centres on the lovely Romanesque abbey church dedicated to St Savin, a hermit priest who settled here in the 6th century. His life is illustrated in a series of magnificent 15th-century paintings inside the church, alongside many other treasures, including an unusual organ cabinet exquisitely decorated with grotesque faces which move when the organ is played.

Beyond the arcaded village square, with its central fountain and pretty stone cottages ornamented with flowers, can be found one of the best restaurants in the region, Le Viscos.

Provence & the Côte d'Azur

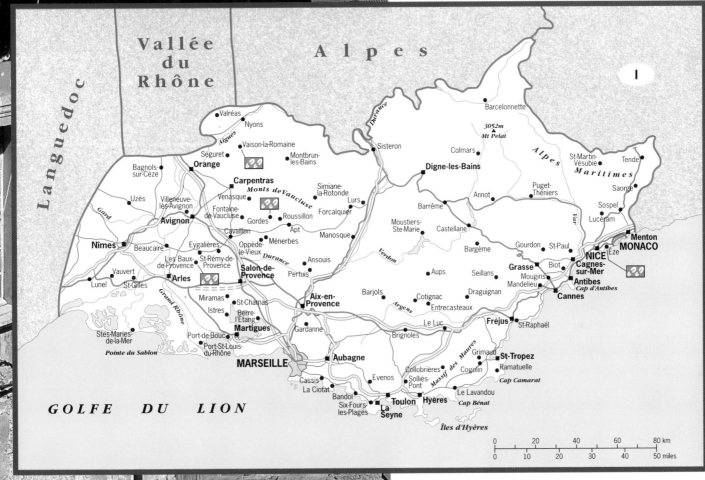

Away from its breathtaking coastline, Provence hides a wealth of historic villages set amongst olive groves, vineyards and scented fields of lavender – pure inspiration for artists and writers.

Èze

(Alpes-Maritimes)

ÈZE IS UNDOUBTEDLY ONE OF THE PRETTIEST AND BEST-PRESERVED PROVENÇAL VILLAGES PERCHÉS, ONLY 10 MINUTES FROM NICE AND MONACO, WITH SPECTACULAR VIEWS OVER THE RIVIERA FROM ITS STEEP, COBBLED STREETS.

This magnificent village, known as the Nid d'Aigle (Eagle's Nest), lies at the point where the mountains meet the Côte d'Azur. Perched high on a rocky pinnacle, crowned with the ruins of a Saracen fortress, and still surrounded by its 17th-century walls, it is a perfect base for exploring the region.

HIGH ABOVE THE AZURE COAST

Like so many Provençal villages, Èze sleeps in winter and buzzes in summer. On entering through the only gateway in the ancient ramparts (once approached via a drawbridge), you will be struck by the tall golden houses clinging to the rocks and the labyrinth of tiny vaulted passages and stairways climbing to the once massive fortress. Lining the cobbled streets, craft shops resembling caves are famous for their treasure troves of antiques, ceramics, pewter and olivewood carvings.

Surrounded by splendid formal gardens, ornamental wrought-iron gateways, terracotta pots bursting with flowers and occasional

Narrow streets that hindered medieval enemies are no barrier to the enjoyment of today's visitors

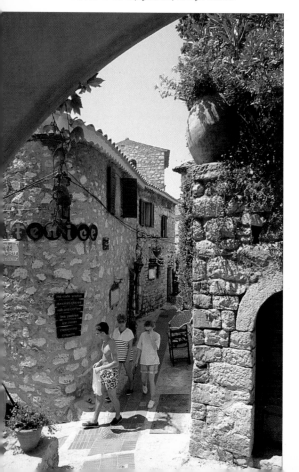

glimpses of the dazzling blue sea, iIt is easy to forget that the medieval ramparts and 14th-century gateway were not built to defend boutiques and restaurants, and the narrow streets and stairways were designed not to charm but to hinder the enemy.

Tall and slim, squat and rotund cacti populate the castle garden, above. Looking out from the garden, right, the view is of sparkling sea and distant isles

ROYAL CONNECTIONS

The settlement records of Èze date back as far as the 11th century, although the site has been occupied since the Bronze Age. Fortified in the 14th century, the village belonged to the Counts of Savoie for hundreds of years. Frequent French invasions culminated in the destruction of the castle in 1706, ordered by King Louis XIV. In 1792, following the creation of the Alpes-Maritimes, Èze became part of the principality of Monaco. Only after the plebiscite of 1860 –

when the villagers voted in the Chapel of the White Penitents for annexation to France – did peace finally come to the village.

This century, the village played host to an entire Russian colony fleeing from the 1917 Revolution, including a Russian prince who made Cap Estel his romantic residence. Today it is a luxury hotel, one of several top-class hotels at Èze, which also include Château Eza, the former residence of Prince William of Sweden, and the village's top restaurant, and another gourmet paradise, the Hôtel Château de la Chèvre d'Or.

Surprisingly for its size, Èze has two churches. The Chapelle des Pénitents Blancs at the top of the rue Principale is a simple

The Walk

1

Start at the car park at the foot of the village. Zigzag up the path through a series of arches, alongside the Auberge du Vieux Village and into the rue Principale.

2

Go down a flight of steps to the left, under the arched entrance to the Hôtel Château de la Chèvre d'Or and round to the right into rue du Malpas. Climb the steps and go straight on at the junction, up to the rue Principale.

3

Turn left, up past a pretty square on the right, then go right at the next junction past the Chapelle des Pénitents Blancs, under vines and arches.

4

Turn left at the shops up rue du Château to the Jardin Exotique. Return to the shops and continue downhill.

5

Circle the church, descend the steps and zigzag back down to the car park.

i

▷ Length of walk: 2km
▷ Approximate time: 1 hour
▷ Terrain: Surfaced but too steep for wheelchairs and pushchairs
▷ Parking: Free at the foot of the village
▷ Open: Jardin Exotiqu: 9am–10pm (summer), 9–12, 2–7 (winter)
▷ Refreshments: Bars, cafés, restaurants

14th-century chapel, decorated with enamelled tiles illustrating the life of Christ and containing an unusual 13th-century crucifix of Catalán origin, with Christ smiling on the cross. The second church, built in 1764, is more classical and contains a beautiful 18th-century statue of the Assumption. A short distance from the church is the cemetery, where Francis Blanche, a celebrated French comedian, is buried.

PERFUMES AND PALMS

As it is only a short distance from Grasse, the perfume capital of Provence, Èze counts perfumeries among its main attractions. Two famous names, Galimard and Fragonard, have factories and museums here. Guided tours explain the secrets of perfume production, traditional and modern, and the role of perfume over the centuries.

But the crowning glory of Èze is the striking exotic garden surrounding the ruins of the castle. Designed by engineer-agronomist Jean Gastaud in 1949, the garden contains magnificent rare palms, cacti and succulents, mostly native to South America. Set at the highest point in the village, the garden commands a superb view over the sparkling Côte d'Azur, with Corsica visible on a clear day.

Below Èze is the former fishing village of Èze-Bord-de-Mer, now a popular coastal resort. The Chemin de Nietzsche, named for the German philosopher zigzags steeply down from the place du Centenaire through open countryside to the beach.

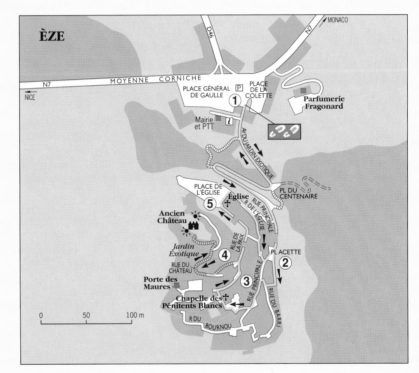

Les Baux-de-Provence (Bouches-du-Rhône)

OFTEN CALLED 'THE POMPEII OF PROVENCE', LES BAUX-DE-PROVENCE WITH ITS ANCIENT RUINED CITADEL IS SITUATED 31KM SOUTH OF AVIGNON, ON A ROCKY OUTCROP OF THE ALPILLES MOUNTAINS.

Winding through the wild, rugged wasteland of thorny brushwood, silvery olives and dark pines of the Alpilles Mountains, a narrow road leads up to the barren heights of Les Baux. Clinging to one of the highest ridges like an eyrie, its ruined buildings are hardly distinguishable from the milky-white crags of limestone which surround it. The village, which takes its name from the Provençal *baou* or high rock, is divided in two: the bustling inhabited lower part with elegant Renaissance houses lining the shiny cobbled streets, and the deserted Ville Morte perched high above, with breathtaking views which stretch from the ominously named Val d'Enfer (Valley of Hell), immediately below, out to the Mediterranean.

FROM RICHES TO RUINS

There has been a settlement here since the earliest of times, but the village became prominent during the Middle Ages as the seat of the seigneurs de Baux, one of the most powerful families in southern France. They ruled from here for many generations, waging war and patronising the troubadours.

Carefully hand-fashioned santons, wearing Provençal prints, show traditional village occupations

Their 12th-century Cour d'Amour (Court of Love), a dazzling society of lords, ladies and wandering troubadours, was renowned throughout the Midi, and for centuries Les Baux was considered a romantic mecca for poets and painters.

During the 14th century Les Baux fell into the hands of robber-baron Raymond de Turenne, enemy of the papacy and the Counts of Provence. He made Les Baux his base for looting and kidnapping, throwing his prisoners to their deaths from the top of the castle at sunset. The village remained in Protestant hands until Cardinal Richelieu had the castle destroyed in 1632, after which the town began to crumble into decay.

The village was almost entirely abandoned until the start of the industrial age, when rich mineral deposits were discovered which became the principal source of aluminium; the mineral was named bauxite after the village. The present-day population

Startlingly white against the scrub, rocks dot the craggy landscape, which held an abundance of bauxite

is largely dependent on tourism, with artists, craftsmen and restaurants round every corner. Indeed, Les Baux has become something of a gastronomic centre and boasts one of France's most outstanding restaurants, the Hôtel Oustaù de Baumanière. Tourists can also enjoy a feast of cultural events, including a summer art and folklore festival in June.

OLD AND NEW

During Les Baux's height of glory, it is believed that the now 'dead' town contained more than a hundred buildings. Today, at over a thousand metres above sea level, the remains are assaulted by the harsh and howling mistral wind. It is said that when this wind blows, the normally smiling and carefree people do strange and irrational things. One man, it is claimed, put his wife in a barrel and hurled it off the summit of the castle.

The Walk

Starting from the Porte Mage, walk along rue Porte Mage. At the start of the Grande Rue, branch right downhill to the ramparts and climb up rue de la Calade, past the 16th-century Porte d'Eyguières on the right. Turn right at the Hôtel des Porcelets to the Église St-Vincent, the Chapelle des Pénitents Blancs and the Galerie St-Vincent (not shown on the map), with its changing exhibitions of local artists' work.

From place de l'Église, return to the Hotel and continue along rue de l'Église and into rue des Fours (not named on the map). Turn right at the junction into rue du Trencat, hewn out of the rock, and up to the paying entrance to the old village.

Once inside, pass Chapelle St-Blaise on the left and go straight ahead to the breathtaking viewpoint near the Monument Charloun Rieu. Continue round past the old hospital and up to the château. The Tour Paravelle is further ahead and there is another viewpoint round to the right before the Tour Sarrasine. Return to the entrance to the old village, turning right at the hospital, and go down rue du Château. Bear right at the tourist office, past the Mairie and back down to the Porte Mage.

> **i**
> ▷ Length of walk: 3km
> ▷ Approximate time: 1½ hours
> ▷ Terrain: The ruined old village (point 3) is unsuitable for wheelchairs
> ▷ Parking: Choice of car parks
> ▷ Open: Old village: 8:30am–9pm (summer), 8:30–dusk (winter)
> ▷ Refreshments: Restaurants, bars and café

Despite everything, the Romanesque chapel of St-Blaise remains relatively intact, housing an Olive Tree Museum and slide show presenting some of the Provençal works of Van Gogh, Gauguin and Cézanne. Beyond the chapel and the ruins of a 16th-century hospital is a terrace affording one of the finest views of the whole region, across the Rhône Valley and the Camargue to the distant sparkling sea. Equally good views can be had from the ruins of the massive romantic castle, carved out of the solid rock, on a crag behind the terrace. In the moonlight, the eerie shadows and sinister silhouettes make a haunting scene.

The lower village is a shopper's paradise. The beautifully restored Renaissance houses, including the Hôtel des Porcelets and the elegantly vaulted Mairie, boast fine architectural details, occasionally decorated with the Baux coat of arms. This contains the Star of Bethlehem, as the family claimed to be descended from Balthazar, one of the Three Kings. At the top of the village, the Romanesque church of St-Vincent still keeps alive the ancient Provençal tradition of *pastrage* (Midnight Mass on Christmas Eve), with the arrangement of a medieval mystery play and a Nativity pageant.

The place Louis Jou, seen from the Musée des Santons, offers relaxation after exploring the hilly streets

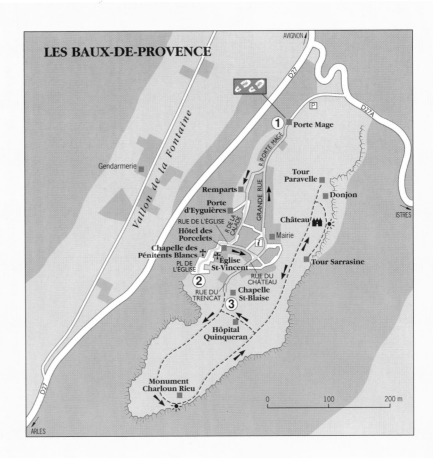

LES BAUX-DE-PROVENCE

AVIGNON

Gendarmerie

Vallon de la Fontaine

D27

D27A

P

① Porte Mage

GRANDE RUE

R. PORTE MAGE

Tour Paravelle

Donjon

ISTRES

Remparts

Porte d'Eyguières

RUE DE L'ÉGLISE

R. DE LA CALADE

Hôtel des Porcelets

Château

Mairie

Chapelle des Pénitents Blancs

Église St-Vincent

PL DE L'ÉGLISE

②

RUE DU CHÂTEAU

Tour Sarrasine

RUE DU TRENCAT

③

Chapelle St-Blaise

Hôpital Quinqueran

Monument Charloun Rieu

0   100   200 m

D27

ARLES

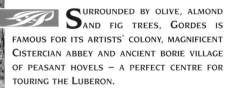

Gordes

(Vaucluse)

SURROUNDED BY OLIVE, ALMOND AND FIG TREES, GORDES IS FAMOUS FOR ITS ARTISTS' COLONY, MAGNIFICENT CISTERCIAN ABBEY AND ANCIENT BORIE VILLAGE OF PEASANT HOVELS – A PERFECT CENTRE FOR TOURING THE LUBERON.

This hilltop village, situated 17km north-east of Cavaillon, is dominated by its massive church and an 11th- to 16th-century castle. Often described as resembling an acropolis as it rises from its golden plinth on a spur of Mont Ventoux – with stunning views of the Luberon, narrow cobbled streets and tiers of sand-coloured houses spilling down the steep slopes – Gordes is rated one of the most beautiful villages in France.

Like many other Provençal châteaux, the castle is an extraordinary cross between feudal fortress and Renaissance manor, mullioned windows contrasting with pepper-pot towers. Growing up round this medieval fortress, Gordes became famous for its tanneries and silk-weaving industry during the 16th and 17th centuries.

A few poppies project above a sea of dreamy lavender, above, the sight and scent of which spells Provence for many people. Cultivated fields of lavender surround the secluded Cistercian abbey of Sénanque, below, where the monks make a liqueur called Sénancole. Opposite, time for a well-earned drink with friends

NEW BEGINNINGS

During World War II, the village suffered severe damage as a result of being the local centre of the Resistance movement. With so

many buildings either ruined or abandoned, Gordes fell into decline until the 1960s. Then, led by Cubist André l'Hote and, later, abstract painter Victor Vasarély, a group of artists and intellectuals were attracted to the village. These new arrivals brought a new lease of life to the village, restoring the delightful Renaissance houses and setting up attractive galleries, studios and boutiques. Nevertheless, the lower slopes serve as a reminder of Gordes' troubled past, with numerous ruined houses and part of a tiny chapel, its unusual stone altar still embedded in the cliff face.

It was Hungarian-born Victor Vasarély, one of the most important artists of Constructivism, who renovated the château and did so much to restore the town's fortunes. The castle is now his home, and the Musée Vasarély here contains over a thousand of his vivid abstract paintings and dazzling geometric designs in vibrant colours.

UNIQUE BORIE VILLAGE

Just south of Gordes, down a narrow, winding lane through dusty scrubland, lies the most famous collection of *bories* in France. These extraordinary vaulted beehive-shaped huts, built of large flat *lauzes* (limestone roofing stones), with thick dry-stone walls and no windows or chimneys, sheltered the earliest farmers and semi-nomadic shepherds, as far back as the 3rd century BC, from snow, rain and the mistral wind.

There are over 3,000 such stone dwellings in the Vaucluse and Luberon, with 350 in and around Gordes alone. This particular village, inhabited as recently as the last century, is believed to date from the Middle Ages to the 18th century – contemporary with Gordes castle and village, whose style and construction could hardly be more different. It is said that the villagers of Gordes fled here to save themselves during the plague.

The *borie* village at Gordes, the largest and most complete of its kind in the world, was restored in the 1960s and is classified as part of the national heritage.

LAVENDER AND LIQUEUR

In a valley just beyond Gordes is the 12th-century abbey of Sénanque, an important medieval studies centre whose sun-bleached stone walls contrast beautifully with the surrounding lavender fields. Along with Silvacane and Thoronet, this was one of the 'Three Sisters of Provence', the finest Cistercian monasteries in the region. Thanks to this secluded position, it was never subjected to attack and remains a perfect example of the Provençal Romanesque ecclesiastical style. The monks here still follow a secret medieval recipe to concoct a pungent, herb-flavoured yellow liqueur called Sénancole.

Near by, the Musée du Vitrail is a most unusual museum of stained glass. Originally established to honour the work of Frédérique Duran, it has a resident stained-glass maker and also illustrates the history of stained-glass window production. Next door, the 16th-century olive mill stands as a reminder of how the area was once famous for its oils.

The Walk

Start by the château at the place du Marché. Go down the little lane by the Cercle Républicain bar and turn right at the Aumônerie St-Jacques, down some steps and under the arch. Turn right again under the next arch and continue down to the end of rue Jean Deyrolle.

Turn sharp left at the bottom along the cobbled rue de la Fontaine Basse, which winds down to the village *lavoir*. Turn right here, then branch left along a shady unpaved path lined with ruined houses.

At the end of the lane, follow the narrow path on the left, curving round the house on the corner, and climb steeply up to the road. Turn left, sharp right and up another bumpy track, past the ruined chapel. Bear left under a large fig tree and zigzag up steps past the Théatre des Terrasses to rue de l'Église.

❹

Turn left up to some shops under the arches, then first right down to a viewpoint and rue André l'Hote. Turn left and climb the second flight of steps to the left. Bear left at the top and return to the château.

ℹ️

▷ Length of walk: 1.5km
▷ Approximate time: 1 hour
▷ Terrain: Points 2 and 3 are unsurfaced, frequently steep and unsuitable for wheelchairs and pushchairs
▷ Parking: Free at place du Château
▷ Open: Monastery, 10–12, 2–6, Sundays 2–6 (Mar–Oct); afternoons only in winter. *Bories* village: 9–sunset daily. Stained-glass museum and olive mill: 9–12, 2–6
▷ Refreshments: Restaurants, bars and café terraces

GORDES

The Walk

From the Parking du Pasquier, walk along rue des Bourgades and turn second left up rue des Lauriers to the main square.

Following signs to the belfry, turn left, then immediately right, through an arch, up rue de l'Église. Take the first left to a viewpoint across to the Valley of Fairies.

From here turn left up a tiny lane to place de la Forge. Cross the square and continue alongside the church to another viewpoint.

4

Retrace your steps to the square, turn left down rue de l'Église and back to the main square. Go straight ahead, then right at the T-junction, following signs to the Sentier des Ocres. The marked footpath, Chaussée des Géants, leads you through the ochre cliffs and quarries. Return along the same route to the car park.

Roussillon
(VAUCLUSE)

This unique village, perched on a platform of rust-coloured rock called Mont Rouge, takes its name from *roux*, meaning rust. Situated 10km north-west of Apt, at the heart of the richest deposits of ochre in France, surrounded by jagged cliffs of every shade imaginable from pale yellow to blood red, punctuated by dark green pine forests, Roussillon is one of the most striking villages in France.

The village was founded by Raymond d'Avignon. According to legend, on discovering that his wife loved his pageboy, he killed the page and served her his heart on a platter. In her distress she leapt off a cliff, and her blood formed a spring which coloured the surrounding earth. This quality makes it one of the most spectacular areas in all Provence, with multicoloured needles in the Valley of Fairies, the Cliffs of Blood and the deep gullies of the Giants' Causeway, where visitors can explore the old quarries.

The ochre industry began here at the end of the 18th century, and soon Roussillon was known worldwide for its dyes. Prosperity reigned until the middle of this century, when competition from synthetic pigments became too great. Nevertheless, villagers still hold a three-day Ochre Festival at Ascensiontide, when the village is a riot of celebrations.

Beautifully restored houses present the full palette of ochre shades, from apricot, pink and burgundy to gold, mustard, orange, russet and brown. The hub of the village, and a popular meeting place, is the small village square, with its outdoor cafés beside the Mairie, overlooked by a clock tower, formerly a defence tower. From here narrow lanes and winding stairways lead up to a Romanesque church and viewpoint, offering a magnificent panorama of the mountains, hill villages and countryside of the Vaucluse.

The warm earth tones of the Giants' Causeway, left, are repeated in the colours of Rousillon's houses,

Fontaine-de-Vaucluse
(VAUCLUSE)

Fontaine-de-Vaucluse is tucked at the end of a narrow, enclosed valley – the *vallis clausa*, after which the whole *département* is named. The village is famous for an emerald-green spring gushing from a huge cave-like abyss at the foot of a 230m cliff; pagan Gauls believed it to be the home of a god, while Christians named it the Devil's Hole. In the Middle Ages, the pool was said to contain a dragon.

Only relatively recently have geologists and speleologists traced the flow of the water, to find that it is one of the largest and most powerful springs in the world, consisting of a vast underground labyrinth of rivers covering over 2,000sq km. What no one can explain is why the spring is sometimes an explosion of water, producing about 200,000 litres per second, but almost disappears at other times of the year. The history of exploration here is displayed in re-created caves, the Monde Souterrain de Norbert Casteret.

This remarkable spring is joined by five secondary springs as it tumbles over the rocks and develops into the lake of the River Sorgue, right in the village. Needless to say, local specialities include trout and crayfish.

At the edge of the village is the last remaining paper mill. The last commercial paper mill her closed in 1968, this one still turns within a small museum, demonstrating medieval paper-making and evoking memories of a once thriving industry.

Other attractions in the village include two further museums: one presents the history of the Resistance from 1870 to 1940, the other is dedicated to Petrarch, the famous 14th-century Italian poet. Petrarch lived in Fontaine-de-Vaucluse for 16 years, writing most of his poetry here, inspired by the solitude and wilderness he found here.

Cassis
(BOUCHES-DU-RHÔNE)

This cheerful fishing port and resort is set in a semicircular bay, between Europe's highest sea cliffs and the breathtaking *calanques* to the west. Surrounded by hills clad with olive, almond and fig trees and the famous terraced vineyards which yield a highly reputed white wine, it is a popular weekend retreat for the people of Marseille.

Once the Roman port of *Portus Carcisis*, Cassis started to thrive in the 17th century when the Cassidains abandoned their old perched village near the medieval château to settle beside the quay. Since then, it has entranced artists and writers, including the Impressionist painters Dufy and Matisse.

At the heart of the village, beside a local history museum, the narrow streets converge on a small, dusty square where *boccia* is played under the shade of ancient plane trees. At the waterfront, fishermen spread their nets out on the quayside while locals look on from the colourful cafés. The speciality here is a plate of sea urchins – black and spiny and served raw in the shell, washed down by a glass of Cassis wine. A landing stage along the quay is the starting point for boat trips to see the superb cliffs and bays.

The biggest attraction of Cassis is an awesome series of fjord-like inlets formed at the end of the Ice Age. These *calanques*, magnificent creeks of sheer white limestone bite into the coast, plunging down to the transparent turquoise sea. They are best seen on foot, following a well-marked footpath from the car park, although reaching the tiny sandy beach at the third and most spectacular *calanque* is a serious test of rock-climbing skills.

Discreetly chic yet down-to-earth, Cassis is the starting point for discovering inlets known as calanques

Vaison-la-Romaine (Vaucluse)

VAISON IS BISECTED BY THE JADE-GREEN RIVER OUVÈZE. THE TRANQUIL UPPER VILLAGE CONTRASTS DRAMATI-CALLY WITH THE LOWER DISTRICT, AN EXTRA-ORDINARY COMBINATION OF 'MODERN TOWN' AND FORMER ROMAN CITY.

Vaison-la-Romaine, nestled in a wooded valley at the foot of Mont Ventoux, 30km north-east of Orange, is a town with village proportions. Its rich past emerged only at the start of this century, when excavations unearthed extensive Roman remains.

The hill was inhabited by a Celtic tribe as far back as 2000 BC. Following the Roman conquest, the people of *Vasio Vocontiorum* (the Roman name for Vaison) moved to the plain below. The end of the 12th century saw the villagers returned up the craggy hill to seek refuge in the château built by Raymond V,

Roman ruins in an exceptional state of preservation abut the roadside bustle of cars, cafés and shops

Count of Toulouse, using stone from the Roman ruins. Only in the 19th century did the villagers return to the lower district.

Today Vaison plays an important argicul-tural role in the Vaucluse, renowned for black truffles, lavender-scented honey and Picodon cheese on sale at the large weekly market. The tourist office contains a museum of Rhône wines, with tastings every Wednesday.

ROMAN LEGACY

The majority of Roman cities in the region have disappeared entirely beneath the crim-son soil, making the extent of Vaison's ruins all the more remarkable. Together with the nearby Roman capital of Orange, it is one of the richest Roman sites in all Provence. Excavations have been carried out here with-out pause since the turn of the century. In Roman times Vasio had no great military or strategic role but led a peaceful, prosperous life reflected in its fine villas, colonnaded streets, shops and public baths. One of the main finds was the Maison des Messii, with its colonnaded courtyard and mosaic floors. Near by, the Roman theatre still seats 7,000 people during the July festival. A visit to the Roman Museum is highly recommended.

The most famous Roman legacy and one of the most resilient is a single-span bridge, 18m wide, which crosses hight above the river to join the two halves of the town. Over 2,000 years old, the Pont Romain still carries traffic. Restored after flood damage in 1616, the surrounding roadway was destroyed by

the Germans in 1944, and in 1992 it miraculously withstood an immense flood which reached several metres above the bridge. Today, among the tranquil Ouvèze and pretty pastel houses, it is hard to believe that lives were lost in that tragic freak flood.

THE ANCIENT HIGH VILLAGE

Clinging to a lofty jagged rock high above the river, its maze of twisting cobbled streets free from traffic, the upper walled village is a pleasant spot for a stroll The fine medieval and Renaissance façades of the sand-coloured houses, draped with knotted vines, Virginia creeper and pomegranate bushes, have been beautifully restored by artists and craftsmen who have also brought life to the cafés of the market square. The climb up to the ruined 13th-century château is steep, but the snow-capped Alps, the Ouvèze Valley

An elegantly slim cypress points to the blue sky, as the cathedral belfry points human hearts to heaven

The Walk

 ①

From the tourist office, go towards the river along avenue Général de Gaulle, then across into Grand' Rue and across the Pont Romain. Turn right up a narrow lane through the gateway to the ancient village.

 ②

Turn sharp left up a cobbled street, through another gateway and under the arched belfry into rue de l'Horloge, which leads round to the former Hôtel de Ville. Turn left and climb gently up to place de l'Église.

 ③

Passt the church and go round to the right. Continue to place du Vieux Marché.

 ④

Turn right along rue de l'Evêché, past the former bishop's palace and 17th-century chapel, back to the Hôtel de Ville. Branch left and go back across Pont Romain.

 ⑤

Turn left, then fork right, back along Grand' Rue. At the main crossroads, bear left down avenue Jules-Ferry to the cathedral. Behind the *cloître* entrance, follow a small lane, go left, then right along chemin du Couradou to the tourist office, alongside excavations of the Roman village (Fouilles de la Villasse).

 ℹ

▷ Length of walk: 3km
▷ Approximate time: 1¼ hours
▷ Terrain: All surfaced, some slopes
▷ Parking: Choice of car parks
▷ Refreshments: Bars and café terraces

and the vineyards of the Côtes du Rhône prove a remarkable backdrop. Beyond the village, waymarked rocky paths lead into the hills towards the mountains and 'the Giant of Provence', the awesome Mont Ventoux (1,909m) – the Windy One'.

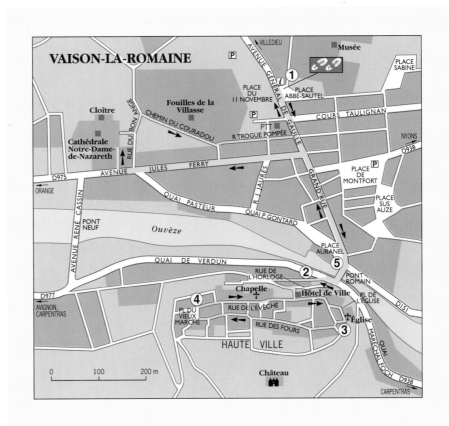

Biot
(ALPES-MARITIMES)

Set in a typical Provençal landscape of cypresses, olives and pines, the village of Biot boasts medieval ramparts and a delightful arcaded square dotted with cafés and antique shops.

This pretty village is wrapped round a small hill 5km north of Antibes. Its first residents were Greeks, who settled here over 2,000 years ago. In the 15th century, following the Black Death which devastated the village, it was repopulated by 50 families from Genoa. Many of the families resident today are descendants of those Italian settlers, who cultivated orange trees, previously unknown in Provence, as well as vines and olives. The production of fruit gave way to lavender, and the village also became a thriving pottery

The Walk

1

Start at the tourist office. Turn right into rue du Portugon, first left along a narrow alleyway, then right again.

2

Descend steeply to the junction and continue straight down the rue de la Regouaro along the village ramparts, following signs to the gateway, the Porte des Tines.

3

Continue past the gateway to the left up the rue des Tines, then left along the narrow rue des Orfèvres following signs to the church (église).

4

Turn left at the next junction along rue de la Poissonnière, into the place des Arcades, and under the arch to the church. Return across the square, turn right and follow the road round to the tourist office.

centre, producing the huge earthenware jars still to be seen in the streets, filled with tropical plants and geraniums, as well as in gardens throughout the Riviera.

Despite floods of summer tourists, Biot still has the power to charm. With its steep, bumpy streets and delightful sand-coloured houses capped with orange-tiled roofs, the village is known today for its gold- and silverwork, ceramics, olivewood carving and thriving glassworks. At the Verrerie de Biot, visitors can watch the glass-blowers at work on their creations, including the famous Biot *verre bullé* or bubble glass.

Twenty minutes' stroll from the old village is a museum devoted to the Cubist painter Fernand Léger, with its huge, brilliantly coloured mosaic façade and monumental stained-glass window. Léger bought a villa here in 1955, intending to make Biot his home, but sadly he died 15 days later. His widow founded the Musée Fernand Léger in 1959, the first major museum in France to be dedicated entirely to one artist.

Haut-de-Cagnes
(ALPES-MARITIMES)

Haut-de-Cagnes, set on a conical hill just inland from the resort of Cagnes-sur-Mer, is undoubtedly one of the prettiest Riviera hilltop villages. Winding alleyways and vaulted streets cloak the hill, and geraniums and bougainvillaea overflow from the windows of brightly coloured houses, which look out across cypresses, mimosas and orange trees to the sea. Above the village sits a fortified

In Biot, massive arches form a cool, airy arcade – a retreat from the heat when it's time to eat

An ancient lion sits like a sentinel on guard beside a stepped walkway in Haut-de-Cagnes. Renoir lived near by, taking inspiration from light and landscape

stronghold, built in the 14th century by Admiral Rainer Grimaldi to watch for pirates. Four centuries later Heinrich Grimaldi had the citadel remodelled into a magnificent castle, adding a splendid Renaissance courtyard and an opulent frescoed banqueting hall.

The Château Musée is divided into various permanent exhibitions including the Solidar collection – an unusual series of portraits of Suzy Solidar, a celebrated Parisian cabaret star – and the Musée Méditerranéen d'Art Moderne, dedicated to the painters who have worked on the coast during the last hundred years. This sun-bleached landscape of olive groves, cooled by a breeze scented with thyme and rosemary, has inspired many great artists including, Chagall, Matisse and Renoir, and is often called the 'Mecca of Modern Art'. Haut-de-Cagnes has played host to a modern art festival of international repute every summer since 1969.

Cagnes's most famous painter is without doubt Pierre-August Renoir, who spent the last 11 years of his life less than a kilometre away at the Domaine des Collettes. Rheumatism had forced him to move to the sunny south, where he spent hours at his easel in the shade of his beloved olive trees. In later years rheumatism him forced to paint with the brush strapped to his hand, but despite great physical difficulties he produced many canvases. Today his beautiful villa is a museum, and although it contains few of his paintings, it remains a moving tribute to this great artist.

St-Paul
(ALPES-MARITIMES)

This *village perché*, draped gently over a hill surrounded by palm trees and enclosed within ramparts, lies just in from the coast, 20km north-west of Nice. Beyond the popular shady *pétanque* arena, the village welcomes you with a cannon, double gateway and portcullis, leading into a maze of cobbled streets flanked by 16th- and 17th-century façades. St-Paul was designated a royal town by Francois I in the 16th century, and the wealth of the village is still apparent.

In the 1920s two impoverished and unknown young artists by the names of Soutine and Modigliani visited St-Paul and stayed at the modest La Colombe d'Or, paying their bill with their paintings. Word of the *auberge* spread, and soon other artists and young intellectuals arrived. Today, the exclusive Hôtel La Colombe d'Or boasts an impressive past guest list and one of the finest private collections of modern art in France, with works by Braque, Picasso, Matisse and others.

The village is still an artists' colony, with painters gathered round the fountains in the picturesque squares. The many shops are best visited early in the morning, or at night when the alleys are lit by tiny lanterns.

The main attraction of St-Paul is the Foundation Maeght, one of Europe's most significant collections of modern art, set on a wooded hill. Two main buildings – designed by Catalán architect José-Luis Sert, a pupil of Le Corbusier – house works by Kandinsky, Chagall, Braque and Miró and contemporary artists Adami and Viallat. Other important exhibits are scattered about the terraces and pavilions which overlook the Gulf of Antibes.

The streets of St-Paul are crammed with little shops, which makes browsing a pleasure at less crowded times

AUPS

This tiny walled village basks in a wide valley, surrounded by undulating countryside of vines and olive groves, its name deriving from the Celto-Ligurian *alb* or hill pasture. With its friendly people, medieval gateways, shady streets and archways and tiny, peaceful squares dotted with fountains, Aups offers a perfect getaway from the tourist routes of Provence. The village enjoys a local reputation for its wine, honey, oil, black truffles and other regional specialities sold at the local Thursday-morning market. An old convent is now the small but interesting Simon Ségal Museum, devoted to modern art.

COGOLIN

Cogolin's economy is rooted in the traditional crafts of making cane furniture, briar pipes, silk yarn, wool carpets and, above all, reeds for wind instruments, attracting musicians of international renown. The village is alive all year round, and visits to the craft factories can easily be arranged at the tourist office. The local museum of carpets and fabrics is one of the most unusual in Provence.

Behind the square lies the true heart of Cogolin, with its brightly coloured medieval houses, cobbled streets, and tiny hidden squares or *placettes* bursting with flowers – a welcome escape from the tourist hordes encountered in nearby St-Tropez.

COLLOBRIÈRES

Known throughout France for its production of corks and *marrons glacés*, the hillside village of Collobrières lies at the heart of the wild Massif des Maures, surrounded by a dense forest of cork-oaks and chestnut trees whose fruits are the size of tennis balls.

Collobrières is reputed to have learned about corkage from the Spanish in the Middle Ages, the first place in France to do so. Cork production is still the major industry in the village, together with *marrons glacés* and other sweet chestnut confectionery. Strolling under plane trees alongside the River Collobrier in the tranquil village, it is easy to forget that the famous bustling resort of St-Tropez is only 25km away.

COTIGNAC

Tucked at the foot of a sheer 80m cliff, honeycombed with caves and dominated by the ruins of a

A window in Provence, open to the warm scented air and dazzling sunlight

medieval castle, Cotignac has a truly Provençal feel with its ochre-coloured houses, terracotta-tiled roofs, old-fashioned shop fronts and ornamental fountains splashing in the squares. From the place de la Mairie, with its impressive four-storey houses, rue de l'Horloge leads under the clock tower up to the church and the cliffs beyond.

Village life revolves round the Cours, a broad esplanade lined with café tables set out under the massive plane trees. Near by, the village wine cooperative, Les Vignerons de Cotignac, sells various excellent regional wines.

EYGALIÈRES

Picturesque Eygalières lies off the tourist track 10km south-east of St-Rémy-de-Provence, on a gentle slope sheltered behind the Alpilles Mountains and surrounded by a wild, dusty landscape of olive and cypress trees.

Creamy stone houses with sky-blue and acquamarine shutters line the interlacing lanes leading up to the ruined château, village church and 17th-century clock tower with sweeping views towards the mountains.

This sleepy village improbably bursts to life during the first weekend of August, for a splendid torchlit Arlésienne parade with horses and a merry fête.

MOUSTIERS-STE-MARIE

Moustiers, set on a ridge near the foot of sheer cliffs and surrounded by lavender, thyme and cork-oaks, marks the start of the great gorges of the River Verdon, among the most extraordinary land formations in the whole of France.

Hard against the rock face above the village is the 5th-century chapel of Notre-Dame-de-Beauvoir, affording a breathtaking view of the region. Above the chapel, suspended on a 227m chain, hangs a famous star presented to the village by a knight called Blacas to celebrate his release from captivity during the Crusades.

The village was famous worldwide in the 17th and 18th centuries for its white decorated earthenware pottery. Faïence de Moustiers has recently been revived, and the *faïence* shops spill their wares out into the little cobbled squares throughout the village.

OPPÈDE-LE-VIEUX

Oppède nestles high above vineyards on the steeper slopes of the Petit Luberon near Apt. In appearance it seems a typical Provençal village, with a maze of narrow streets, flights of steps and attractive, cream-coloured houses spilling down the hillside, all crowned by an impressive ruined château. Oppède, however, suffered a grim period in its history when, at the end of the last cen-

tury, the tyrannical Baron Oppède sold over 800 villagers as slaves in Marseille and the village was abandoned. Even today, many of the houses are gutted ruins overrun with weeds.

Some of the picturesque old dwellings and the Romanesque church have recently been restored by resident artists, and Oppède is gradually returning to its former glory, vying with the neighbouring villages of Ménerbes, Lacoste and Bonnieux for the title of prettiest village in the Luberon.

SÉGURET

This delightful circular hilltop village is set against the jagged backdrop of the Dentelles de Montmirail. Lying at the heart of the famous Côtes du Rhône wine region, Séguret carries the distinction of having its own individual *appellation contrôlée*. Where better to taste the local wines than on a cool shady terrace, with views stretching across vineyards to the neighbouring hilltop villages of Sablet and Gigondas.

Among the many medieval charms of the village is a one-handed clock on the ancient belfry, the Porte Reynier, and an unusual 15th-century fountain with gargoyles. The ochre cottages, with their turquoise shutters draped with vines and Virginia creeper, house the local craftsmen, famous for their *santons* – traditional Christmas crib figurines of hand-painted terracotta – and dried flowers. On Christmas Eve, in place of the standard Provençal crib, the villagers perform a living re-enactment of the Nativity.

VENASQUE

The pretty village of Venasque enjoys a lofty perch on a steep rock 11km south-east of Carpentras. Protected by an imposing medieval gateway and curtain wall, the site has been occupied since the earliest times. During the 6th century, the bishops of Carpentras sought refuge from the Saracens here, and for hundreds of years the village was an episcopal seat. One of the bishops, St Siffrein, built the magnificent baptistery dedicated to the Blessed Virgin. The 13th-century church beside it was erected on the site of a previous church, also from the 6th century.

Visitors come to Venasque not only for its religious connections but also for its gastronomic reputation, and in May and June the village holds a daily cherry market.

Corsica

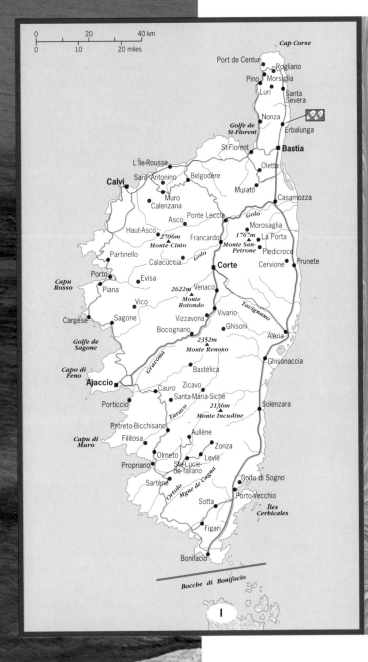

Map of Corsica:

Cap Corse
Port de Centuri
Rogliano
Pino · Morsiglia
Luri · Santa Severa
Nonza
Golfe de St-Florent
Erbalunga
St-Florent · **Bastia**
L'Île-Rousse
Oletta
Sant'Antonino · Belgodère
Calvi
Murato
Casamozza
Muro · Calenzana
Asco · Ponte Leccia
Golo
Morosaglia
Haut-Asco · Francardo
1767m · La Porta
2706m · Monte San-Petrone
Monte Cinto · Piedicroce
Partinello
Golo
Cervione · Prunete
Calacuccia
Corte
Porto
Evisa
Capu Rosso
Piana
2622m
Venaco
Vico
Monte Rotondo
Tavignano
Cargèse · Sagone
Vizzavona · Vivario
Bocognano · Ghisoni
Golfe de Sagone
Alèria
2352m
Monte Renoso
Ghisonaccia
Capo di Feno
Bastélica
Ajaccio
Cauro · Zicavo
Santa-Maria-Siché
Porticcio
Taravo
2136m · Solenzara
Petreto-Bicchisano
Monte Incudine
Capu di Muro
Filitosa
Aullène
Zonza
Olmeto
Levie
Propriano
Ste-Lucie-de-Tallano
Golfo di Sogno
Sartène
Mgne de Cagna
Porto-Vecchio
Ortolo
Sotta
Îles Cerbicales
Figari
Bonifacio
Bocche di Bonifacio

Scale: 0 — 20 — 40 km / 0 — 10 — 20 miles

A fascinating diversity of cultures complements varied landscapes, spectacular cliffs and white sandy beaches.

Erbalunga

(Haute-Corse)

OCCUPYING A TINY PENINSULA ON THE SHELTERED EASTERN COAST OF MOUNTAINOUS CAP CORSE – ITSELF A LARGER PENINSULA POINTING FINGER-LIKE FROM THE NORTH-EAST CORNER OF CORSICA – ERBALUNGA IS A SMALL FISHING VILLAGE STEEPED IN HISTORY.

As you approach from Bastia, capital of Haute-Corse, Erbalunga appears as a jumble of stone houses jammed on to a rocky spit of land, at the end of which sits a 16th-century Genoese watchtower, one of scores dotted round this coast. Although there has been a road round Cap Corse for 150 years, Erbalunga retains a strong sense of isolation and self-sufficiency.

This identity was forged some thousand years ago. Indeed, Erbalunga's days of glory were over by the time the watchtower was built. Inhabited since prehistoric times, it presumably came into its own with the flourishing Greek and Etruscan trade in olives, oil, corn and wine. The Pisan occupation of Corsica in the 11th century strengthened links with nearby Tuscany, and Erbalunga was the primary port, far more important than Bastia.

OUTWITTING THE WINDS

These days the village has one harbour, but the secret of its ancient importance and prosperity lay in its having not one harbour but two. In Corsica generally, and Cap Corse in particular, the many and variable winds are the stuff of legend. At Erbalunga, if wild winds threatened one harbour, the boats were transferred over land to the other. The

A roughly arched passageway to the Pian di Fuor

big piazza at the head of the village is still called Pian di Fuor, 'the space outside' over which the boats were hauled.

Erbalunga had a further advantage over Bastia in those days: abundant pure water welling up from the rocks on which the village was built. The village women would row to and from Bastia with that town's linen, soiled one way, famously clean the other.

Genoa succeeded Pisa as ruler of Corsica, and the ruling family at Erbalunga was the da Gentile. Power led to power struggles and when, in the 1550s, one da Gentile was opposed by another backing an unholy French-Turkish alliance, Erbalunga was bombarded from the sea and all but destroyed. So, for all its history, Erbalunga has just one building – the tall turreted house – older than the 16th century. After this time of turmoil, coastal watchtowers were built and Bastia fortified to protect Corsica from Muslim raiders. Bastia's rise confirmed Erbalunga's fall.

TRUE TO ITSELF

Early this century the village harboured a colony of artists, two of whom lived here and have places named after them. This artistic heritage lives on in the open-air music festival held every August. The most famous event in the calendar, however, is the Good Friday procession, which takes in all the villages of the commune.

Although appealing to tourists, Erbalunga has not compromised its character. It remains a real community that does not depend on tourism for its identity. Cars have been excluded without the usual accompanying proliferation of boutiques and craft shops (there are none) and 'Heritage', it seems, has yet to reach this very independent part of Europe.

Houses bordering the sea viewed from the south, above, and the harbour today, in morning light, below

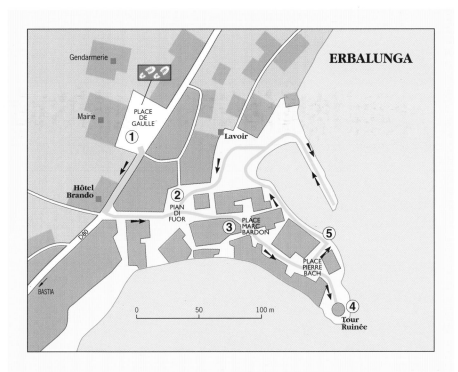

ERBALUNGA

1

From the car park in place de Gaulle behind the Mairie, walk back a little way to the entrance to the old village, opposite the Hôtel Brando.

2

Entering the main square from the road, you see several lanes leading out of it. Take the one directly ahead, which leads to the tower through an arch into the small place Marc Bardon. Having left the Pian di Fuor, you are now in the village proper.

3

In place Marc Bardon there is a roofless church ahead and the island of Elba on the horizon. Turn right into the spacious place Pierre Bach, looking back for the best view of the strange turreted house which dominates the village (only this turreted section pre-dates the great disaster of 1553). To the left, a few steps lead down to the harbourside duckwalk. Proceed straight ahead, up a few steps, where another arch takes you through to the tower (Tour Ruinée).

4

At the tower itself there are wide views south to Bastia, while to the left a few steps take fishermen, and the surefooted, down to the rocks.

5

From the tower return to place Pierre Bach and take the steps down to the duckwalk under the lee of the harbourside houses. Here you can either go on to the bars at the head of the harbour for snacks or a meal, sitting in sun or shade, or first take a promenade along the breakwater for the main view of the village with the mountains behind (best in the morning). Before leaving the harbour, note behind the plane trees the portico which houses the once-famous village *lavoir* (wash-house). Just behind, a lane leads through to the main beach. Leaving the harbour area past the souvenir shop, you re-enter Pian di Fuor with its two Italianate palazzos.

i

▷ Length of walk: About 500m
▷ Approximate time: 1 hour
▷ Terrain: All surfaced, but not uniform or even; several sets of steps
▷ Parking: Place de Gaulle; no car access to village
▷ Refreshments: Bars and restaurants

The Walk

1

Sturdy shoes are advised. Go through the arched gateway at the end of the piazza and turn left. Take the right-hand fork at the narrow house; at the last house on the left, turn left down steep steps, then right. Do the same at the end of the next section.

2

Carry on after the last house until the paving ends. Behind to your left is a grassy path leading down. Continue to a rock formation overhung with giant cacti.

3

Turn right immediately (ie, ahead in front of the rock). Keeping the stone wall to your left, after a few minutes you reach an open area of smooth stone, a good resting or picnic place. Look back to see the village and a hillside of cactus (Barbary figs).

4

Here you make a choice: turn back, or carry on round the cliff where some 800m ahead, down by the water, stands a ruined 13th-century church, the former convent of St Francis. In either case, retrace your steps to meet the paved path again. This time carry straight on, with houses to your right, to the arched gateway and the piazza.

Nonza
(HAUTE-CORSE)

Nonza is the star village of Cap Corse: thrillingly sited on a spectacular promontory on the rugged west coast of the Cap, with a Genoese watchtower capping the promontory itself, set high above a vast stretch of iron-grey beach fringed with white. At the bend in the road – the apex of the village – sits a lovely pink- and blue-fronted church, with a restaurant on one side and a piazza opposite. There are houses clustered along the road and between the church and rocky heights behind, but the village proper begins through the piazza on the south-facing slopes beneath the watchtower.

Three stories, two ancient and one modern, are attached to this singular place. The first concerns Nonza's patron, Ste Julie. The exact details vary from one version to the next, but all agree she was an 8th-century Christian, possibly born here, barbarously murdered for her faith. She is credited with a miraculously flowing spring now enshrined and reached by 164 steps leading down from the road which lies just north of the church dedicated to her.

The second story describes the amazing exploit of a single elderly man who lived in Nonza during the heady days of the native rebellion against the French in the 1760s; while the town was under attack, using a clever system of cables to manipulate a line of muskets and a cannon, he managed to convince the thousand-odd besieging force that a whole company of soldiers was inside the Genoese watchtower training a barrage of cannonballs and small fire on them, thus bringing about a French truce.

The third story concerns a phenomenon barely 30 years old. Before then, the extraordinary beach below the village did not exist. On the next headland to the north, one sees mine workings (now derelict) which for years gouged millions of tonnes of asbestos-bearing rock from the headland and dumped the waste offshore. By the time this huge operation was shut down (an economic disaster that reverberated through the whole of the Cap), the spoil had accumulated to such

a point that the sea began to throw up a beach of grey stone, now 3km long and looking a millenium old.

Nonza is illuminated for a procession on the Feast of the Assumption, 15 August.

Cargèse
(CORSE-DU-SUD)

From its position perched on the clifftop overlooking a bay, Cargèse exudes a certain lazy charm that obviously appeals to the hundreds of affluent summer residents attracted by its whitewashed houses. This seeming tranquillity, however, belies the village's turbulent past. Around a thousand Greek refugees landed on the island in the 1670s, following an agreement between the people of Zitylos in the Turkish-occupied Peloponnese and the Genoese. The Genoese plan to weaken Corsican resistance through colonization with different nationalities involved large monetary rewards in return for protection from hostile natives objecting to their presence.

Settling in the nearby Paomia, within a year the Greeks had established five hamlets and were extremely successful farmers and cultivators of grapes, olives and fruits. Facing increasing resentment from the local people, Paomia was eventually ransacked by patriots and, after much bloodshed, the Greeks fled to Ajaccio, remaining there for 40 years until the French brought temporary peace. In 1773 Count Marbeuf, a French nobleman, tried to integrate the communities by forming a united Greek/Corsican regiment and offered the Greeks Cargèse as compensation for Paomia – a gesture which again provoked the locals into attacking the Greeks, this time forcing them into hiding.

Attacked once again in 1793, the Greeks then fled to Ajaccio, with two-thirds returning a few years later, gradually joined by Corsicans in an uneasy coexistence, leading, eventually, to integration mainly through intermarriage.

The village's double split loyalties and old conflicts are reflected in the two churches at its heart. One is a large neo-Gothic Orthodox church housing an outstanding iconostasis decorated with 17th-century icons brought over with the original settlers. The accompanying 19th-century baroque Catholic church features a *trompe l'oeil* ceiling, and a magnificent terrace view.

Although now well assimilated, the Greek population still conducts ceremonies such as weddings in traditional style, and the festival of St Spiridon in December is distinctly Greek. More peaceful in September, Cargèse is an ideal starting point for a boat trip to the spectacular pink and orange rock masses and pinnacles of the Calanche, a protected site of unusual rock formations.

What's mine is yours: Nonza's beach, left, created from spoil from a mine. Below, Nonza from the tower

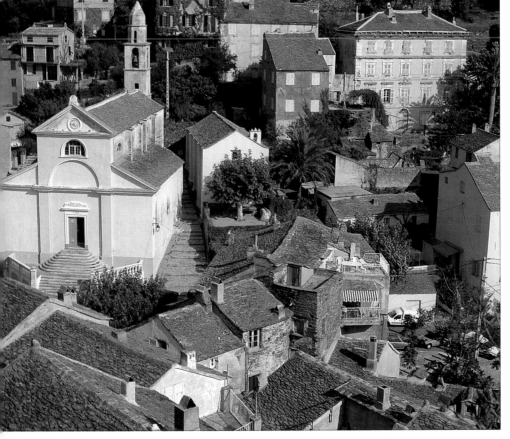

Far from aloof, a feline resident of Piana welcomes a brief encounter with a friendly stranger

Piana
(CORSE-DU-SUD)

Piana, a small but welcoming hamlet, lies north of Cargèse and about 8km south-west of Porto. Occupying a prime site overlooking the Calanche, Piana can be very busy in summer but somehow manages to retain a sleepy village atmosphere – alleys winding through a cluster of houses with outside stairways and shallow, red-tiled roofs. Add an 18th-century church with graceful bell-tower, a few hotels (one an old house with high wooden ceilings and a leafy garden) and restaurants and the picture is complete.

This is an outstanding area for excursions, with Capo d'Orto, 10km east, a fairly demanding five- or six-hour walk requiring sturdy footwear over the rocky terrain. The effort is well worth the glorious view from the summit (1,294m).

South of the village is the Col de Lava, a notable viewing platform for the gulf. Also worth a detour, and a short walk from the end of the route de Ficajola (the D624), are the pleasures of the Anse de Ficajola, a delightful little cove of red rocks accessible via a stone stairway.

Index

Page numbers in **bold** refer to illustrations

Acknowledgements

The Automobile Association wishes to thank the following photographers and libraries for their assistance in the preparation of this book.

The Bridgeman Art Library 81 (Musée d'Orsay, Paris, Giraudon)
Michael Busselle front cover (Peillon), back cover (a, La Couvertoirade), 1, 2/3, 4a, 4b, 4c, 4d, 4f, 4h, 4i, 5b, 5c, 5d, 5e, 5f, 5g, 5h, 5i, 5j, 10a, 11, 25, 39a, 45a, 61, 68a, 85, 97a, 117a, 133a, 142, 145a, 157a, 169a, 179a, 191, 203, 217a
Julian Cotton Photographic Library back cover (c, Provence), 10b
CDT 05 163b (E Negret), 163c (S Passeron)
Teresa Fisher 26a, 26b, 32b, 32c, 33, 214b
The Mansell Collection Ltd 34a, 34b, 35a
John Millar 40b, 40d, 46, 72/3, 72, 162a, 162b, 163a, 164a
Pictures Colour Library 186b, 187b
Spectrum Colour Library 196, 215
Jean-Charles Spindler 56a, 56b, 57a, 57b, 57c

The remaining photographs are held in the Association's own photo library (AA Photo Library) with contributions from:
A Baker 204b, 204c, 205, 206a, 206b, 208c, 209, 210, 210/1, 213; **P Bennett** 201b; **S Day** 16/7, 126a; **J Edmanson** 63a, 63b, 66a, 66b, 71a, 71b, 73, 74a, 74b, 107b;

P Kenward 5a, 13, 14a, 14b, 14c, 15, 18c, 19, 24a, 62, 64b, 64/5, 76a, 80a, 94a, 98a, 107a, 108b, 108c, 109, 110/1, 111a, 111b, 112b, 112/3, 113, 114a, 114b, 115, 116a, 116b, 118b, 118c, 119, 120a, 120b, 120c, 121, 122a, 122b, 122c, 123, 124, 125b, 126b, 126c, 127, 128b, 128c, 129a, 130a, 130/1, 131a, 132b, 146a, 158a, 169b, 170b, 170c, 171, 172a, 172b, 173a, 174b, 175, 176, 177a, 177b, 178b, 184b, 184c, 185, 194a, 194b, 194c, 195, 197a, 200, 201a, 218a; **J Millar** 197b, 202a;
R Moore 27a, 27b, 28a, 31, 32a, 34c, 38a, 64a, 67a, 66/7, 68b, 68c, 69, 70, 86a, 117b, 125a, 133b, 134a, 134b, 134c, 135, 136a, 136b, 136c, 136d, 137, 139a, 140, 141a, 141b, 142/3, 143, 144a, 144b, 145b, 146b, 146c, 147, 148a, 148b, 149, 150, 151a, 151b, 152a, 152b, 153, 154, 156a, 156b, 157b, 158b, 158c, 159, 161a, 161b, 164c, 166/7, 167, 168a, 168b, 180a, 180b, 181a, 181b, 183a, 183b, 184a, 186a, 188a, 188b, 190a, 192b, 192c, 193, 198a, 198b, 198c, 199, 202b, 207, 214a, 217b, 218b, 218c, 218/9, 220, 220/1; **R Moss** 28b, 29a, 29b, 30, 36, 37a, 39b, 40a, 42a, 42b; 42c, 43a, 43b, 44b, 47, 48b, 50a, 50b, 50c, 51, 54a, 54b, 54c, 55, 58b, 58c, 59, 76b, 76c, 77, 78a, 78/9, 79, 82/3, 82, 83a, 83b, 84b, 88c, 89, 90/1a, 94b, 96b, 100/1, 102a, 102b, 102c, 103, 104, 106a; **D Noble** 80b, 80c; **T Oliver** 4e, 45b, 46/7, 49, 52a, 58a, 60a, 60b, 138a, 138b, 139b, 182, 187a, 189, 190b; **K Paterson** 128a, 174a; **I Powys** 52b; **D Robertson** 3, 40c, 41, 44a, 48a, 53; **C Sawyer** 26c, 30/1, 35b, 37b, 38b, 75a; **M Shales** 131b, 132a; **M Short** 75b, 86b, 86c, 87, 88a, 88b, 90/1b, 90b, 90c, 92a, 92b, 92c, 93, 94/5, 95, 96a, 97b, 98b, 98c, 99a, 99b, 101a, 101b, 105a, 105b, 106b, 192a; **B Smith** back cover (b, geese in the Dordogne), 10c, 48c, 129b, 170a, 173b, 174c, 178a, 212a; **A Souter** 84a, 108a, 118a, 179b; **R Strange** 12a, 12b, 12c, 17, 18a, 18b, 20b, 21a, 21b, 22a, 23b, 24b, 112a, 155, 160/1, 164b, 165, 204a, 206c, 208a, 208b, 211, 212b, 212c, 216a, 216b; **B Toms** 221; **R Victor** 12d, 16, 20a, 22b, 23a.